WITHDRAWN

INSTINCTUAL STIMULATION OF CHILDREN:

from common practice to child abuse

VOLUME 2

INSTINCTUAL STIMULATION OF CHILDREN:

from common practice to child abuse

by

JOHN LEOPOLD WEIL, M.D.

Judge Baker Guidance Center
Harvard Medical School

VOLUME 2
CLINICAL CASES

INTERNATIONAL UNIVERSITIES PRESS
Madison   Connecticut

Copyright © 1989, John L. Weil, M.D.

All rights reserved. No part of this book may be reproduced by any means, nor translated into a machine language, without the written permission of the publisher.

Library of Congress Cataloging-in-Publication Data

Weil, John Leopold, 1920–
    Instinctual stimulation of children.

    Includes bibliographies and index.
    Contents: v. 1. Clinical findings — v. 2. Clinical cases.
    1. Sensory stimulation — Case studies.   2. Child psychopathology — Case stud-
ies.   3. Mental illness — Etiology — Case studies.   4. Child abuse — Case studies.
I. Title.   [DNLM: 1. Child Behavior Disorders — etiology — case studies.   2. Phys-
ical Stimulation — in infancy & childhood.   3. Psychoanalytic Interpretation.
WS 350.6 W422i]
RJ507.S44W45   1989   618.92'89071   88-32788
ISBN 0-8236-2885-X (v. 1)
ISBN 0-8236-2886-8 (v. 2)

Manufactured in the United States of America

PUBLISHED UNDER THE AUSPICES OF
THE WATERS FOUNDATION
FRAMINGHAM, MASSACHUSETTS

TABLE OF CONTENTS

FOCUS: **SYMPTOMS ASSOCIATED WITH CHILDREN'S EXPOSURES TO EROGENOUS AND/OR TO MORE HIGHLY EROTIC VISUAL AND TACTILE CONTACTS WITH THE ADULT BODY**

FUGUES OR DAYTIME HALLUCINATORY REACTIONS

FOCUS: **SYMPTOMS ASSOCIATED WITH CHILDREN'S EXPOSURES TO PUNITIVE CONTACTS WITH ADULTS**

DESTRUCTIVENESS AND/OR DELINQUENT BEHAVIOR

FANTASIES OF DEATH

SELF-DESTRUCTIVENESS WITH OR WITHOUT SUICIDAL TENDENCIES

SECTION 3   CASES 65-86

FOCUS: **SYMPTOMS ASSOCIATED WITH CHILDREN'S EXPOSURES TO BOTH EROTIC AND PUNITIVE CONTACTS WITH ADULTS**

SYMPTOMS PERTAINING TO SEX, DESTRUCTION, AND FIRE

xiv

SECTION 4   CASES 87-100

FOCUS: **SYMPTOMS ASSOCIATED WITH CHILDREN'S EXPOSURES TO ANAL AND FECAL STIMULATION**

ACKNOWLEDGMENTS

The following cases are synopses derived from the classical psychoanalytic literature:

Case 1: Synopsis of Sigmund Freud's "Little Hans" — S. Freud (1909), Analysis of a phobia in a five-year-old boy, *Standard Edition,* 10:5-149, London: Hogarth Press, 1955.

Case 2: Synopsis of Leo Rangell's "Paul" — L. Rangell (1950), Treatment of nightmares in a seven-year-old boy, *The Psychoanalytic Study of the Child,* 5:358-390, New York: International Universities Press.

Case 19: Synopsis of David Crocker's "S" — D. Crocker (1955), The study of a problem of aggression, *The Psychoanalytic Study of the Child,* 10:300-335, New York: International Universities Press.

Case 20: Synopsis of Michael Robbins's "Alan" — M. Robbins (1969), On the psychology of artistic creativity, *The Psychoanalytic Study of the Child,* 24:227-251, New York: International Universities Press.

Case 21: Jenny Waelder Hall's "Anton" — J. W. Hall (1946), The analysis of a case of night terror. *The Psychoanalytic Study of the Child,* 2:189-227. New York: International Universities Press.

Case 22: Synopsis of Erna Furman's "Danny" — E. Furman (1962), *J. Amer. Psychoanal. Assn.,* 10:258-268.

Case 23: Synopsis of Selma Fraiberg's "Sally" — S. Fraiberg (1952), A critical neurosis in a two-and-a-half-year-old girl. *The Psychoanalytic Study of the Child,* 7:173-215. New York: International Universities Press.

Case 24: Synopsis of Amy Katan's "Margaret" — A. Katan (1951), The role of displacement in agoraphobia. *Internat. J. Psycho-Anal.,* 32:45-46.

Case 28: Synopsis of Margaret Gerard's "Robert" — M. W. Gerard (1946), The psychogenic tic in ego development. *The Psychoanalytic Study of the Child,* 2:133-162. New York: International Universities Press.

Case 29: Synopsis of Berta Bornstein's "Sonya" — B. Bornstein (1946), Hysterical twilight states in an eight-year-old child. *The Psychoanalytic Study of the Child,* 2:229-240. New York: International Universities Press.

Case 31: Synopsis of Coren and Saldinger's "Hank" — H. Coren & J. Saldinger (1967), Visual hallucinosis in children. *The Psychoanalytic Study of the Child,* 22:331-356. New York: International Universities Press.

Case 32: Synopsis of Kolansky and Moore's "Dick" — H. Kolansky & W. Moore (1966), Simultaneous analysis of a father and his adolescent son. *The Psychoanalytic Study of the Child,* 21:237-268. New York: International Universities Press.

Case 68: Synopsis of Edith Buxbaum's "Poldi" — E. Buxbaum (1935), Exhibitionistic onanism in a ten-year-old boy. *Psychoanal. Quart.,* 4/1:161-189.

Case 75: Synopsis of Selma Fraiberg's "Roger" — S. Fraiberg (1962), Technical aspects of the analysis of a child with a severe behavior disorder. *J. Amer. Psychoanal. Assn.,* 10:338-367.

INTRODUCTION

The one hundred clinical cases contained in this volume provide the in-depth source material upon which the conclusions of *Instinctual Stimulation of Children* are based. These cases include the synopses of twenty-one children's analyses and two adult analyses reported in the classical psychoanalytical literature as well as the author's own diagnostic and clinical cases. The clinician and research investigator are invited to turn to individual cases which focus upon specific areas of clinical concern and interest. To facilitate an inquiry into the one hundred clinical cases, the Table of Contents has been designed as a directory for locating cases which illustrate children's symptom constellations associated with certain forms of instinctual stimulation.

Cases illustrating children's exposures to *instinctual stimulation* have been grouped in the Table of Contents along a continuum extending from common practice to child abuse and include intimate forms of bed sharing; children's observations of adult intercourse; children's visual and/or tactile erotic contacts with the adult genitalia; anal stimulation; and mounting levels of parental yelling and physical beatings.

Cases illustrating children's *symptom constellations* associated with particular forms of instinctual stimulation are listed in the Table of Contents under the headings of school phobias (cases 1-8); sexual, hysterical, and/or phobic symptoms (cases 9-20); night terrors and sleep-walking (cases 21-28); the hallucinatory intrusion of night terrors and sleep-walking into waking life (cases 29-31); firesetting (cases 66, 73, 74, 80, 81, 82, 83, 85); learning problems (cases 32-45); delinquent destructiveness (cases 46-54); suicide attempts (cases 60-64); and obsessions with respect to excrement, sickness, and death (cases 87-96, and 98-100).

In general, cases involving minimal and moderate levels of instinctual stimulation are presented at the beginning of each section, while cases involving maximal levels of instinctual stimulation are presented toward the end of each section. Such an arrangement favors a comparison of symptom formation among mildly versus severely overstimulated children.

Supplementing these functions of the Table of Contents, the twenty-two tables in Appendix 1 provide an index of all positive and all negative findings, minor as well as major, regarding the relation of specific forms of overstimulation and specific symptoms and dream content.

With respect to the presentation of the one hundred case synopses in this compendium, marginal notations draw attention to the presence or absence of specific stimulus conditions, symptoms, and dream content within each case history. Ratings were determined upon the basis of operational definitions presented in Volume 1, chapter 2 and designated by the symbols:

(+)   referring to *rated present*, 100% consensus;

(+ / −)   referring to *rated present*, majority consensus;

(−)   referring to *rated absent*, 100% consensus;

(− / +)   referring to *rated absent*, majority consensus.

Marginal notations *with asterisks* indicate those variables which were selected for quantitative investigation in the One Hundred Clinical Case Study. Marginal notes *without asterisks* refer to material which is of clinical interest but was not quantitatively investigated because the pertinent variables could not be measured with sufficient accuracy (see Volume 1, chapter 2).

A coding profile located at the end of each case presentation summarizes positive stimulus and positive symptom ratings for each case. In turn, the index tables in Volume 1, Appendix 2 summarize the combined data for the total one hundred clinical case profiles.

SECTION 1
CASES 1-31

Focus:

SYMPTOMS ASSOCIATED WITH CHILDREN'S EXPOSURES TO EROGENOUS AND/OR TO MORE HIGHLY EROTIC VISUAL AND TACTILE CONTACTS WITH THE ADULT BODY

Case 1: Synopsis of Sigmund Freud's "Little Hans"

Freud's classic patient, five-year-old Little Hans, suffered from incapacitating fears of big horses in the street and fears of stepping outside of his home. Hans's personal conversations and activities with his parents for the period January 1st through May 2, 1908 were recorded by his father and sent by mail to Professor Freud (Standard Edition, 1909: p. 23-98). The recordings provide an excellent direct source of information about a family's personal customs and a child's symptoms, presented without an onslaught of theoretical interpretations. Fortunately, the freedom of Little Hans's thoughts was encouraged by his parents who were determined to let him grow up to express himself without being intimidated (p. 6).

Sources of Stimulation:
children's tactile and visual erogenous contacts with the adult body

−/+ sleeping in bed with adults* (only cuddling mornings)

1. Hans shared his parents' room until he was four years old (p. 99). Then, even after he was given his own room, he still insisted upon getting into bed with his father or mother. He especially liked to *"coax in bed"* with his mother (p. 23, 26, 28, 39, 43, 47). Hans's father accused the mother "not without some show of justice, of being responsible for the outbreak of the child's neurosis on account of her excessive display of affection for him and her too frequent readiness to take him into her bed" (p. 28). The father added (p. 39): " 'Hans always comes in to us in the early morning, and my wife can not resist taking him into bed with her a few minutes. Thereupon I always begin to warn her not to take him in bed with her . . . and she answers . . . rather irritated . . . that it's all nonsense . . . one minute is after all of no importance, and so on.' " Hans, however, would not let himself be forbidden to visit in bed with his mother. When the father pointed out to Hans, " 'As long as you come into our room in the mornings, your fear of horses won't get better,' " Hans was defiant and replied, " 'I shall come in all the same, even if I *am* afraid' " (p. 47).

+ adult nudity

2. Hans's mother undressed in front of him (p. 9, 62). The father reported (p. 9-10): Hans "was looking on intently while his mother undressed before going to bed. 'What are you staring like that for?' she asked." Hans answered, " 'I was only looking to see if you'd got a widdler too . . . I thought you were so big you'd have a widdler like a horse.' "

−/+ view adult coitus*
−/+ adult genital erotic*

Whether Hans had witnessed his parents' coital activities while he had shared his parents' room throughout most of his life, i.e., for four years, is not

1

known. Also, it is not known how intense were the "coaxings" between Hans and his mother in bed each morning, coaxings which reportedly disturbed even Hans's liberal-minded father.

Behavioral Symptoms correlated with
tactile and visual erogenous contacts with the adult body

1. Hans displayed a separation problem at night and day (p. 23, 24, 43-4). At the age of four and three-quarters, he woke up from an anxiety dream crying: " 'When I was asleep, I thought you were gone and I had no Mummy to coax with' " (p. 23). During the day (p. 23, 24), he became upset when he was taken out into the street and cried to be taken home "saying he wanted to 'coax' with his Mummy . . . Till the evening he was cheerful as usual. But in the evening he grew visibly frightened; he cried and could not be separated from his mother." Likewise, (p. 25) "On the first walk with the nursemaid . . . he said that in the street he missed his mother whom he could coax with and that he did not want to be away from her."

+ separation phobia*

Hans summarized his separation problem as follows as he complained to his father, " 'When I'm not with you I'm frightened; when I'm not in bed with you, then I'm frightened' " (p. 43-4).

2. At the time of his referral Hans suffered from a constant array of fears. He was afraid of going into the street (p. 22, 24, 34, 43, 48, 53) and afraid that a horse would bite him (p. 22, 24). Following an attack of influenza which kept him in bed two weeks, his fears increased to the point that he could not be induced to go out of his house at all or at most would venture only onto the balcony (p. 29). Somewhat later he became irrationally afraid of animals in the zoo (p. 33) and "absolutely refused to go into the house in which the giraffe was kept nor would he visit the elephant which formerly used to amuse him." His fears spread to horses making a row with their feet (p. 50), horses falling (p. 50, 46, 55), and coal carts and buses drawn by horses (p. 53, 54).

+ irrational fears*

3. Angry antics were mentioned once in Hans's history; the reference involved his early bowel training (p. 54) about which his father noted: " 'In very early days when he had to be put on the chamber and refused to leave off playing, he used to stamp his feet in a rage, and kick about, and sometimes throw himself on the ground.' " Hans still would make "a row with his feet" when he was cross, or when he wanted to play rather than do "lumf" (p. 54).

+ irrational tempers*

4. At night Hans compulsively masturbated (p. 27, 30), a practice which was directly associated with thoughts of his mother's nudity: during a conversation with his father, he acknowledged that he played with his "widdler," then immediately went on to speak of seeing his Mummy quite naked in her chemise.

+ sexual problems*

Compounding the problem of Hans's sexualized reaction toward his mother, was his parents' attitude toward his masturbatory activity. Both parents went to great lengths to stop his masturbation: " 'If you do that,' " his mother threatened, " 'I shall send for Dr. A to cut off your widdler; and then what'll you widdle with?' " (p. 7-8). In turn, Hans's father gave him a sack to sleep in so as to control the disturbing behavior (p. 31).[1]

+ biting*

5. Hans's presenting problem, his persistent irrational phobias, featured a preoccupation with animals *biting*. The father first summarized Hans's problem by the statement, " 'Hans is afraid in the street that a horse will bite him' " (p. 22, 24). His father tried to assure him that horses do not bite, but to no avail (p. 29). Hans also was particularly afraid of horses with a black "thing on their *mouths*" (p. 49, 41). At other times, he would play horse, repeatedly running up to his father and biting him (p. 52).

+ eyes*

(+ obsessions and compulsions*)

6. Preoccupation with "eyes" and "looking" as an anxiety symptom also troubled Little Hans. His fear of horses became converted more and more into an obsession of looking at them. He said: " 'I *have* to *look* at horses and then I'm frightened' " (p. 29). Shortly thereafter, Hans revealed that he was particularly bothered by " 'what they wear in front of their eyes.' "[2]

Sources of Stimulation:
adult punitive and excretory contacts

+ adult defecation

1. Hans's mother in his presence would defecate into the toilet. His father asked the mother whether Hans was often with her when she went to the toilet. " 'Yes,' she said, 'often. He goes on *pestering* me till I let him. Children are all like that' " (p. 57).

+ anal stimulation*

2. Enemas and aperients were administered frequently to Hans "from the very first" because he had such trouble with his stools (p. 55-56).

− / + beatings*

3. The mother often threatened to beat Hans with the carpet beater (p. 81). Apparently her threats generally were not carried out in this family which was determined to be "modern" and understanding. Freud notes (p. 6): Hans's parents had agreed that in bringing up their child "they would not use more coercion than might be absolutely necessary for maintaining good behavior." That Hans probably did get some whacks from his mother is suggested by the report that on occasion the mother would whack Hans's baby sister on her bare bottom so as to make the little girl scream (p. 72).

Behavioral Symptoms correlated with
adult punitive and excretory contacts

− / + closing down upon destructively*

1. Hans expressed occasional phantasies about whipping. However, this sadistic theme had not invaded the area of his symptoms. In one phantasy Hans reported: " 'Once I had the whip and whipped the horse and it fell down and made a row with its feet' " (p. 79). In another, he referred to his mother and explained, "I should just like to beat her" (p. 81).

+ excretory
symptoms*

2. Hans's preoccupation with excrement permeated his fears and phantasies. Hans explained to his father that according to his thinking, *lumf (feces) is white or black* (p. 55). On the other hand, Hans was quite upset by *black* horses (p. 51, 67), carts of *black* coal (p. 54), his mother's *black* panties (p. 56, 63, 67), *black* leather (p. 67), and *dark* food (p. 68). Thus, one day he remarked: " 'I spit because (Mummy's) black drawers are black like lumf.' " Another day, he complained of dark food as looking like lumf: "he saw a piece of liver in the soup and exclaimed, 'Ugh! A lumf!' " (p. 68). Meat croquettes too he ate with evident reluctance because their form and color reminded him of lumf (p. 68). Similarly, when he accompanied his parents in a second class train carriage, he looked at the black leather upholstery of the seats and said, " 'Ugh, that makes me spit!' " and then went on to speak of lumf (p. 67). Toilets also disturbed Hans and he complained of being frightened by the noise of the flushing toilet (p. 63-64).

+ falling*

3. The theme of "falling" made its appearance over and over again in Hans's symptoms and phantasies. He was afraid of noises which reminded him of excrement falling into the toilet (p. 66). He also was troubled by fears of himself, Hans, falling into the bath water (p. 66), his baby sister, Hanna, falling from the balcony (p. 68); and horses falling (p. 49-50), e.g. when they were teased (p. 79) or when their carts were loaded with black coal (p. 55).[3]

NOTES

[1] Hans's mother could keep arousing Hans's sexual feelings, yet Hans was not supposed to indulge in masturbatory discharge.

[2] Hans's primitive concerns about *looking, touching,* and *mouthing* the body, the sexual fore-pleasures, became increasingly clear: Hans obsessively had to *look* at horses' big bodies (p. 29). Additionally, his horse phobia initially was triggered by a little girl friend's father saying not to *touch* the white horse (p. 29). Finally, the phobia consistently focused upon the theme of horses *biting* flesh (p. 22).
Whereas Hans's neurosis focused upon the actions of looking, touching, and biting, so also it focused upon certain objects, e.g. the big bodies of horses which in many ways were equivalent to the big bodies of his mother and father: Hans was preoccupied with the white horse just as he was preoccupied with the white body of his father. Thus he exclaimed to his father: "Daddy you are lovely. You're so white" (p. 53). On another occasion, Hans even spontaneously referred to his father in the same terms as he would a horse as he called out: "Daddy don't trot away from me" (p. 45). Similarly, he equated the bodies of horses with his mother's nude body: "I thought you were so big," he said to her, "you'd have a widdler like a horse" (p. 10).

[3] Hans connected in his mind thoughts about (1) horse carts loaded with black coal; (2) fecal loads; and (3) an unborn baby lodged within the abdomen (p. 73).

[4] Of note, Freud reported two of Hans's dreams. Except for a reference to his separation problem (see above), these dreams displayed no direct reference to the symptom-dream-content variables being statistically evaluated by the 100 Case Study. However, these

two dreams do direct attention to two sources of stimulation taking place in Hans's life: (a) coaxing, (b) the penis. These dreams as reported by Freud are as follows:

(a) "When I was asleep, I thought you were gone and I had no Mummy to *coax* with" (p. 23).

(b) "Some one said, 'who wants to come to me?' Then some one said, 'I do.' Then he had to make him *widdle*" (p. 19)

Freud's "Little Hans"

1

Stimulation-Symptom-and-Dream-Profile

	+ Separation Phobias	
	Night Terrors, Twilight States	
− / + Sleep in Bed with Adult	+ Irrational Fears: Other	
	+ Irrational Tempers	
− / + Adult Genital Erotic	+ Sexual Symptoms	
	+ Biting/Cutting, etc.	} *content of*
− / + View Adult Coitus	+ Eyes	} *dreams and*
	Fire	} *symptoms*

	Learning Problems (levels 2 or 3 etc.)	
Punitive Yelling	Lying and Delinquency	
	Reversal of Affect	
− / + Beatings	Closing Down Upon, Kill	} *content of dreams and*
	+ Falling	} *symptoms*

	+ Excretory Symptoms and Dreams	
	Anal Masturbation	
Preoccupation with Child's BM	Enuresis	
	Illness, etc.	} *content of*
+ Anal Contacts	Pain	} *dreams and*
	Death	} *symptoms*
	+ Compulsions	

Case 2: Synopsis of Leo Rangell's "Paul"

Leo Rangell (*Psychoanalytic Study of the Child,* Vol. V, 1950, p. 358-390) presents the case of seven-year-old "Paul" who, according to his parents, was a bright, outgoing, social, witty and happy appearing child during the day (p. 360). However, at night Paul suffered from an unrelenting series of nightmares and fears (p. 358). The home atmosphere was described as harmonious, warm, and permissive (p. 365) and the parents went out of their way to assure Paul of their love and understanding (p. 362).

Sources of Stimulation:
children's tactile and visual erogenous contacts with the adult body

+ sleeping in bed with adults*

1. Shortly after Paul's little sister Ann was born, Paul's parents began their nightly practice of lying down with him in bed. The mother reasoned that in this way Paul would feel loved and then would be able to develop a sense of security. It became more and more difficult for Paul's parents to resist his pleas for them to sleep with him (p. 359).

Dr. Rangell conducted therapy with the parents from a geographical distance via an interchange of letters. In these letters, he urged the parents to control their practice of resting in bed with their son: "Please try very, very hard not to sleep in his bed. . . . It is all too stimulating to him and perpetuates the problem. Sit up next to his bed when put to the task and make repeated attempts to return to your own room" (p. 366). Despite such kindly advice from Dr. Rangell, the parents for one reason or another continued the bed-sharing custom on and off for many months before they finally were able to institute consistent controls (p. 367).

− / + view adult coitus*

− / + adult genital erotic*

2. Paul's family spent their vacation in a small log cabin where they found it "necessary" to share the same bedroom throughout the summer months. Dr. Rangell noted that these sleeping arrangements invited repeated exposure to primal scene material (p. 379). However, no reports pertaining to this matter were received from Paul's parents. The nature and range of Paul's observations remain unknown.

+ adult nudity

3. Paul did refer to "the big size of his grandpa's penis, the big size of his daddy's penis" (p. 380).

Behavioral Symptoms correlated with
children's tactile and visual erogenous contacts with the adult body

+ separation
phobia*

1. Paul's separation problems appeared most obtrusively at night. If he could not get a parent to lie down with him, he pleaded with them to remain at least where he could see them. "When I see you I feel better," he would say (p. 367). These separation fears were reflected in his dreams. In one dream he was separated from his father in the subway station and awoke panic-stricken upon not being able to find him (p. 378).

Separation fears were also beginning to invade his daytime activities. The parents noted (p. 359) that Paul "for the last few months . . . has taken a dislike to school, whimpers, 'Must I go?,' gets terribly cold, shivers," even though "he happens to be one of the brightest children in the class." Paul admitted that when he worked hard in school he got a headache, especially when he wanted to be home with his parents.

+ night terrors*

2. It was Paul's "nightmares" of wild animals which motivated his parents to seek psychiatric help for him. He would awaken every single night without exception in a state of panic. Only immediate comforting by his parents in the form of lying down in bed beside him or remaining in the room with him was able momentarily to quiet his surge of nightly fears (p. 358-59, 361).

+ irrational
tempers*

+ nightmares

3. Paul suffered from temper tantrums though tempers were not listed as a presenting problem. Paul would be "difficult" when he did not have his own way (p. 377). Additionally, he became increasingly angry at night as his fears abated with therapy. Whereas at one time "he was quite willing to go to sleep but would have nightmares, later he would refuse altogether to go into his bedroom and would have outbursts of loud crying and yelling. . . ." These yelling tantrums subsided as bed-sharing was completely discontinued (p. 380).

+ biting/cutting/
stomach*

4. Paul's nightmares featured the presence of flesh-biting animals: lions, tigers, foxes, and wolves (p. 359, 363) (animals who would evoke the warning: "Don't touch or they'll bite"). Other dreams involved a gorilla with an open mouth (p. 363) or a squirrel who grabbed nuts in his mouth (p. 372).

If, at night, Paul dreamt of animals with sharp teeth, during the day he complained of aches in his stomach. The mother realized that these stomach complaints were emotional in origin but *hoped that the security of the parental bed would relieve both his fearful dreams* and his stomach tensions (p. 360). Unfortunately, the reverse was true: Paul's nightmares about animals with big teeth as well as his persistent stomach complaints did not disappear until the parents unreservedly refused to let Paul come into bed with them (p. 374-75).

Sources of Stimulation:
adult punitive and excretory contacts with children

+ preoccupation with child's BM*

    1. Paul's mother was preoccupied with inspecting his bowel movements, and wrote Dr. Rangell about Paul's extremely large bowel movements. For example, one day she was concerned that Paul had three large bowel movements and that maybe they were related to some salmon she had given him for lunch, etc., etc. The mother concluded: "But I don't know that this whole thing is not an emotional problem" (p. 360).

Behavioral Problems correlated with
adult punitive and excretory contacts with children

+ falling*

    1. Paul's dreams featured the theme of falling: e.g., "The gorilla was chasing me through the jungle. I ran and just reached the ship in time . . . the gorilla jumped after the ship and caught on to the back end. But the ship went too fast and he *fell* into the water" (p. 364). Paul also dreamed that the father was killed as he *fell* off the subway platform; and that nuts *fell* from a hole in a tree and hit a fox on the nose (p. 372, 382).

+ killing*

    Paul's dream that his father was killed by falling off a subway platform, followed a dream that "Daddy was shot and killed by a cowboy" (p. 382).

+ excretory symptoms and dreams*

    2. Prior to "therapy," Paul experienced bouts of diarrhea and soiling in school as well as concern about his bowel movements (p. 359-360, 365). He also dreamed about the *back-end* of a ship and the *back* of a horse.

+ death and dying*

    3. On six reported occasions, Paul's conversation directly referred to dying. He persisted in his questions about death of family members: "When did grandmother die? . . . when did grandfather die?" (p. 368) ". . . would father?" (p. 369, 370, 380). He also expressed the phantasy wish that his mother might go away or die (p. 372).

+ pain*
+ illness non-organic*

    4. In school, Paul suffered from headaches when he was upset over his separation from home and parents (p. 368).

Rangell's "Paul"
2

Stimulation-Symptom-and-Dream-Profile

	+ Separation Phobias
	+ Night Terrors, Twilight States
+ Sleep in Bed with Adult	Irrational Fears: Other
	+ Irrational Tempers
− / + Adult Genital Erotic	Sexual Symptoms
	+ Biting/Cutting, etc.
− / + View Adult Coitus	Eyes
	Fire

content of dreams and symptoms

	Learning Problems (levels 2 or 3 etc.)
Punitive Yelling	Lying and Delinquency
	Reversal of Affect
Beatings	+ Closing Down Upon, Kill
	+ Falling

content of dreams and symptoms

	+ Excretory Symptoms and Dreams
	Anal Masturbation
+ Preoccupation with Child's BM	Enuresis
	+ Illness, etc.
Anal Contacts	+ Pain
	+ Death
	Compulsions

content of dreams and symptoms

Case 3: Brian

Brian, a bright, eight-year-old boy with an I.Q. of 145 and with a pale, frail body, was referred to the clinic for severe school phobic symptoms. Even though he loved learning, wanted to go to school, and received top grades, he panicked upon separating from his mother and could not remain in school.

Sources of Stimulation:
children's tactile and visual erogenous contacts with the adult body

+ sleeping in bed
with adults*

1. When Brian was asked whether he ever would wake up frightened and want to get into his mother's bed for comfort, Brian answered that he *didn't get up* to get into his mother's bed because he was *there* all the time. He slept regularly with his mother, this despite the fact that they lived in a fourteen room mansion. Possibly one reason the mother might have insisted upon sleeping with her boy so constantly was her fear that her husband, a harmless enough man whom she had divorced, might come and take Brian away from her. In any case, Brian found sharing his mother's bed no hardship. He enjoyed waking up knowing that, at any time he wished, he was able to touch her.

Brian's mother could not see bed-sharing with her son as much of a problem. When her social worker indicated surprise and pointed out that perhaps this arrangement contributed to Brian's difficulty in being separated from her, she seemed singularly uninterested in changing. "Oh stop making so much of it," she claimed initially. Yet at the end of the hour she volunteered to see if she could get a separate cot for Brian.

+ adult nudity

2. Sharing the same bedroom and bathroom with his mother, Brian frequently would see her unclothed. In addition he was permitted to wash his mother while she was taking her bath.

Behavioral Symptoms correlated with
children's tactile and visual erogenous contacts with the adult body

+ separation
phobia*

1. Each morning when it was time for Brian to leave for school he would be overtaken by a state of panic, stomachache and nausea. This school phobic symptom kept him glued to his mother. As part of the school's effort to help Brian remain in school, his mother was at first allowed to be present in the classroom. However, when the mother was asked to wait in the library, Brian refused to remain in the classroom and ran up to the library to make sure that his mother was still there.

+ biting/cutting/
  stomach*

2. The stomach reactions which accompanied Brian's separation panics at school also appeared when he was separated from his mother at the clinic. Even though he was able to remain alone with his therapist during his diagnostic interviews, nonetheless he complained of trembling inside with butterflies in his stomach.

Sources of Stimulation:
adult punitive and excretory contacts with children

+ adult
  preoccupation
  with child's
  BM*
+ anal
  stimulation*

1. Although Brian was eight years old, his mother continued to wipe him at the toilet. Furthermore, she pulled his pants down for him when he was in a hurry. Occasionally she assisted him at the toilet by putting suppositories into his rectum. Consistent with these activities which erogenously rewarded Brian for passivity, the mother would also wash him in his bath.

+ hitting

2. The mother admitted that she *used* to fly off the handle and would swat Brian and his brother. The father had threatened that if she hurt the boys he would "kill" her.

Behavioral Symptoms correlated with
adult punitive and excretory contacts with children

+ hurting
− / + closing
down upon
destructively* (no
symptoms)
+ pains*
+ illness non-
  organic*

1. Brian was afraid of being *hurt* by the tough boys in school. This concern about being hurt was also reflected in his associative material at the end of his second diagnostic hour when Brian drew a picture of tanks charging down upon a man.

2. As already noted, Brian's separation panics in school were accompanied by attacks of stomachaches and nausea.

Brian

3

Stimulation-Symptom-and-Dream-Profile

	+ Separation Phobias	
	Night Terrors, Twilight States	
+ Sleep in Bed with Adult	Irrational Fears: Other	
	Irrational Tempers	
Adult Genital Erotic	Sexual Symptoms	
	+ Biting/Cutting, etc.	⎫ *content of*
View Adult Coitus	Eyes	⎬ *dreams and*
	Fire	⎭ *symptoms*
	Learning Problems (levels 2 or 3 etc.)	
Punitive Yelling	Lying and Delinquency	
	Reversal of Affect	
Beatings	Closing-Down-Upon, Kill	⎫ *content of*
		⎬ *dreams and*
	Falling	⎭ *symptoms*
	Excretory Symptoms and Dreams	
	Anal Masturbation	
+ Preoccupation with Child's BM	Enuresis	
	+ Illness, etc.	⎫ *content of*
+ Anal Contacts	+ Pain	⎬ *dreams and*
	Death	⎭ *symptoms*
	Compulsions	

Case 4: Chippy

Chippy's school phobia, a presenting symptom when he was referred to the clinic at the age of thirteen, persisted on and off until he was sixteen. His mother had always kept him an infant by physically rewarding him for passive submission. *At the age of nine she was still wiping him at the toilet, and at the age of thirteen he was still being helped to wash and dry himself.* It is not surprising, therefore, that Chippy could do little for himself other than sit and study or go to bed. He would attempt no sports and was so restricted that he even found it difficult to talk. The situation was made all the worse by his mother's overpermissiveness. Chippy was allowed, for example, to eat whenever and wherever he wanted. His father's attempts to offer help and correction only brought forth the mother's constant opposition and blame. The principal work of therapy focused upon teaching Chippy how to be active, creative, and independent.

It was upon such a background that the following stimulus patterns and reactions were superimposed.

Sources of Stimulation:
children's tactile and visual erogenous contacts with the adult body

+ sleeping in bed with adult*

1. Chippy slept between his parents until he was ten. Furthermore, until the age of thirteen he continued to get into bed with his mother while his father was away.

+ adult nudity

2. When Chippy was thirteen years old, the mother was still allowing him to see her without clothes. Although he had not recently seen his father nude, Chippy, when he was little, showered together with his father.

Behavioral Symptoms correlated with
children's tactile and visual erogenous contacts with the adult body

+ separation phobia*

1. Chippy struggled with his school phobia from his twelfth to his sixteenth year. One week he would be threatening not to go to high school where he was a top A student; the next week, he would be out of school completely. Then one day he wrenched his leg, required a cast and thereafter stayed out of school for over three months. Chippy could be motivated to return to school only after he was faced with the alternative of attending his school as required by law or being sent to boarding school away from home.

Chippy's fears of making friends, it turned out, also reflected a separation problem. As he explained to his therapist: "My unconscious doesn't want me to make friends: with no friends I could stay home all the time. I wouldn't want to go out into the unknown . . . I might be with strange people and be uncomfortable."

+ irrational
tempers*

2. At the age of thirteen, Chippy explained that he still loved to scream, especially when "there was nothing else to do." His father complained that Chippy would easily fly off the handle and his mother noted that almost anything could upset him. Often he would break out sneezing, coughing, and crying during his rages.

+ sexual
symptoms*

3. Compulsive masturbation was a problem for Chippy. His parents would find him masturbating and would constantly tell him not to touch his penis. Chippy himself became very worried when he would see his penis become irritated and red.

Sources of Stimulation:
adult punitive and excretory contacts with children

+ adult
preoccupation
with child's
defecation*
+ punitive
yelling*

1. Until he was nine years old, Chippy was wiped by his mother at the toilet.

2. In Chippy's presence, the parents would frequently argue and yell at one another. First, the father would get upset at Chippy for doing things the wrong way. Then the mother would explode at the father for attacking her son.

Behavioral Symptoms correlated with
adult punitive and excretory contacts with children

+ negative
behavior

1. Chippy was withdrawn from children other than his cousins, though at one time he did have one "friend." Furthermore, prior to therapy he was restricted in his activities and interests; and when he did begin coming to the clinic, he found it very difficult to talk with his first therapist.

+ negative
emotion

2. Chippy objected to everything in school: he did not like his teachers and did not like his classmates. He also complained that the teachers did not like him. His mother pointed out that this attitude was not realistic since the teachers always seemed to like him.

In favor of Chippy's positive qualities, at the age of thirteen he did cooperate positively with his therapist's recommendations that he stop sleeping in bed with his mother and seeing her nude; and eventually he did respond positively to his therapist's endeavors to help him gain ego mastery of his separation problems.

Chippy
4

Stimulation-Symptom-and-Dream-Profile

+ Separation Phobias

Night Terrors, Twilight States

+ Sleep in Bed with Adult   Irrational Fears: Other

+ Irrational Tempers

Adult Genital Erotic   + Sexual Symptoms

Biting/Cutting, etc.   } *content of*

View Adult Coitus   Eyes   } *dreams and*

Fire   } *symptoms*

Learning Problems (levels 2 or 3 etc.)

+ Punitive Yelling   Lying and Delinquency

Reversal of Affect

Beatings   Closing Down Upon, Kill   } *content of*

Falling   } *dreams and symptoms*

Excretory Symptoms and Dreams

Anal Masturbation

+ Preoccupation with Child's BM   Enuresis

Illness, etc.   } *content of*

Anal Contacts   Pain   } *dreams and*

Death   } *symptoms*

Compulsions

Case 5: Aaron

On two occasions, Aaron, age ten, had recently "run out of school without his coat, across a busy highway to get home." Despite Aaron's conscientiousness and his attachment to his "favorite teacher" he persistently was reluctant to attend school subsequent to his weekends at home. Sometimes separation was so upsetting for Aaron that he became nauseated in school.

Aaron was angry at himself for not being able to remain in school. He told his mother he "didn't want to run home in the first place." He was worried that he would miss his homework assignments and that he no longer would be able to keep up his high standards of school performance.

Aaron lived with his mother from the time his parents were divorced two years prior to the diagnostic referral. His father was alcoholic and epileptic (though EEG findings were normal even during seizures). Aaron was eight years old the last time he saw his father experiencing a seizure: "The bed was shaking and he had to have something in his mouth." After his parents' divorce, Aaron visited his father for a few hours each Sunday, this despite his mother's concern.

Sources of Stimulation:
children's tactile and visual erogenous contacts with the adult body

+ sleeping in bed with adults*

1. For a month prior to his referral, Aaron had been frequently kissing his mother on the mouth. He also liked to cuddle in bed with her. Sometimes the mother would wake up at night to find Aaron sleeping next to her. Aaron confided that at such times he liked to rest close to his mother's body. Aaron explained: "If I were really scared, my mother would let me stay in bed with her for the night; but if she thought I wasn't scared, she'd only let me stay there until she wanted to go to bed . . . Her unconscious[1] wants me there but her smart part don't . . . I get in her bed about three or four times a week."

+ adult nudity

2. Aaron recalled "two" occasions when he saw his mother nude: "When I was about two my mother brought me in with her to a toilet when we were on a trip driving. I saw how she looked between the legs when she was sitting on the toilet." The second occasion occurred when Aaron was five years old at which time Aaron took a bath with his mother.

Aaron recalled his penis getting hard as he looked at *Playboy* magazines.

16

Behavioral Symptoms correlated with
children's tactile and visual erogenous contacts with the adult body

+ separation
   phobias*

1. Aaron's chief presenting problem consisted of school phobic symptoms accompanied by nausea. Despite his conscientious interest in his school work, something made him suddenly get up in the middle of his class and run impulsively home.

+ irrational fears*
+ nightmares

2. As already noted, Aaron was allowed to sleep with his mother when his night fears had gotten the best of him. When he was younger Aaron experienced daytime fears of dogs and would have nightmares of them biting him.

+ sexual
   symptoms*

3. Aaron confided that his "hot dog" would get stiff when he was watching TV; this occurred frequently enough that his mother took him to the hospital for a checkup. She worried that his former hernia was acting up.

+ biting/cutting*

4. Aaron presented two dreams during his diagnostic: (a) "When I used to be afraid of dogs I would dream of dogs *biting* people"; (b) "About sharks eating people."

Sources of Stimulation:
adult punitive and excretory contacts with children

+ punitive
   yelling*

1. In answer to the opening diagnostic question: "What do you think are your problems?" Aaron answered, "My mother goes hollering at me a lot. . . . My mind is over-active because I'm scared of being hollered at." Similarly, Aaron described his first memory taking place at the age of four: "I would do things wrong by accident and I'd get hollered at." The mother in return reported she "yelled and picked on Aaron all day long."

+ beatings*

2. Aaron's mother also hit him on the hand or arm about once a week. Sometimes she hit him on his back hard enough to *leave a mark the rest of the day*. Aaron concluded, however, that "her hollering is worse than the hitting."

Violence also stemmed from Aaron's father's explosions and wild rage prior to the parents' divorce. On one occasion, the father hurled a brick through the windshield of the family car so as to scatter broken glass over the mother.

+ anal
   stimulation*

+ adult
   defecation

3. "About thirty times" the mother put suppositories into Aaron's rectum to help him with constipation when he was five or six years old. Aaron also recalled the occasion when he saw his mother's legs wide open as she defecated into the toilet.

Behavioral Symptoms correlated with
adult punitive and excretory contacts with children

+/− negative
behavior

1. When asked what were his earliest memories, Aaron answered "When I was four, I would do things wrong by accident and I'd get hollered at." Since that time an authority battle continued to rage between Aaron and his mother

at home. Aaron complained "My friend can get away with stuff and I can't."
Aaron's mother explained that for three months prior to the diagnostic, Aaron
had been rebelling against her authority, while in return she had been yelling
and picking on him all day long. These battles led to Aaron's *lying* to his mother,
for which he would get two or three whacks on his bottom.

+ lying*

+ illness non-
organic*

2. Aaron suffered from periods of nausea and constipation. He remembered when he was five or six years old he would not go to the toilet for two
weeks at a time.

+ excretory
symptoms*

On occasion, Aaron would have "BM" accidents in his pants. He related
how his mother would not get mad if he told her directly about his accidents.
Sometimes he messed himself on purpose. At such times his mother would make
him stay in his room and miss one of his favorite TV shows.[2]

+ hurting

3. In answer to his therapist's inquiry as to how Aaron's anger eventually
got discharged *when his mother yelled and hit too much,* Aaron answered: "I
might make trouble for someone. I might hurt someone, not meaning to. Then
they'd think I did it on purpose and we'd get in a real fight."

NOTES

[1] A word he had learned during his diagnostic.

[2] For other examples of excretory symptoms among children who have been yelled at
excessively, see cases 37, 58, 64, 65, 67, 70, 71, 72, 76, 77, and 78. It is possible that
frightening noises among children activate defecation much as electrical shocks activate defecation among mice and other experimental animals.

Aaron

5

Stimulation-Symptom-and-Dream-Profile

+ Separation Phobias

Night Terrors, Twilight States

+ Sleep in Bed with Adult   + Irrational Fears: Other

Irrational Tempers

Adult Genital Erotic   + Sexual Symptoms

+ Biting/Cutting, etc.   } *content of*

View Adult Coitus   Eyes   } *dreams and*

Fire   } *symptoms*

Learning Problems (levels 2 or 3 etc.)

+ Punitive Yelling   + Lying and Delinquency

Reversal of Affect   } *content of*

+ Beatings   Closing Down Upon, Kill   } *dreams and*

Falling   } *symptoms*

+ Excretory Symptoms and Dreams

Anal Masturbation

Preoccupation with Child's BM   Enuresis

+ Illness, etc.   } *content of*

+ Anal Contacts   Pain   } *dreams and*

Death   } *symptoms*

Compulsions

Case 6: Darryl

Darryl, at the age of fifteen, was beset by a severe school phobia. For three months prior to his diagnostic evaluation he had been unable to leave home to attend school. In an effort to help him return to his classes the school arranged for him to sit in the principal's office each day. However, he could do no better than attend an art class each week for two hours.

When Darryl was twelve, his father and both of his grandmothers died within a span of two weeks. Darryl was left to live at home alone with his mother. This lady was a dominant woman who had gloried in the weakness of her husband and of her son. She spoke of the father's sperm being "weak" as she proudly claimed, "I was too strong for him." In keeping with this attitude she completely took over decisions while the father was alive. With pride, she told how she "put up the screens, paid the bills, and arranged for repairs." She also interfered with any attempts by the father to discipline Darryl.

Likewise, the mother took over Darryl's ego functions: she drove the fifteen-year-old boy to school "to save time" and thereby rewarded him for being passive. On the other hand her punishments for Darryl consisted of her making him walk to school. In this way she linked his positive ego functions with situations of punishments. When Darryl's therapist attempted to encourage him to take an active stance, tears came into Darryl's eyes. He explained to his therapist that if his mother drove him around in a car it was because he did *not* like to walk; his aunt did not like to walk either; she lived with *her* father and he drove her wherever she wanted, so why shouldn't his mother do the same for him?

Sources of Stimulation:
adult punitive and excretory contacts with children

1. The mother stated that Darryl's father had been "too severe" and lost control of his temper when he was angry. She, therefore, had interceded when the father tried to discipline Darryl. At such times the mother and father would argue angrily.

+ punitive
  yelling*

The mother also admitted that she herself would get upset with Darryl and let her anger out by screaming at him.

+ adult
  defecation

2. The mother allowed Darryl to be in the bathroom with her while she was defecating (see below).

20

Behavioral Symptoms correlated with
adult punitive and excretory contacts with children

+ enuresis*

1. Darryl's early development was uneventful beyond a somewhat late appearance of urinary control: following a brief hospitalization for a tonsillectomy, Darryl wet his bed from the age of two and a half to three and a half years.

+ learning
(level 1)

2. Darryl's capacity to learn declined from the time his father died, three years prior to his diagnostic referral. Darryl reflected, "I don't mind school when marks come easy without my doing any work, but I don't want to put out the effort."

+ negative
emotion

3. Darryl found fault continually with the food his mother prepared for him to eat. Darryl's negative emotions also were reflected by his disinterest in receiving any kind of therapy to help him with his problems.

Sources of Stimulation:
children's tactile and visual erogenous contacts with the adult body

1. Darryl and his mother held hands while they watched TV at home alone together.

+ adult nudity

2. Darryl explained that the doors of his mother's room and his room were open at night. This arrangement made it possible for this teenager to see his mother in various stages of undress approximately once a month. Just two weeks prior to his referral, he saw his mother completely naked.

− / + adult genital
erotic*

Additionally, Darryl would be allowed in the bathroom while his mother was on the toilet. Conversely, the mother would come into the bathroom while Darryl was urinating. Thus, the mother and her fifteen-year-old adolescent son saw each other's genitalia regularly despite the sexual temptations which such exposures entailed.

Behavioral Symptoms correlated with
children's tactile and visual erogenous contacts with the adult body

+ sexual
symptoms*

1. The mother pin-pointed Darryl's withdrawal from his peer groups as occurring when the boys first started to become interested in girls.

+ irrational fears*

2. Darryl was afraid of going to the barber and stayed as far away as possible from the barber shop.

+ biting/
cutting*(teeth)

3. During his diagnostic, Darryl recalled one dream which he reported as: "I was in the barber's chair. I turned around and the barber was bald. He had colored *teeth* like a xylophone." Darryl's associations led to memories of a barber *cutting* his ear.

+ separation
phobia*

4. Darryl's severe school phobia necessitated his referral for diagnostic evaluation. He became totally unable to attend school although he had previously

been an A student and had always enjoyed his classes until his phobia erupted. He had also been a favorite of his teachers and enjoyed helping them with chores.

At home, Darryl did not want to be separated from his mother. He would try to keep her from going out at night on the basis that he did not like staying alone.

Darryl
6

Stimulation-Symptom-and-Dream-Profile

	+ Separation Phobias	
	Night Terrors, Twilight States	
Sleep in Bed with Adult	+ Irrational Fears: Other	
	Irrational Tempers	
− / + Adult Genital Erotic	+ Sexual Symptoms	
	+ Biting/Cutting, etc.	*content of*
View Adult Coitus	Eyes	*dreams and*
	Fire	*symptoms*

	Learning Problems (levels 2 or 3 etc.)	
+ Punitive Yelling	Lying and Delinquency	
	Reversal of Affect	
Beatings	Closing Down Upon, Kill	*content of*
		dreams and
	Falling	*symptoms*

	Excretory Symptoms and Dreams	
	Anal Masturbation	
Preoccupation with Child's BM	+ Enuresis	
	Illness, etc.	*content of*
Anal Contacts	Pain	*dreams and*
	Death	*symptoms*
	Compulsions	

Case 7: Elmer

Elmer, a thin, eight-year-old boy of high average intelligence, looked rather sad and small when he arrived at the clinic for his diagnostic interviews. His presenting problems included "temper tantrums," "poor school performance" and "need for attention."

Sources of Stimulation:
children's tactile and visual erogenous contacts with the adult body

+ sleeping in bed with adults*

1. Elmer was in the habit of waking up at 3 a.m. and proceeding to get into bed with his parents. His mother would try to put him out of the room, but because he would throw terrible temper tantrums at such times she would capitulate and allow him to remain in her bed an hour or so until he fell asleep. Elmer explained that actually he would often sleep between his mother and father. At other times, he would sleep in bed with his sister, age fourteen, or with his big brother, age seventeen.

+ adult nudity

Elmer was accustomed to seeing both his father and his twenty-six-year-old sister, Sally, unclothed.

Behavioral Symptoms correlated with
children's tactile and visual erogenous contacts with the adult body

+ separation phobia*

1. Elmer continually "hung around" his mother. The degree of his separation problem was reflected by his refusal to go to the second floor of his house without her, e.g. he refused to go upstairs to the bathroom alone.

+ sexual symptoms*
+ hysterical conversion*
(+ pain*)

2. As Elmer spoke of seeing his twenty-six-year-old sister Sally nude, he became nervous and told how seeing her that way made his "dinky" get stiff.

3. Elmer displayed a classical hysterical conversion symptom during one diagnostic session: no sooner had he spoken of his penis getting stiff in the presence of his nude twenty-six-year-old sister, than he began to complain of a painful stiffness[1] suddenly appearing in his neck.

+ eyes* (looking)

4. The one dream reported by Elmer included a reference to "looking." In the dream, Elmer explained: "Me and my brother Clark Kent, my mother and Superman and Sally went to the beach. There was a big aquarium there. You could *sleep and look* at the fish because they were electrified."

+ biting/cutting*

5. Before family controls were established, Elmer would *bite* adults,[2] especially when anyone attempted to interfere with his temper tantrums.

23

+ irrational
tempers*

6. It was Elmer's wild temper tantrums which motivated his family to bring him to the clinic. Whenever he was corrected, he would throw a tantrum during which he would scream, and kick anyone near him. A month following the parents' decision to put an end to bed-sharing and exposure to adult nudity, Elmer's mother phoned to offer the cheerful news that he was no longer having temper tantrums.

Sources of Stimulation:
adult punitive and excretory contacts with children

+ early
deprivation

1. During the first six months of pregnancy, Elmer's mother was very upset, nauseous, and exhausted. She described the pregnancy as "simply awful." Elmer was born when his mother was forty years old. She had been looking forward to being free of responsibilities after having raised three other children and became very angry at her husband for burdening her with another child. The mother admitted it was the truth, she did not want Elmer. She complained that as a baby he would push his parents away and did not want to be picked up. As a baby he also displayed difficulty in accepting solids and remained a poor eater up to the present.

+ punitive
yelling*

2. Elmer was *constantly yelled at* by his father, "a very high strung, impatient man . . . a nervous wreck" who relentlessly demanded perfection.

Behavioral Symptoms correlated with
adult punitive and excretory contacts with children

+ freezing of
affect

1. Elmer's emotional life was characterized by an inhibition of affect, especially when he was hurt. He refused to admit to anyone that he was upset even when he was suffering.

+ learning*
(level 2)

2. Elmer did well in the first grade of school. However, he decided he did not like his second grade teacher, flunked, and then when he repeated the year, managed to do even more poorly.

NOTES

1 See Selma Fraiberg's case of Roger, case 75.
2 Not in the playful way that "Little Hans" had bitten his father.
3 It is uncertain whether Elmer reported a dream about a bottle that was cracked over his brother's head and stuck in his back.

Elmer

7

Stimulation-Symptom-and-Dream-Profile

+ Separation Phobias
+ Night Terrors, Twilight States
+ Sleep in Bed with Adult   Irrational Fears: Other
+ Irrational Tempers
Adult Genital Erotic   + Sexual Symptoms
+ Biting/Cutting, etc.   } *content of*
View Adult Coitus   + Eyes   } *dreams and*
Fire   } *symptoms*

+ Learning Problems (levels 2 or 3 etc.)
Lying and Delinquency
+ Punitive Yelling   Reversal of Affect
Closing Down Upon, Kill } *content of*
Beatings   Falling   } *dreams and*
} *symptoms*

Excretory Symptoms and Dreams
Anal Masturbation
Preoccupation with Child's BM   Enuresis
Illness, etc.   } *content of*
Anal Contacts   + Pain   } *dreams and*
Death   } *symptoms*
Compulsions

Case 8: Francis

Francis, a top notch student of thirteen with an I.Q. of 135, was forced by his mother to come to the clinic because of his psychosomatic symptoms: stomach upsets, headaches and diarrhea. He presented the impression of a highly learned and cultured member of the diplomatic corps. He was thought of most highly by his teachers and other adults.

Sources of Stimulation:
adult punitive and excretory contacts with children

+ early
deprivation

1. Francis experienced a particularly painful first three years of life during which his mother suffered prolonged depressions, withdrawal, and crying spells. She had no social contacts during these years and spent most of her time in bed. It was difficult for her to provide physical care for Francis especially since, according to her own report, she was disoriented and confused during these years of his infancy. Often she would leave Francis helplessly screaming and crying for hours in his crib.

+ punitive
yelling*

2. Unfortunately, his mother's problems continued to plague the family as Francis grew up. When Francis was three years old, the mother pulled out of her state of withdrawal and depression, but to compensate for her own feelings of helplessness she became relentlessly controlling. She would use anger, tears, and threats of depression and emotional breakdown as a means of worrying her family to the point that they would always give in to her. The mother also would continually blame, yell and scream at her husband so as to direct the focus of attention away from her own inadequacies.

+ anal
stimulation*

+ preoccupation
with child's BM*

3. The parents required Francis to submit to frequent enemas when he was four and five years old. His father would hold him on his lap while the mother would insert the tube. Francis reported being very frightened of these procedures. Additionally, Francis's mother was reported to have been preoccupied with Francis's loose bowels.

Behavioral Symptoms correlated with
adult punitive and excretory contacts with children

+ negative
behavior and
negative
emotion

1. At the age of thirteen, Francis found it very difficult to trust[1] (and never did so during his three years of therapy). He often withdrew from his peers and preferred to play quietly alone or to spend time with the elders at the church prayer-meetings.

26

Additionally, Francis was obsessed with inner narcissistic feelings of devalued self-worth.[1] He frequently expressed to his mother that he could not understand why she loved him at all, he was *"no good,"* etc. And to compensate for this diffusely negative self-concept, he rigidly demanded A+ work from himself in school. Actually, Francis offered as his presenting problem his dissatisfaction with his school work: he had only received three A+'s and one A−. Francis otherwise insisted that he had *no* problems and was convinced that he needed *no* therapy.

+ enuresis*
+ excretory
  problems*

2. Francis wet himself until he was seven years old. He also suffered from constipation for many years; later he was troubled by diarrhea. Medical examination revealed that these bowel disturbances were emotionally determined.

+ preoccupation
  with illness*
+ pain*

3. Francis generally suffered from hypochondriasis. He would go to bed with headaches and stomachaches and also complained of hot and cold flashes along with his diarrhea. Francis's headaches continued to disturb him for many years. These headaches appeared when he was most upset. Their intensity warranted EEG studies which revealed no organic basis for the symptom.

Sources of Stimulation:
children's tactile and visual erogenous contacts with the adult body

+ sleeping in bed
  with adults*

1. Francis, up to the age of ten, would crawl into his parents' bed at night and sleep between his mother and father.

+ adult nudity

2. He regularly saw his mother dressing and undressing even at the time of his diagnostic study when he was thirteen years old. His mother would tell Francis and his sister not to look while she was undressing. Francis would yell at her to shut the door but it did no good.

At the age of thirteen, Francis would still shower with his father under the same spray in order "to save time" when they both were in a hurry to use the bathroom. Francis could not see that their close body proximity at such times might serve as a possible source for stimulation (this despite his dreams of long snakes; see below).

Behavioral Symptoms correlated with
children's tactile and visual erogenous contacts with the adult body

+ separation
  phobia*

1. Francis developed a school phobia during the early months of kindergarten and refused to be separated from the mother. The mother handled the situation by walking him to school and then leaving him to "scream it out." Hints of this school phobia kept reappearing up to the time of his referral for therapy. Despite his excellent work in school, Francis would have periods of stomach upsets and headaches (see above) necessitating his staying home. At such times, his symptoms would disappear as soon as school was closed for the weekend.

+ nightmare   2. Francis recalled a frightening nightmare of a long snake. In order to stop the nightmare he forced himself to wake up, so that he could proceed to climb in bed with his parents.

+ irrational   3. Francis would "take terrible fits" during which he would keep hitting
tempers*   himself when he failed to get a perfect mark. Shortly before his referral to the clinic, he became so furious that he hit the wall with his fists and tore his hair while calling himself dumb and saying he knew better than to act this way.

                  4. During kindergarten, the teacher reported that Francis would bite little
+ biting/cutting/   girls. One day the mother caught him biting a child. She handled this by holding
stomach*   him and in turn biting him on the back. He was never known to bite anyone again. However, at the age of thirteen, Francis still was preoccupied with biting. During his diagnostic interviews, he related his phantasies about the dangers of being born: "There could be something bad out there like an alligator who could bite one's head off. It would be better to come out with one's legs first; then the head would be protected, while just the feet would be chopped off."

+ stomach*   Francis's psychosomatic stomach disorders have already been mentioned: recurrently he experienced severe stomach cramps each time he was overwhelmed by fears of going to school and of leaving his mother.

NOTES

1 These feelings are in keeping with Francis's severe early deprivation of positive empathic care. The devalued feelings also must have been related to the mother's custom of continually finding fault with her family.

Francis

8

Stimulation-Symptom-and-Dream-Profile

+ Separation Phobias

Night Terrors, Twilight States

+ Sleep in Bed with Adult   Irrational Fears: Other

+ Irrational Tempers

Adult Genital Erotic   Sexual Symptoms

+ Biting/Cutting, etc.   } *content of*

View Adult Coitus   Eyes   } *dreams and*

Fire   } *symptoms*

Learning Problems (levels 2 or 3 etc.)

+ Punitive Yelling   Lying and Delinquency

Reversal of Affect

Beatings   Closing Down Upon, Kill } *content of dreams and*

Falling   } *symptoms*

+ Excretory Symptoms and Dreams

Anal Masturbation

+ Preoccupation with Child's BM   + Enuresis

+ Illness, etc.   } *content of*

+ Anal Contacts   + Pain   } *dreams and*

Death   } *symptoms*

Compulsions

Case 9: Greta

Greta, a cultured, attractive and "sophisticated" young girl, was seen in psychotherapy once a week from the time she was eight until she was twelve years old. Her referral problems as listed by her pediatrician, included "separation fears accompanied by stomachaches, tenseness, and skin scratching."

Sources of Stimulation:
children's tactile and visual erogenous contacts with the adult body

−/+ sleeping in bed with adults* (frequency?)
+ adult nudity

1-2. When, at the age of eight, Greta would awake from bad dreams of snakes, spiders, etc., she would get into bed with her parents.

Greta would see her father nude in bed and in the bathroom. It was not unusual for her to barge in on him when he was attending to toilet functions or showering.

+ adult genital erotic*

Mornings she would also like to get into bed with her father while he was completely nude. At such times she especially enjoyed allowing him to squeeze her between his legs near his exposed penis. The father rationalized his permissiveness about his nudity by emphasizing the importance of "modern" psychology and noting that the body should be seen as something fine and good, a source of pride rather than shame.

Behavioral Symptoms correlated with
children's tactile and visual erogenous contacts with the adult body

+ separation phobia*

1. A school phobia was one of Greta's three presenting problems. At the time of her referral to the clinic she would be struck by *stomachaches* when it was time for her to leave home for school. In spite of her phobia, however, she managed to get to school where she was helped a great deal by a sympathetic teacher. Medical examination revealed that Greta's disturbance was emotionally determined.

+ sexual symptoms*

2. Since the age of two and a half, Greta would masturbate in front of the family and would become particularly involved in masturbating with her younger brothers. She would touch their genitals and they would touch hers. At other times, the youngest brother would end up getting on top of her, an act which set Greta complaining of being smothered. Greta and this younger brother would also get into bed together. The mother was finally able to see that Greta would pick at her skin most frequently during these periods of close bodily contact

30

and that the skin picking did subside when a stop was put to the children's bed activities. The mother confided that Greta went "too far" when it came to sexual permissiveness, but then claimed, like her husband, she did not want her daughter to become afraid or ashamed of her body.

Unfortunately, the same behavioral trend generally infiltrated Greta's relationships with men. The father reported that she was exhibitionistic in the presence of any male. Since the age of two and a half years, she would "rub up against men and would want to touch their penises."

Of particular interest were Greta's reactions during her diagnostic interview when there occurred a reference to children's interest in the bodily differences between girls and boys and the word "penis" was mentioned. For a moment Greta responded by claiming that she didn't know anything about a penis, then suddenly she ceased to be a shy, demure little girl and began talking more and more loudly and brashly with an unusual display of envy. She was going to have *big* things and be powerful; she was going to have *big* money and get very rich; she was going to be an astronaut. She didn't want to stay home and be a cook, rather she was going to go around the world. "I want to be on a destroyer like my father, and I want to have a big gun; I want to play football; I want to be a man like daddy."

+ irrational tempers*

3. Greta broke loose with temper tantrums at home whenever she heard any kind of negative comment about herself. Her hysterical bursts of rage, a presenting problem, continued to appear regularly during the first year of therapy. Such displays would also be triggered when Greta did not want to come to the clinic for her hour of therapy. At such times, Greta gave vent to screaming, crying, and to running up and down stairs with an intensity far beyond what would be expected for even the most resistant child.

+ hysterical twilight states*

4. During her second and third year of therapy, Greta began writing over and over again on her therapist's blackboard the words "FEAR, FEAR, FEAR." At this time she ventured to tell her therapist about her acute attacks of fear which overwhelmed her frequently and during which she did not know what was happening around her. No actual loss of consciousness occurred during these attacks. However, she appeared to suffer altered states of consciousness during which external stimuli neither were perceived clearly nor could be recalled. Her mother reported that Greta's spells were characterized by extreme panic, such that Greta would run to her screaming hysterically.

Greta's therapist became concerned that these spells might be the result of a temporal lobe epilepsy due to brain damage. However, a series of EEG studies revealed negative findings and Greta's neurologist recommended librium to calm her nervousness. This medication did decrease the frequency of her attacks. Unfortunately, the relation between (a) these panic states of overwhelming excitement and (b) the excessive erotic stimulation to which Greta was exposed when she cuddled near the exposed penis of her nude father was not considered.

It is not suprising therefore that her spells of fear reappeared soon after her librium medication was discontinued.[1]

5. Just prior to the period when her *panics* became most evident, Greta began to draw during her therapy hours. She drew faces remarkable in that they contained no eyes. When her therapist took note of this, Greta became uncomfortably silent. She later began to make rhymes about these faces, and dwelt upon a particular rhyme about "weird, wicked, witches who jump out of ditches, they tear out your *eyes,* they tear out your *eyes,* they tear off your breeches."

+ eyes*

6. Greta's school phobic reactions were accompanied by stomachaches which her pediatrician described as completely emotional in origin (for details see below under "preoccupation with illness"). Greta also related a dream about "turtles, snakes, and spiders" (which snap and bite).

+ biting/cutting/
stomach*

Sources of Stimulation:
adult punitive and excretory contacts with children

1. The mother, depressed and lonely following Greta's birth, found it extremely difficult to enjoy her baby or to offer her comfort and tenderness. To make matters worse, the mother was frequently overcome by *feelings of rage* activated by criticisms of her efforts to care for Greta. Repeatedly her husband criticized her, the pediatrician criticized her, while Greta ended up screaming at her.

+ early
deprivation

In turn, Greta cried constantly during the first two months of life and was slow in gaining weight. According to her parents' report, Greta suffered from "heart trouble" which caused some blueness of her skin. Although the attacks of blueness disappeared when she was three months old, Greta continued to show signs of emotional disturbance: she displayed feeding difficulties until she was two years old and from infancy onwards she suffered from skin rashes. Even at the time of her referral, Greta continued to scratch and pick at minor sores, insect bites and pimples which irritated her skin.

Greta's reactions to deficient emotional care during her infancy also persisted in the form of an inability to trust. Her defective trust intruded into her therapeutic sessions during her first two years of therapy as was reflected by a quote from her therapist: "Communication was very difficult to establish. During the early sessions Greta was shy, withdrawn, and uncommunicative. At first it appeared this was due to an inability to verbalize readily. However, Greta soon indicated directly that she *did not want* to communicate and resented having to talk about herself. She stated that she did not like being asked questions by nosey doctors and resented people prying into her life.[2]

2. The rage which the mother experienced during Greta's infancy did not fade as the years went by; instead her excited upsets became more and more intense. Greta and her brother took the brunt of her punitive explosions. The

+ punitive
yelling*

father described how Greta's mother would yell at the children, threaten to "kill them," and threaten to force them to submit to all kinds of punishment if they didn't do one thing or another. Even after years of therapy during which the mother was able to understand her own behavior as a function of her own upbringing in an atmosphere of fighting, yelling and poverty, she still was not able to control her yelling. The best she could do was t˞ explain to her children that she really did not mean what she said when she was screaming. She was even willing to take tranquilizing drugs to control her explosions.

Behavioral Symptoms correlated with
adult punitive and excretory contacts with children

+ pain*
+ illness non-
organic*

1-2. When Greta developed stomachaches prior to her leaving home each day for school, she would double up with pain to the point that she was not able to stand up. Her pediatrician was convinced that these pains were emotional in origin.

+ reversal of
affect*

3. At times, Greta displayed periods of sporadic uncontrolled giggling which irritated and provoked those about her.

+ negative
emotion

4-5. On the other hand she was bored by everything except watching a few TV programs. She was not interested in school and claimed that school was boring like everything else. Although she performed "quite adequately" in school, the teacher felt her performance was well below her capabilities.

+ learning
(level 1)

+ negative
emotion

The extent of Greta's negative feelings became evident during her first two years of therapy. Her first therapist noted that she hurled epithets at him and even verbalized death wishes. In addition to these negative comments directed at the therapist, Greta declared her hate for her father and also for all boys and all men.

NOTES

1 The *"limbic" temporal lobes* are the seat of both complex *sexual* activities and of temporal lobe epilepsy. Therefore, it is understandable that functional epilepsies derived from *excessive sexual stimulation of the limbic temporal lobes* in the absence of appropriate channels for discharge, might easily be confused with epilepsies derived from *organic damage within the limbic temporal lobes*.

2 Of note, although Greta suffered from a deficiency of contented, tranquilizing and comforting stimulation during her infancy, there apparently was never a lack of color, excitement and interest in her life from the very beginning. It is, therefore, not surprising that her lack of emotional trust was counter-balanced by a precocious perceptual-motor development. According to the mother, Greta crawled at three months, walked at nine months, and was saying phrases like "how pretty" by the age of seven months.

Greta
9

Stimulation-Symptom-and-Dream-Profile

	+ Separation Phobias
	+ Night Terrors, Twilight States
Sleep in Bed with Adult	Irrational Fears: Other
	+ Irrational Tempers
+ Adult Genital Erotic	+ Sexual Symptoms
	+ Biting/Cutting, etc. ⎫ *content of*
View Adult Coitus	+ Eyes ⎬ *dreams and*
	Fire ⎭ *symptoms*
	Learning Problems (levels 2 or 3 etc.)
+ Punitive Yelling	Lying and Delinquency
	+ Reversal of Affect
Beatings	Closing Down Upon, Kill ⎫ *content of* ⎬ *dreams and*
	Falling ⎭ *symptoms*
	Excretory Symptoms and Dreams
	Anal Masturbation
Preoccupation with Child's BM	Enuresis
	+ Illness, etc. ⎫ *content of*
Anal Contacts	+ Pain ⎬ *dreams and*
	Death ⎭ *symptoms*
	Compulsions

Case 10: Grant

Grant, a seven-year-old brother of Greta (see case 9), entered therapy as his sister terminated. His presenting problems included excessive masturbation, temper tantrums, severe stomach cramps, tenseness, hyperactivity, bed-rocking and soiling.

Sources of Stimulation:
children's tactile and visual erogenous contacts with the adult body

− / + sleeping in bed with adults*

+ adult genital erotic*

1-2. In the morning Grant would get into his father's bed. As the father stretched out in the nude, he and Grant would tickle one another and wrestle. Grant's little brother would often join in the excitement and the two boys would enjoy crawling all over the father's nude body. Grant liked to climb onto his father's chest or to slide down his legs. He and his father would also play a game called "Harbor" during which Grant would be the boat while the father's spreading legs and exposed penis formed the port. At first Grant did not see this activity as a problem for it in no way consciously bothered him.

Grant saw his mother without clothes less frequently and without the accompaniment of exciting games of body contact.

Behavioral Symptoms correlated with
children's tactile and visual erogenous contacts with the adult body

+ sexual symptoms*

1. Grant and his sister frequently would exhibit their genitals to one another (Grant was eight, his sister ten) and then would proceed to masturbate together. Frequently they would climb in bed together. Grant also would wrestle with his younger brother as his father wrestled with him. The wrestling eventually would lead to mutual masturbation.

Despite his protestations as to how good an athlete he was, Grant demonstrated a wish to be a girl. His mother was concerned that at the age of four Grant liked to dress in girl's clothes. His homosexually oriented behavior also was reflected by his seductiveness to men. During his first diagnostic interview he practically tried to crawl onto his therapist's lap. This behavior turned out to be a generalization of his behavior at home: at the age of eight Grant still enjoyed sitting on his father's lap. Both parents were aware that Grant was preoccupied with penises.

+ irrational tempers*

2. Grant's temper tantrums motivated the family to seek help for him at

the clinic. On one occasion he suddenly poked his father in the face as hard as he could and broke the father's glasses simply because he had lost TV privileges for the night.

+ eyes*

3. Grant boasted that he knew where to hit his father: "in the back and in the *eyes*." Likewise, Grant "loved" attacking his sister by sending pieces of fruit flying across the table into his sister's *"eye."*

+ biting/cutting/
stomach*

4. Grant began to suffer from stomach cramps when he was three and four. The cramps still troubled him at the time of his diagnostic referral. G.I. series and further medical examination revealed no organic basis for this disturbance.

In addition to being troubled by stomach cramps, Grant found it difficult to eat meat.

In line with these symptoms, a "chopping" theme appeared in Grant's material during his first year of therapy. During the same hour in which he referred to his concerns about his father's hairy body and penis, Grant presented a phantasy about the father as a "monarch who would *chop* his head off."

Sources of Stimulation:
adult punitive and excretory contacts with children

+ early
deprivation

1. Grant, like Greta, suffered from early deprivation of cuddling and comforting. The mother felt she was even less able to relate positively to Grant, her second baby, than to Greta, her first. Often she wanted to pick him up from the bed but instead left him crying helplessly. She found herself hating Grant in these early years because he made her feel inadequate. To make matters worse, Grant was hospitalized at the age of three months for an "allergic" respiratory complaint. During his stay in the hospital, his mother was unable to hold Grant even once or make other contacts with him. "Because he was asleep" each time she visited, she could not bring herself to disturb him.

+ punitive
yelling*

2. The more Grant's mother was criticized for being "emotional and destructive" the more she would yell and scream. She realized that she overreacted to Grant, jumped on him and was too quick to punish him. As reported within Greta's history, the mother threatened the children with all kinds of disastrous punishments if they didn't do one thing or another. Then, most of the time she never followed through on any of her threats. Unfortunately, Grant increasingly became the target of his mother's attacks once his sister improved in therapy. Most pathetic for Grant was the mother's intolerance of his head banging and bed rocking at night. When she heard him banging and rocking she would angrily try to force him to stop. Finally, the father persuaded her that this was the worst way to try to control him.

Behavioral Symptoms correlated with
adult punitive and excretory contacts with children

+ excretory
symptoms*

1. Grant soiled regularly until he was seven and thereafter soiled on occasion or stained his undershorts. The soiling plus his bed-rocking added up to a

+ anal
masturbation*

+ hurting

+ closing down
upon
destructively*
+ non-organic
illness*
+ pains* (and
aches)
+ hurt self

+ falling*

steady source for anal self-stimulation. Eventually, he scratched his anal orifice and used his fingers to masturbate anally. His mother was aware of this activity but did not want to prohibit it for fear that Grant would develop guilt feelings.

2. Grant liked to hurt children who were weaker than he was. "I hate a certain girl," he confided, "I take a chance to hit her in the face." Similarly, Grant reported that one of his first memories in life had to do with his "throwing stones at a fat boy."

3. Grant also displayed many signs of masochistic behavior. Psychosomatic headaches and severe stomach pains were a presenting complaint. His two dreams focused upon his falling and being injured. In one dream he *fell* off a cliff. Associating to his dream, he recalled *breaking his leg* when he was quarterback on a football team. In the second dream, "a boy *broke his glass arm* as he caught the ball and *fell* over the grandstand."

NOTES

Grant
10

Stimulation-Symptom-and-Dream-Profile

	Separation Phobias	
	Night Terrors, Twilight States	
Sleep in Bed with Adult	Irrational Fears: Other	
	+ Irrational Tempers	
+ Adult Genital Erotic	+ Sexual Symptoms	
	+ Biting/Cutting, etc.	*content of*
View Adult Coitus	+ Eyes	*dreams and*
	Fire	*symptoms*
	Learning Problems (levels 2 or 3 etc.)	
+ Punitive Yelling	Lying and Delinquency	
	Reversal of Affect	
Beatings	+ Closing Down Upon, Kill	*content of* *dreams and*
	+ Falling	*symptoms*
	+ Excretory Symptoms and Dreams	
	+ Anal Masturbation	
Preoccupation with Child's BM	Enuresis	
	+ Illness, etc.	*content of*
Anal Contacts	+ Pain	*dreams and*
	Death	*symptoms*
	Compulsions	

Case 11: Homer

Homer was an extremely bright seven-year-old boy who had lived with his aunt and uncle since infancy. Now the aunt and uncle had just been divorced. The aunt requested psychotherapy for Homer because he was so unhappy about the divorce and was "taking it out" on his little stepsister by hitting and punching her.

Sources of Stimulation:
children's tactile and visual erogenous contacts with the adult body

+ sleeping in bed
with adults*

1. Prior to the divorce Homer occasionally slept in bed with his aunt throughout the night. Frequently, he would sneak into his uncle's bed while the uncle was sleeping. Said Homer: "I'd get into his bed. He never woke up. When he started to snore I'd go back into my bed." After the aunt and uncle's divorce, Homer would sleep in bed with the uncle during weekend visits.

+ adult nudity

2. Everyone in Homer's family would appear before each other without clothes. Homer still took baths together with his younger "brother" and "sister."

(latency child and
adult in bath)

The children would see his aunt completely nude at close range since she was accustomed to taking off her pajamas to give them their bath. On occasion she herself would take a bath with Homer.

The uncle often would sleep in the nude, even when Homer shared the bed with him. Homer reported there were nights when he became aware of his un-

+ adult genital
erotic*

cle's penis sticking out.

The uncle also was not ashamed to leave his bed in the morning, then walk down to the dining room without putting on any clothes. He seemed undisturbed that the children would view his penis partially erect.

Following the divorce, the uncle reported that Homer would peek to watch him having intercourse with his new "girl friend." The uncle did not take steps to prevent this peeking. However, Homer, who was extremely open and honest

−/+ view adult
coitus*

about referring to sexual matters, stated that all he saw was his uncle and the girl friend as they kept kissing in bed.

With respect to observing sexual activities, Homer also was exposed to seeing his uncle dress up in women's clothes.

Behavioral Symptoms correlated with
children's tactile and visual erogenous contacts with the adult body

+ irrational fears*

1. Homer was obsessed by fears that his aunt would cut him up and throw him into the stove. This information was offered by the aunt and by Homer himself. The intensity of these fears resulted in a state bordering upon delusion: Homer was convinced his aunt actually tried to do this once but that he managed to get away. A year or so prior to his referral Homer also was beset by fears that under his bed there was a ghost who would pick him up and throw him down the stairs.

+ sexual
symptoms*

2. Homer confided a presenting problem: "I don't know why my unconscious[1] makes me hit my sister and kiss my brother." Sometimes Homer would put on his aunt's clothes and wiggle while directly admitting he wished he could be a girl and get married to his boy friend, Randy. His phantasies included "making a baby" with his sister and then bringing the baby to his boy friend.

Homer's penis frequently was in a state of excitement. The uncle reported that Homer would masturbate by rubbing his penis on the floor until it was red and sore. The relation of Homer's sexual excitement to his uncle's exhibitionistic activities was reflected by his associative flow of thoughts: "I see him without clothes a lot. When he sleeps he takes off his clothes and when he wakes up he walks downstairs naked. Then he gets his underwear downstairs. My dinky gets hard. My mouth starts to water when I pass this restaurant where his girl friend works."

+ biting/cutting*

3. The activation of flesh-biting reactions was directly reflected in his delusionary thoughts and fears that his aunt was going to *cut* him up and cook him in the oven, i.e., like food to be eaten. Homer also presented a related dream: "me and her . . . passed this old lady's house and this cat came down the pipe and was just about to *bite* me."

Sources of Stimulation:
adult punitive and excretory contacts with children

+ early
deprivation

1. Homer's aunt and uncle were regularly absorbed with smoking marijuana at the time they took three-month-old Homer into their home. They were also busy partying with friends at the time. As a result Homer was often "left alone crying for hours without being picked up." Then, when Homer was seven years old the aunt and uncle became deeply involved experimenting with new sexual partners. During this period, Homer again was often neglected.[2]

+ beatings*

2. While Homer's uncle was the seducer, his aunt was administrator of punishment. In Homer's words: "She hits hard. I'm used to it. She hits and hits with her hand. Sometimes she leaves a bruise mark. Sometimes she whacks me in the ass. It happens about two to three times a week."

+ punitive
   yelling*

Yelling also was prominent in the home prior to the divorce. The aunt and uncle were getting on poorly and let it out by accusing one another, or by yelling at the children. Even after the divorce, the aunt kept up the fighting with Homer. Homer complained that she would scream at him what to do, what not to do.

Behavioral Symptoms correlated with
adult punitive and excretory contacts with children

+ negative
   behavior

1. When Homer was asked during his first diagnostic what he thought were some of his problems, one of his answers went as follows: "In school I say, 'nah, I don't want to play,' but I really do want to play."[3]

+ reversal of
   affect*

2. Homer told his problems with little emotion. In fact, one would think he were enjoying himself gossiping with a friend as he related his worst difficulties. This inhibition-and-reversal of affect became even more apparent during his first year of therapy when he could only smile or giggle and for a long time was unable to show sadness or tears in relation to the death of his best friend, the loss of his uncle after the divorce, and the loss of his therapist at the end of the year.[4]

Homer indicated he would like to look down on people. He wanted to go to the top of a building and look down on all the little[5] people below — thus attempting to reverse his feelings of being very little and helpless.

+ hurting

3. Homer regularly teased and hurt his little "sister," a "chief complaint" at the time of his referral. Homer admitted he "bashed" her. His aunt in turn joined in the fray by hitting him.

+ falling*

Homer also suffered from fears of being hurt, e.g., by falling. He noted: "I thought a ghost would come to my bed and would pick me up and throw me down the stairs." He then presented the following associations: "The other day my unconscious made me do something strange. We were climbing up on a box near the stairs. I began slipping, and smash, I fell off and went bump, bump down the stairs."

+ death*

Homer was beset with a morbid upset over a young cousin's death at the hands of a hit-and-run driver. Whereas one might expect such an event to disturb a child for a few days, a week or a month, Homer was still perseverating about the boy's death a year later.

1 Homer's therapist defined the unconscious as that part of our minds which makes us do things when we do not know why we do them.

2 Fortunately, Homer's aunt was a bright and highly educated woman who responded well to therapy and was able to stop exposing the children to bed-sharing and nudity. She also was able to stop her own sexual acting out and her intake of marijuana, all of which had covered up her own intense needs for someone to take care of her.

3 Fortunately, at the time of his referral, Homer's negativism had not invaded his capacity for learning.

4 With a lot of work on his therapist's part, Homer was finally able to bring up his upset feelings regarding these losses. Then the intensity of the feelings became so great, Homer momentarily believed he was falling apart.

5 This thought was expressed shortly after Homer had told of his uncle's penis sticking out, i.e., a memory which made him feel so small. Looking down from the top of a high building in turn would help him feel bigger.

Homer
11

Stimulation-Symptom-and-Dream-Profile

	Separation Phobias	
	Night Terrors, Twilight States	
+ Sleep in Bed with Adult	+ Irrational Fears: Other	
	Irrational Tempers	
+ Adult Genital Erotic	+ Sexual Symptoms	
	+ Biting/Cutting, etc.	*content of*
View Adult Coitus	Eyes	*dreams and*
	Fire	*symptoms*
	Learning Problems (levels 2 or 3 etc.)	
+ Punitive Yelling	Lying and Delinquency	
	+ Reversal of Affect	
+ Beatings	Closing Down Upon, Kill	*content of*
		dreams and
	+ Falling	*symptoms*
	Excretory Symptoms and Dreams	
	Anal Masturbation	
Preoccupation with Child's BM	Enuresis	
	Illness, etc.	*content of*
Anal Contacts	Pain	*dreams and*
	+ Death	*symptoms*
	Compulsions	

Case 12: Ira

Mr. and Mrs. F claimed that their son, Ira, had always been a "perfect boy." He had been a conscientious student who had earned all A's and B's; always minded his parents; and always had been their favorite spoilt darling. They were, therefore, astounded when at the age of ten, Ira suddenly refused to attend school. By the time Ira was seen for a diagnostic evaluation he had already been absent from school for three weeks. All attempts of the parents to drag him there were met by violent outbursts of fighting, kicking and yelling.

Ira's initial appearance during his evaluation was not of a child with problems. He was a quiet, pleasant-looking, slightly chubby boy, neatly dressed. He smiled a lot, was quite cooperative and generally worked rapidly and effectively. His Full Scale WISC intelligence scoring was 107, Performance I.Q. 113, Verbal I.Q. 101.

Sources of Stimulation:
children's tactile and visual erogenous contacts with the adult body

+ adult nudity

1. Ira's adolescent brother, age sixteen and sexually well developed, would regularly appear without any clothes in front of ten-year-old Ira.

The father was worried about the adolescent brother's display of possible "homosexual tendencies" when he danced around the house like a "fruit." Actually, the father himself enjoyed doing "striptease acts" in the morning while removing his pajamas in front of the adolescent brother.

Of note, Ira had permission to go through the stack of "nudie" magazines in the father's bureau drawer. In fact, the father had just invested in one of the "girlie" magazine publishing companies and very proudly brought Ira to the printing firm for a tour of the building. He wanted to be sure to let Ira know that the firm in which he had invested was something about which he could be very proud.

− / + adult genital erotic* (no proof)

2. At the same time that Ira's school phobia erupted, the adolescent brother, unknown to the parents, had been reported in school to be experimenting with pot and "acting out sexually" (presumably homosexually). It was therefore likely that this teenage brother who had been aroused by the father's exhibitionism was in turn exposing himself sexually to Ira.[1]

Behavioral Symptoms correlated with
children's tactile and visual erogenous contacts with the adult body

+ separation
phobias*

1. Ira's school phobia was sudden, explosive and unrelenting. A letter from his school principal, a visit from the probation officer, attempts at dragging him into the family car to cart him to school, as well as diagnostic visits to the clinic, were all unsuccessful in countering Ira's wild and desperate refusal to separate from home and attend school. Also, Ira was not able to attend Sunday school and even refused to go out to play with friends.

+ irrational
tempers*

2. "Both parents could not get over the intensity of the anger with which Ira exploded as they tried to push him to go to school." Ira also demonstrated his temper at the clinic during a family conference. He had been the model of a "golden boy" at the meeting until he was crossed. Suddenly, he slouched, pouted and then had a full fledged temper tantrum when it was pointed out to him that the law required his going to *some* school. He ended up crying and knocking over a chair as he tried to run out of the room.

3. Ira's tempers were not only triggered by a reference to his attending school. He was "over-sensitive" to any teasing at home and "if anyone touched him playfully he would scream back as if he had been physically assaulted."

− / + eye*

4. In one of Ira's early screen memories, he was playing hide-and-go-seek with his brother. "The game ended with the crib falling and the crank of the crib poking into his eye." Ira's case history, however, contained no reference to symptoms pertaining to the eye.

+ biting/cutting/
stomach*

5. During his school-phobic panics, Ira often complained of pains in his stomach.

Sources of Stimulation:
adult punitive and excretory contacts with children

+ punitive
yelling*

1. A conference note pertaining to Ira's home atmosphere read as follows: "The household picture is filled with nagging, screaming, and inconsistencies." At one time the mother described herself as getting hysterical, crying and yelling at everyone. The father admitted that many times he was so tired from all of the fighting at home that he did not bother disciplining at all.

− / + beatings*

2. While Ira's adolescent brother was the butt of his parents' wrath, Ira was their darling. The mother would hit the brother for the slightest failure to go along with her whimsical demands and the father would beat him black and blue. In turn, the brother would "beat up" Ira. The severity of these blows, however, is uncertain.

Even though Ira was his parents' darling, the father apparently had periods of exploding at him and hitting him too. For example, one of Ira's earliest memories had to do with his punching his brother right into a glass window. Then his father "killed" Ira.

Behavioral Symptoms correlated with
adult punitive and excretory contacts with children

+ excretory
symptoms*

1. At times, Ira did not wipe himself after bowel movements so that his mother would regularly find his undershorts "stained."

+ negative
emotion

2. Ira stated he had *nothing* to live for. He felt he should be in school and worried that something *bad* would happen to him if someone saw him out in the streets during school hours. He began to feel that everyone in the family was *mean* to him. Then, he decided he *hated* his teacher because she was too strict, and he ended up *hating* school itself. Similarly, Ira began finding *something wrong* with each of his friends.

+ falling*

3. Ira recalled four of his first memories pertained to falling: (a) "I *tripped* and laughed my head off"; (b) "I *fell* in the cement when they were fixing the cement in the back of the house"; (c) "There were big long steps to get up to the house. I *fell* and scratched both legs"; and (d) (already noted) "Me and my brother played hide-and-go-seek. I thought he was in the crib. The crib *fell* and the crank went into my eye."

+ pain*

+ non-organic
illness*

4. As his school phobia erupted, Ira complained of severe stomach pains. His mother brought him to the family pediatrician who found no organic basis for the pains and suggested that Ira needed psychiatric rather than medical help for the stomach symptoms.

NOTES

[1] Such contacts with the exhibitionistic adolescent brother could easily have placed Ira in a homosexual panic and thus triggered his school phobia.

Ira

12

Stimulation-Symptom-and-Dream-Profile

	+ Separation Phobias	
	Night Terrors, Twilight States	
Sleep in Bed with Adult	Irrational Fears: Other	
	+ Irrational Tempers	
− / + Adult Genital Erotic	Sexual Symptoms	
	+ Biting/Cutting, etc.	} *content of*
View Adult Coitus	Eyes	*dreams and*
	Fire	*symptoms*

	Learning Problems (levels 2 or 3 etc.)	
+ Punitive Yelling	Lying and Delinquency	
	Reversal of Affect	
Beatings	Closing Down Upon, Kill	} *content of*
		dreams and
	+ Falling	*symptoms*

	+ Excretory Symptoms and Dreams	
	Anal Masturbation	
Preoccupation with Child's BM	Enuresis	
	+ Illness, etc.	} *content of*
Anal Contacts	+ Pain	*dreams and*
	Death	*symptoms*
	Compulsions	

Case 13: Joel

By the age of six, Joel had developed stomachaches, depression and a compulsion to pull his hair. His mother had recently separated from his father who had been acting out homosexually in the community. Subsequent to her divorce, the mother lived in a small apartment with Joel and his four-year-old sister.

Sources of Stimulation:
children's tactile and visual erogenous contacts with the adult body

− / + sleeping in bed with adults* (occasionally?)

1. At the time of his diagnostic evaluation, Joel explained: "Sometimes I sleep all night in Mommy's bed and sometimes I don't. . . . I'm almost getting married to my mother. . . . No."

+ adult nudity

2. Joel offered details of seeing his mother without her clothes and referred anxiously to his mother's genitals and pubic hair. In particular, Joel was aware of seeing his mother unclothed while she was sitting on the toilet with her legs spread apart. The mother would remain on the toilet for extended periods of time in the morning when it was necessary for Joel to wash before leaving for school.

− / + adult genital erotic*

Joel mentioned that he had also been accustomed to seeing his father without clothes and noted "me and him wanted to take a shower but I was scared."

3. The mother expressed concerns that the father may have acted out sexually with Joel. She was concerned, for example, that after a Sunday visit with his father, Joel would return home in a state of agitation during which he would be overcome with bouts of vomiting. However, there was available no direct evidence of sexual interactions between Joel and his father.[1]

Behavioral Symptoms correlated with
children's tactile and visual erogenous contacts with the adult body

+ nightmares

1. At night Joel had bad dreams which would awaken him. Often he would go to his mother at such times to tell her about the dreams.

+ sexual symptoms*

2. What reactions Joel could not discharge upon his mother's exposed vagina, he discharged upon his little sister's vagina, i.e., he completed sexual-looking-touching-mouthing with the little sister. Anxiously, Joel confided, "I tickle and *lick Lu-lu's place when we are in the bathroom together.* She sees mine but I won't let her lick it." Joel next confided that he was acting out sexually with several little boys in the neighborhood. He allowed "Bill" to stick

46

his penis into Joel's "bum." With another boy, he practiced mutual fellatio following which he would "spit to get rid of the germs."

+ biting/cutting/
stomach*

3. Psychogenic stomachaches constituted one of the principal reasons for Joel's referral to the clinic for psychiatric help.

4. When Joel spoke of seeing his mother's genitals, he elaborated: "I see her hair. It looks like she has *eyes there.*"[2]

+ eyes*

During his second diagnostic hour, Joel presented the following *nightmare* which also had to do with eyes: "My *eyes* was looking; they was going chk-chk-chk like a man was breaking in a window." In line with this dream, Joel later told of funny feelings he experienced when he watched TV: "When I watch TV all the time, it's hard on my *eyes*. It's *scary*. I block my *eyes.*"

Likewise no sooner had Joel spoken of seeing a boy's erect penis than he perseverated about "blinded eyes." He added, "If I look at something it's like a light, my *eye* gets something the matter. Indians have their *eyes* hurt (a color print of an Indian stood on the office cabinet) . . . the sun shines into the eyes . . . cowboys wear black suits and *black eye*-things."[3]

− / + fire*

5. Joel demonstrated no symptoms pertaining to fire. However, his one association pertaining to fire was of particular interest. Joel's conversation had just led the therapist to inquire as to whether Joel was ever worried when he would see his father's penis. In response, Joel suddenly answered: "*Fire* blows the whole world apart. If someone would break a big building, even the police couldn't help."[4]

Sources of Stimulation:
adult punitive and excretory contacts with children

+ adult
defecation

1. The mother's bathroom habits have already been mentioned. Joel would find her on the toilet defecating. "She needs help," Joel noted, "she's not good at flushing the toilet and it smells."

+ beatings*

2. Joel's mother was a cripple whose legs were immobilized by a "slipped disc of the back." Her illness, however, did not keep her from belting both of her frail children. "If she hits me, I'll get angrier and angrier," Joel explained, "and then she hits me worser; then I will go away. Once my mother kept on spanking me harder and harder." The mother wanted little part of the clinic's psychiatric understanding or advice with respect to limiting the beatings. At first, she unwillingly followed the clinic's recommendations but by the end of the first year of treatment, she withdrew Joel from therapy because of her disapproval of the clinic's attitudes. At one time, her back was so crippling that she could not reach Joel and his sister with her belt. Then she simply yelled at the children while she threatened to strike them with a crutch.

+ punitive
yelling*

The parents' battles prior to their separation added to the noisy screaming to which Joel was exposed. The first "problem" Joel could think of had to do with divorce: "that thing when you get married and you don't get along well; my father was getting mad." Joel later told how his heart pounded "when his mother and father started fighting."

Behavioral Symptoms correlated with
adult punitive and excretory contacts with children

+ negative
   behavior

+ learning*
   (level 2)

1. Joel was a restricted little boy who "seemed lost in day dreams in school." His mother complained of his negativism; she could not understand why he so frequently insisted upon doing the opposite from what she requested. In relation to his negative opposition and restriction, Joel developed a learning problem which necessitated his being left back in the first grade.[5]

+ excretory
   symptoms*

+ anal
   masturbation*

2. Joel and his friends showed "bottoms" while they were having bowel movements (note the relation to scenes of Joel viewing his mother defecate at the toilet). Joel also confided: "I stuck a stick up my rear; it hurt," then he went on to tell how it also hurt when one of his friends stuck his penis into his "bum."

+ falling*
+ hurt

3. Another "presenting problem" was verbalized by Joel: "I fall a lot on my head when I block my eyes." The theme of "hurt" also appeared in the following *nightmare*: "My father was about to *hurt* my little sister. I didn't know how to stop him."

+ obsessions and
   compulsions*

4. Joel dreamed of and repetitively spoke of a "clck-clck noise" which clicked him out of his mind. He also compulsively pulled at the hair on his head to the extent that he developed bald spots.

+ preoccupation
   with illness*
   (poison)
+ pain* (aches)

5. During his diagnostic interview Joel stated that one of his main worries had to do with "when I try to eat some poison apples — If I did — If I do — there's a dirty spot and I eat the dirty spot. I don't even know what to do; I keep eating the dirty spot." Joel's psychogenic stomachaches were possibly related to his concerns about eating "dirty," "poisonous" substances.[6]

NOTES

[1] Hence, Joel's adult genital erotic contacts were rated $(-/+)$, the statistical equivalent of a $(-)$ rating.

[2] This primitive communication involves (1) pubic hair and (2) eyes. It is *his* eyes which are so preoccupied with staring at *her* pubic hair. However, the image becomes a unified focus upon "eyes and hair" without the elaboration of syntax.

[3] Compare these thoughts with those of Little Hans who was frightened by the black shields above the horse's *eyes*, and who like Joel would stare while his mother defecated into the toilet (see case synopsis 1).

[4] The intensity of Joel's response suggested that he had seen his father expose himself sexually. However, no confirmation of this conjecture was obtained. Joel did mention

that he had seen his father walk and wiggle like a girl.

5 Joel did respond well to therapy and recovered from his learning problem. In fact, the teacher was so impressed with his progress that she wanted to send a batch of Joel's classmates for psychiatric help. This course of events confirmed the clinic's belief that Joel's learning problem was not organic in nature.

6 If sexual forepleasure among children pertains to *looking-at-touching-mouthing* the body parts and body products, then Joel's custom of closely looking at his nude mother as she defecated spread-eagle into the toilet could have activated sexual forepleasure reactions pertaining to looking at, touching or grasping and mouthing his mother's pubic hair and ano-genital regions. In that case, it is possible (a) the overstimulated reactions of grasping the pubic hair were compulsively discharged by his pulling the hair on his own head, while (b) the overstimulated reactions of mouthing the anal and genital regions were discharged by his mouthing the sister's ano-genital region (and mouthing his boy friend's penis) thus providing one source for his concerns about eating dirty spots and poison.

Joel
13

Stimulation-Symptom-and-Dream-Profile

	Separation Phobias	
	Night Terrors, Twilight States	
Sleep in Bed with Adult	Irrational Fears: Other	
	Irrational Tempers	
Adult Genital Erotic	+ Sexual Symptoms	
	+ Biting/Cutting, etc.	} *content of*
View Adult Coitus	+ Eyes	*dreams and*
	Fire	*symptoms*
	+ Learning Problems (levels 2 or 3, etc.)	
+ Punitive Yelling	Lying and Delinquency	
	Reversal of Affect	
+ Beatings	Closing Down Upon, Kill	} *content of dreams and*
	+ Falling	*symptoms*
	+ Excretory Symptoms and Dreams	
	+ Anal Masturbation	
Preoccupation with Child's BM	Enuresis	
	+ Illness, etc.	} *content of*
Anal Contacts	+ Pain	*dreams and*
	Death	*symptoms*
	+ Compulsions	

Case 14: Karen

Karen was seven and a half years old when she was first brought to the clinic. She was beset by hysterical fears of dogs, frequent crying, babyish dependency and difficulty in being accepted by other children. Despite these problems, Karen's teachers reported that she was a very capable little girl who was a model student both behaviorally and academically.

Sources of Stimulation:
children's tactile and visual erogenous contacts with the adult body

− / + bed-sharing
with adults*
(infrequent)

1. Prior to therapy, Karen on occasion slept in bed with her mother. She would also lie on the couch next to her father.

+ adult nudity

2. Karen would regularly see her mother, father and adolescent sister unclothed. In therapy she told how her father's penis "looked so terrible. It looked so white." At the age of ten Karen also shared showers with her sexually developed sixteen-year-old sister. During these showers the sister soon found it fun to run her hands over Karen's buttocks.

+ adult genital
erotic*

+ adult genital
erotic*

Karen was ten during a period when her mother copulated with another woman's husband, in the woman's presence. Shortly thereafter, the mother came home one night drunk from a family outing and explained to the children that she had had too much to drink. She thereupon asked the children to undress her. As Karen and her sister were taking their mother's panties off, the mother, in a spread-eagle position, began to urinate openly in front of them.

Behavioral Symptoms correlated with
children's tactile and visual erogenous contacts with the adult body

+ separation
phobias*

1. One of Karen's presenting problems was her tendency to cling to her mother in preference to the company of other children.

Additionally, Karen displayed some signs of a school phobia prior to the first year of therapy. Mornings, she would consistently complain about having to go to school, even though she actually always managed to get there. Then when Karen began sharing showers with her sister, school phobic symptoms intensified and she began to suffer from stomachaches each morning as it came time to leave home.

+ irrational fears*

2. Karen's fear of dogs biting her was so extreme that the sight of a dog would send her running in a panic. On one occasion, in order to get away from

a dog, she ran in front of a car and barely escaped being hit. At other times, she would run to strange men for protection.

Dramatic improvement of Karen's fear of dogs took place early in treatment after her therapist, in Karen's presence, explained to her mother that bed-sharing and exposure to adult nudity often activated, in the "baby part" of the brain, thoughts of looking at the body, touching it and putting it into the mouth and that these upset thoughts, therefore, provided a likely source for Karen's fears pertaining to biting. The mother was then asked to help Karen by controlling these sources of physical contact. She responded in a kindly way and said she would be more than happy to do anything that she could to help her daughter. She then proceeded immediately to maintain privacy in the home. Dramatically, two weeks later Karen was found patting a dog in the clinic lobby without any fear of being bitten. She continued her progress and a month later she was still unafraid of dogs. Additionally, her mother reported she had never before seen Karen so happy.

Then, alas, as in Dr. Rangell's case of "Little Paul," (case synopsis 2) circumstance conducted an experiment: the mother once again began letting herself be seen in the nude. During this period, the mother would walk into the bathroom without any covering and would tell Karen to turn her back if she didn't want to look at her. This was also the time that Karen began sharing showers with her adolescent sister. In brief, this inadvertent experiment revealed that with Karen's re-exposure to adult nudity, there immediately occurred an aggravated resurgence of her fears of biting dogs. Furthermore, following the subsequent episode of the mother exhibitionistically urinating in a spread-eagle fashion in front of the children, Karen's fears erupted still more explosively. Her school phobia and dog phobia intensified during the day while at night she

+ nightmares

was troubled by a series of nightmares. In one nightmare, "the Pope was going down a flight of stairs; the Pope fell, was dying and the vultures were eating him up." Another of the nightmares, which equally frightened her, had to do with "peeping toms" (looking), "werewolves" (biting flesh), and "the mummy."

+ irrational
tempers*

3. Karen showed the first signs of overt temper tantrums shortly after she had begun sharing showers with her sister. Months later she was still flying into rages over minor incidents to which previously she would not have reacted intensely. If her mother wouldn't keep a promise, she would now start screaming at the top of her lungs whereas in the past she would only cry or whimper.

+ sexual
symptoms*

4. Following Karen's mother's exposure of herself urinating, Karen and her sister discharged upon one another what could not be completed upon the mother's body; erotic looking was superceded by touching, grasping and biting. Karen was able to tell her therapist that she and her adolescent sister became involved hugging one another both dressed and undressed. They would also play a game called "Piggy" consisting of jumping, tickling and biting one another in the nude. Asked where they would bite, Karen replied, on the leg, arm,

the rear or anywhere.

5. As can be seen, the biting theme permeated Karen's symptoms and associative material: her day fears, her night fears and her sexual activity. The theme of flesh-biting was central in her fears of *being bitten by dogs*. So was this theme reflected in her nightmares of *werewolves biting* and of vultures *eating* the Pope's flesh. The theme was directly expressed in her sexual behavior with her sister when Karen *actively bit* erogenous areas of the body.

+ biting/cutting/
stomach*

Karen spoke of other aspects of her biting preoccupations. She presented thoughts of worms which would bite and which would crawl on the ground and stay alive after their heads had been *cut* off. Accompanying a preoccupation with these flesh-biting reactions, there appeared overt "psychosomatic" symptoms involving Karen's stomach. Stomachaches appeared during the period of sharing showers with her sister. They reached a peak of intensity following the mother's urinating on the bed in front of Karen.

+ eyes*
+ fire*

6-7. Following Karen's exposure to her mother's exhibition of her genitals, Karen experienced her nightmare about sexualized looking and fire: "the *peeping tom*" dream, about a mummy who was in a house and "the house caught *fire* and the mummy died."

Sources of Stimulation:
adult punitive and excretory contacts with children

+ early
deprivation

1. The mother experienced post-partum depressions following the birth of each of her children including Karen. In turn, Karen repeatedly refused to accept sufficient amounts of milk from her bottle and by the age of seven still resisted eating the food placed before her.

+ beatings*

2. Prior to therapy, Karen's mother, who once had been an abused child herself, would react to her children's misbehavior by giving them beatings.[1] Fortunately, once therapy had been instituted the mother was able to stop beating Karen. However, it was more difficult for the mother to control her yelling: even after two years of therapy had passed, she could not refrain from screaming at Karen. She would try to ask Karen "nicely" to do things, but found that only by screaming could she achieve obedience. To make matters worse, in front of Karen the father would castigate the mother with explosive outbursts of anger.

+ punitive
yelling*

+ adult
defecation

3. Karen's mother would continually leave her large deposit of feces in the toilet. She then would be constantly after Karen to clean the toilets.

Behavioral Symptoms correlated with
adult punitive and excretory contacts with children

+ negative
behavior

1. Karen would get very negativistic at home and seemingly would not hear her mother when corrected. Just when Karen was behaving well and was being

praised, she would do something "to spoil things."

2. At the time of her referral for therapy, Karen suffered from a phobia of toilets. She was particularly concerned that any of the water from the toilet might get on her face.

+ excretory
  symptoms*

3. Stomachaches accompanied Karen's most severe school-phobic symptoms.

+ pains*

+ preoccupation
  with illness*

+ closing down
  upon
  destructively*
  (crush)

4. Karen *ran in front of a car* without looking in order to escape a barking dog. The mother complained that, in general, Karen did not stay away from situations where she could get hurt. Karen dreamt of bloody destruction: "a man tore a car apart. It became a *bloody* car because *blood* came out where *gas* should and the children died."

+ excretory
  dream* (gas)

+ falling*

+ death*

5. Karen's nightmares contained the following references to falling and dying: a) "The Pope was going down a flight of stairs; the Pope *fell* and was *dying* . . . ," b) "blood came out . . . and the children *died*." c) "The mummy was in the house, she caught on fire and *died*."

NOTES

1 Personal communication from the mother's social worker. This information was not included within Karen's record.

Karen
14

Stimulation-Symptom-and-Dream-Profile

	+ Separation Phobias	
	Night Terrors, Twilight States	
Sleep in Bed with Adult	+ Irrational Fears: Other	
	+ Irrational Tempers	
+ Adult Genital Erotic	+ Sexual Symptoms	
	+ Biting/Cutting, etc.	⎫ *content of*
View Adult Coitus	+ Eyes	⎬ *dreams and*
	+ Fire	⎭ *symptoms*
	Learning Problems (levels 2 or 3, etc.)	
+ Punitive Yelling	Lying and Delinquency	
	Reversal of Affect	
+ Beatings	+ Closing Down Upon, Kill	⎫ *content of*
		⎬ *dreams and*
	+ Falling	⎭ *symptoms*
	+ Excretory Symptoms and Dreams	
	Anal Masturbation	
Preoccupation with Child's BM	Enuresis	
	+ Illness, etc.	⎫ *content of*
Anal Contacts	+ Pain	⎬ *dreams and*
	+ Death	⎭ *symptoms*
	Compulsions	

Case 15: Lee

The father and stepmother sought psychiatric treatment for nine-year-old Lee who they claimed suffered from a "split personality," "inappropriate affect," "problems in motor development," "dyslexia," "day fears" and "night fears."

Although Lee was well adjusted in school and was well liked by his teachers, at home he was described as impossible to get along with. It was on the basis of his contrasting behavior at home and at school that the parents concluded Lee was suffering from a "split personality."

Lee's father and stepmother were intelligent, college-educated people brought up in a "restricted," "emotionless," "Victorian" atmosphere. In rebellion, they turned as adults to a "free," "mod," "hippie" way of life.

Sources of Stimulation:
children's tactile and visual erogenous contacts with the adult body

1. Both parents regularly kissed Lee on the mouth. Lee remarked that his father's lips were "very hard" in contrast to his mother's.

+ adult nudity

No bed-sharing was reported. However, the children, two boys and two girls, often would sit around the house in the nude and regularly Lee would see his stepmother and father appearing without clothes. At such times, Lee was allowed to *cling to his stepmother's exposed breast.* Conversely, one of Lee's

+ adult genital erotic*

sisters would be allowed to hug the father so tightly that she openly began to display copulatory movements while in contact with him. The family physician suggested that for this reason the father should try to limit his close contacts with the daughter. However, the parents, with their "modern" philosophy, were determined not to subject their children to the restrictions and inhibitions that were forced upon themselves as children. They greatly resented interference with the liberty and freedom of themselves or of their children as "individuals."

Behavioral Symptoms correlated with
children's tactile and visual erogenous contacts with the adult body

+ nightmares

1. Lee suffered from nightmares during which he tossed and grunted. One nightmare Lee reported had to do with a rock which came out from an earthquake and grabbed him.

+ irrational fears*

Lee also displayed irrational fears during the day, fears of death and fire.

Whenever he heard anyone speak a word referring to death he would scream and cover his ears. One day he stopped eating because the teacher had mentioned obesity can cause death. Also Lee's fear of fire seemed to make no sense. The family pointed out that there were no indications whatsoever of his ever having experienced trauma in connection with either death or fire.

+ irrational
   tempers*

2. "Terrible" temper tantrums were a chief complaint at the time of Lee's referral. He would scream and scream, sometimes ten times a day. These episodes of screaming would be easily triggered by any disagreement or by small frustrations in completing a task.

+ sexual
   symptoms*

3. Lee was absorbed with lip-kissing: he would go around the house with lips pursed in an effort to procure more kisses from his stepmother. He also actively kissed his little two-year-old brother on the lips.

More seriously, both parents spoke with concern of Lee's pattern of open masturbation in the midst of the family. Often he would masturbate while he was clinging to his stepmother's breast.

+ biting/cutting*

4. Lee demonstrated bizarre eating habits. He would force down food he hated, saying he loved it although he would be gagging. He also would gulp his food to the point of *vomiting* at the table. He would not *bite* into his food nor would he *cut* his meat.

+ eyes* (reading
   problem)

(+ learning*
   level 1; referral
   symptom)

5. Despite his otherwise excellent work in public school, Lee suffered from a specific reading problem. Prior to his referral to the clinic for one and a half years he attended a reading disability school in an effort to obtain help with this reading difficulty. The special school claimed that he suffered from "dyslexia" based upon a "disability in visual-motor coordination." However, a medical evaluation revealed that there were no organic disturbances present to account for Lee's visual disability: his "eye" troubles were found to be psychosomatically determined.

+ fire*

6. The parents could not understand Lee's irrational preoccupations with fire.

Sources of Stimulation:
adult punitive and excretory contacts with children

+ early
   deprivation

1. Lee lived with his natural mother and father until he was four years old, at which time his natural mother deserted the family. Even though she delighted in the attention she received while pregnant, Lee's natural mother did not want Lee once he was born. She never cuddled him and managed to get rid of him by putting him to bed at 5:00 P.M. Both this original mother and the father had felt that Lee needed nothing beyond physical care in these early years.

2. When Lee at the age of four came under the care of his stepmother, he was described as a "frightened animal" and in particular was extremely fearful

– / + beatings*

of punishment. It is assumed that Lee had been subjected to beatings prior to his father's remarriage.

Behavioral Symptoms correlated with
adult punitive and excretory contacts with children

+ enuresis*

1. Lee indulged in bed-wetting until he was six and a half years old.

2. Lee's capacity for inappropriate affect was described by the parents during their first interview. As an example they told how on one occasion Lee's brother had an accident in which he "split his head open." Even though at the time Lee was in the same room, he paid no attention. Rather he continued to

+ freezing of
affect

watch TV as if oblivious to the brother's screaming and bleeding![1]

The parents also indicated that Lee would inappropriately laugh with a "weird" indescribable quality to the laughter. Likewise, during his diagnostic

+ reversal of
affect*

visits Lee demonstrated evidence of inappropriate reversal of affect. Although he had so much to be unhappy about, Lee spent much time referring happily to "lovely" themes. Even one of his dreams accentuated the "everything is lovely" theme: "We went to a park where there were beautiful flowers. My brother and sister and I jumped in them. We were in a beautiful tunnel. We saw psychedelic birds and then we went home again." Or again, Lee reported an early memory: "When I was about four (at the time his mother deserted) I was watching a cartoon. I got dressed and made my bed. Then I watched TV again and then I took a nap. My sister went to a birthday party. My father came over on his motorcycle and I got a ride on it," etc., etc.

+ lying*

According to his parents' complaints: "Lee lies and if caught in a lie will speak of himself in the third person. . . . "

+ hurting

3. The parents added: "Lee also loves negative attention and spankings. He will be happy all day if he is spanked in the morning." Lee, they claimed, enjoyed being beaten up by the kids and being hurt. In turn, he was prone to hurt himself. The parents concluded, "Lee remains a very clumsy accident-prone

+ closing down
upon
destructively*

youngster." As an example of Lee's capacity to hurt himself, the parents told of one of his accidents when he had managed to jam a steel spike into his cheek. Additionally, Lee dreamed: "I was walking around the street and an *earthquake* came and a rock came out. It was a monster that grabbed me and I woke up."

+ preoccupation
with illness*
+ pain*

+ death*

4. Sickness concerned Lee to the point that he would "always" be complaining at home about his aches and pains. According to the parents, he "enjoyed being sick" and would be unaware of the discomfort involved. On the other hand, Lee displayed intensely phobic reactions about death: it will be recalled, he would scream and cover his ears whenever he heard even a word which referred to death.

NOTES

1 It is interesting that Lee's parents were rebelling against their parents' lack of feeling. Yet they ended up with little empathic feeling for Lee, while Lee in turn displayed an inhibition or reversal of appropriate affect. As Harlow's studies indicate: parents who have been emotionally deprived in their own infancy grow up without a capacity to react with care and positive empathy toward their own offspring. In such a way, lack of empathy often becomes handed down generation to generation.

Lee
15

Stimulation-Symptom-and-Dream-Profile

	Separation Phobias	
	Night Terrors, Twilight States	
Sleep in Bed with Adult	+ Irrational Fears: Other	
	+ Irrational Tempers	
+ Adult Genital Erotic	+ Sexual Symptoms	
	+ Biting/Cutting, etc.	} *content of*
View Adult Coitus	+ Eyes	*dreams and*
	+ Fire	*symptoms*
	+ Learning Problems (levels 2 or 3, etc.)	
Punitive Yelling	+ Lying and Delinquency	
	+ Reversal of Affect	
− / + Beatings	+ Closing Down Upon, Kill	} *content of*
	Falling	*dreams and symptoms*
	Excretory Symptoms and Dreams	
	Anal Masturbation	
Preoccupation with Child's BM	+ Enuresis	
	+ Illness, etc.	} *content of*
Anal Contacts	+ Pain	*dreams and*
	+ Death	*symptoms*
	Compulsions	

Case 16: Muriel

Muriel, age eleven, was referred to the clinic because of her nervousness, nightmares and learning problems.

During therapy, Muriel reported many details pertaining to her home and family. However she discussed upsetting matters "with a precocious distance as though she were discussing someone else's family. She revealed no appropriate engagement of feeling, sign of hurt, disappointment or sadness. She denied that any of her family's attitudes concerned her and insisted she had no problems."

Sources of Stimulation:
children's tactile and visual erogenous contacts with the adult body

1. Whenever the parents sat on their couch, there would be little Muriel sitting between them.

+ sleeping in bed with adults*

By the age of six Muriel also would regularly climb into bed between her parents. Eventually, she became very upset if she were not allowed to sleep with them. In an attempt to persuade Muriel to sleep in her own bed, the mother would first sit in Muriel's room until eleven and twelve o'clock at night. Exhausted, she would then try to go back to her own room. But Muriel would scream and fight until in desperation the mother would finally allow her to join the parents in bed. It was during this period that Muriel's severe nightmares first appeared. These in turn drove her all the more actively to the parents' bed.

+ adult nudity

2. *Even at the age of eleven, Muriel regularly would see her mother and father undressed.* The father would "try" to shoo her out of the bathroom when he was washing in the nude but Muriel would come back giggling to look at him. After three years of therapy, Muriel's therapist reported that fourteen-year-old Muriel was continuing her voyeuristic excursions into the parents' bathroom.

− / + adult genital erotic*

− / + view adult coitus*

3. Muriel reported to her teachers in school how she would find her mother and father together in bed upon her returning home in the afternoon. Considering the parents' permissive and exhibitionistic attitudes, it is therefore likely that they did not go out of their way to ensure sexual privacy.

Behavioral Symptoms correlated with
children's tactile and visual erogenous contacts with the adult body

− / + separation phobias*
(homesick but no fears expressed)

1. Not only did Muriel refuse to separate from her parents at night but at times she found it inappropriately difficult to separate from them during her

59

waking hours. For example, at the age of eleven, she was extremely homesick at camp: one day she wrote her parents six letters pleading with them to bring her back home to them.

+ irrational fears*

+ night terrors*

2. Night fears of robbers and witches headed the list of Muriel's presenting problems. At the age of six, nightmares began. Her terror would keep her awake on into the night and sometimes she would not be able to sleep at all. In one dream, "people were in bed and there was a big bad thing at the window." The mother wondered how Muriel, with so little sleep, could have functioned in school and was most disturbed by her pediatrician's advice to forget the idea of seeking psychotherapy. The pediatrician kept assuring her that Muriel would outgrow her symptoms. It was five years later that the mother finally did bring Muriel to the clinic. Unfortunately, by that time pathological restriction and negativism (see below) kept Muriel from getting help with her fears.

+ irrational tempers*

3. Muriel hysterically screamed when her parents attempted to keep her from sleeping with them. This screaming anger soon became vented almost anytime her family refused to acquiesce to her wishes.

+ sexual symptoms*

4. Muriel often put on her father's clothes. Even after two years of therapy, the father found it difficult to say "No" to Muriel on this subject.

− / + fires*

5. Muriel went through a "phase" during which she was preoccupied with setting fires during her therapy interviews. Over a period of many sessions, she continued to use her therapist's ashtray to build one fire after another.

+ eyes*

6. In school, Muriel developed a severe reading problem. Although she suffered from an incapacitating learning problem in general (see below under "learning"), reading remained her most troublesome disability.

Sources of Stimulation:
adult punitive and excretory contacts with children

+ early deprivation

1. Muriel's history was not a happy one from the very beginning when her upward-striving middle-class mother conceived her out of wedlock unwanted. The mother had always been much preoccupied with her own immediate pleasures and became depressed by the burden of caring for this baby even though she and Muriel's father married soon after her conception. In turn, Muriel would drink only one and a half ounces of milk at a time before spitting up. She would not take solids. The mother laughed as she recalled her determination not to let this stir up her own tensions.

During much of Muriel's infancy the mother slept late into the morning and saw little of her family. Similarly, Muriel's father displayed little interest in his wife or children and spent much time away from home. This rejection and lack of empathy continued throughout Muriel's childhood. Repeatedly Muriel's parents would fail to keep her home from school when she was sick.

− / + beatings*

2. Muriel's father had trouble in "handling" her. He, therefore, spanked

her frequently. He felt this approach was most helpful. In turn, the mother was in the habit of hitting Muriel in the face even when Muriel had reached fourteen.

+ punitive
yelling*

3. Muriel's mother yelled at everyone in the house; she fought with her husband, Muriel's little sisters and Muriel. Muriel realized that she "got it" the worst from her mother when her father was at home.

Behavioral Symptoms correlated with
adult punitive and excretory contacts with children

+ negative
behavior

1. At home, Muriel was so negative that if one would say "black" she would say "white." Additionally, Muriel would do the opposite from what she was told. Her opposition to authority became a central source of fighting with her mother.

Muriel's negativism interfered with her working on problems in therapy. Her "no-nos" were pervasive. Even when she lay down to sleep at night she would repeat to herself that she had *no* problems as a way of telling herself she was okay. This negative reaction to looking at her problems was rigidly maintained over a period of three years' therapy. To the chagrin of her therapists, Muriel would often leave in the middle of her therapy hour.

+ learning*
(level 3)

However, the most devastating effect of Muriel's negativism appeared in the form of inhibition and restriction of learning. During a five-year period, her I.Q. fell from 91 to 80, this despite her endowment with a high-average intelligence potential. Even in a special school for children with severe learning problems, she made slow progress. At the age of fourteen, she was only able to perform at a fifth-grade level in reading and arithmetic.

+ negative
emotion

+ reversal of
affect*

2. Muriel regularly reflected negative affect; for example, she would endlessly repeat how she "hated" school because it was "boring." She flunked math because her teacher "hated" her. She "had no problems" but her teacher was "crazy," etc. In class, she provoked the teachers with her inappropriate silliness and clowning.

+ death*
+ non-organic
illness*

3. Many of Muriel's fears pertained to sickness and dying. At night she feared that she would die if she fell asleep. Likewise, during the day if she heard any stories of sickness and death, she would become hysterical.

Muriel
16

Stimulation-Symptom-and-Dream-Profile

	Separation Phobias	
	+ Night Terrors, Twilight States	
+ Sleep in Bed with Adult	+ Irrational Fears: Other	
	+ Irrational Tempers	
Adult Genital Erotic	+ Sexual Symptoms	
	Biting/Cutting, etc.	} *content of*
View Adult Coitus	+ Eyes	} *dreams and*
	Fire	} *symptoms*

	+ Learning Problems (levels 2 or 3, etc.)	
+ Punitive Yelling	Lying and Delinquency	
	+ Reversal of Affect	
Beatings	Closing Down Upon, Kill	} *content of*
		} *dreams and*
	Falling	} *symptoms*

	Excretory Symptoms and Dreams	
	Anal Masturbation	
Preoccupation with Child's BM	Enuresis	
	+ Illness, etc.	} *content of*
Anal Contacts	Pain	} *dreams and*
	+ Death	} *symptoms*
	Compulsions	

Case 17: Ned

The parents referred to their seven-year-old son's problems as follows: "He has a learning problem; he needs attention; and he acts older than his age." Unfortunately, the statement regarding acting older than his age reflected the parents' reversal of the facts: in school Ned was hyperactive, disruptive and defiant; he did no school work, crawled on the floor and walked around the classroom much of the day.

Ned could not miss being affected by his parents' negative behavior and negative emotion:

(a) Because both parents had been brought up in "harsh and repressive homes" where Victorian rigid rules were the norm, they made a fetish of *opposing rules*, especially with respect to the control of their son's primitive language and behavior. Their concept of loving Ned involved their "okaying" whatever he did or said, until a point was reached when they would *explode* at him. The result, of course, was a catering to Ned's narcissism and his narcissistic entitlements. Ned had learned to think of nobody but himself. When the family started therapy after the diagnostic had been completed, the father told Ned he could do anything and say anything at the clinic *he* wanted. Ned took full advantage of his father's advice.

(b) The parents' *negative emotion* was so extreme it could only be described as paranoid: the parents repeatedly found fault and blamed others. In their negativism, the parents did the opposite of what their therapists recommended, then they attacked their therapists as incompetent for not curing Ned's problems. They were sure the clinic either was "babying Ned or torturing him." Their accusation that Ned was not helped with his problems was matched by their opinion that there was *"nothing"* wrong with him.

Another aspect of the parents' negative emotion was their lack of feeling beyond the emotions of dislike and hate. Their inhibition or freezing of affect approached schizoid proportions. The mother stated that it was difficult for her to be spontaneous except when she was drinking wine or beer. Even when she told the clinic that Ned's therapist was "torturing Ned," her demeanor and affect were noted to be "bland." She described herself as always having felt more "inert and lifeless" than she should have been.

Ned's father also displayed an "inappropriate blandness." He admitted that he would often fall asleep in a group situation if the group were not talking about topics particularly interesting to him. The mother felt his falling asleep in such situations was "insulting." The father also responded with frozen affect when his friends and creditors became upset at him for refusing to pay them his debts amounting to thousands of dollars.

Sources of Stimulation:
children's tactile and visual erogenous contacts with the adult body

−/+ sleeping in bed with adults* (not weekly)
+ adult genital erotic*
+ adult nudity

1-2. Every two or three weeks Ned would *sleep in bed with his father for the night.* Sometimes the father would sleep *in the nude*[1] with Ned. Additionally, Ned was accustomed to seeing his father nude every day.

Ned explained that he also saw his mother without clothes, though he was not allowed to bring his friends in to see her. In summer, his mother wore a very thin nightgown, Ned said; it was easy for him to see through it. The father could see nothing wrong in Ned's seeing both parents nude even though Ned at the age of seven had been overly preoccupied with sex in school and had been too familiar with his mother sexually (see below).

Ned regularly saw soft-core pornography. His father, against the advice of the clinic, gazed at the nude pictures with him. The father felt it was wise to encourage Ned's expressions of interest in nude women as normal and healthy. The father also did not hesitate to let Ned know that he "went out" with women other than Ned's mother.

−/+ view adult coitus*

It is not known whether or not Ned observed his parents engaged in primal scene activities. The mother and father did sleep with their bedroom door open, and mornings Ned often would be found sleeping on the floor near his parents' bed.

Behavioral Symptoms correlated with
children's tactile and visual erogenous contacts with the adult body

+ separation phobia*

1. Even after a year of therapy, Ned "put up quite a fuss" about going to school.

+ irrational fears*

2. Ned spoke of his fears of being poisoned by paint.

+ irrational tempers*

3. Ned's diffuse tempers were combined with destructive hurting: he exploded at his therapist continually while he spit, kicked and hit her (see below).

+ sexual symptoms*

4. The school principal complained that Ned constantly was drawing pornographic pictures in class, e.g., of figures which possessed both breasts and a penis. He also was found passing around stories he had written "full of sexual content." On one occasion, he made breasts for himself out of paper and inserted a pencil between his legs as he went about kissing the girls in class.

The Cub Scout leader similarly complained that Ned was making a pest of himself at meetings where he would continue to draw nude women.

This same obsession permeated Ned's therapy hours: he demanded that his therapist undress and stand nude in the window. He also begged her to get *Playboy* pictures for him.

Even Ned's mother noticed that Ned had been initiating sexual contacts with her. She also noticed that Ned and his brother were participating in sexual play. Ned and his brother liked to snuggle in bed with their bodies close together; then they would jump up and down on the bed until it broke down.

Ned confided that he played sexually with his boy friend. He would let the boy put his penis to Ned's anal orifice. He also would allow the boy to put his fingers into Ned's rectum. Ned stated that his father would "murder" him if he found out.[2]

+ biting/cutting*

5. Ned nearly *cut* his thumb off with a knife. He was preoccupied with telling his therapist the bloody details of this event. He also *perseverated* over the details as to how he might avoid cutting himself again. In school, Ned was reported for *cutting* a little girl's sweater.

+ eyes*

6. The parents noticed that when Ned was *reading*, he displayed overt signs of tenseness and nervousness.

− / + fire*

7. When asked what he *liked and disliked about his father*, Ned answered in primary process language similar to that one would find in a dream: "Once my father had a brand new Volkswagen. Something went wrong. The car caught on *fire*. I did not like that because I like the car." However, he presented no symptoms or actual dreams pertaining to fire.

Sources of Stimulation:
adult punitive and excretory contacts with children

+ / − early
deprivation of
empathic care

1. Ned's history, as reported by his parents, contained no information which directly indicated deprivation of maternal care during his infancy. However, a question does arise in relation to his parents' frozen, unempathic emotion, i.e., it is most likely that the parents' lack of warm tender emotion appeared during Ned's infancy as well as at the time of his referral when he was seven years old.

The mother did state that when Ned was "small" she went through a period of *extreme depression* during which she gave him no controls and let him do whatever he wanted.

+ beatings*

2. The mother would pull down Ned's pants when she hit him, but finally stopped the custom when she found he seemed to enjoy it. Additionally, "two or three times a year" when she found herself particularly frustrated, the mother hit Ned with a belt. She stated that when he was disorderly, no technique short of beating him would get him to pick things up at home.

Behavioral Symptoms correlated with
adult punitive and excretory contacts with children

+ enuresis*

1. Ned was accustomed to holding in his urine for long periods until he would find himself urinating upon himself before he could finally make it to the toilet.

+ excretory
symptoms*

Ned confided that he played with feces[3]; so did his brother and sister. As Ned spoke of playing with his feces, he associated directly to fears that paint would poison him.

Most striking, Ned's sexual play, as noted, was directly anal. He submitted to his boy friend's attempts to perform anal intercourse upon him and allowed the boy friend to stimulate his rectum with his finger, the equivalent of anal masturbatory activity.[3]

+ reversal of
affect*

2. Ned *laughed* when his mother *hit him* with his pants down.

+ negative
emotion

When his first therapist asked Ned how he would prefer to be addressed, "He vehemently responded with a resounding 'FUCK.' " Ned stated that he did not want to come to the clinic and intended to do everything in his power to make life miserable for his parents and therapist.

Ned let it be known in no uncertain terms that he hated his female teachers and therapists. He would complain: "I haven't really had much fun in school today because I really think that stupid fucking teacher of mine is a real shit-head; she's so crabby, she's really a bitch. I think she's a bitch. Oh, she's sometimes nice but right today she's a bastard; I hate her." When his therapist commented that he seemed quite angry at this teacher, Ned retorted, "Why don't you shut up."

To his therapist's mortification, Ned started calling out "Black Pig" to the black lady who was working in the clinic cafeteria. In a similar fashion, Ned derided his therapist with the taunt, "Jingle Bells, Jingle Bells, Miss P. smells."

+ negative
behavior

3. Ned's negativism was reflected directly within his therapy hours. He would poke his fingers into his ears to avoid conversations he did not want to hear. He also rejected all positive overtures of his therapist. For example, although Ned "graciously" accepted a gift from his therapist and "thoughtfully and gratefully" read the therapist's note, he rejected the present at the last minute and threw it down on the floor.

+ learning*
(referral
problem)

Ned did not follow directions in school nor did he finish his assigned work. The teacher stated that he was absolutely not motivated to learn. His most recent report card showed that he was barely passing his subjects, this despite his earning a full-scale Bellevue Wechsler I.Q. score of 108. Though he was placed in the lowest group in math, Ned still ended up the slowest of all the students. It was for this learning problem that Ned was referred for help at the clinic.

+ illness* (poison)

+ closing down
upon
destructively*

4. Ned's fears of *poison* pertained to substances like paint which could make him sick.

Ned also acted out his problems. At the clinic, he would throw a ball at the lights on the ceiling and would knock over any object within his grasp. While he ran through the hall, he would hit his therapist with his ball. Once when a young boy happened to pick up the ball, Ned turned enraged upon his therapist, kicked her hard on the leg and spit at her face. Ned's therapist was not the only butt of his aggression. The librarian, for example, was exasperated when she found Ned pouring coke on her floor. Ned remarked to his therapist that the librarian "sure was crabby!"

Addendum

Fortunately, Ned's therapist decided upon firm controls, come hell or high water. She wrote: "Realizing that if I were to survive this relationship, a change had to occur. Ned and I could not benefit from our violent and unpleasant encounters. . . . I made it clear that there would be no more kicking and spitting directed towards me. In retrospect, it was a victory for both of us when Ned realized that I was big enough and strong enough to prevent his physical abuse by holding him firmly from behind with both arms pressed comfortably but securely against his back." Interestingly, Ned's mother reported some improvement in Ned's behavior at home and school during this period. Ned's therapist was offering him help by imposing controls counter to the direct "narcissistic" discharge of his primitive emotions. Unfortunately, his parents could not do the same.

NOTES

[1] In this way, the father increased the chances of Ned being exposed to his nocturnal erections and emissions.

[2] Yet it was the father who was stimulating Ned's sexual responses: the father was still sleeping in bed nude with Ned and was still gazing at pictures of nude women with him.

[3] Ned reported the following dream: "I went to get a drink of water, I had a plastic cup; and when I turned on the cold-water faucet *lava and acid* came out." Burning lava and acid are substances which have features in common with *hot feces* with which Ned played: *tactile* contact with feces would result in a hot, irritating and burning sensation suggestive of contact with acid or lava.

Ned
17

Stimulation-Symptom-and-Dream-Profile

	+ Separation Phobias	
	Night Terrors, Twilight States	
Sleep in Bed with Adult	+ Irrational Fears: Other	
	+ Irrational Tempers	
+ Adult Genital Erotic	+ Sexual Symptoms	
	+ Biting/Cutting, etc.	} content of
View Adult Coitus	+ Eyes	} dreams and
	Fire	} symptoms

	+ Learning Problems (levels 2 or 3, etc.)	
Punitive Yelling	Lying and Delinquency	
	+ Reversal of Affect	
+ Beatings	+ Closing Down Upon, Kill	} content of dreams and
	Falling	} symptoms

	+ Excretory Symptoms and Dreams	
	Anal Masturbation	
Preoccupation with Child's BM	+ Enuresis	
	+ Illness, etc.	} content of
Anal Contacts	Pain	} dreams and
	Death	} symptoms
	Compulsions	

Case 18: Owen

At the age of eight, with a reported I.Q. of 150, Owen was having a difficult time in school. He displayed a crippling reading problem as well as more generalized learning difficulties which made it necessary for him to repeat the second grade. Also, he was on the verge of being expelled from school because of his disruptive behavior.

Owen's parents both were highly successful professional specialists who graduated from college, Phi Beta Kappa. Their capacity to succeed professionally, however, was not matched by their emotional ability to care for their two children. Their intellectual determination to bring up the children correctly culminated in failure: their negativism, in the form of their constantly doing the opposite from what their superior intelligence dictated, continually kept them from protecting Owen. For example, despite Owen's failure to learn and his disturbed behavior in school, the father insisted that Owen was "perfectly normal." The father agreed to "go along with" a diagnostic only because Owen's principal had insisted that he do so. Even after Owen became involved sexually with an adult homosexual, the father panicked for only a few days before he once again insisted that Owen needed no help. Coldly resistant to therapy for a year, he finally withdrew the boy from treatment.

The mother also did the opposite from what her prolific psychological reading and good sense dictated. In spite of her intellectual interest in "understanding children" she continually found fault with Owen's behavior. "Don't do this. . . . Don't do that. . . . Stop that. . . . Will you come here!" etc. was her constant theme song until Owen's initiative became highly restricted. The mother's negativism interfered with Owen's therapy and led to her opposition to the diagnostic team's recommendations: (a) The mother refused to allow Owen to have a room separate from his little brother who suffered from hemophilia, (b) she refused to consider moving from an area of the city where drugs and perversion were rampant and where there was little opportunity for outdoor play activities, and (c) she refused to stop appearing in the nude in front of Owen. She found an excuse for evading each one of these suggestions.

The mother's behavioral negativism was reinforced by an inhibition of maternal empathic emotion. In particular, she had no feelings which would allow her to take into account Owen's need for feelings of adequacy. Owen, for example, stated: "My mother is good but she *does not really understand what I feel about things*: she lets other people use my bike without asking me." Additionally, the mother would not allow Owen to grow up. She frequently could not resist bathing the eight-year-old boy; she insisted upon washing his body, especially "if he missed a piece." Such contacts put Owen in the position of the passive, helpless baby. No wonder he would crawl around the classroom floor at times when he was severely upset.

Sources of Stimulation:
adult punitive and excretory contacts with children

+ early
deprivation

1. The mother was quite upset when she learned she was pregnant with Owen. She compared herself with her own mother: "a cold, angry and disapproving woman who was never relaxed with her own children." However, she became aware of how much she wanted this baby when she was faced with a possible miscarriage.

Following delivery, Owen's mother could not care for him because of her professional commitments. Owen was therefore sent for a month to the "cold, angry and disapproving" grandmother.

When Owen returned home, his mother found confinement to a small apartment and a baby "a little trying and tense." Then when Owen was three years old another baby was born. This time the mother suffered from marked feelings of depression and self-immolation derived from the burden of remaining confined in the apartment with both children. The discovery that Owen's brother was afflicted with hemophilia made the situation all the worse.

+ punitive
yelling*

2. Owen's mother admitted that she was "the one who had a temper" in the family. The father felt that the whole family had bad tempers and that the mother was no exception. Later, however, the father confessed that when his wife was drinking she poured out her rage upon himself and the two boys.

− / + beatings*

It is most likely that Owen's parents not only yelled at Owen but also hit him. Although they denied hitting him, Owen would lie on the floor in school and ask the children to spank him while he would cry out, "I'll cut it out, Daddy; I'll cut it out."

+ adult
defecation

3. At the age of eight, Owen still watched his mother on the toilet as she urinated and defecated.

Behavioral Symptoms correlated with
adult punitive and excretory contacts with children

+ negative
behavior

+ learning*
(level 2)

1. Owen displayed a proclivity for withdrawing and turning away from all but direct sources of pleasure. He withdrew from children the moment they did not please him; likewise, he turned away from learning the moment things did not go his way. A crippling learning problem soon developed. "On certain days he sat at his desk and did absolutely nothing." On other occasions in the middle of a quiet period, Owen would say: "It's too noisy here; I can't do the work." If his teacher then tried to help him, Owen ignored her by turning away from

her. All efforts to help him in his learning were eventually negated. Owen's father would drill him on his lessons but then Owen would "forget." After the father drilled him on his spelling, Owen would be nervous all day at school until his test was finally given. Often he would come to his teacher with an urgent declaration such as: "I can spell 'house'; I'll tell you," and then would forget how to spell the word. Owen's teacher suggested that he be excused from spelling tests, but his parents rejected the idea because they "didn't want Owen to be different." Significantly, within a year, Owen's verbal I.Q. fell from 147 to 125.

+ negative
emotion

2. Owen turned away from any references to his own frailties by focusing upon the frailties of others. This tendency reached paranoid proportions. His finding fault with others did not make him popular. Owen blamed "this boy," "that boy," "this teacher," "that teacher." Thus, Owen expressed his presenting referral problem as follows: "The boys bother me so I got left back." Likewise he complained about his teachers in school: "Miss A won't let me get ahead. . . . Miss B had no discipline. . . . Miss C told me I could do something special and she never let me do it," etc.

Owen's "don't likes" extended eventually to everyone who in any way interfered with his wishes. "I don't like my therapist asking me silly questions; I don't like to go to doctors; I don't like to feed the ducks; I don't like the boy who sits near me in school."

+ hurting

3. Owen displayed many thoughts and reactions having to do with being hurt and hurting others. He asked the children in school to *spank* him. On the other hand, he hit and hurt children. He found pleasure in stepping on their feet, taking their work papers and poking them with sticks.

+ closing down
upon
destructively*
(crush)

In this regard, Owen reported one of his first memories as follows: "I was in the backyard playing when I was a baby. My mother was washing the dishes. I dug a hole in the fence and almost got *run over by a car*; the wheel came so close to me." Also, Owen dreamed: "I was riding in a car and a gust of wind blew and broke a wall and we were all drowned."

− / + excretory
symptoms*

4. Owen stated that he watched his "brother and a friend put a plastic tube in their 'butts' and then put it in their mouths." It is likely that Owen was talking of himself as well as of his brother although he did not dare to admit any involvement.

During an extended period of his year's therapy, Owen regularly passed flatus.

+ preoccupation
with illness*

5. Owen suffered from a hypochondriacal fear of catching chicken pox and the pox lodging upon the retina of his eye.

Sources of Stimulation:
children's tactile and visual erogenous contacts with the adult body

+ adult nudity

1. Owen regularly saw his mother without clothes and spoke of seeing her pubic hair.

Approximately once a month he *shared showering* with his father. The father described Owen as being "*very physical.*"

+ adult genital
erotic*

2. During his year of therapy, Owen came across a homosexual in an alley. The homosexual exposed his penis and stimulated Owen's penis.

Behavioral Symptoms correlated with
children's tactile and visual erogenous contacts with the adult body

+ separation
phobias*

1. Following his experience with the homosexual, Owen became school phobic for several weeks.

+ irrational fears*

2. At the same time Owen suffered from phobic panics that he would get chicken pox from his brother and that a pox would lodge on the retina of his eye.

+ irrational
tempers*

3. The school complained of Owen's temper. His teacher wrote: "When I reprimanded him, he would push chairs over, knock books off the tables. . . . One day there was no milk for lunch. Owen could not accept this and screamed: 'It's not fair. I ordered milk. Now where is it?' whereupon he kicked a chair, threw books, etc. . . . During a spelling test he went to the bathroom and was gone a very long time. When he returned, he said: 'Why didn't you wait?' His face got very red and he spat at me when I went near him. He finally did his work after I ignored him."

+ sexual
symptoms*

4. Owen busied himself exploring and poking the "cracks" of two or three girl friends. He tried to stroke his teacher's breasts, arms and legs and would find excuses for pressing his body very close to her body.

Then, during his year of therapy, approximately six months after his diagnostic evaluation, Owen permitted a stranger to expose himself and to stimulate Owen's penis (see above).

+ biting/cutting*

5. Owen dreamed, "lobsters were all around; they were about to *bite* me."

+ eyes*

6. Owen attacked children with his fist, usually aiming for their *eyes*. On one occasion he poked a child's *eyes* with a toy truck.

As already mentioned, he became terrified that he would come down with chicken pox and that a pox would lodge on the *retina of his eye.*

Significantly, it was the *visual* aspect of learning which was the most striking aspect of Owen's severe learning problem. Despite his superior intelligence, Owen, at the age of eight, was unable to read.

Owen's sexual encounter with the man who exposed his penis contributed to the intensity of these problems: a week following his voyeuristic experience, Owen clung to his teacher while desperately crying: "I can't work; I can't play; I can't do anything."

Owen
18

Stimulation-Symptom-and-Dream-Profile

	+ Separation Phobias	
	Night Terrors, Twilight States	
Sleep in Bed with Adult	+ Irrational Fears: Other	
	+ Irrational Tempers	
+ Adult Genital Erotic	+ Sexual Symptoms	
	+ Biting/Cutting, etc.	} *content of*
View Adult Coitus	+ Eyes	} *dreams and*
	Fire	} *symptoms*
	+ Learning Problems (levels 2 or 3, etc.)	
+ Punitive Yelling	Lying and Delinquency	
	Reversal of Affect	} *content of*
Beatings	+ Closing Down Upon, Kill	} *dreams and*
	Falling	} *symptoms*
	Excretory Symptoms and Dreams	
	Anal Masturbation	
Preoccupation with Child's BM	Enuresis	
	+ Illness, etc.	} *content of*
Anal Contacts	Pain	} *dreams and*
	Death	} *symptoms*
	Compulsions	

Case 19: Synopsis of David Crocker's "S"

Although S was gifted with a superior intelligence, he had fallen far behind his class at school by the time he was thirteen years old. He failed to adjust in school because of his inability to read and work and because of his intolerable aggressive acting out (*Psychoanalytic Study of the Child,* Vol. X, 1955, p. 300). From the age of six, S displayed uncontrollable bouts of destroying property; in school he "defied all rules and authority and became a leader in delinquent acts, inciting other children to destructive behavior" (p. 303).

Sources of Stimulation:
adult punitive and excretory contacts with children

+early
deprivation

1. The mother unsuccessfully attempted to abort while she was carrying S. She was depressed and felt inadequate to become a mother once again, for she was already burdened by a daughter of two and a half who was subject to temper tantrums and stubborn behavior (p. 301, 303). From the time of his birth, S "had an awful life," she reported, "I neglected him and he suffered from not getting enough" (p. 303). To make matters worse she received little support from her husband who worked nights in a "vital" factory in order to escape military service (p. 302). It is not surprising, therefore, that S developed signs of irritability, hyperactivity, depression and a proneness for colds and infections (p. 303).[1]

+beatings*

2. S was spanked from the time he was a baby. At the age of two when he persisted in sucking his thumb, his parents spanked him and put varnish on his thumb (p. 303). Later the parents, in an effort to be "loving," permissively encouraged S to express his emotions indiscriminately, but then when S got completely out of hand they put him into isolation and beat him (p. 302, 304).

The mother, believing that permissiveness was the modern solution to children's problems, would encourage S to hit her, to slap her on the face and body while she explained, "I know you hate me and this might make you feel better" (p. 305). The father also attempted to relate to S by bribery and seduction with lack of controls until the father's anger finally led to harsh controls and physical beatings (p. 302). In this way, the parents set up a vicious cycle of priming S's rage by alternately hitting or beating him for being bad, and then permitting him to act out his hate by giving him no controls and encouraging him to hit his mother.

3. S was exposed to hearing his parents fight. On one occasion, he recalled,

74

+ punitive
yelling*

he was so upset by their prolonged yelling at one another that he defecated directly into his undershorts (p. 330).

+ anal
stimulation*

4. S witnessed scenes during which his mother administered enemas to the father. (p. 330).

Behavioral Symptoms correlated with
adult punitive and excretory contacts with children

+ killing*

1. At the age of seven, S suffered from nightmares of his sister being killed in accidents (p. 304). At this time, *he* got into an accident: he ran into a car and broke his arm (p. 304). Later, at the age of thirteen, S suffered recurrent

+ death*

dreams that his family all had *died* violently (p. 323).

+ hurting and
destruction

Meanwhile, S developed a proclivity for destroying property, a symptom which became increasingly severe. By the time he was placed in a residential treatment home, S had destroyed hundreds of dollars worth of property (p. 305). S continued to display such behavior at the residential center. "His cottage parents became afraid of him because . . . he . . . turned the cottage into pandemonium" (p. 306). On one occasion he defiantly broke up to fifty windows (p. 309). He would even blow up if he were praised for his school work, and then would try to destroy his work (p. 307).

+ pain*(aches)
+ hypochondria*

2. At different times of his life, S suffered from numerous physical complaints of emotional origin: a) when he was five he suffered from "headaches and stomachaches for which no organic causes could be found" (p. 303); b) at the age of thirteen he expressed worries about his nose bleeding and fears that "he was going blind" (p. 317).

+ excretory
symptoms*

3. S soiled on an occasion when his parents were fighting (p. 330). Later he developed a tendency for compulsive neatness (p. 309) along with fears of dirt (p. 330).

+ compulsions*

4. S compulsively pulled out his hair (p. 305). He also suffered from compulsions during which he "had" to go back to be certain that doors were closed (p. 318).

+ learning*
(level 3)

5. Despite his superior intelligence, S entered the residential school four to five grades behind in every subject except mathematics (p. 300, 305).

The emotional origin of his learning problem was demonstrated by resolution of his learning inhibitions during psychoanalytic treatment: by the time S left the residence he had caught up in all school subjects except reading in which he achieved scores still one to two years behind those of his class (p. 334).

S's negative delinquent defiance to social authority also improved with therapy but not until the end of his stay at the residential school. It will be recalled that S's defiance of all rules and authority in grammar school was one of the principal complaints precipitating his placement in a residential treatment center. This defiance continued during the first half of his stay at the residence where he became identified with boys who stole, gambled and destroyed property, boys who aimed to prove that they were above the law as they broke into the store and the offices of the administration (p. 306).

+ delinquency*

Sources of Stimulation:
children's tactile and visual erogenous contacts with the adult body

1. When S was six years old (i.e., at the time of the acute outbreak of his disturbing symptoms) his mother decided upon a "modern," "liberal," "permissive" approach for bringing up her children. At the time, she was in the process of receiving psychiatric treatment for herself and became convinced that it would be best not only to let S express his emotional anger and to encourage him to hit her, but also to encourage him "to know all" by freely seeing his parents naked (p. 303). Thereafter, the mother seductively titillated S with her body (p. 322). On one occasion S recalled getting an erection while his mother exposed herself to him in the bathroom and asked him to look at her. He tried to turn away but saw her in the mirror. At this time S became uncontrollably excited to the point that he started yelling and throwing things at the mother. Then to punish S for his misbehavior, the father proceeded to beat him (p. 333).[2]

+ adult nudity

+ adult genital erotic*

S also recalled sexually exciting memories of taking showers with his father, memories focusing upon his father's penis (p. 331).

+ view adult coitus*

Furthermore, S was reported to have seen "primal scene" activities while he slept in his parents' room (p. 323). Unfortunately, within the residential home where he was placed, S was overtly exposed to the homosexual play and excitements of the teenage boys in the bedrooms and showers. S became so involved that there was a concern that he would become a confirmed homosexual (p. 306).

Behavioral Symptoms correlated with
children's tactile and visual erogenous contacts with the adult body

+ irrational fears*

1. S expressed many fears: of going insane (p. 304); of becoming blind (p. 317); of not being able to control his radio and his thoughts (p. 317-18). He also suffered from nightmares of violent death (p. 323).

+ nightmares

+ irrational tempers*

2. S broke out into a rage when his mother seductively exposed herself (p. 333). He spontaneously informed his therapist "When I think about sex and get excited, then I get angry" (p. 323). As already noted, S's tempers soon became discharged conjointly with severely destructive behavior. At the beginning of therapy, his tempers would end in his "overturning the desks, breaking the drawers, and turning the room into shambles" (p. 314, 316).

3. S was terrorized by his inability to control his driven masturbation and

+ sexual
   symptoms*

his homosexual feelings which he felt were making him weak and crazy (p. 318-19, 321, 323). "He became obsessed . . . with the thought of having a hole, a vagina and of being raped" (p. 330). To counter his fears of being different in not being able to control his own homosexual thoughts and behavior, he incited other teenagers to act out homosexually (p. 321).

+ biting/cutting*

4. Prior to his residential placement, S was threatening his siblings with knives (p. 305).

+ eyes*
+ hysterical
   conversion
   symptoms*

5. S was enraged at the "lousy" eye doctor for assuring him that there was nothing organically wrong with his *eyes*. Rather he was convinced that he was going *blind* (p. 317).

+ eyes* (reading)

At the time he was recalling memories of looking at his father's penis in the shower, S became aware that he had been *afraid to look at* words (p. 331). It, therefore, is understandable that in all school subjects dependent upon reading, S was three to four years behind his age level in grade school (p. 304), although he received satisfactory grades in mathematics. Even when his learning problems were clearing after his treatment at the residence, the slowest of all his subjects to recover was his reading (p. 334).

+ fire*

6. Prior to therapy, S would give vent to bouts of excitement during which "he would throw [his] clothes into the burning fire in the fireplace" (p. 304).

Addendum

It is significant that S began to form a positive relationship with his therapist as he realized that in analysis he could talk over his "crazy," sexual thoughts and activities and could begin to understand them. S responded to Dr. Crocker's plea: "Let's talk about it" (in place of acting it out). S later indicated that "what helped him the most in analysis and formed the core of his understanding of analysis, was this reminder: 'Let's talk about it' " (p. 311). This approach in behalf of control provided the antithesis of his parents' pathological priming, permitting and encouraging S's acting out instinctual behavior.

NOTES

1 See Spitz on "hospitalism" (*Psychoanalytic Study of the Child,* Vol. I, 1945, p. 59).

2 Note, these events provided an association between eroticized pleasure and anger.

Crocker's "S"
19

Stimulation-Symptom-and-Dream-Profile

	Separation Phobias	
	+ Night Terrors, Twilight States	
Sleep in Bed with Adult	+ Irrational Fears: Other	
	+ Irrational Tempers	
+ Adult Genital Erotic	+ Sexual Symptoms	
	+ Biting/Cutting, etc.	⎫ *content of*
+ View Adult Coitus	+ Eyes	⎬ *dreams and*
	+ Fire	⎭ *symptoms*
	+ Learning Problems (levels 2 or 3, etc.)	
+ Punitive Yelling	+ Lying and Delinquency	
	Reversal of Affect	
+ Beatings	+ Closing Down Upon, Kill	⎫ *content of* ⎬ *dreams and*
	Falling	⎭ *symptoms*
	+ Excretory Symptoms and Dreams	
	Anal Masturbation	
Preoccupation with Child's BM	Enuresis	
	+ Illness, etc.	⎫ *content of*
+ Anal Contacts	+ Pain	⎬ *dreams and*
	+ Death	⎭ *symptoms*
	+ Compulsions	

Case 20: Synopsis of Michael Robbins's "Alan"

"Alan was seventeen years old when he was referred to the hospital from a local private school. . . . He was suffering from an acute psychosis" (*Psychoanalytic Study of the Child*, Vol. XXIV, 1969, p. 233).

Since early childhood, Alan had been able to induce what appeared to be hallucinatory experiences. At the time of his hospitalization, Alan had lost control of his hallucinations and became overwhelmed by depersonalized feelings of identity loss and a passive sensation of paralysis (p. 235).

This case illustrates the effects of parental sexual overpermissiveness superimposed upon the effects of early deprivation and a severe lack of empathic care.

Sources of Stimulation:
children's tactile and visual erogenous contacts with the adult body

+ adult nudity

1. Open nudity was sanctioned in Alan's home, with parents and siblings alike freely going about without clothes (p. 239). Alan still possessed a picture he had drawn at the age of five — a drawing of his father with a gigantic penis (p. 245).

+ adult genital
erotic*
(− / + observe
adult coitus*)[1]

2. At the age of six, previous to his father's death, Alan *"had been striving to have intercourse with his mother the way his father did"* (p. 237-38). Alan's stepfather later described Alan's relation with his mother as being inappropriately seductive: the two did not appear as mother and son but rather as lovers.

Behavioral Symptoms correlated with
children's tactile and visual erogenous contacts with the adult body

+ irrational fears*
+ twilight state*
+ hallucinations*
+ nightmares

1. Since his early childhood, Alan was terrified by feelings of paralysis and loss of identity (p. 235) and was able to induce hallucinatory experiences, e.g., of a "green, frog-like jelly mass under tables" (p. 235). Alan experienced nightmares about monsters and war (p. 243).

+ sexual
symptoms*

2. Alan began sexual experimentation in early puberty (p. 234). Then for a period of three years during adolescence he developed incestuous relationships with his sisters. Sexual contacts with the sisters included ejaculation without penetration (p. 239).

+ biting/cutting*

3. Alan experienced delusions that "his flesh was being torn apart and eaten" (p. 241).

4. In a dream, Alan was "lying on the floor of a large cave and *staring* at the ceiling" (p. 243). After his father died, Alan claimed his survival was made possible by his *eyes* looking at the world until "everything" became equivalent to an hallucination (p. 243-44). Alan's preoccupation with looking replaced any attempts on his part to relate to the lives of other people.

+ eyes*

Sources of Stimulation:
adult punitive and excretory contacts with children

+ early
deprivation
(continuing
throughout
childhood)

1. Alan's mother oscillated between being (a) "domineering and control-ling" or (b) "depressed and withdrawn." She had been "unable to create a se-cure, warm . . . environment for her children" (p. 233), a maternal defect which must have exerted its most disastrous effect upon Alan during his infancy.[2]

As Alan grew into latency, the mother continued to evidence little capacity for supplying Alan nurturance. It was his father, not his mother, who would wake Alan up in the morning and prepare breakfast for him (p. 235)

The mother resorted to seduction as a replacement for care and protection. As a child Alan recalled staying up with his mother late at night in her bedroom where she would tell him stories of Nazi atrocities and talk a great deal about sex (p. 236).

The father also displayed little capacity for relating to Alan. For example, "Alan recalled a long, silent motor trip across Canada alone with his father. . . . There was no verbal communication except for occasional remarks by the father about the beauty of the landscape and little interaction except for occa-sional stops for the father to photograph trees" (p. 236). Despite the father's distant personality, however, he was Alan's idol. Therefore, Alan was exposed to a shattering trauma at the age of seven when he learned that his father had been killed in a head-on automobile accident. To make matters worse, after the father's death, the mother was "emotionally unavailable to Alan" so that he had no one to share his disturbed feelings and grief (p. 238). When Alan asked for help during his adolescence, his mother would not even allow him to see a psychiatrist (p. 240).

+ punitive
yelling*

2. Alan recalled that his mother did not discipline the children but would repeatedly let them fight things out until she became so angry she would explode (p. 239). At the same time, one of Alan's last memories of his father was of the father yelling at the children for not going to bed on time (p. 236). Alan also recalled his stepfather, Mr. O, and his mother having "explosive and frightening arguments, each vying for power and trying to get the children on his or her side."

+ anal
 stimulation*

3. As a child, Alan suffered from pinworms, a source for direct stimulation of his anal mucous membranes and for anal itching and scratching (p. 239).

Behavioral Symptoms correlated with
adult punitive and excretory contacts with children

+ negative
 behavior
+ learning*
 (level 2)
+ lying*

+ delinquency*

1. At the age of seven, following his father's death, Alan "gave up and sat passive and depressed watching television" (p. 238). He could not do his school work for a whole year after the father's death and was not promoted from the second grade (p. 238). By the age of thirteen, Alan was considered "lazy" and "undisciplined" (p. 240). He was described as "sneaky and untruthful" and often ran away from his parents (p. 239). On one occasion he became involved in stealing a car (p. 240).

+ death*

Alan was obsessed with fall landscapes which to him looked empty and dead. He experienced hallucinations of skulls lying under the table (p. 240) and hallucinations of his being buried (p. 241). After the father's death, Alan felt he was destined to go to hell (p. 237). At the age of fifteen he began to experiment with drugs and to become increasingly involved with marijuana and LSD (p. 240). In treatment he realized his "flip-outs" were a hell with punishments he felt he had merited (p. 237). He dreamed of monsters and *war* (p. 243).

+ hurting
+ killing*

A year prior to treatment he became preoccupied with suicidal thoughts and attempted suicide by slashing his wrist (p. 240).

NOTES

1 "Alan had been very physical in bed with his mother when his father was away. However, he had not observed his parents copulating"; personal communication from Dr. Robbins.

2 Many of Alan's principal symptoms — defective concept of self and body, defective differentiation of self, as well as unstable regulation of his self-esteem — are all problems regularly associated with earliest deprivation in infancy.

Robbins's "Alan"
20

Stimulation-Symptom-and-Dream-Profile

<table>
<tr><td></td><td>Separation Phobias</td><td></td></tr>
<tr><td></td><td>+ Night Terrors, Twilight States</td><td></td></tr>
<tr><td>Sleep in Bed with Adult</td><td>+ Irrational Fears: Other</td><td></td></tr>
<tr><td></td><td>Irrational Tempers</td><td></td></tr>
<tr><td>+ Adult Genital Erotic</td><td>+ Sexual Symptoms</td><td></td></tr>
<tr><td></td><td>+ Biting/Cutting, etc.</td><td>} content of</td></tr>
<tr><td>View Adult Coitus</td><td>+ Eyes</td><td>} dreams and</td></tr>
<tr><td></td><td>Fire</td><td>} symptoms</td></tr>
<tr><td></td><td></td><td></td></tr>
<tr><td></td><td>+ Learning Problems (levels 2 or 3, etc.)</td><td></td></tr>
<tr><td>+ Punitive Yelling</td><td>+ Lying and Delinquency</td><td></td></tr>
<tr><td></td><td>Reversal of Affect</td><td></td></tr>
<tr><td>Beatings</td><td>+ Closing Down Upon, Kill</td><td>} content of dreams and</td></tr>
<tr><td></td><td>Falling</td><td>} symptoms</td></tr>
<tr><td></td><td></td><td></td></tr>
<tr><td></td><td>Excretory Symptoms and Dreams</td><td></td></tr>
<tr><td></td><td>Anal Masturbation</td><td></td></tr>
<tr><td>Preoccupation with Child's BM</td><td>Enuresis</td><td></td></tr>
<tr><td></td><td>Illness, etc.</td><td>} content of</td></tr>
<tr><td>+ Anal Contacts</td><td>Pain</td><td>} dreams and</td></tr>
<tr><td></td><td>+ Death</td><td>} symptoms</td></tr>
<tr><td></td><td>Compulsions</td><td></td></tr>
</table>

Case 21: Synopsis of Jenny Waelder Hall's "Anton"

Jenny Waelder Hall's "An Analysis of a Case of Night Terror" was the first case of a child analysis ever to be reported in detail. Originally read at the Vienna Psychoanalytic Society in 1930, it was eventually published in English in 1947 (in the *Psychoanalytic Study of the Child*, Vol. II, 1946, p. 189-227).

Dr. Hall's young patient, Anton, was seven years old when treatment began. His presenting symptoms included severe night terrors, piercing heart pains of emotional origin (organic disturbance having been ruled out) and an inability to remain alone in a room (p. 189, 190).

Sources of Stimulation:
children's tactile and visual erogenous contacts with the adult body

+ sleeping in bed with adults*

1. Anton's home consisted of one bedroom and a kitchen. He slept in his parents' bed. His parents expressed some concern over their boy sleeping between them: even though their small quarters necessitated his remaining in the same room, they wondered whether he should nonetheless have his own bed. At the beginning of treatment, immediate steps were taken to institute this change despite Anton's protests (p. 193).

+ adult genital erotic*

2. The parents often indulged in sexual intercourse while Anton was sharing their bed (p. 218, 192). "Anton claimed that he had never actually seen anything. 'It was too dark for that' " (p. 218). However he described the noises and movements which must have been a source of much excitement for him. He also easily described in detail the preliminaries of his parents' lovemaking (p. 193). Anton complained " ' Father torments mother, there is no peace when he is around; he tickles her on the neck in bed' — Anton did not like that — he could not stand it — He grew quite hot and excited during this recital." Often he would wake up at night after he had been placed in his own bed and would see his mother in bed with the father. He would begin to cry and ask his mother to come into his bed or else would call out sharply to her " 'Go away

(+ view adult coitus* in the dark)

from father, you have no business there.' All of this was confirmed by his mother." He was particularly afraid of the father beginning to tickle his mother because then " 'the rest would follow' " (p. 218-19).

Additionally, the slums of Vienna invited Anton and his street friends to watch overt sexual activities "in dark doorways, courtyards, and stairways" (p. 192).

Behavioral Symptoms correlated with
children's tactile and visual erogenous contacts with the adult body

+ separation
phobia*

1. At the beginning of treatment Anton could not remain alone in a room or sleep alone. He offered the excuse that there had been a burglary in the neighborhood and he was frightened by the thought of a surprise attack (p. 190).

+ irrational fears*

2. Anton's ongoing state of fearfulness consisted of more than his exaggerated concerns about burglars. Much more disturbing were his attacks of night

+ night terrors*

terror which had occurred for about a year at irregular intervals (p. 189). Anton would "wake up screaming or sit up and cry out in terror. He took no notice of what went on about him, nor did he respond to attempts by his mother to calm him. The mother would apply cold compresses to his heart to calm him. After a while the child would quiet down and fall asleep, without having been fully conscious at any point. He had no memory of the attacks afterward" (pp. 189-90). The mother reported how Anton would frequently appear at night in a state of somnambulism (p. 207) during which he would talk, sing, laugh or cry and eventually erupt with shrieks of fear (p. 207).

The relation of Anton's night terrors to bed-sharing with his mother was demonstrated when Anton and the mother secretly reverted to bed-sharing following a year of abstinence. Anton's night terrors had disappeared completely once the mother had taken Dr. Hall's initial advice that Anton sleep in a separate bed. However, after mother and son shared a bed together again, the night terrors directly reappeared (p. 194, 202, 211).

+ / − irrational
tempers*

3. One episode of temper tantrums was reported during Anton's analysis. This appeared at the time of his reversion to bed-sharing with his mother. At that time the mother reported that she had given in to his wishes because he screamed so much (p. 210).

+ sexual
symptoms*

4. A boy, Franky, who repetitively had witnessed his widowed father's sexual activities with street women, became Anton's friend. The two boys, prior to and during Anton's analysis, became intensely involved in sexual activities with the neighborhood children (p. 196). Every child contributed a new variation for their sexual games "the result being that Anton had gone through the whole gamut covering practically every possible form of sexual activity" (p. 197-98).

Compulsive masturbation was also a problem for Anton. Even though his father punished him severely for masturbation, he could not control it. In particular he would masturbate under the blanket while he was in bed with his mother and then "ask for his mother's hand when he had enough of it" (p. 218).

+ biting/cutting/
stomach*

5. Anton was preoccupied with worries that Dr. Hall would *cut* open the "breast" of one of her male patients; then drinking water would not come out of the patient's *penis* any more but would come out of his *heart* (p. 203).[1]

Also, Anton spoke about: a) fears of a biting shark which might eat him up (p. 212); b) phantasies of a priest who cuts off his big toe (p. 220); c) a dream that Father came from Dr. Hall's office and "brought a long pencil with him. I took a hatchet and *cut* the pencil in two so that only a tiny bit was left; then I got some glue and stuck a bit on it" (p. 221).[2]

Sources of Stimulation:
adult punitive and excretory contacts with children

+ beatings*

1. Anton's father was described as kind and thoughtful to his boy but also ambivalent and inconsistent: "from tender affection he would pass to sudden rage and menace the child." "When a firm hand was needed he would be soft" but for trifling faults he would whip the child (p. 191). "Often when father and son began to wrestle[3] as comrades and they became too rough, the father would discover an insult to his dignity. The play that had seemed to begin in friendly equality thus would end in a sound whipping."

+ punitive
yelling* and
violence

2. Anton was also exposed to his father's rages toward his mother (p. 206, 207). The mother described wild scenes which Anton as a little child had to witness. During one battle the father knocked the mother down to the floor while Anton stood by helplessly.

Behavioral Symptoms correlated with
adult punitive and excretory contacts with children

+ closing down
upon
destructively*

1. Sadistic hurting was included in Anton's repertoire of symptoms. On one occasion, for little apparent reason, Anton became enraged at his young female cousin and proceeded to hit her savagely on the legs with a whip (p. 210).[4] Whipping was also reflected in one of Anton's dreams about dogs and a sled. Anton reported the dream as follows: "I drove in a sled with Karli. Two dogs were harnessed to it. I had a *whip* in my hand and a cord, and I *tied* the cord around the dogs' bellies like a saddle girth and *whipped* the dogs with my *whip*.

+ falling*
+ killing*

There was a steep mountain; it got steeper and steeper and we *tumbled down*. The other boy was *killed* and I was wounded" (p. 221).

These problems involving sadism were reflected in Anton's preoccupation with a news story about a boy, Artmann, who killed his parents. Sadism also tended to be acted out in therapy, and Dr. Hall found it necessary to institute firm controls to prevent Anton from hurting her, e.g., when he attempted to throw coal at her head (p. 201).

+ pain*
+ non-organic
illness*

2. Anton's piercing "heart attacks" were emotional in origin (p. 189). In this regard, Dr. Hall wrote, "One day the children were almost caught at their sexual game; they shook with fright and their hearts beat violently. Anton noticed the heart poundings of one of his playmates who was very thin. Anton knew that he also got palpitations when he was sexually excited" (p. 219). In brief, Anton's heart poundings appeared to be associated with perceptions of

excessive sexual excitement as well as expectations of punishment.

Fortunately, Anton's "talking out" his upset memories, together with Dr. Hall offering him understanding, controls and protective care, resulted in the complete relief not only of his cardiac symptoms but also his anxiety and night terrors as well. A follow-up study, seven years after termination of his analysis, revealed that Anton's symptoms had not recurred (p. 226-27).

NOTES

1 Note the associative connection of "heart" and "penis" suggesting a possible connection between pains in the penis and pains in the heart.

2 There occurs the possibility that Anton's thoughts about *cutting* could have been a function primarily of his father's threats to cut off his penis (see p. 217). However, according to the cumulative findings from this investigation, cutting symptoms are characteristic of children exposed to excessive erogenous contacts with the adult body (including primal scene stimulation) with or without a history of castration threats. The father's castration threats therefore are understood not to be the only source for Anton's fears about "sharks biting" and thoughts about "toes," "breasts" and "pencils" being cut.

3 See cases 32, 46 and 78 for other examples of wrestling in association with sexual stimulation and sadism.

4 Anton discharged upon this little girl what his father had discharged upon him: child abuse was in the making.

Hall's "Anton"
21

Stimulation-Symptom-and-Dream-Profile

	+ Separation Phobias	
	+ Night Terrors, Twilight States	
+ Sleep in Bed with Adult	+ Irrational Fears: Other	
	+ Irrational Tempers	
+ Adult Genital Erotic	+ Sexual Symptoms	
	+ Biting/Cutting, etc.	} *content of*
+ View Adult Coitus	Eyes	} *dreams and*
	Fire	} *symptoms*
	Learning Problems (levels 2 or 3, etc.)	
+ Punitive Yelling	Lying and Delinquency	
	Reversal of Affect	
+ Beatings	+ Closing Down Upon, Kill	} *content of* / *dreams and*
	+ Falling	} *symptoms*
	Excretory Symptoms and Dreams	
	Anal Masturbation	
Preoccupation with Child's BM	Enuresis	
	+ Illness, etc.	} *content of*
Anal Contacts	+ Pain	} *dreams and*
	Death	} *symptoms*
	Compulsions	

Case 22: Synopsis of Erna Furman's "Danny"

Danny's analysis with Erna Furman started when he was four years old and was still in progress at the time of his case presentation in the *Journal of the American Psychoanalytic Association* (Vol. 10, 1962, p. 258), when Danny was eight.

Danny presented serious referral problems. Although it was shown that he suffered from neither mental deficiency nor demonstrable neurological damage, Danny "spent most of his time withdrawn and preoccupied with . . . (inanimate) objects, e.g., fans and cigarette boxes" (p. 259); he would speak "only disconnected spontaneous words; mostly he repeated parts of sentences after his mother." Danny's cognitive development actually had advanced beyond these surface manifestations, e.g., "when Danny talked in his sleep, he used the personal pronouns correctly and referred to himself as 'I' " even though he did not speak in this fashion during states of wakefulness (p. 262).[1]

Danny also presented a severe eating disturbance, absence of bowel or urine control, outbreaks of uncontrollable temper tantrums (p. 259) and "spells of aggressive hyperactivity" which upset his mother's overly neat household (p. 260).

Danny's history of being infantilized served as a background for his emotional problems. The mother, unfortunately, had joined the ranks of mothers who are overpreoccupied with their children's bodies and body products, mothers who infantilize their children to the point of rendering them weak and helpless. Danny's mother was still feeding him when he was almost four (p. 259); she still helped him urinate by holding his penis upon which she would pour warm water (p. 260). She also allowed Danny to sleep in the parental bedroom until he was six and a half years old (p. 263).

Fortunately, Danny's mother responded to an educationally oriented preparatory period of therapy aimed "to help her alter her handling of Danny." "The mother proved to be an astute observer; she learned to utilize her insight in some respects and in line with Danny's initial rapid progress, was able to talk with him about some of his difficulties" (p. 261).

Sources of Stimulation:
children's tactile and visual erogenous contacts with the adult body

+ sleeping in bed
with adult*

1. "In the evenings Danny made his mother lie down with him for hours before he fell asleep. During the night, he would wander into his parents' bedroom where he went to sleep in his father's bed while the father moved to another bed in the same room. When the parents attempted to return Danny to

88

his room, he . . . disturbed them throughout the night to such an extent that they . . . decided to accept his nightly company" (p. 260).

At the age of six and a half years, Danny "prevailed upon his parents to lock their bedroom door . . . and stopped trying to enter their room at night." Prior to this time, "the parents had never been able to accept the therapist's advice in this respect" (p. 263).

+ adult nudity

2. Danny was present during his parents' baths, especially during his mother's baths. He also would be allowed to remain in the bathroom while the parents urinated and defecated. On his visits to his grandparents, Danny would also be exposed to his grandmother's nudity (p. 260). With great anxiety he recalled seeing his grandmother's genitalia (p. 265).

+ adult genital
  erotic*
+ view adult
  coitus*

3. Danny was so terrified by exposure to his parents' copulating that his mother was driven to wrap him up in a blanket and carry him out of the room (p. 265).[2] For a long period Danny tried to deal with memories of these events "by excited, bizarre behavior and incoherent talk" (p. 265).[3]

Behavioral Symptoms correlated with
children's tactile and visual erogenous contacts with the adult body

+ separation
  phobia*

1. Danny was afraid of masturbating when he was alone. Therefore he always had to accompany his mother "everywhere" (p. 268).

+ night terrors*

2. During the period when he shared his parents' bedroom, Danny was plagued by night terrors. "Not long after falling asleep . . . he would talk in his sleep" and then would "wake in panic" with complaints that "his shadow [had] threatened to attack him in his sleep." Danny's fears of his shadow also would disturb him during waking hours, "around dinnertime" (p. 261-62).

+ irrational fears*

+ night terrors*
+ sleepwalking*

When Danny was placed in his own room and no longer was permitted to enter his parents' bedroom, he at first suffered almost nightly pavor nocturnus sometimes coupled with *sleepwalking* (p. 264).

Eventually, "Danny's pavor nocturnus was replaced by repetitive nightmares in which he was threatened by a mechanical figure called 'the theatigator' " (presumably "the alligator"). Danny also dreamed of "eleficient [which] frightened Danny by appearing, flying, and thundering . . . to warn Danny of 'bad things' " (p. 268). Danny begged Mrs. Furman to help to make dreaming impossible for him. He feared he would have the " 'worst dream in the whole world' " (p. 264).

+ irrational
  tempers*

3. Danny's tantrums, a presenting problem, erupted whenever his activities of the moment were interrupted (p. 259).

+ sexual
  symptoms*

4. Danny "masturbated openly, exhibited, and provocatively used sexual language in public" (p. 267).

His sexual panics also appeared during his therapy hours. As he faced his upsetting sexual memories, Danny suddenly called out to Mrs. Furman, " 'I have to run to the bathroom, I have to leave my pishi [penis] there . . . I'll pick it up another time.'[4] He dashed off to the toilet and returned much calmer" (p. 266).

+ biting/cutting*

5. Danny's nightmares repetitively featured the "theatigator" (the classic alligator with big teeth) (p. 264).

+ eyes*

6. Still another "terribly scary" nightmare focused upon his mother's head and her eyebrows. (p.263).[5]

Danny exclaimed that he *couldn't* even *see* a certain dream. His associations to the dream led to his upset memories of *seeing* his grandmother's genitals (p. 265).

− / + fire*

7. Danny knew what to do about his night terrors: "if they start to act up, *one calls* the *fire* department"; one spits the dreams out and the *fire department* takes them away (p. 269). However, Danny experienced no symptoms or dreams pertaining to fire.

Sources of Stimulation:
adult punitive and excretory contacts with children

+ early
  deprivation (of
  appropriate
  care)
+ punitive bowel
  training

1. Danny "was born prematurely, and barely survived." He failed to thrive insofar as he did not begin to walk until the age of sixteen months (p. 259).

2. The mother tried to bowel-train Danny by wrapping him in a blanket and then "holding him on a chamber-pot . . . in front of the TV for periods of an hour" (p. 260).

+ punitive
  yelling* and
  hitting

3. At times of Danny's hyperactivity, his mother would either break loose with "uncontrollable outbursts of anger, [while] shouting threats of desertion, blaming Danny for ruining her life, and spanking him harshly; or she would passively sit by, allowing him to become overwhelmed with his impulses" (p. 260). The mother also could not tolerate Danny's masturbation and would slap him when she found him masturbating (p. 260). Thus, Danny's mother could hold his penis and pour warm water over it (p. 260); furthermore, she could copulate with her husband in front of him; yet Danny was not to do sexual things in front of her and he was to be punished for masturbating (p. 260). Danny, therefore, was placed in the helpless position of being expected to suppress instinctual behavior which his parents were actively priming.

Behavioral Symptoms correlated with
adult punitive and excretory contacts with children

+ enuresis*
+ excretory
  symptoms*
+ learning*
  (referral
  complaint)

1. Danny still wet himself and soiled (p. 259).

2. Danny suffered from a severe learning inhibition to the extent that at the beginning of therapy he could speak only disconnected words.

+ reversal of
affect* (silly
inappropriate-
ness)

3. "In his daily life . . . Danny had persistently warded off . . . [sexual] memories by excited, bizarre behavior and incoherent talk" with an insistence that everything was nonsense (p. 265).

Addendum

The formulation that Danny's psychotic-like symptoms stemmed from his history of exposures to erotic and punitive overstimulation as well as infantilization is supported by the progress which he displayed when these sources of emotional disturbance were dealt with in therapy. Mrs. Furman reported that even though Danny at the age of eight was still in analysis, he had already "become more independent." He became able to go shopping for his mother and to visit the barber on his own. He showed "increasing signs of true sublimations" involving "geography, nature study, and reading. This, together with his vastly improved behavior . . . helped him to be promoted to the second grade of his public school" (p. 268).

NOTES

1 Presumably Danny was tranquilized sufficiently during states of sleep that his states of excitement then did not overwhelm his higher cognitive processes (p. 262).

2 It is of interest that in relation to observing the primal scene, Danny dreamed of ". . . a tiny boy, wrapped in a blanket and being carried in and out of the noisy aeroplane in which he was traveling" (p. 265): much as he was wrapped in a blanket and carried out of the bedroom during parental intercourse.

3 See case 84 of Mrs. Furman's Carol; also case 77 of Kurt Junior with respect to bizarre speech and behavior among children exposed to adult-genital-erotic contacts.

4 In other words, Danny was implying that the feelings of *sexual excitement in his penis* were so great and unmanageable that his penis felt ready to break. He must have hoped he could dispose of his penis or at least get rid of the intense feelings in his penis.

5 Note this image of "eyebrows" refers to "eye" and to the "brows," i.e., to *"eye"* and to *"hair."* As expected, Danny's associations indicated a memory of (his *eye*) seeing his mother's genitalia, the most prominent aspect of which would be her pubic *hair.*

Furman's "Danny"
22

Stimulation-Symptom-and-Dream-Profile

	+ Separation Phobias
	+ Night Terrors, Twilight States
+ Sleep in Bed with Adult	+ Irrational Fears: Other
	+ Irrational Tempers
+ Adult Genital Erotic	+ Sexual Symptoms
	+ Biting/Cutting, etc. ⎫ *content of*
+ View Adult Coitus	+ Eyes ⎬ *dreams and*
	Fire ⎭ *symptoms*

	+ Learning Problems (levels 2 or 3, etc.)
+ Punitive Yelling	Lying and Delinquency
	+ Reversal of Affect
Beatings	Closing Down Upon, Kill ⎫ *content of*
	⎬ *dreams and*
	Falling ⎭ *symptoms*

	+ Excretory Symptoms and Dreams
	Anal Masturbation
Preoccupation with Child's BM	+ Enuresis
	Illness, etc. ⎫ *content of*
Anal Contacts	Pain ⎬ *dreams and*
	Death ⎭ *symptoms*
	Compulsions

Case 23: Synopsis of Selma Fraiberg's "Sally"

Selma Fraiberg's case, "A Critical Neurosis in a Two-And-A-Half-Year-Old Girl," presents detailed clinical material pertaining to the environmental stimulation and the behavioral disturbances of Mrs. Fraiberg's little patient, Sally (*Psychoanalytic Study of the Child*, Vol. VII, 1952, p. 173-215).

Sally, the extremely bright and precocious child of modern intellectual parents, developed symptoms following a month's visit at her grandparents' home. For the first two weeks of this visit, the parents remained with Sally. Then, during the second two weeks, they took a vacation and left Sally to be cared for by the grandparents. During this period Sally, unfortunately, was exposed to viewing her grandparents copulating. When she returned to her parents, Sally displayed an ever-increasing barrage of terrors culminating in panics and the appearance of hallucinatory "noises" (p. 173, 174, 180).

The mother could not understand the source of Sally's symptoms and decided that they must somehow be related to Sally's "sibling rivalry" toward her three-month-old baby brother. With no success the mother devoted herself to reassuring Sally that she was loved. Unfortunately, the mother did not seek therapy for a period of four months, not until Sally's condition had become disturbingly grave (p. 173).

Sources of Stimulation:
children's tactile and visual erogenous contacts with the adult body

+ sleeping in bed with adults*

1. During the outbreak of her terrors, Sally begged her mother to sleep with her. On one occasion, "the mother found Sally crawling on top of her in bed, clutching and embracing her sensually" (p. 178). At night Sally went from one bed to another to seek solace for her terrors.

+ adult nudity

2. Sally observed her mother's vagina, pubic hair and clitoris and insisted that, contrary to what she had been told, her mother *did* have "a little piece" of penis skin in her genital area (p. 191, 190). It turned out that Sally was referring to her mother's clitoris.

(menstrual display)

Permissiveness in Sally's home extended to the mother's leaving her bloody sanitary napkin in the wastebasket where it was available for Sally to discover (p. 184). Several months prior to the onset of Sally's symptoms, Sally had found the used napkin in the wastebasket and brought it blood-stained to her mother. Thereupon the mother "explained to Sally that this was what happened to grown-up ladies and that when Sally grew up she would have this too" (p. 182).

3. When Mrs. Fraiberg inquired about Sally's sleeping arrangements, the mother offered her assurances that during the visit to the grandparents, Sally had had a room by herself. However, a letter from the grandparents revealed that following the parents' departure, the grandparents had insisted that Sally sleep in their room so that Sally would not be "lonely" (p. 174). It was during this period that Sally at the age of two and a half witnessed her grandmother and grandfather copulating (p. 193). Sally reported the grandmother saying at the time, "Do you think she saw anything?" to which the grandfather answered, "No she couldn't see." Sally eventually was able to tell her mother, "I *did* see. And I heard the noise" (p. 193).

+ adult genital erotic*

(+ view adult coitus*)

Behavioral Symptoms correlated with
children's tactile and visual erogenous contacts with the adult body

1. Shortly after Sally returned from her visit to her grandparents, she began to awaken screaming after an hour or two of sleep and could not be induced to sleep again. Also, during the day the slightest noise produced a startle reaction and set her screaming. However, by the time Sally came for treatment, she no longer awakened in anxiety but left her bed like a sleep-walker. She would wander dazedly for hours and then, exhausted, she would seek out other beds in the house in which to sleep. She ended up changing beds four or five times within the course of a single night. As she would leave each bed she would whisper: "noises in de bed" (p. 173). It became evident that Sally was experiencing terrifying hallucinatory sounds. That these phobic hallucinatory reactions were not due simply to some organic, psychotic predisposition was confirmed by their disappearance once Sally was able to talk directly of her frightening primitive experiences.

+ night terrors* (sleepwalking, twilight hallucination)

Sally displayed many other phobias. These pertained to the noises from the vacuum cleaner (p. 196); sight of the front door of the house (she insisted upon entering the house via the back door) (p. 181); and contact with electric wall sockets (p. 202). Thus, "Sally would scream in terror for long periods even if she heard a vacuum cleaner in other parts of the building" (p. 196). When the bulb in her closet failed to light up, Sally again went into a panic (p. 204).

+ irrational fears* (phobias)

2. With the onset of her phobic hallucinations, Sally developed a compulsion to suck her thumb violently while she rubbed and massaged the area just above the genital region (p. 173-74). Sally's sexual reactions were also vented upon her mother. One night, as has been noted, "the mother found Sally crawling on top of her in bed, clutching and embracing her sensually" (p. 178). On another occasion, Sally entreated her mother to lie on the floor with her. When the mother refused, Sally tugged at her with such unexpected strength that the mother fell sprawling down onto the floor. Instantly, Sally jumped on top of her and sat astride her (p. 190). Still another time, Sally deliberately urinated on the mother's lap (p. 184).

+ sexual symptoms*

Sally's penis envy, her thoughts of possessing a penis, her rage that males had a penis, were activated to the highest pitch. She was determined to have a penis for herself one way or another: she talked of her doll swallowing a penis so that she could become an ice cream man (p. 198). She contradicted her therapist's statement that girls do not have a penis and insisted that she and her mother *did* have a piece of penis down there as she referred to her mother's clitoris.

Sally also accused her mother: " 'You have a penis! You hid it inside; you thought you would hide it so I wouldn't know. But I *do* know! I think that's clever of me to find out!' With this ringing accusation, Sally marched out of the room. Her mother made explanations in vain" (p. 190). Unfortunately, Sally's excessive penis envy was accompanied by a rage against her little brother. Not only did she try to bite his penis (p. 201) but also attacked him with such violence that "the baby was in tears and terrified all day" (p. 198).

+irrational
tempers*

3. Sally not only awoke at night with fear, but was reported to have exploded during the day with shrill tantrums (p. 177). As therapy proceeded, Sally's temper continued to be easily triggered. When the mother would not allow Sally to straddle her upon the floor, or when Sally was particularly disturbed that girls and women do not have penises, she would break out in tirades of angry screaming (p. 190).

+biting/cutting/
stomach*

4. "Sally actually attempted to bite her little brother's penis." When her mother sternly prohibited her from indulging in such activities, Sally suddenly refused to eat for almost two weeks. With encouragement from her mother she would nibble apathetically at anything, but then indulged in episodes of forced vomiting (p. 201). Symptoms pertaining to biting flesh were expressed not only in relation to her brother's penis but also her own lips: Sally developed a compulsive type of lip-biting during which she would tear the skin (p. 199).

Sally's severe symptoms also focused upon *cutting*. For example, she suffered a "severe set back" when she became aware that her mother had accidently inflicted a superficial *cut* upon her own finger, even though the scratch only needed a bandaid (p. 195). Even after a year of therapy when the hallucinated noises and her phobias had essentially disappeared, there continued a long period of Sally's preoccupation with scratches and minor cuts (p. 207, 206). And at the age of five or six, Sally still resorted to displays of aggressively *cutting* up quantities of paper (p. 208).

+eyes*

5. Sally developed a temporary eye tic after therapy had terminated. The tic disappeared a while later without any specific treatment (p. 208).

Sources of Stimulation:
adult punitive and excretory contacts with children

+anal
stimulation*

1. Enemas were periodically administered to Sally from earliest infancy for the treatment of a bowel infection.

+ hitting

2. Sally was angrily *spanked* by her grandparents for wetting herself at the time she had witnessed (and interrupted) the grandparents' copulatory activities (p. 179). Another source of painful and therefore punitive stimulation was the needle injections which Sally received for a staph infection three months after the outbreak of her neurosis. Unfortunately, this series of needle injections ended with a needle breaking under Sally's skin at the point of injection with the result that the broken piece of needle remained lodged in her flesh (p. 212). These events served to intensify Sally's illness (p. 212).

Behavioral Symptoms correlated with
adult punitive and excretory contacts with children

+ excretory
symptoms*

1. Prior to therapy, Sally often would withhold her feces (p. 180). Later, during therapy, withholding of feces alternated with displays of soiling. For example, on two occasions when she was three, Sally defiantly defecated in the bathtub (p. 202, 203). Then, when she was punished for behaving this way, she retained her stools even under the duress of much pain. She would cry out asking to go to the toilet but then refuse to have a bowel movement (p. 204). When Sally was assured she would not be punished for soiling, there followed several days during which she anxiously soiled in her pants (p. 205). "On some occasions the mother was certain Sally deliberately wet her bed after waking up, and a few times deliberately urinated on the floor" (p. 206). As already noted, on one occasion, Sally purposefully urinated on her mother's lap.

+ pain*

+ enuresis*

+ compulsions*

2. Sally "had acquired certain rituals. She would go about the house to see that all the faucets were turned off. Frequently, she would pick up a certain wastebasket and absentmindedly present it to her mother."

+ hurting

3. Sally was preoccupied with thoughts that the grandfather had been hurting the grandmother during sexual intercourse (p. 180).

+ negative
perceptions

4. One of Sally's presenting symptoms involved her negative reaction to entering the front door of the house. Sally, upon returning home after a walk, refused to enter the front door and insisted, "This is *not* our house" (p. 173). Similar negative reactions continued to plague her during the early months of treatment. She would repeat, "Mamma dis is *not* our house," and "Mamma, I'm *not* me!" (p. 184).[1]

+ freezing of
affect

5. Sally's emotional states fluctuated between (a) wild panic already described and (b) emotional inhibition, *freezing, restriction* and *withdrawal* (p. 176, 177, 207): during the early months of treatment, Sally presented the picture of an ill child. "Her face was solemn and unexpressive, totally unchildlike. The detachment, the vagueness of her manner, the fixed stare indicated that the child had only the frailest contact with reality" (p. 176). Even though Mrs. Fraiberg's therapy eventually helped to restore appropriate affect, the withdrawn frozen state once again became reinstated in full force when the topic of Sally's needle injections was first discussed in therapy. Following the discussion of her needle

injections, Sally's eyes became dull and staring; she spoke little, "and when she did speak her voice was noticeably flat and without affect" (p. 181). Sally's affect also was completely disturbed following a spanking: at first Sally reacted to the punishment by crying for hours. Later her mother tried to reassure her to no avail; Sally was overcome by a depression which lasted for several days (p. 203).

Of note, Mrs. Fraiberg discovered that when her therapeutic approach was predominantly *passive*, Sally's emotional withdrawal and consequent ego disintegration became more severe. Conversely, she found that *actively helping* Sally deal with her disturbed reactions to recent traumatic stimulus experiences (both sexual and punitive) was effective in steering Sally's course into a more healthful direction (p. 183). Sally responded well to therapy. Despite her having to struggle with critical events following therapy, Sally displayed no return of her disturbing symptoms, even after she was hospitalized for four months with poliomyelitis and was required to adjust to the birth of another baby brother (p. 208).

NOTES

1 The responsiveness of this symptom to therapy directs attention to its emotional origin.

Sally
23

Stimulation-Symptom-and-Dream-Profile

	Separation Phobias	
	+ Night Terrors, Twilight States	
+ Sleep in Bed with Adult	+ Irrational Fears: Other	
	+ Irrational Tempers	
+ Adult Genital Erotic	+ Sexual Symptoms	
	+ Biting/Cutting, etc.	} *content of*
+ View Adult Coitus	+ Eyes	*dreams and*
	Fire	*symptoms*

	Learning Problems (levels 2 or 3, etc.)	
Punitive Yelling	Lying and Delinquency	
	Reversal of Affect	
Beatings	Closing Down Upon, Kill	} *content of*
	Falling	*dreams and*
		symptoms

	+ Excretory Symptoms and Dreams	
	Anal Masturbation	
Preoccupation with Child's BM	+ Enuresis	
	Illness, etc.	} *content of*
+ Anal Contacts	+ Pain	*dreams and*
	Death	*symptoms*
	+ Compulsions	

Case 24: Synopsis of Anny Katan's "M"

Dr. Anny Katan presented the case of an unnamed forty-one-year-old woman, who for convenience will be called Margaret. Margaret's focal symptom was a severe agoraphobia from which she had suffered since the age of fourteen (*International Journal of Psycho-Analysis,* Vol. 32, 1951, p. 45).

Sources of Stimulation:
children's tactile and visual erogenous contacts with the adult body

+ adult genital erotic*
(+ view adult coitus*)

− / + sleeping in bed with adults*

1. *Up until her tenth year,* Margaret slept in her parents' room where she was exposed to "reoccurring nocturnal primal scenes" (p. 46). After the age of ten, she slept in an adjoining room separated from her parents only by a thin wall. "She remembered having consciously eavesdropped on her parents intercourse," observations which had been accompanied by "terrifying anxiety attacks and profuse perspiration" (p. 45). By screaming, Margaret regularly succeeded in getting her father to leave his activities in the conjugal bed and come to her bed in order to calm her with his caresses (p. 45).

Behavioral Symptoms correlated with
children's tactile and visual erogenous contacts with the adult body

+ night terrors*

1. Margaret, as "a child of three or four . . . had suffered from grave nocturnal anxiety attacks, nightmares and screaming spells" (p. 45).

+ irrational fears*

Her agoraphobia began when she was fourteen under the following circumstances: "During a lesson given by a man teacher, she suddenly developed anxiety, left the classroom hurriedly, and for the first time had the idea, 'How shall I get home?' For the first time the idea of 'walking the streets' aroused anxiety" (p. 45).

A serious aggravation of her agoraphobia occurred at the age of sixteen when she panicked and left a theatrical performance of "Oedipus Rex." "Tottering from anxiety" she ran out on the street to "accost" somebody with the request to bring her home. She met a couple and accosted the man. The people responded by insulting her since they believed she was a drunken prostitute (p. 46).

Margaret also developed a fear of bridges: she could not allow herself to walk across a bridge, but was "compelled to run, as if she were chased or persecuted." As she would cross a bridge, she staggered, knocked herself against the rails, stumbled and "threatened to fall any moment" (p. 46). She experienced the sensation that "she was *running on a soft padding*." Her associations during analysis led Margaret to recall the following childhood scene: "at a very early age she awakened one night in her crib which was standing in her parents' bedroom. She watched their intercourse and began to scream. Her father, infuriated, rushed to her crib to spank the little girl." Thereupon she took a few steps upon the *soft padding, staggered, knocked against the bars* of the crib, "until she was seized by her father and spanked" (p. 46).

+ sexual
symptoms*

2. "At the age of eight, a classmate seduced her to masturbate." For a brief period, she practiced masturbation alone, then became involved in mutual masturbation with a younger girl. During their sexual activities, the two girls imitated intercourse, wherein Margaret always played the feminine role (p. 45).

At the age of fourteen, Margaret no longer masturbated with this girl, but rather masturbated alone. Despite her vehement wish to control the compulsive masturbation her struggle against it proved futile (p. 45).[1]

Sources of Stimulation:
adult punitive and excretory contacts with children

+ hitting

1. The father angrily hit Margaret when her screaming disturbed his coital activities.

Behavioral Symptoms correlated with
adult punitive and excretory contacts with children

+ falling*

1. When Margaret as an adult woman attempted to cross a bridge, it will be recalled, she staggered, knocked herself on the rails, became weak-kneed and threatened to *fall* any minute. This symptom brought back early memories not only of witnessing the parents in the act of sexual congress, but also of her attempt to escape from her father as he proceeded to hit her for disturbing his sexual activities (p. 46). Clearly, Margaret's perception of crossing the bridge served to trigger the disturbed reactions and feelings of running on soft padding, staggering and knocking herself against bars, once associated with the erotic and punitive excitation she had experienced in her crib.

NOTES

[1] Note, her agoraphobia began at the age of fourteen, i.e., when Margaret forced herself to stop her homosexual activities. The phobic conflictual neurosis replaced her acting out.

Katan's "M"
24

Stimulation-Symptom-and-Dream-Profile

	Separation Phobias	
	+ Night Terrors, Twilight States	
Sleep in Bed with Adult	+ Irrational Fears: Other	
	Irrational Tempers	
+ Adult Genital Erotic	+ Sexual Symptoms	
	Biting/Cutting, etc.	*content of*
+ View Adult Coitus	Eyes	*dreams and*
	Fire	*symptoms*

	Learning Problems (levels 2 or 3, etc.)	
Punitive Yelling	Lying and Delinquency	
	Reversal of Affect	
Beatings	Closing Down Upon, Kill	*content of dreams and*
	+ Falling	*symptoms*

	Excretory Symptoms and Dreams	
	Anal Masturbation	
Preoccupation with Child's BM	Enuresis	
	Illness, etc.	*content of*
Anal Contacts	Pain	*dreams and*
	Death	*symptoms*
	Compulsions	

Case 25: Pierre

Pierre, a nine-year-old lad of average intelligence, was brought to the clinic because of a series of disturbing symptoms: night terrors, enuresis, fire setting, headaches, as well as exhibitionistic masturbatory behavior in school.

Sources of Stimulation:
children's tactile and visual erogenous contacts with the adult body

+ sleeping in bed with adult*

1. Pierre often slept between his father and mother.

+ adult nudity

2. He also regularly saw his parents without clothes. Sometimes his mother would tell him not to watch her undress, but he peeked from under the covers to see her disrobe.

Pierre reported that when his father was out, he liked to be in bed with his mother and tickle her "titties, her hair, the big hole and the little hole." It was uncertain whether this report was true or whether it resulted in part from the mental completion of his sexual reactions to his mother's exposing herself to him. However, this report was consistent with Pierre's mother's description of her own mother "who lived with many men openly and immorally."

+ adult genital erotic*
(+ view adult coitus*)

3. Pierre at the age of three saw his mother and father "wrestling" with each other without clothes. When he was eight, he again witnessed bouts of parental sexual intercourse.

Behavioral Symptoms correlated with
children's tactile and visual erogenous contacts with the adult body

+ separation phobias*

1. The mother reported that Pierre displayed school-phobic reactions to separation during his early school years.

+ night terrors*

2. Night terrors headed the list of Pierre's problems. To quote the intake report: "Night terrors were very severe, with the child crying out and shaking." These terrors were accompanied by increasingly severe episodes of sleep-walking. During these episodes he would begin to go toward the bathroom but often would change his course, put on his sweater and walk out of the house. On other occasions when he did enter the bathroom, Pierre would urinate on the towels.

+ sexual symptoms*

3. Pierre's school was about to expel him because of his exhibitionistic masturbation in class. He also sprayed water into the classroom cupboards.

102

+ eyes*

4. At the age of four, Pierre required stitches for an injury incurred following his falling on a hockey stick which penetrated just over his eye.[1]

+ biting/cutting*

5. Pierre was frequently found *spitting* on children in school. He also ruined school books by *biting* them.

+ fire*

6. Pierre set his sister's closet on fire. He confessed to his parents that he did this so that their house would burn down. Then he would be able to move back to their old home where he could play once again with his cousin, a boy whom the mother said he "idolized." After the fire, the father took Pierre to the chief of police who delivered him a serious lecture on his fire-setting.

Sources of Stimulation:
adult punitive and excretory contacts with children

+ early
  deprivation

1. Until the age of four and a half, Pierre experienced difficulty in feeding and vomited a great deal.

+ punitive
  yelling*

2. Both parents had a problem about yelling at Pierre. His mother yelled at him until he went to bed with headaches. Pierre's father admitted that he always expected too much from Pierre and would get angry and hit him if Pierre did not do his bidding. Five minutes after exploding, the father would feel badly that he had reacted so intensely, especially since he felt the upsets were precipitated by insignificant incidents.

Behavioral Symptoms correlated with
adult punitive and excretory contacts with children

+ enuresis*

1. Since the age of two and a half, Pierre wet his bed. Even at the age of nine when he shared a bed with his brother, Pierre and the brother would wet upon each other.

+ learning
  (level 1)

+ reversal of
  affect*
+ lying*
+ hurting
+ falling*

2. Pierre at first adjusted well in school and earned good grades. Then his grades consistently began to go down while his behavior became increasingly disruptive. His teachers complained of his incessant talking and whispering, his need to clown in class, and his "lying about everything."

3. Pierre showed some evidence of a sadistic pleasure in hurting others. He told how he hit and *tripped* the children in school. Also Pierre liked to make his sister cry: "It's *fun*," he explained. "She is unhappy anyway and that's why I hit her."

+ pain*

+ non-organic
  illness*

4. Pierre suffered from recurrent headaches, severe enough to be referred to as a presenting problem. He and his parents each reported that his headaches regularly appeared in relation to his being yelled at and scolded. In Pierre's words, "I get headaches when I get mad and I get mad when my mother yells at me, when my father yells at me and when my sister yells at me." The headaches often kept Pierre awake "half of the night." Medical examination revealed

them to be of psychogenic origin.

NOTES

[1] See cases 99 and 100 of Philip and Ronny, section on "eyes," for other examples of sexually overstimulated children who poked pointed objects into the eyes.

Pierre
25

Stimulation-Symptom-and-Dream-Profile

	+ Separation Phobia	
	+ Night Terrors, Twilight States	
+ Sleep in Bed with Adult	Irrational Fears: Other	
	Irrational Tempers	
+ Adult Genital Erotic	+ Sexual Symptoms	
	+ Biting/Cutting, etc.	} *content of*
+ View Adult Coitus	+ Eyes	} *dreams and*
	+ Fire	} *symptoms*
	Learning Problems (levels 2 or 3, etc.)	
+ Punitive Yelling	+ Lying and Delinquency	
	+ Reversal of Affect	
Beatings	Closing Down Upon, Kill	} *content of*
	+ Falling	} *dreams and*
		} *symptoms*
	Excretory Symptoms and Dreams	
	Anal Masturbation	
Preoccupation with Child's BM	+ Enuresis	
	+ Illness, etc.	} *content of*
Anal Contacts	+ Pain	} *dreams and*
	Death	} *symptoms*
	Compulsions	

Case 26: Randy

Randy was referred to the clinic for diagnostic evaluation at the age of twelve with the following presenting symptoms: a) he put on his mother's underclothing in bed "because it felt good"; b) he attempted to cut himself with razor blades and threatened suicide by the ingestion of aspirin.

Sources of Stimulation:
children's tactile and visual erogenous contacts with the adult body

+ sleeping in bed
  with adults*

1. Randy would sleep in bed between his mother and father until he was six years old.

+ adult nudity

2. At the age of twelve, Randy continued to see his mother nude approximately once a month. Randy noted that his mother felt it was not bad for him to see her without clothes. She also encouraged him to read soft-core pornographic magazines and to hang the magazine pictures on the wall.

+ adult genital
  erotic*
  (+ view adult
  coitus*)

3. Both Randy and his mother referred to his having observed his parents during coitus. In particular Randy was aware of being very upset at seeing his father's erect genital.

Behavioral Symptoms correlated with
children's tactile and visual erogenous contacts with the adult body

+ separation
  phobias*

1. At the time of Randy's diagnostic, his mother decided to take a brief trip to California. When she started to leave, Randy began to "carry on." When she did return home after three days, Randy again lost his temper at her for leaving him.

+ nightmares
+ night terrors*
+ irrational fears*

2. Randy frequently suffered from "very serious nightmares" during which he would scream out in his sleep. He also suffered from daytime fears, e.g., he was continually fearful that he might have injured a joint or broken a bone.

+ irrational
  tempers*

3. Both parents referred to Randy's "temperamental" tantrums and the ease with which he would "blow up," especially when he was criticized.

+ sexual
  symptoms*

4. Randy was obsessed with taking his mother's underclothing and her diaphragm and contraceptive jellies. He would bring them into his room at night and then wear her underclothing to bed. When Randy's mother confronted him with these activities he said he didn't know why he was taking the mother's personal things but enjoyed the feeling of her panties on him.

Randy responded well to the diagnostic team's explanations and recommendations regarding the disturbing effects of excessive sexual stimulation upon children and the need for appropriate controls. Following the diagnostic, the family did manage to establish controls with respect to exposing their twelve-year-old son to adult nudity and to sexual intercourse. Randy was helped to understand how his seeing "soft-core porno" magazines only reactivated his past overwhelming memories of viewing intercourse and that it would therefore be best to stay away from it. He was also helped to understand his looking-touching sexual forepleasure reactions: since he could not complete them upon the female body of his mother, he tried to discharge them instead upon his own body dressed as a female substitute for the mother. In this way he set himself up as a female even though from the point of view of his body development he was solidly masculine, and even though he was really expressing heterosexual feelings aroused by his own mother.

Although Randy gave up his transvestite masturbatory activities, still other disturbing sexual symptoms were to appear on the horizon. At the age of sixteen, four years after his last contact with the diagnostic unit, Randy suddenly, "out of the blue," phoned his "therapist" in a panic one night at 2:00 A.M. He begged for help: he had just had intercourse with his girl friend without using contraceptives and was sure the girl friend would become pregnant . . . what should he do? This was the last thing in the world he needed. Fortunately, this sexual episode did not eventuate in disaster: the therapist was able to refer Randy to a medical clinic where his girl friend could be checked for pregnancy and could receive help with her problem. However, Randy's acting out sexually and his phone call in the middle of the night suggested that he was again acting out his panic and forbidden impulses associated with having observed his parent's coital activities: this time he set it up so that he and his girl friend were the active participants performing sexual intercourse, while his doctor was the third party awakened in the middle of the night to "observe" the scene.

+ biting/cutting/
stomach*

5. Randy "accidentally" went through a glass door while he was playing with friends and *cut* both his wrist and stomach. Also, as already noted, Randy was brought to the clinic because of his threats to *cut* himself with a razor.

Sources of Stimulation:
adult punitive and excretory contacts with children

+ punitive
yelling*

1. Randy told how his mother and father were continually fighting. He added that he knew part of the fighting had to do with their not having sex recently. The parents also yelled accusingly at one another for going out at night with other partners. The father stated the problem was the mother's fault; the mother claimed it was the father's fault; and Randy answered them, "It's both of your faults." Often these fights would eventuate in the father's beating his

− / + beatings*
(observed)

wife in front of the children. Sometimes the battles became so violent that Randy and his siblings would have to call the police.

Behavioral Symptoms correlated with
adult punitive and excretory contacts with children

+ negative
 behavior

    1. Randy was described by his mother as a "very stubborn" child who would not do what she requested. The mother also noted that Randy was inflexible with his peers. Fortunately, at the time of his diagnostic, Randy's opposition to authority had not disrupted his capacity to learn at school.

+ preoccupation
 with illness*
+ pains*
+ falling*

    2. The mother's "deep concern" also was aroused by Randy's preoccupation with physical complaints in a "kind of hypochondriacal way." At the age of three he began complaining about many and various aches and pains such as stomachaches and headaches. Furthermore, when he would *fall,* he was always fearful that he might have sprained a joint or broken a bone.

+ hurting

    3. Randy's nightmares focused upon hitting, hurting and death. Randy recalled one nightmare as follows: "My friend was in the car and his father was there. They were speeding around the block. There was this little brook there and they *crashed* into it and everybody came. My brother came and I was telling what happened to the police. Then he kept telling me to shut up and kept hitting me." In another nightmare which was fixed in Randy's mind, his "friend's *mother died.*"[1] Randy directly acted out this preoccupation with dying: he eventually ingested an overdose of aspirin himself and threatened to cut his wrists with a razor.

+ closing down
 upon
 destructively*

+ death*

+ killing*
 (self)

NOTES

[1] Recall that Randy called the police when he feared *his mother* might die from his father's beatings.

Randy
26

Stimulation-Symptom-and-Dream-Profile

	+ Separation Phobias	
	+ Night Terrors, Twilight States	
+ Sleep in Bed with Adult	+ Irrational Fears: Other	
	+ Irrational Tempers	
+ Adult Genital Erotic	+ Sexual Symptoms	
	+ Biting/Cutting, etc.	} *content of*
+ View Adult Coitus	Eyes	*dreams and*
	Fire	*symptoms*

	Learning Problems (levels 2 or 3, etc.)	
+ Punitive Yelling	Lying and Delinquency	
	Reversal of Affect	
Beatings	+ Closing Down Upon, Kill	} *content of dreams and*
	+ Falling	*symptoms*

	Excretory Symptoms and Dreams	
	Anal Masturbation	
Preoccupation with Child's BM	Enuresis	
	+ Illness, etc.	} *content of*
Anal Contacts	+ Pain	*dreams and*
	+ Death	*symptoms*
	Compulsions	

Case 27: Stanley

Stan's intake summary read as follows: "eight-year-old boy, not reading, forgets alphabet, stuttering for the past two years, active non-conforming child who does not seem able to accept structure or authority."

Sources of Stimulation:
children's tactile and visual erogenous contacts with the adult body

1. Stan and his younger brother each were assigned to their own bunk beds. However, Stan usually slept with the brother in the lower bunk bed "because it was too hot" up on top. Occasionally, he had bad dreams which led him to climb in bed between his mother and father. At times, his father had to leave the bed in order to accommodate him.

2. Stan saw everyone in his family without clothes: his mother, father, brother and little sister. Showers with his father were a regular custom. Magazines displaying nude adults were readily available to all the children. With uncertainty, the mother attempted to limit Stan's exposure to adult nudity. However, she felt hamstrung in the face of her husband's conviction that one should not grow up with negative feelings about the human body.

3. When he was approximately five years old, Stan witnessed his parents copulating.

Behavioral Symptoms:
children's tactile and visual erogenous contacts with the adult body

1. Stan suffered from night terrors. He was also plagued by one recurring nightmare in which he was "cut in half and stuck into a barrel of tar."

2. When Stan was five, the parents began their search for psychiatric help for him. At that time their principal concern involved the ease with which he would fly into a screaming rage.

3. Stan compulsively acted out sexually, e.g., he regularly practiced fellatio (with one of his girl friends) and sexually stimulated her rectum.

4. With discomfort, Stan's mother reported how she had found a *razor blade* Stan had carefully hidden in the folds of her dress. On another occasion she found a *broken light bulb* he had placed in her shoes. Stan's recurrent nightmares of his "being cut in half and stuck in a barrel of tar" coincided with this

---

Margin notes (left column):

- -/+ sleeping in ed with adults* occasional)

- adult nudity

- + adult genital erotic*
  + view adult coitus*)

- + night terrors*

- + irrational tempers*

- + sexual symptoms*

- + biting/cutting*

symptomatic behavior.

Of note, three of Stan's screen memories also pertained to sharp objects with a capacity to cut. Stan's earliest memories involved (a) *broken glass* taken into the mouth, (b) *splinters* lodged in the throat and (c) a jab with a *knife*.

+ eyes* (reading problem)

5. Stan, at eight and a half still could not read; this despite his normal intelligence and absence of any neurological pathology.[1]

+ fire*

6. Stan dreamed of fire: "There was a man and he had a *torch* and the black cloud looked at him and he hid in a cave."

At the age of five, Stan set a brush fire and although he presumably set no other fires thereafter, he did continue to be preoccupied with lighting matches.

Sources of Stimulation:
adult punitive and excretory contacts with children

+ early deprivation

1. Following Stan's birth, his mother was depressed and exhausted. At night she began to be haunted by a fear of killing him. When Stan was one year old, she sought psychiatric help because she was still *tormented by her impulses to kill her child*.

The father who was also depressed at that time became reticent, egocentric and preoccupied with work. He had been "abominable" to his wife because he had been "an only child" and presumably resented loss of attention when Stan was born. The mother wondered whether her preoccupation with killing had been activated by her feelings toward her husband and then displaced onto the baby. In any case, the mother's bouts of depression, rage and fear functioned antithetically to empathic and contented emotional care for little Stan.

+ punitive yelling*

2. Battles between the parents often resulted in an uproar in the house. Stan reported that he was scared when both parents screamed at him that he was a "lousy brat" or "little bastard." The father admitted that he had become more and more aware of his yelling at Stan and was trying to modify it.

Behavioral Symptoms correlated with
adult punitive and excretory contacts with children

+ negative behavior

+ learning* (level 2)

1. Stan's presenting symptoms included an opposition to authority and a restriction in his capacity to learn. The mother was aware that Stan was negative about learning from the time he was four. She felt that this problem was connected with his not liking to be told what to do. In school it had been necessary to place him in a special class for slow learners.

+ enuresis*

+ excretory symptoms*

2. Until his eighth year, Stan would purposefully urinate on the bathroom floor. Constipation and soiling also were problems. Stan told how his mother

would "get mad" at him when he made a mess in his pants. The mother euphemistically described his soiling as "staining." She stated it had persisted since he was three years old.

Stan's sexual activities were apparently influenced by his excretory problems, i.e., as has already been mentioned, Stan indulged in stimulating his girl friend's rectum.

3. Stan's nightmares often involved death and killing, e.g., in one nightmare he stated: "We had a porch outside, and I ran out with my brother and some friends. There was a moth out there like a bat. There was a monster under it. The monster grabbed me or something." More significantly, in another dream, "There was a black cloud. It went around the neighborhood. It was a book. It

+ killing* killed people . . . and threw up and died. . . ." Stan's dreams, it would seem,
+ death* were not that different from his mother's concerns about killing him during his first year of life.

NOTES

1 Stan's reading problem responded excellently to therapeutic controls in relation to bed-sharing, adult nudity, showering with adults and exposure to adult sexual intercourse. With controls and with help directed toward understanding his symptoms, Stan soon displayed a spurt in his interest in learning. When interviewed several years later, he had caught up with his class in his reading ability.

Stanley
27

Stimulation-Symptom-and-Dream-Profile

	Separation Phobias
	+ Night Terrors, Twilight States
Sleep in Bed with Adult	Irrational Fears: Other
	+ Irrational Tempers
+ Adult Genital Erotic	+ Sexual Symptoms
	+ Biting/Cutting, etc.
+ View Adult Coitus	+ Eyes
	+ Fire

content of
dreams and
symptoms

+ Punitive Yelling	+ Learning Problems (levels 2 or 3, etc.)
	Lying and Delinquency
	Reversal of Affect
Beatings	+ Closing Down Upon, Kill
	Falling

content of
dreams and
symptoms

	+ Excretory Symptoms and Dreams
	Anal Masturbation
Preoccupation with Child's BM	+ Enuresis
	Illness, etc.
Anal Contacts	Pain
	+ Death
	Compulsions

content of
dreams and
symptoms

Case 28: Synopsis of Margaret Gerard's "Robert"

Robert, aged ten, I.Q. 136, was referred for analysis because of "generalized anxious behavior. He was a tall, sturdily-built boy, shyly friendly, with meticulous manners, and a quiet mien. He exhibited a marked mouth tic in which he pursed his lips tightly together and grunted. According to the mother, his fears reached panic proportions whenever he was expected to be on his own" (*Psychoanalytic Study of the Child*, Vol. II, 1946, p. 146).

Sources of Stimulation:
children's tactile and visual erogenous contacts with the adult body

+ adult nudity

1. Robert reported he had seen large penises "lots of times," his father's and that of his adolescent brother, Richard (p. 148).

+ adult genital
erotic*

2. Robert was five and a half when he first developed a tic shortly after the following traumatic experience. Robert "had been watching his brother Richard play with his electric trains in the basement playroom when an older teen-age boy joined them. . . ." It was later learned that the teen-ager had attempted to force fellatio upon Robert. In therapy Robert began to talk about this event by asking his therapist why penises sometimes become enormous and stiff and then began to tell how the teen-age boy had put his penis up to Robert's mouth but had not been able to penetrate his pursed lips. Robert had kept his lips clamped tightly shut (p. 148).

Behavioral Symptoms correlated with
children's tactile and visual erogenous contacts with the adult body

+ separation
phobia*

1. At the time of his referral, Robert was unable to remain at home without his parents. "The final straw" which led the parents to treatment occurred one afternoon when they left Robert alone in the house for one hour. When they returned he cried hysterically, trembled and was quieted only after he had been given a sedative at the doctor's office (p. 146).

+ night terrors*

2. Following the attempted fellatio incident when he was five and a half years old, Robert experienced night terrors during which he talked incoherently in his sleep. Thereafter, the terrors reappeared, according to the mother, whenever Robert was overly tired or had an exciting or anxious day (p. 148). Within his nightmares, Robert was repetitively "attacked by enormous men trying to push a *penis,* or a club, sometimes a sword *down his throat.* He was always alone in the dream and would try to scream for help" but found himself unable

+ sexual
concerns*

to utter a sound (p. 149).

+ biting/cutting*
+ eyes*

3. Robert dreamed of sinking "his *teeth* into a figure's hand and then *saw* that it was his brother. He was trembling when he awakened but he remembered saying to himself: 'I'd kill him, I'd *chew* him all up' " (p. 149).

Also, when Robert was first able to talk about his fears engendered by the sight of the teen-ager's penis, he asked Dr. Gerard, "Why does it get so stiff?" and, "Why doesn't it get *bitten*?" (p. 149). Robert's mouth tic appeared directly associated with this wish to *bite* a penis as well as his fear of this behavior, i.e., the tic was ushered in directly after the attempted *fellatio experience* and *terminated* following his direct verbal expression of thoughts about *biting and chewing* flesh (p. 148, 149).

Sources of Stimulation:
adult punitive and excretory contacts with children

1. During his first seven years of life, Robert was cared for by a rigid, perfectionist nurse who pleased the mother with her insistence upon strict discipline. "The mother was proud of the fact that the nurse had prevented the development of any aggressive problems and that Robert preferred to play quietly. . . . The mother knew of no incidents of masturbation but was sure the nurse would have punished him if she had noted any masturbatory activity" (p. 147).

+ punitive
scoldings

During latency, Robert's sexual experience involved punitive overtones. The teenager who had attempted fellatio with him threatened to kill him if he cried or told (p. 148). Then when Robert finally did blurt out to the mother the details of the adolescent boy's sexual advances, the mother scolded Robert (p. 148).

− / + beatings*

Also, Robert recalled that one day, sometime after his experience with the teen-ager, he purposefully broke into the bathroom to stare at his father's penis. Even though Robert pretended this intrusion was an accident, the father dealt with it by giving Robert "a licking" (p. 149).

Behavioral Symptoms correlated with
adult punitive and excretory contacts with children

+ killing*

1. Robert remembered saying to himself, " 'I'd kill him,' " as he woke from his nightmare of sinking his teeth into the hand of a figure who was about to grab him (p. 149).

+ reversal of
affect*

+ negative
emotion
+ learning
(level 1)

2. Robert *giggled* as he told of the incident during which his father licked him for breaking into the bathroom. However, Robert complained, "I can't do anything right, Richard is an expert. I'm a fumbler" (p. 149).

3. Robert's restrictiveness led to a learning problem in school. Despite his superior I.Q. of 136, Robert was barely able to keep up with his class. "He was

conforming in school," his teacher explained, "but at the bottom of the class instead of the top where his I.Q. of 136 would place him" (p. 148). The emotional determination of this learning problem on the basis of Robert's restrictiveness was reflected by his improvement during therapy. As restrictiveness became replaced by the expression of open negative defiance to his mother, Robert demonstrated a marked improvement in his learning performance (p. 149-50), this despite his mother's complaints about his defiance at home, and his unwillingness to perform the many favors he previously had automatically done for her (p. 149).

Gerard's "Robert"

28

Stimulation-Symptom-and-Dream-Profile

	+ Separation Phobias	
	+ Night Terrors, Twilight States	
Sleep in Bed with Adult	Irrational Fears: Other	
	Irrational Tempers	
+ Adult Genital Erotic	+ Sexual Symptoms	
	+ Biting/Cutting, etc.	} *content of*
View Adult Coitus	+ Eyes	} *dreams and*
	Fire	} *symptoms*
	Learning Problems (levels 2 or 3, etc.)	
Punitive Yelling	Lying and Delinquency	
	+ Reversal of Affect	
Beatings	+ Closing Down Upon, Kill	} *content of dreams and*
	Falling	} *symptoms*
	Excretory Symptoms and Dreams	
	Anal Masturbation	
Preoccupation with Child's BM	Enuresis	
	Illness, etc.	} *content of*
Anal Contacts	Pain	} *dreams and*
	Death	} *symptoms*
	Compulsions	

Case 29: Synopsis of Berta Bornstein's "Sonja"

Berta Bornstein's "Hysterical Twilight States in an Eight-Year-Old Child," focuses upon the uncontrollable and repetitive fugues experienced by Berta Bornstein's patient Sonja (*Psychoanalytic Study of the Child*, Vol. II, 1946, pp. 229-40).

Sonja had been diagnosed as an incurable psychotic prior to her analysis with Berta Bornstein. She had suffered from "spells" during which she reacted in a state of somnambulism with the following repetitive behavior: she would go out to the street, "beckon men who were driving by in cars, and in a very coquettish manner would ask for a ride. If her mother prevented her from leaving the house she would become hostile, threaten her with a knife and eventually turn it against herself. She responded when she was called by name and recognized everybody but her father. . . . Afterwards she showed complete amnesia for these events" (p. 229).

On the other hand, during her normal state, Sonja "seemed well adjusted, though somewhat shy and subdued." She was intelligent and loved school (p. 229).

Sources of Stimulation:
children's tactile and visual erogenous contacts with the adult body

−/+ sleeping in bed with adults*

1. When her sister was born, four-year-old Sonja started to rest in bed with her adolescent uncle and cuddle with him (p. 236).

+ adult genital erotic*

2. Gradually the bed-sharing led to the uncle's initiation of sexual activity. These sexual episodes resulted in the uncle infecting little Sonja with a chronic case of vaginal gonorrhea (p. 237). For the next two years Sonja received vaginal douches for the gonorrhea. Her father would hold her and spread her labia while her mother would insert the douche nozzle. Sonja recalled her sexual excitement during these repetitive procedures. When Sonja was eight years old, her gonorrhea once more erupted and necessitated a reinstatement of the douche treatments (p. 232).

Behavioral Symptoms correlated with
children's tactile and visual erogenous contacts with the adult body

+ separation phobias*
+ irrational fears*

1. Sonja at approximately the age of eight was temporarily sent to boarding school where she was panic-stricken to be separated from her mother. In particular, she was afraid that in the mother's absence, no one would be able to

116

prevent her from killing herself (p. 230).

+ hysterical
twilight states*

2. During her fugues, Sonja coquettishly tried to "pick up" men who were driving by in cars and, when thwarted by her mother, she threatened to kill her mother or herself.

+ irrational
tempers*

3. Sonja's aggression broke through her twilight states. As soon as the mother would stop her from signaling a passerby in the street, Sonja became violent as she tried to free herself from the restraint (p. 229).[1]

+ sexual
symptoms*

4. In her twilight states Sonja repetitively responded like a street-walker, motioning to men to pick her up (p. 229).

5. Sonja's recall and disclosure of her uncle's sexual activities was associated with the following nightmare: "Sonja, her young uncle and her parents are in one room. She is lying on a table. Suddenly it is not she who is lying there but her little sister who has to undergo some kind of treatment. The sister opens her *mouth*, two *matches* are put into her *throat*. Her uncle plays with *fire*" (p. 232).

+ biting/cutting*
(and throat)
+ fire*

Sources of Stimulation:
adult punitive and excretory contacts with children

+ / − anal
stimulation*

1. Sonja would watch her mother hit her sister for soiling and would watch her sister submit to enemas (p. 231).

Whether or not Sonja herself had been subjected to punishment for soiling or had a history of submitting to enemas was not reported. However, her vaginal douches were most painful. Like enemas, Sonja's douches for her burning gonococcal infection served as a source for both erogenous and painful stimulation (p. 231).

Behavioral Symptoms correlated with
adult punitive and excretory contacts with children

+ excretory
dreams*

1. Sonja's memories of witnessing her sister's enemas were reported in association to the following dream which focused upon *brown* chocolate: "Lying on her sister's bed is a tennis racquet of chocolate." The brown color of the chocolate reminded her of feces (p. 231).

+ killing*

2. Sonja was preoccupied with killing. During her twilight states she threatened to kill her mother. At other times she experienced fears of killing herself (p. 229, 230).

NOTES

[1] This behavior on the one hand involved a diffuse temper tantrum: rage characterized by screaming and noisy threats. On the other hand it was accompanied by specific threats of killing her mother.

Sonja
29

Stimulation-Symptom-and-Dream-Profile

	+ Separation Phobias	
	+ Night Terrors, Twilight States	
Sleep in Bed with Adult	+ Irrational Fears: Other	
	+ Irrational Tempers	
+ Adult Genital Erotic	+ Sexual Symptoms	
	+ Biting/Cutting, etc.	} *content of*
View Adult Coitus	Eyes	} *dreams and*
	+ Fire	} *symptoms*
	Learning Problems (levels 2 or 3, etc.)	
Punitive Yelling	Lying and Delinquency	
	Reversal of Affect	
Beatings	+ Closing Down Upon, Kill	} *content of*
	Falling	} *dreams and symptoms*
	+ Excretory Symptoms and Dreams	
	Anal Masturbation	
Preoccupation with Child's BM	Enuresis	
	Illness, etc.	} *content of*
+ Anal Contacts	Pain	} *dreams and*
	Death	} *symptoms*
	Compulsions	

Case 30: Terry

It was only after Terry's sister had been seen in therapy at the clinic for two years that Mrs. T. and her husband were able to admit that their eight-year-old son Terry was struggling with severe problems requiring help. Terry's presenting symptoms at this time were stated to be "bizarre mannerisms; effeminate posturing, compulsive talking, inappropriate laughing spells in school where his performance was dropping; extremely poor peer relationships, and enuresis." The ominous cast of these presenting symptoms, suggestive of psychosis, indicated that Terry was suffering from a disorder which possibly might be too severe for once-a-week psychotherapy. However, to the contrary, Terry proved to be a positive, trusting, conscientious patient. Over a period of two years he responded dramatically to psychotherapy aimed at controlling his exposure to sources of sexual and punitive overstimulation, and helping him to understand his "crazy" thoughts and behavior activated by this stimulation.

Sources of Stimulation:
children's tactile and visual erogenous contacts with the adult body

+ sleeping in bed with adults*

1. Terry often frequented his mother's and father's bed when he was "frightened." His mother clung tenaciously to the conviction that there was nothing wrong about taking frightened children into bed with parents. She supported her position by maintaining that all of her relatives did it and "their children were well adjusted" (actually her sister's daughter was on drugs while her sister's adolescent son acted out homosexually with Terry, see below). Mrs. T.'s conviction regarding the normality of bed-sharing with her son was determined by her own inability to remain in bed alone. She had slept in bed with her own mother till the day she married. Now, when her husband worked at night, it was necessary to have either one of her two children in her bed. It was she who needed Terry in her bed when she was frightened: when Mrs. T. agreed to keep Terry out of her bed, she substituted his sister Mary, and when sleeping with Mary was prohibited, she substituted the family dog to fill the empty space.

+ adult nudity

2. At the time of his diagnostic interviews, Terry was accustomed to taking showers with his father. Earlier in his life he had taken showers with his mother. Additionally, Terry confessed that he liked to peek through a crack in his parents' bedroom door and watch his parents disrobe. He spoke of seeing his mother's "goochies" (her breasts) and her "belly button."

In the bathroom, Terry's father, his adolescent cousin Marty and Terry

119

would urinate criss-cross together into the toilet. At such times each would wiggle his penis in order to win "squirting" races.

+ adult genital
erotic*

3. Terry reported seeing his father having an erection while they showered together: "Daddy's pee-pee sometimes was like a bone, sometimes it was all wrinkled, and sometimes it stuck out like a board." Additionally, when he peeked through the crack in his parent's bedroom door, Terry frequently observed his parents grunting and wriggling under the covers during the act of intercourse.

(+ view adult
coitus*)

The sexual responses activated as the result of Terry's seeing his father's erect penis and his parents' coital movements later became discharged with his adolescent cousin. *The fifteen-year-old cousin and eight-year-old Terry became involved in mutual masturbation and fellatio.* Terry thus was exposed to highly activated visual and tactile sexual stimulation in relation to the adult genitalia.

Behavioral Symptoms correlated with
children's tactile and visual erogenous contacts with the adult body

+ eyes*

1. For many years Terry complained about "dizzy eyes." The mother alternated between a conviction that this symptom was organic and a conviction that it was emotional. It became most prominent during the period when Terry was compulsively "sneaking a peek" through the crack of his parents' bedroom door. Not until both Terry and his parents were helped to control Terry's observations of the parents' sexual activities did Terry finally gain relief from his dizzy-eye symptoms.

+ sexual
symptoms*

2. Sexual discharge (and charge) took place not only via fellatio and masturbation with Terry's adolescent cousin. Terry found he could discharge his activated reactions upon the family dog and upon himself. "By mistake" he would poke his finger up the dog's rear end and rub the dog's penis which caused the dog to "jump all over the place." In addition, Terry repeatedly poked himself in a similar fashion leading to the onset of anal masturbation.

+ irrational fears*

+ nightmares

+ night terrors*

3. Terry suffered from fears of monsters and wolfmen consuming people, fears of dogs biting, fears of poison, fears of germs, fears of losing his penis; nightmares of Wolfman, Frankenstein, Dracula; nightmares of heads being chopped off. These nightmares often were accompanied by episodes of sleepwalking and sleep-talking.

+ twilight states*

During one period, his dream states were activated to the point of invading his waking life. He would experience daytime periods of confusion during which his mind wandered. He then "forgot things," could not concentrate, and felt in an "unknown world." Sometimes during these periods he saw things like a monster or a Martian with long ears and teeth.[1]

+ irrational
tempers*

4. Terry admitted that when his "Mr. Monster" blew his top, a switch went off, his hair went flying and he really went wild. His mother recalled having

been concerned about Terry's violent temper since he was four years old. His tempers contributed to his poor peer relationships in the neighborhood and at home, a presenting problem at the time of his referral to the clinic. It was only after several years of therapy and the institution of controls regarding exciting body stimulation, that Terry's tempers, his "Mr. Monster," quieted down.

− / + separation phobias*

5. Terry at the age of nine was very "emotional" when his mother visited him at camp and could not stop crying as she left. Subsequently, it was with a great deal of effort that Terry could be induced to go to camp at all. This homesickness in itself, however, did not appear phobic.

+ biting/cutting/ stomach*

6. Terry's dreams, fears and hallucinations contained key references to *biting*. His hallucinatory dream material involved "a Martian with long ears and *teeth*." An illusion of a ghost or witch at night in his mother's room contained a big mouth ready to *gobble* him up. His associations to his own primitive part, "Mr. Monster," led him to explain: "Mr. Monster has *teeth*; . . . he's worried that if you *bite* someone he will kill you." His nightmares often focused upon Wolfman (who bites) and upon monsters. In one nightmare, "the monster was a guy who was coming around *chopping people's heads* off, whoever came close to him gets his head *chopped*." It is not surprising that during waking hours Terry expressed direct concerns that his penis "might get *cut* off."

Terry's concerns about cutting and biting often accompanied his references to his father's penis. For example, when Terry began talking of his showers with his father he freely associated to thoughts about his dog wriggling and *biting* him.

+ fire*

7. Irrational fears of fire troubled Terry. He brought home "bizarre" reports of fires occurring in Maryland near the home of his adolescent cousin Marty (with whom he had acted out homosexually). He also was preoccupied with the thought that their new house would be set on fire because the radiator was "too hot" and was placed "too high" on the wall. Terry's resistance to all rational assurances underscored the irrationality of these fears of fire.

Sources of Stimulation:
adult punitive and excretory contacts with children

+ punitive bowel training

1. Bowel training was achieved at the age of two when Terry's father repeatedly made the screaming child sit on the toilet for three hours at a stretch.

+ beatings*

2. The father, prior to therapy, used a *"tough," long belt to beat Terry.* This form of dispensing discipline to his son was in keeping with the father's own history of having been severely beaten as a child.[2] Fortunately, during three years of therapy the father learned to control these beatings and finally was very pleased to report that he was dealing with his children in an intelligent manner instead of "knocking their heads together."

Terry's mother did not belt him; she "simply" whacked Terry with her hand when she would break loose in a temper tantrum. In general, however, she saved her "affection" for Terry while she discharged her "hate" upon Terry's sister whom she had beaten from infancy.

+ punitive
yelling*

3. The mother frequently yelled and screamed at the whole family. Terry told his mother that he never would want to get married because all she did was yell at his father.

Behavioral Symptoms correlated with
adult punitive and excretory contacts with children

+ enuresis*

1. The "intake" summary of Terry's presenting symptoms noted that Terry was still wetting himself when he was eight years old.

(+ anal
masturbation*)

Terry poked his rear end for almost a half year at the beginning of therapy.[3] (Terry's anal poking, as noted above, was discharged not only upon himself but also upon his dog.)

+ excretory
symptoms*

At the time of his referral to the clinic, Terry was soiling several times a week. There also had occurred an episode of fecal play during his earlier childhood when Terry recalled taking his feces from the toilet and rubbing it into his hair. On other occasions he would like to smell the excrement and had gotten some of it in his mouth.[4]

+ non-organic
illness*

2. Terry developed frequent stomachaches at times of frustration, e.g., when he was not invited to a neighbor boy's birthday party. Terry's stomach complaints were so troublesome that the family thought that he might be suffering from appendicitis. A medical exam revealed that the problem was psychosomatic.[5]

+ reversal of
affect*

3. As the years passed by, Terry began to laugh with pleasure when his father subjected him to frequent beatings. In Terry's words: "I *don't* mind him beating me. I *don't* cry. I laugh." In other words, Terry's beatings led to the inhibition of unpleasurable affect and the reciprocal activation of *opposing*, pleasurable affects. This inhibition and reversal of affect were manifest in other instances of his history: Terry boasted that *nothing* frightened him . . . he *never* cried . . . he only laughed; needles and hospitals, oh, he laughed at them . . . he was *not* afraid . . . , etc. (This despite Terry's intense phobia of hospitals at the age of three after he had been exposed to extremely painful ear probing at the hospital.) This information pertaining to reversals of affect suggests that Terry's "inappropriate giggling and laughing spells" reflected the reverse emotions of grief and depression.

+ learning*
(referral
problem)

4. In the midst of all these problems there occurred a drop in Terry's performance of school work, a referral problem.

+ hurting

5. Prior to the onset of therapy, Terry had a knack for turning "kids" against him. Defending himself by "belting" some of the children made him

even more unpopular. This unpopularity was all the more striking in light of his basically cheerful and friendly disposition.

Terry also frequently hurt himself. The mother reported that at the age of two and a half he was extremely accident-prone, and on many occasions required stitches.

+ closing down
   upon
   destructively*
+ excretory
   dream* (black)
+ kill*
+ die*

6. Terry experienced many sado-masochistic dreams. He dreamed of *Frankenstein* and *Dracula,* and at the time that his *anal masturbation* was most active, he dreamed of being *"whipped* by four guys with *black* jackets" and of being beaten on the head with chains. Terry also dreamed of a guy who *"kills* people — wants to kill everybody in the world because he's from another planet. Whoever gets close to him gets his head chopped off. Only his people won't *die* because they are good to this man."

+ death*

In line with these sado-masochistic concerns appearing in his dreams, Terry suffered from similar waking fears. For example, he had fears of being poisoned (especially in relation to getting some excrement in his mouth); and he was afraid of dying in the event that his penis would break.

NOTES

1 These hallucinatory dream reactions were directly controlled by a temporary course of Mellaril and were then fully resolved once sexual stimulation (including autoerotic stimulation from anal masturbation) became controlled.

2 The tendency of parents to re-enact past traumas, as illustrated by most child-abuse cases, was reflected in this history.

3 It was during this period that he experienced daytime hallucinations. It is of interest that as the anal masturbation finally became controlled, hallucinatory activity ceased.

4 The reader might be satisfied to call out "psychotic" and thereupon forget environmental sources of Terry's symptoms. The label "psychotic" directs attention to constitutional factors rather than to controllable sources of environmental stimulation. But Terry's "psychosis" subsided with therapy and application of kindly and understanding control of sexual and punitive stimulation (including his anal self-stimulation) and in that sense was not some rare organic constitutional disease.

5 Adding a little more stimulation in the life of this frenzied child, his doctor followed the routine procedure for checking appendicitis by giving him a rectal exam.

Terry
30

Stimulation-Symptom-and-Dream-Profile

	Separation Phobias	
	+ Night Terrors, Twilight States	
+ Sleep in Bed with Adult	+ Irrational Fears: Other	
	+ Irrational Tempers	
+ Adult Genital Erotic	+ Sexual Symptoms	
	+ Biting/Cutting, etc.	} *content of*
+ View Adult Coitus	+ Eyes	} *dreams and*
	+ Fire	} *symptoms*
	+ Learning Problems (levels 2 or 3, etc.)	
+ Punitive Yelling	Lying and Delinquency	
	+ Reversal of Affect	
+ Beatings	+ Closing Down Upon, Kill	} *content of* / *dreams and*
	Falling	} *symptoms*
	+ Excretory Symptoms and Dreams	
	+ Anal Masturbation	
Preoccupation with Child's BM	+ Enuresis	
	+ Illness, etc.	} *content of*
Anal Contacts	Pain	} *dreams and*
	+ Death	} *symptoms*
	Compulsions	

Case 31: Synopsis of Coren and Saldinger's "Hank"

Hank, a five-year-old boy, was admitted to the Mt. Zion pediatric inpatient services because he was experiencing intense anxiety and continuing to "see snakes" (*Psychoanalytic Study of the Child*, Vol. XXII, 1967, p. 332). Clinical attention focused upon two disturbing events which had directly preceded Hank's hallucinations: (a) four months previously, he had been hospitalized three days for a cardiac catheterization to investigate a heart murmur which turned out to be functional (p. 333); and (b) the day hallucinations began, Hank had witnessed a mouse running up his mother's slacks. The mouse next ran under the carpet but was caught by Hank's aunt who killed it with her shoe and threw it away in the garbage (p. 334).

Sources of Stimulation:
children's tactile and visual erogenous contacts with the adult body

+ / – sleeping in bed with adults*

1. For the first five years of his life, "Hank had often slept with his mother because *she* was afraid to sleep alone. He would often go to sleep in his own bed . . . but when his mother was ready to retire "or when her boy friend had left the house, she would usually pick Hank up and take him into bed with her. Occasionally, he would come into her bed on his own initiative" (p. 332, 334). The evening hallucinations began, Hank clutched his mother while lying directly on top of her (p. 334).

+ adult nudity
+ adult genital erotic*
(+ view adult coitus*)

2. "Hank was frequently exposed to an intense amount of visual sexual stimulation in his home" (p. 340). He was repeatedly exposed to female sexual anatomy when he slept with his mother (p. 340-41). Additionally, through an open door, Hank would watch his mother and her boy friend copulating in bed (p. 340).

Added to this, Hank and his brother were absorbed with the "father's" pornographic photos (p. 336).

Behavioral Symptoms correlated with
children's tactile and visual erogenous contacts with the adult body

+ night terrors and hysterical twilight states*

1. On the night of the "mouse" incident, Hank's mother and "father" had sent him from their bed to his own, but he returned almost immediately. He appeared wide-eyed and very frightened in their room while "screaming that he had seen a big black snake in his brother's bed." Thereafter, Hank's snake panic continued for many days. Hank insisted on lying directly on top of his mother

because there was a "snake" on the sheet (p. 334). He "complained that the 'snakes' were after him" (p. 335). The "snakes" kept him from sleeping (p. 335). Later, in the pediatric ward, he screamed with fear that there was a devil in his pants (p. 335). He referred to snakes in his mother's bed, in his brother's bed and "small ones in the baby's crib" (p. 336).

+ irrational
tempers*

2. Hank's temper was demonstrated during his therapy hours. At such times, he would try to break things in the office. "He would also untape the stapler at times and bang it with his fist" (p. 337).

+ biting/cutting/
stomach*

3. Hank told his mother that they "should *chop* up the baby" (p. 337). During therapy, his concern about sharp scissors and even a toy rubber knife was great enough to motivate him to tape them up. He also played a game with this therapist during which he *cut off* his therapist's hand and then *ate it* (p. 340). It was not too surprising, therefore, that he would complain about feelings that there was "a man inside his *stomach*" (p. 336).

+ sexual
symptoms*

4. Prior to his admission to the hospital, Hank frequently peeked under the skirts of neighborhood girls (p. 341).

At the hospital he was observed masturbating frequently. One night he masturbated and screamed that there was "something on his legs" (p. 335).

− / + eyes*

5. Hank drew a man and woman with very large and prominent eyes. The woman's eyes, breasts and hair were the only body features represented (p. 338-39). However, no dreams or symptoms pertaining to eyes were reported.

Sources of Stimulation:
adult punitive and excretory contacts with children

None reported.

Behavioral Symptoms correlated with
adult punitive and excretory contacts with children

+ enuresis*

1. Hank began to wet his bed when he was four years old (p. 333).

+ killing*
+ dead*

2. On the night his panic first erupted, Hank was perturbed by a delusion that there was a little boy in the room ready to *kill* him (p. 334, 336). Hank also *hallucinated* on one occasion about a *dead* rat.

Coren and Saldinger's "Hank"
31

Stimulation-Symptom-and-Dream-Profile

	Separation Phobias	
	+ Night Terrors, Twilight States	
+ Sleep in Bed with Adult	Irrational Fears: Other	
	+ Irrational Tempers	
+ Adult Genital Erotic	+ Sexual Symptoms	
	+ Biting/Cutting, etc.	} *content of*
+ View Adult Coitus	Eyes	*dreams and*
	Fire	*symptoms*

	Learning Problems (levels 2 or 3, etc.)	
Punitive Yelling	Lying and Delinquency	
	Reversal of Affect	
Beatings	+ Closing Down Upon, Kill	} *content of* *dreams and*
	Falling	*symptoms*

	Excretory Symptoms and Dreams	
	Anal Masturbation	
Preoccupation with Child's BM	+ Enuresis	
	Illness, etc.	} *content of*
Anal Contacts	Pain	*dreams and*
	+ Death	*symptoms*
	Compulsions	

SECTION 2
CASES 32-64

Focus:

SYSTEMS ASSOCIATED WITH CHILDREN'S EXPOSURES TO PUNITIVE CONTACTS WITH ADULTS

Case 32: Synopsis of Kolansky and Moore's "Dick"

"At the beginning of analysis, Dick was thirteen years old and had recently celebrated his Bar Mitzvah. He was referred for analysis because of poor academic performance and lack of any initiative and responsibility.[1] Both parents expressed concern about the effect of the father's frequent beatings of Dick," beatings which began when Dick was six or seven years old (*Psychoanalytic Study of the Child*, Vol. XXI, 1966, p. 244).

When Dick first appeared for analysis he gave the impression of a "passive, reluctant, affectless mass" who appeared "somewhat detached and very disinterested in treatment" (p. 243).

Sources of Stimulation:
adult punitive and excretory contacts with children

+ beatings*

1. Dick was relentlessly chased and beaten by his father. First the father would strike Dick who would then fall limp upon the floor. The father would proceed to jump on Dick and punch the boy in the head or to "kick him in the torso as Dick tried to roll out of the way" (p. 244-45). These beatings would be triggered by Dick's attempts to beat up his two younger brothers during wrestling bouts (p. 244) or by his criticism of his mother's cooking (even though the father himself repeatedly complained about the cooking)[2] (p. 246).

The mother also would beat Dick (p. 245) and, by adamantly informing the father of Dick's unsatisfactory behavior, set the stage for the boy to get more punishments (p. 247).

"Both parents expressed concern about the effect of the father's frequent beatings of Dick" (p. 244). They knew the beatings would have to stop but were afraid that if they did stop, Dick would "get out of control" (p. 245).

Behavioral Symptoms correlated with
adult punitive and excretory contacts with children

+ negative
behavior

1. Dick directly opposed therapy. " 'It [therapy] won't do no good,' " he repeated. " 'I don't see wasa use' " . . . "he had tried a psychiatrist before, but it ended up the same way. 'Nuffin is complished. Ya coont get nowhere. Ya coont change nuffin.' Following this he became sullen and silent" (p. 244).

Dick actively opposed his father's requests: " 'He can't make me do nuffin.' " " 'He can beat me all he wants. I won't eat. I won't let my brothers alone. I won't study. I won't do nuffin he wants' " (p. 247). Even in the area of sports, Dick refused to comply with his father's recommendations. The father tried to interest Dick in golf and skiing for example, but Dick "would stop before he got started" (p. 244). Dick ended up withdrawing from competitive situations and from making friends (p. 244).

Such withholding and opposition to authority contributed to the formation of a discouraging learning problem. Dick seemed to have no interests at all. He "failed physical education and did poorly in all school subjects" (p. 244). Dick actually received pleasure in opposing his father, by failing. On one occasion, Dr. Moore noted that Dick was displaying a mysterious smile. Dick responded, " 'You will find out why.' " The answer was Dick's latest report card which was his "worst ever." " 'I fooled you,' he laughed, 'see nuffin does no good. Nuffin ever can' " (p. 249).

+ learning*
(level 1; referral
problem)

Dick's learning problem was further exacerbated by his proclivity for *forgetting*. Dick became quite impressed when he began to realize how many things had happened that he had forgotten. He was most impressed to find he could not even remember the full names of five friends. He also began to realize "he could not remember what he read even though he was a voluminous reader. Nor could he memorize any material for tests." With alarm, he commented, "No wonder I never do any good. I study and forget everything" (p. 247-48). Thus, excessive punishment resulted in the inhibition of *memory* rather than in the inhibition of the disturbing behavior.

+ freezing of
affect

2. At the beginning of therapy, Dick displayed an inhibition or "freezing" of emotion. To requote Dr. Moore: "Dick [first] appeared in the office, a passive, reluctant, *affectless* mass. He seemed somewhat detached and was very disinterested in treatment" (p. 243).

+ negative
emotion

Only after analysis had progressed to a somewhat positive phase was Dick able to say for the first time that he hated his father: " 'I will never like him 'til he dies no matter how he treats me now. It's too late. The hate is too much' " (p. 249).

+ hurting

+ falling*

3. Prior to his analysis, Dick's only activity seemed to be beating up his two younger brothers only to be beaten in turn by his father (p. 244). As already noted, Dick would purposefully *fall* to the floor as his father would strike him, a move which was followed by his father's jumping upon him and punching him (p. 245).

+ excretory
symptoms*
+ non-organic
illness*

4. Dick had a long history of periodic diarrhea. On several occasions a diagnosis of spastic colitis was made. The final medical diagnosis indicated the symptoms to be emotional in origin (p. 245).

Sources of Stimulation:

children's tactile and visual erogenous contact with the adult body[3]

1. Dr. Moore drew attention to the pleasure both Dick and his father obtained from tangling with one another wrestling (p. 257).

− / + sleeping in bed with adult* (no sleeping or cuddling reported)

2. Another possible source for tactile erogenous contacts with the adult body was the mother's inclination to watch television in bed with Dick (p. 259).

Behavioral Symptoms correlated with

children's tactile and visual erogenous contacts with the adult body

No pertinent symptoms were reported.

NOTES

[1] Dick attained an I.Q. score of 105. Because of his intense intellectual negativism this score must have reflected an achievement well below his actual capacity.

[2] Simultaneous analysis of the father and son revealed that the father's beatings reflected his own history of having been beaten when he was a child. The father's driven need to wrestle with Dick and to beat him also proved to be related to the father's homosexual reactions towards Dick (p. 257, 262, 264).

[3] Dr. Moore notes: "I have presented only those aspects of the case which I feel have a direct bearing on the discussion of a simultaneous analysis of Dick and his father."

Kolansky and Moore's "Dick"
32

Stimulation-Symptom-and-Dream-Profile

	Separation Phobias
	Night Terrors, Twilight States
Sleep in Bed with Adult	Irrational Fears: Other
	Irrational Tempers
Adult Genital Erotic	Sexual Symptoms
	Biting/Cutting, etc.
View Adult Coitus	Eyes
	Fire

content of dreams and symptoms

	+ Learning Problems (levels 2 or 3, etc.)
Punitive Yelling	Lying and Delinquency
	Reversal of Affect
+ Beatings	Closing Down Upon, Kill
	+ Falling

content of dreams and symptoms

	+ Excretory Symptoms and Dreams
	Anal Masturbation
Preoccupation with Child's BM	Enuresis
	+ Illness, etc.
Anal Contacts	Pain
	Death
	Compulsions

content of dreams and symptoms

Case 33: Arnold

The public schools recommended that Arnold, at the age of eleven, be brought to a psychiatrist for a diagnostic evaluation. The school counselor, who had been trying to help Arnold, felt his problems were only getting worse. The mother remarked that his "school work goes up and down." Arnold in turn retorted: "School is an awful place." Arnold's WISC intelligence testing revealed a Full Scale I.Q. score of 107 (a Verbal I.Q. of 95 and a Performance I.Q. of 118).

Of note, when Arnold was three years old, he saw a little girl knocked to the side of a passing train. She had a chunk of her forehead gouged out but was not severely injured. Arnold stayed calm and brought the little girl's mother to the scene. On future occasions, the little girl and Arnold played a great deal with one another.

Sources of Simulation:
adult punitive and excretory contacts with children

+ punitive yelling*

1. Arnold's mother was a strong, buxom woman who expressed her wishes and opinions in a loud voice, a woman who did not hesitate to be directly outspoken whether her audience liked it or not. She told her social worker, "Look lady, how would you like to be taking care of six children? Well, I've had it!" The mother described her *temper as "fierce."* She was accustomed to yell at "all the kids," but she felt she had to yell the most at Arnold's oldest brother. Next in line, she "let loose" on Arnold because of the messiness of his bedroom.

Arnold explained that his mother was not the only *"screamer"* in the house. His father also regularly yelled at him. Arnold was convinced that his father found real pleasure in "blasting out" at him.

+ beatings*

Arnold was particularly upset by his mother hitting him in the face. One time she gave him a bloody nose. He was equally upset when his mother hit his brother in the face. Arnold stuttered, "She should not hit so hard like that."

Behavioral Symptoms correlated with
adult punitive and excretory contacts with children

Arnold described his problems as follows:

+ negative behavior

a) "Nothing"[1]

b) "Sometimes I study and sometimes I d*on't* study"

c) "Sometimes I *don't* obey my mother"

(opposites)
d) "I want to go to Catholic Church even though my mother doesn't want me to because we're Jewish." The accent here on negative behavior hardly could be missed.

The parents recalled that Arnold's first episode of negativism occurred when he was about three years old. Arnold had not wanted to eat in a restaurant but was required to go along with the family's plans to eat out. In the restaurant Arnold filled his mouth with food, held in the food until after they left the restaurant, then spit it out. It was not until Arnold was seven, however, that the parents began to feel that his stubbornness had become hard to manage.

Arnold did well in school until the year of his diagnostic referral. The year before, he often brought home papers marked 100, whereas just prior to his referral Arnold frequently seemed *to do nothing* and only cried when he was asked about school. In class, he was described as lazy; he would look out the window and would not finish his work. On the other hand, periodically Arnold would still bring home excellent papers.

+ learning*
(level 2)
Unfortunately, the family did not accept the diagnostic team's suggestions that Arnold and his parents receive therapy: one year later Arnold had to be placed in a special school for severe learning disabilities.[2]

+ stuttering
Of note, Arnold occasionally stuttered, a possible sign of his being hit on the face.

+ reversal of affect*

+ negative emotion
2. The teacher reported that Arnold was acting as the class *clown* and would mock and make faces at her. Arnold directly complained that he *disliked* school every day and *disliked "everything"* about it. He also *disliked* himself and asked, "Why was I born *'stupid?'* "

+ falling*
3. "Arnold did a fair amount of falling as a young child." It was thought that his falling might have been due to eye astigmatism. In any case, he refused to wear his glasses. Arnold had a scar under his lip as the result of his falls.

Of note, at the end of his last diagnostic hour, it was suggested to Arnold that perhaps he could draw a picture which would help both him and his therapist understand his problems and worries. He first refused; but when his therapist was willing to bypass the request, Arnold immediately complied. He deftly drew a picture of a "railroad bridge which had *collapsed* so that a train was *falling* into a ravine" (also see introduction).

Sources of Stimulation:
children's tactile and visual erogenous contacts with the adult body

− / + sleeping in bed with adults*
1. Arnold would climb into bed with his thirteen-year-old brother, and when he was scared would sleep with his brother for the night.

−/+ adult genital
erotic* (brother
only age 13)

2. Arnold stated that his brother's penis was already getting big. The two would have tickle fights during which Arnold would experience an erection. Arnold would complain to his parents that his brother always wanted to kiss him.

Behavioral Symptoms correlated with
children's tactile and visual erogenous contacts with the adult body

+ irrational fears*

1. As noted, Arnold's night fears sent him in to sleep with his brother.

+/− sexual
symptoms*

2. Arnold's erections during the wrestling fights with his adolescent brother and the brother's attempts to kiss Arnold gave evidence of a mounting homo-sexual interaction between the two brothers — a likely source for the development of homosexual panic.[3]

+ eyes* (reading
problem)

3. The mother exaggerated when she stated: "Of course Arnold can't read." Yet, Arnold was reading "at least a year below his grade level." His reading difficulties of course exacerbated the mounting severity of his learning problem.

NOTES

[1] Note here the frequent reference to negative words "not," "never," etc. in parallel with Kolansky and Moore's case of Dick, see synopsis case 32.

[2] It is not difficult to understand that when a child has to listen to a parent's punitive lectures at home, the child may easily turn away from listening to a teacher's long lectures in school.

[3] Since both boys were equally hit and yelled at by their parents, it is understandable how each might cling to the other as an only source of comfort or pleasure.

Arnold
33

Stimulation-Symptom-and-Dream-Profile

	Separation Phobias	
	Night Terrors, Twilight States	
Sleep in Bed with Adult	+ Irrational Fears: Other	
	Irrational Tempers	
Adult Genital Erotic	+ Sexual Symptoms	
	Biting/Cutting, etc.	⎫ *content of*
View Adult Coitus	+ Eyes	⎬ *dreams and*
	Fire	⎭ *symptoms*

	+ Learning Problems (levels 2 or 3, etc.)	
+ Punitive Yelling	Lying and Delinquency	
	+ Reversal of Affect	
+ Beatings	Closing Down Upon, Kill	⎫ *content of* ⎬ *dreams and*
	+ Falling	⎭ *symptoms*

	Excretory Symptoms and Dreams	
	Anal Masturbation	
Preoccupation with Child's BM	Enuresis	
	Illness, etc.	⎫ *content of*
Anal Contacts	Pain	⎬ *dreams and*
	Death	⎭ *symptoms*
	Compulsions	

Case 34: Barry

The intake note indicated that seven-year-old Barry "reads backwards; he reverses letters; his school performance is erratic; he is immature, and he complains of his 'rear end' itching."

Sources of Stimulation:
adult punitive and excretory contacts with children

+ beatings*

1. Barry explained: "Since we moved, the kids were mean and I began to copy them. I swore a couple of times and my father would give me a beating. . . . My brother, he's nineteen, he swears; he says 'f-u-c-k.' But if I say it, I get hit in the face. . . . I'm always mean but I always get hit when I'm fresh."

Following the first diagnostic interview, Barry proudly announced to his mother: "I told my doctor that you spank me," about which the mother complained: "I don't know why he ever told his doctor that. I never whip him, except a tap now and then." It was not until a year later, when Barry had broken his leg and required a brace that the reality of Barry's beatings was finally recognized. The mother had been hitting him so hard with her hand that she complained of hurting herself on Barry's brace. She therefore resorted to hitting him with a stick, "The Stick of Education." She had called the *stick her best friend* and even had a picture of it. She was very upset when Barry managed to cut the stick in three places.

To make matters worse, Barry was disciplined in school by being hit with a rattan.

+ punitive yelling*

2. The mother admitted that she screamed at Barry's baby brother. She screamed so often at him that Barry suggested: "Maybe we shouldn't have gotten a boy for a baby."

+ anal stimulation*

3. Until six months prior to his diagnostic evaluation, Barry suffered from itching all over his body after his evening bath. He complained mostly about his *"rear end itching."*[1] The mother would apply Noxema cream to the itching area, and then send Barry to bed, only to find him returning in a few moments with more itching, requiring more ointment.

Behavioral Symptoms correlated with
adult punitive and excretory contacts with children

+ excretory dream* ("behind")
+ closing down upon destructively*

1. Barry reported one of his dreams as follows: "A giant was after me, but he was right *behind* me, and he dug a hole and *buried* me. But I came up. I

136

seen his foot go on it."

+ enuresis*

2. The mother noted that Barry continued to wet his bed since he was in the first grade.

+ negative
behavior

3. The mother could not understand why Barry did the opposite when she used the word "don't." She explained that if she said: "Put the pencil on the table, don't put it on the chair," he would deliberately proceed to put the pencil on the chair.

Barry's mother also noticed that when she tried to make him do his homework, Barry would write in reverse. Some days he would get 100s on his papers without any reversals, yet on other days everything would be written backwards. She reasoned that he was writing backwards on purpose to show his resentment. Barry also would often read backwards. Neurological impairment was ruled out: (a) Barry was excellently coordinated in all activities; (b) he correctly spelled words forwards when he was in a good mood; (c) he got over his problem of reading and writing backwards after two years of psychotherapy.

Barry's reversal problem was supplemented by his turning away from auditory contact when his mother would be talking and therefore by his "not hearing" what she would be saying. The mother complained: "Sometimes I have to ask him five or six times to do something and I have to put a few pats on his bottom to make him listen."

+ learning*
(level 2)

With this negativism it was no wonder that Barry suffered from a learning problem and had to repeat the first grade.

+ reversal of
affect*

4. Barry also demonstrated a reversal of affect. For example, he reported: "My mother once picked me up and shook me when I got jelly on the floor. But the more she hit me the more I laughed." After his mother would *hit* him, Barry would first hide and then laugh. In the same way, Barry reported as one of his main problems: "If people fall down, I laugh."

+ falling*

5. The word "fall" permeated Barry's diagnostic. Barry recalled catching his foot and falling to the ground from a high fence. He also remembered falling off the roof of his house.

+ non-organic
illness*
+ pains*

6. Prior to therapy, Barry suffered from headaches and stomachaches.

Sources of Stimulation:
children's tactile and visual erogenous contacts with the adult body

− / + sleeping in
bed with adults*
(occasionally)

1. Barry occasionally got into his father's bed. He also liked to wrestle with his nineteen-year-old brother.

2. Barry "occasionally" saw his mother completely nude and regularly saw his nineteen-year-old brother without clothes.

+ adult nudity

Barry was accustomed to hanging around a beach club where the men sunbathed in the nude. One day one of the men, "a guy with one arm," told him: " 'Beat it, get out of here.' "

Behavioral Problems correlated with
children's tactile and visual erogenous contacts with the adult body

+ irrational fears*

1. Even the father, who was generally unconcerned about Barry's behavior, was troubled by Barry's excessive fears of going to bed.

+ eyes* (dream
   content)

+ biting/cutting*

2-3. A dream which Barry brought in during his diagnostic went as follows: "I thought there was a giant cat and after that I was *looking* through the mail box. After that I *saw* my two friends, and the cat put me in his *mouth* and wanted to *eat* me."

+ eyes*

After a year of therapy, Barry began to express some affect. He then cried: "I'm dumb — I'm doufy; I'm doing ok in most subjects but I'm doing doufy in reading. I just can't read."[2]

NOTES

[1] See case 77 of Kurt Junior who also was disturbed by the "itchies."

[2] Barry's problem in reading may be understood to be multi-determined, i.e., a function of (a) excessive punishment stimulation contributing to a learning problem; (b) excessive voyeuristic stimulation at the men's club for nude sunbathing, a source for conflicts pertaining to the use of the eyes.

Barry
34

Stimulation-Symptom-and-Dream-Profile

	Separation Phobias	
	Night Terrors, Twilight States	
Sleep in Bed with Adult	+ Irrational Fears: Other	
	Irrational Tempers	
Adult Genital Erotic	Sexual Symptoms	
	+ Biting/Cutting, etc.	} *content of*
View Adult Coitus	+ Eyes	} *dreams and*
	Fire	} *symptoms*

	+ Learning Problems (levels 2 or 3, etc.)	
+ Punitive Yelling	Lying and Delinquency	
	+ Reversal of Affect	
+ Beatings	+ Closing Down Upon, Kill	} *content of dreams and*
	+ Falling	} *symptoms*

	+ Excretory Symptoms and Dreams	
	Anal Masturbation	
Preoccupation with Child's BM	+ Enuresis	
	+ Illness, etc.	} *content of*
+ Anal Contacts	+ Pain	} *dreams and*
	+ Death	} *symptoms*
	Compulsions	

Case 35: Clancy

When he was fifteen years old, Clancy rather unwillingly allowed his parents to bring him to the clinic for a diagnostic evaluation of his learning problem.

Clancy maintained that he wanted to go to college and was enrolled in the school college course. However, his mother had become concerned as to whether her son was college material. He had struggled through the preceding year in the ninth grade and had barely passed. Although his sixth grade teacher had observed his performance to be erratic, Clancy's overall work actually had been satisfactory until he reached the ninth grade.

Clancy achieved a Full Scale I.Q. rating of 109, Performance 100 and Verbal 115. It is likely his capacity was much higher, for his negativism directly affected his answers. The psychologist noted for example, that with respect to the similarities subtest, Clancy answered almost every even-numbered question with full credit, yet he negatively refused every *odd-numbered* question with the flat statement, "They're *not* alike."

Clancy constantly served as a target for the parents' *negative emotion and control.* The parents admitted they had taken practically all privileges away from Clancy in order to force him to study. In turn, Clancy complained, "My parents fuss too much, sermonize and keep repeating, 'Why don't you do your homework?' . . . My father is like a brick wall; my mother is like a flagpole. Father has no faith in me." Clancy recalled that as a child he started to build something with an erector set only to have his father find fault because he was not doing it according to directions. Likewise, his mother denigrated Clancy: "She finds fault with me when I go out; she finds fault with me when I don't go out." The mother's negativism (and separation problem) kept Clancy from going out camping and "roughing it" with his father. She also kept him from going to overnight camp because she feared "his allergies might act up." Thus, the mother's negativism served the function of negating Clancy's active ego and encouraged the development of his passivity.

Sources of Stimulation:
adult punitive and excretory contacts with children

+ early
  deprivation

1. The mother implied that Clancy was an unwanted baby, for she related that at the time of her pregnancy she and her husband felt both financially and emotionally insecure. Clancy was ill throughout his first two years. He "vomited

almost continuously" and suffered throughout this period with bronchitis and allergic respiratory reactions which eventually developed into asthma. By the time he was one and a half years old, Clancy began to run temperatures frequently and to suffer from sore throats.[1]

+ early bowel
training

2. When Clancy was only four months old, his mother started toilet training by holding him over the toilet. Since this procedure proved a failure, the mother gave up trying to toilet train the infant until he was one year old.

+ beatings*

3. Clancy's father would lose control as he used a strap to beat Clancy's buttocks after he had the boy take his pants down. This form of chastisement still occurred at least every two weeks even when Clancy was almost sixteen years old.

Behavioral Symptoms correlated with
adult punitive and excretory contacts with children

+ negative
behavior

1. Clancy's current problems were precipitated at the age of twelve when he entered junior high school. It was at that time that he began to show evidences of withdrawal from friends and deterioration of his schoolwork.

In his work, Clancy complained of feeling like a failure. He would "try things once, find them difficult, and then give up." The mother whined: "This is the story of his life: he always feels that he cannot do things and doesn't want to try."

+ learning*
(level 1; referral
problem)
+ lying*

By the time Clancy had entered the ninth grade, his learning problem had become severe enough to cause his mother much concern. To make matters' worse, at this time Clancy began *to lie* and falsify reality. For example, Clancy forged his mother's name to a letter which he wrote to the school to excuse himself from gym. Clancy's father pinpointed the onset of this tendency to lie as coinciding with the onset of his learning problem. The father concluded that the lying was "defensive," i.e., geared to prevent further punishment for his poor grades.

Unfortunately, Clancy's negativism kept him from getting therapy. He was not interested in the prospects of the family getting help and felt that therapy would accomplish nothing.[2] All he wanted was his parents to "get off his back."

+ negative
emotion

2. Poignantly, Clancy spoke of the universe containing millions and millions of minute positively and negatively charged ions. He felt like an insignificant, *negatively charged* ion, lost in space.

Clancy's negative emotion was also reflected in his initial presentation of his "problems": (a) "Boston has a *bad* name, there are *terrible* crimes there, and everyone knows about the bookies. I *hate* the city"; (b) "The house I lived in was in a neighborhood *going to pot*. Boston is a *lousy hole.*"

3. The mother noted that Clancy "seemed to hurt himself a lot"; recently
+ hurting
he had given himself a broken knee and a sprained ankle.

Sources of Stimulation:
children's tactile and visual erogenous contacts with the adult body

+ sleeping in bed
with adults*
1. Clancy would get into bed to sleep with his parents until he was eight or
nine years old. However, he said that he could not stand sleeping between them
because his father snored too much.

+ adult nudity
2. Clancy also took showers with his father until he was eleven. Then his
father slipped on a piece of soap and almost broke a leg, at which point the
sharing of showers stopped.

− / + adult genital
erotic*
3. As a teenager, Clancy saw pornographic pictures of a girl indulging in
fellatio. [3]

Behavioral Symptoms correlated with
children's tactile and visual erogenous contacts with the adult body

− / + separation
phobias*
1. One of the mother's first statements during her diagnostic interview pertained to fifteen-year-old Clancy's emotional upset over separating from her.
The mother indicated that he resented her being away from home when she
recently had taken a part-time job. She wondered whether the increase in Clancy's school problems might be due to her taking a job out of the home.

2. The question arose as to whether Clancy was struggling with a homosex-
− / + sexual
symptoms*
ual panic. Shortly after he had spoken of having shared his parents' bed, Clancy
broke out with a report that there was a homosexual man who had been hanging around one of the neighboring colleges. He complained about this man even
though Clancy had not attended nor as yet been accepted at the college where
the homosexual hung out. Clancy also expressed concern over the pornographic
+ compulsions*
pictures he had seen. Compulsively he repeated to himself, "So what . . . but I
am upset. . . . So what . . . but I'm upset. . . ."[4]

+ eyes*
+ tics
3. "When he looks at people" the mother noticed, "Clancy always *blinks
his eyes.*"

In addition, Clancy suffered from a *reading disability*. His school guidance
counselor reported that Clancy's reading was "atrocious."

NOTES

[1] See Spitz, *Psychoanalytic Study of the Child,* Vol. II, 1947, regarding a proclivity for
bodily disease among children exposed to early deprivation of maternal care.
[2] See Kolansky and Moore's case of Dick, case 32.

³ See Table of Definitions in Appendix 2: this exposure was not recorded positively because of Clancy's age.

⁴ Recall that not only had Clancy as a boy been intimately close to his father's nude body as they shared showers, but the father was still taking down Clancy's pants to strap the adolescent boy on the buttocks when Clancy was fifteen years old, i.e., father and son showering nude together under one spray was followed by the father's attacks upon Clancy's bare buttocks. Clancy's exposure to pornographic pictures then could well have ignited Clancy's already aroused homosexual feelings.

Clancy

35

Stimulation-Symptom-and-Dream-Profile

	Separation Phobias	
	Night Terrors, Twilight States	
+ Sleep in Bed with Adult	Irrational Fears: Other	
	Irrational Tempers	
Adult Genital Erotic	Sexual Symptoms	
	Biting/Cutting, etc.	} *content of*
View Adult Coitus	+ Eyes	} *dreams and*
	Fire	} *symptoms*
	+ Learning Problems (levels 2 or 3, etc.)	
Punitive Yelling	+ Lying and Delinquency	
	Reversal of Affect	
+ Beatings	Closing Down Upon, Kill	} *content of dreams and*
	Falling	} *symptoms*
	Excretory Symptoms and Dreams	
	Anal Masturbation	
Preoccupation with Child's BM	Enuresis	
	Illness, etc.	} *content of*
Anal Contacts	Pain	} *dreams and*
	Death	} *symptoms*
	+ Compulsions	

Case 36: Dominic

Dominic, a thin, lanky boy of nine and a half, was quiet in manner, serious and friendly. His speech revealed a slight stutter at the time he started therapy for a severe learning problem. Despite his achievement of a Verbal I.Q. of 116, Performance I.Q. of 99 and overall I.Q. of 109, Dominic had been receiving no better than social promotions ever since kindergarten.

Dominic was very unhappy about his learning problem. In the first place, he was an idealistic lad who was interested in international projects and who wanted to join the diplomatic corps when he grew up. Certainly his "stupidity" in school did not give him much hope of success in that direction. Additionally, Dominic was ashamed of being the stupid inadequate boy in the family who got D's and E's while his brother, Louis, got A's.

At the time of his referral for therapy, the parents expressed their concern that Dominic was "oversensitive" and cried too easily, e.g., when a distant aunt returned to their home to visit after several years' absence.

After four years of therapy, it was revealed that Dominic's mother had been performing functions for him he normally should have been doing for himself. She was still *combing Dominic's hair each morning* and *tying his ice-skate shoelaces.* She sat with him every night to supervise his homework.

The mother constantly countered Dominic's own plans. When Dominic wanted to go skating, his mother planned for him to go swimming. When Dominic brought some candy for his therapist, his mother substituted her chewing gum for the candy which had gotten "too soft." When Dominic wanted to go down to visit his father at work, his mother urged him not to go because he might get lost. The mother's negative oppositional behavior left Dominic *controlled* like a puppet. To strengthen her position, the mother refused to give Dominic an allowance. It, therefore, became necessary for him to turn to her every time he needed to make a five-cent purchase.

Sources of Stimulation:
adult punitive and excretory contacts with children

+ early deprivation and suffering

1. The mother would give Dominic six or seven bottles of milk a day when he was fifteen months old in order to keep him from crying, whereupon he began to vomit his food. The mother concluded that she had "poisoned" him with too much milk.

144

+ beatings*

_2. After two years of therapy, Dominic's father admitted that he would lose control of himself and beat Dominic, sometimes for the sheer pleasure of it. He also admitted that such episodes once occurred frequently. Dominic verified these reports of his father's hitting him with great force and told how his father once grabbed him up by the neck so tightly that a piece of skin came off.

Dominic's mother was "so very upset" on one occasion when her husband without restraint kept hitting Dominic around the head and ears, yet she told Dominic he deserved the beating and the next morning she herself, for some minor offense, gave him a strapping.

On still another occasion, the mother told Dominic not to hit his brother and suggested that perhaps he could hit her instead. When Dominic then did hit her it "really hurt" so that she punched him back. She felt particularly upset at such times and felt as though she and Dominic were two men battling each other. Battles of this sort always ended with the mother finding it necessary to give Dominic a good belting, whereupon Dominic would begin to cry and say that he was sorry. Of course, the mother would then "break down" and could not resist forgiving Dominic and telling him she hoped he'd have a good day. Sometimes "I feel like killing him" the mother told her social worker. "Of course I don't *really* feel like that. . . . *Not* that I feel like killing him with a knife."

+ punitive
  yelling*

3. One thing that bothered Dominic the most about his low grades was his mother's incessantly yelling at him. He explained to his therapist, "The way she yells at me it makes me feel like a goon man from outer space." The mother eventually could see that she "hollered" at Dominic or slapped him in the face for "little nothings" when she was upset at her own mother for criticizing her.

Behavioral Symptoms correlated with
adult punitive and excretory contacts with children

+ enuresis*
+ lying*

1. At the age of ten, Dominic still wet his bed about twice a week. At such times he would say to his mother, "I didn't do it" (an example of his negative behavior, see below).

+ excretory
  symptoms*

According to his mother's report, Dominic had been troubled with constipation.

+ learning*
  (referral
  problem)

2. Dominic's learning problem brought him C's and D's and E's year after year despite his more than satisfactory I.Q. Unfortunately, the family's therapists took no direct steps to help Dominic's mother and father stop beating the boy. Therefore, it was not surprising that Dominic's discharge of excess negativism in the form of a learning problem continued unabated. When he finally left home to attend prep school, his learning eventually did improve.

Some of the "negative" aspects of Dominic's learning problem soon became evident. (a) In the first place, he delighted in doing the opposite from what his mother would ask him to do: he would say, "You can't make me do my home-work, you can't make me do it," until he finally "reached her" and made her explode. Or he would annoy his mother by chanting, "I've done it, I've done it," even though it was obvious he hadn't even started his assignment. The more she would plead with him and nag, the more Dominic would taunt her.

+ negative
behavior

(b) Another aspect of his learning problem was his habit of looking away from his work. His therapist watched him as he built a model and noted that when he came to joining parts together he would turn and *look away*. Some-times he would gaze out of the window as he tried to put the model together. (c) At home he avoided "doing things" and was passive. However, when it came to work that he liked, such as helping out at "Common Cause," Dominic's pas-sivity quickly vanished.[1]

+ negative
emotion

3. Dominic's expression of negative feelings to his mother and father, i.e., his "fresh" talking back to them, continually triggered their belting him.

+ death*

4. Dominic was obsessed with thoughts of death. Repetitively he accused himself for being responsible for the destruction of those with whom he had been close:

+ preoccupation
with illness*
+ death*
+ hurting

(a) Dominic was sure *he had caused the death* of his maternal grandfather (who died in the hospital with cancer). Dominic once ran a temperature during a siege of measles and somehow became convinced that he had given the tem-perature and the disease to his grandfather. In one dream he saw his (dead) grandfather reappear. Dominic became preoccupied with the question as to why people have to hurt other people.

+ killing*

(b) Once again Dominic accused himself of *"magical" destructiveness* when his paternal grandmother slipped on the sidewalk and broke her pelvis. Directly following this incident, Dominic ran to his room and cried, "God kill me."

(c) Dominic also toyed with thoughts that he had been close to *killing his baby brother*. Dominic had given the baby some "bad stuff" the parents had put on Dominic's thumb to prevent thumb-sucking. In later years Dominic persev-erated that "if the baby had eaten that stuff it could have done away with him."

+ closing down
upon
destructively*
(crush)

Dominic remembered actually hitting a child on the head with a shovel when he was six years old. It was immediately after this incident that Dominic failed to protect himself from being *hit by a car,* an accident which resulted in his being hospitalized for a broken pelvis.[2] Interestingly enough, Dominic's mother too was knocked down by a car when *she* was five years old.

Sources of Stimulation:
children's tactile and visual erogenous contacts with the adult body

+ adult genital
erotic*

1. After the father left the house about six o'clock in the morning, *the mother would often wrestle and tickle with Dominic in bed.* When Dominic's

brother would come into the room, the mother or Dominic would say, "Oh here comes jealous." In this connection Dominic told a story of a guy falling on top of his girl: "with a little lovin' and a little murder, it's great."

+ adult nudity

2. Until he was twelve, Dominic took showers with his father.

− / + view adult coitus*

3. Dominic slept in his parents' room until he was two years old, when his brother was born. However, there was no report whatsoever of his having seen his parents during intercourse. Dominic did note that when he was older he'd "like to stay awake at night in order to listen to his parents' fighting," then corrected himself and said he didn't think his parents had really been *fighting*, rather they seemed to be *laughing*. It, therefore, seems likely that he was listening to his parents as they were in the process of having sexual intercourse. This perception was not too different from that of Dominic's own wrestling and tickling in bed with his mother.

Behavioral Symptoms correlated with
children's tactile and visual erogenous contacts with the adult body

− / + separation phobia* (only homesick)

1. Dominic was homesick at camp. He cried when his family came to visit him and came home a day early with his father because he had been so unhappy, this despite all the beatings and punitive screaming to which Dominic had been subjected at home.

+ biting/cutting/ stomach*

One day the teacher had to send Dominic home because of a bad stomachache he had developed after a morning fight with his mother.

+ nightmare
+ eyes* (the word "see" in a dream)
+ irrational tempers*

2. Dominic experienced a nightmare soon after his grandfather died. In the nightmare, he thought he saw the grandfather reappear.

3. Dominic flew into "fits" of temper, especially in the mornings before his going to school. The mother soon would explode in return.[3]

+ sexual symptoms*

4. Dominic wrestled constantly with his brother as he had with his mother. During these "wrestling" bouts, the boys would try to find "things" in each other's clothing, an activity which required considerable handling of each other's bodies.[4]

NOTES

[1] A neurological report noted that the basal muscles of his right arm were weaker than those of his left and that he wrote with his left hand: possible evidence for "minimal brain damage."

[2] Dominic did not lose consciousness. No signs of brain damage were found upon medical examination.

[3] The mother "just couldn't understand" why there was so much more uproar mornings

even though she reported Dominic to be "over-stimulated" after wrestling in bed with her.

4 See synopsis of Rosenblatt's Harold, case 93; and synopsis of Kolansky and Moore's Dick, case 32; also cases 10 (Grant), 46 (Nathan), and 78 (Larry) regarding the acting out of sexualized wrestling.

Dominic
36

Stimulation-Symptom-and-Dream-Profile

	Separation Phobias
	Night Terrors, Twilight States
Sleep in Bed with Adult	Irrational Fears: Other
	+ Irrational Tempers
+ Adult Genital Erotic	+ Sexual Symptoms
	+ Biting/Cutting, etc. ⎫ *content of*
View Adult Coitus	+ Eyes ⎬ *dreams and*
	Fire ⎭ *symptoms*
	+ Learning Problems (levels 2 or 3, etc.)
+ Punitive Yelling	+ Lying and Delinquency
	Reversal of Affect
+ Beatings	+ Closing Down Upon, Kill ⎫ *content of*
	⎬ *dreams and*
	Falling ⎭ *symptoms*
	+ Excretory Symptoms and Dreams
	Anal Masturbation
Preoccupation with Child's BM	+ Enuresis
	+ Illness, etc. ⎫ *content of*
Anal Contacts	Pain ⎬ *dreams and*
	+ Death ⎭ *symptoms*
	Compulsions

Case 37: Earl

Earl, who appeared sturdy, cheerful and cooperative, was eight years old when he was seen at the clinic for a diagnostic evaluation. The pediatrician had discovered large welts on Earl's arm and back and reported that Earl had been subjected to child abuse. The parents admitted that the welts had been caused by the father's habit of whipping Earl for dawdling while eating his meals and for not meeting his father's high expectations for school performance. Actually, Earl was a very bright boy who, according to his teacher, demonstrated the ability to be an honor roll student. When he decided to do his work, he obtained the highest test scores in the class. However, Earl generally did poorly in school. He was "idling his time away, day dreaming, and playing with his pencils"; and although he was a second grade student, his reading skills stagnated at a first grade level.

Sources of Stimulation:
adult punitive and excretory contacts with children

1. Both Earl's father and mother had been beaten severely during their own childhood. The mother claimed she "got whipped for everything, even for eating on the street." The father had been beaten for being "stubborn."

+ beatings*

In turn, the mother beat Earl because he did not obey. She explained, for example, "he knows he is not to play with the TV but he keeps twisting and turning the knobs and everything he touches he breaks." Earl would "keep it up" until she hit him, sometimes with her hand, sometimes with a belt.

The father's beatings were a source of more concern to the clinic. Earl described how the father sometimes gave him fourteen lashes at a time. The mother admitted "it's something terrible." During his diagnostic, Earl showed the welts on his body where he had been struck.

The pediatrician's referral letter summarized the situation as follows: "Earl's father used physical punishment to the extreme in trying to make Earl conform. The father firmly believes that the only way to make people conform is to punish them physically for their transgressions; otherwise 'they will grow up not knowing right from wrong.' "

+ punitive
yelling*

2. In response to the diagnostic question: "What are your problems and worries?," Earl first answered, "My teacher keeps *screaming* at me."

3. The mother's reactions to Earl's soiling had from the start been especially

149

+ punitive bowel
  training

punitive. Earl confided: "My mother *hits* me when I doo-doo in my pants. . . .
And [when] I got doo-doo in my bath, my mother killed me. She takes a stick
and hits me then."

Behavioral Symptoms correlated with
adult punitive and excretory contacts with children

+ negative
  behavior

1. Earl continually withheld completion of his tasks and activities. At home,
he would take "forever" eating. Sometimes he sat at the table as long as three
to four hours without finishing his meal until finally his father whipped him.

Sometimes he seemed not to be listening. His mother claimed that often
she would have to speak to him "five to eight times" before he would do what
he was told.[1]

+ learning*
  (level 1; referral
  problem)

Similarly, at school he would not finish his work. The teacher said that he
waited until the last minute to start his work, then would have to rush through
his papers.

+ lying*

Additionally, it became clear how excessive punishment pushed Earl in the
direction of dishonesty, i.e., reversing his presentation of reality. In order to
avoid the father's beatings, Earl brought home his "good" papers and hid his
"bad" ones. After the father whipped Earl for his "dishonesty" and "trickery"
Earl in a panic became all the more dishonest: he copied a friend's paper to get
a good grade.

+ reversal of
  affect*

2. According to the mother, while Earl's brother was afraid of the father's
beatings, Earl sometimes "looked forward to them." Earl displayed no disturbed
affect during his diagnostic interviews as he recounted the history of his beatings. *His smiling face displayed no emotional signs of child abuse.*

+ hurting

3. Earl's dreams abounded with references to conditions of hurting:

Dream 1: "My mother and father was walking and this guy *shot* them."

+ closing down
  upon
  destructively*

Dream 2: "This guy got *shot* by a policeman . . . he got *shot* and a bottle
went up and splashed in his back and this boy *threw a rock* at the policeman
and the policeman was bleeding."

+ death*

Dream 3: "I was in a house. It had broken windows. This *ghost*[2] came up
and I was running."

+ excretory
  symptoms*

4. Earl got excrement on his hands and in the bathtub as well as in his
pants. Additionally, he did "doo-doo" under his rug in his bedroom. As Earl
put it, "I put doo-doo on the floor and then I put the rug over it. Then I stepped
on the rug. It dried up and it all goes out when my mother shakes the rug out
of the window."

Constipation was also a problem. Earl elaborated: "Every time I go to the
toilet I try to force it out and it won't come."[3]

(+ anal
    masturbation*)

As a result of subsequent soiling, Earl's "rear end" often itched. In turn, he scratched his anal region and poked his finger into his rectum. Earl explained that it felt "yuckey" inside. As Earl was about to tell this information he suddenly stopped to say: "I keep hearing a noise in my ear. Now it's like a motor." Compare this with similar findings in cases 69 (Dwight), 77 (Kurt Junior) and 100 (Ronny): all cases involved extreme punishment and anal masturbation followed by auditory hallucinations.

+ compulsions*

5. Directly following his statement that poking his *finger into his rear end* "feels yuckey," Earl associated "I *had to get a piece of paper to wipe my behind*." Earl then complained: "I get mad at myself because *something makes me get more paper in school* than I need: when I come back to my desk I already have paper on my desk."

+ non-organic
    illness*
+ aches and
    pains*

6. As he began to recall some of the disturbing memories to be reported below, Earl suddenly complained of a stomachache.

Sources of Stimulation:
children's tactile and visual erogenous contacts with the adult body

− / + sleeping in
bed with adults*
(occasional)

1. Earl let his therapist know that he sometimes would get into bed with his mother and father, and once, they let him sleep there all night.

+ adult nudity

2. Both parents made a point of not appearing in front of Earl nude. Earl, however, told how he saw his swimming teacher without clothes. He saw the teacher's "pee-pee" and his "hair down there."

+ adult genital
erotic*

3. Earl saw some hidden pornographic pictures of (a) "a man's dinky sticking way out;" (b) "the hair and titties on a lady;" (c) "a dink with stuff coming out;" (d) "a dinky up a man's behind;" (e) "a man trying to stick his dink up his own behind." (At this point, Earl, without exposing himself, demonstrated how the penis would be pushed between the legs toward the rear.)

What Earl reported next was unexpected: Earl told how he never directly saw his father's penis but "when my daddy did take his pants off I saw his dink through his shorts. *When he beats me, my father says he has to exercise his penis with his hand.* He told me his dink feels funny when he's beating me." On other occasions, the father would tickle Earl's penis instead of beating him.

Behavioral Symptoms correlated with
children's tactile and visual erogenous contacts with the adult body

+ biting/cutting/
stomach*

1. The intensity of Earl's feelings as he referred to this material was reflected by his suddenly complaining of a stomachache and his having to leave the office to go to the bathroom.

+ eyes*

2. Earl dreamed: ". . . When I came upstairs I *saw* my mother and father." Earl's learning problem involved in particular his difficulty in reading.

+ sexual
symptoms*

3. Earl confided that when he got whipped, it made his own penis stick out: "It makes it feel like someone was tickling you there." Thus, hurting and sexual excitement became emotionally associated for Earl, just as they apparently had been for his father.[4]

NOTES

[1] Earl's actual hearing was excellent. His problem appeared to be related to *turning away* from his mother's auditory contacts or doing *the opposite* from what she was requesting him to do.

[2] Ghosts, i.e., shadows returned from the dead.

[3] Note once again the parallel between withholding performance at the toilet and withholding performance of other tasks at home and at school.

[4] Earl's reversal of emotion (as described above) becomes all the more understandable in the light of this history: "pain," usually associated with "fear" and "anger," now in Earl's case became associated with *pleasurable* sexual activation. This reversal of emotion accounts for the absence of directly expressed anger or fear by Earl, despite a continuous history of beatings extreme enough to require a medical report of child abuse.

Earl
37

Stimulation-Symptom-and-Dream-Profile

	Separation Phobias	
	Night Terrors, Twilight States	
Sleep in Bed with Adult	Irrational Fears: Other	
	Irrational Tempers	
+ Adult Genital Erotic	+ Sexual Symptoms	
	+ Biting/Cutting, etc.	} *content of*
View Adult Coitus	+ Eyes	} *dreams and*
	Fire	} *symptoms*
	+ Learning Problems (levels 2 or 3, etc.)	
+ Punitive Yelling	+ Lying and Delinquency	
	+ Reversal of Affect	
+ Beatings	+ Closing Down Upon, Kill	} *content of* } *dreams and*
	Falling	} *symptoms*
	+ Excretory Symptoms and Dreams	
	+ Anal Masturbation	
Preoccupation with Child's BM	Enuresis	
	+ Illness, etc.	} *content of*
Anal Contacts	+ Pain	} *dreams and*
	+ Death	} *symptoms*
	+ Compulsions	

Case 38: Floyd

The mother was "at the end of her rope" and sobbed on the phone as she pleaded for the clinic to help her twelve-year-old boy, Floyd, who had been "failing in school, made no friends, and fought with other boys." She felt that Floyd was "getting worse rather than better"; he already had hurt children to the extent that they required medical attention. Floyd was in "desperate need of help."

When the mother came for her diagnostic interview, however, she presented quite a different picture. She seemed at a loss as to why she was being interviewed and was immediately protective of Floyd in relation to his problems at school. As she spoke of the school principal who made her feel "entrapped," she became quite hostile. She pointed out that the father saw "nothing wrong" with Floyd although he would "not object" to Floyd's diagnostic evaluation. The mother assured her worker that Floyd went to church, never swore and simply "like some boys, did not like school."

Sources of Stimulation:
adult punitive and excretory contacts with children

1. Floyd's father, as a young man, was known to have had a violent temper. He claimed that he once split a washboard over his brother's head. His tempers continued into his adult life. During one fight he hit another man on the head with a hammer.

+ beatings*

Subsequently, the father beat Floyd with a big strap so as to raise welts. Sometimes the father would get so excited whipping, he would lose control of himself and according to the mother he would "break wild."

Floyd's mother tried to cover up for the father (who refused to be interviewed) but admitted that she too hit Floyd "too often and too hard." She "used the belt on him" in order to scare him, yet she was convinced Floyd knew "her real love" for him. Floyd confided how his mother hit him on the face when he displayed a facial tic.

+ tic

Behavioral Symptoms correlated with
adult punitive and excretory contacts with children

+ negative
  behavior

1. Despite an I.Q. score of 93, Floyd was failing in school where he was reported to be extremely passive and restricted. Floyd responded especially

153

poorly to strict teachers and failed the fifth grade which had been taught by a teacher he disliked. Concerned about Floyd's behavior, the school recommended a neurological workup. However, the neurosurgeon examining Floyd found no sign of a neurological problem.

+ learning*
(level 2)

2-3. Floyd began his first diagnostic hour: "If I sit down here, is this an electric chair?" His preoccupation with harm coming from all sides was also reflected by his presentation of his chief problem: "The kids pick on me and they use *knives.*" However, Floyd felt that as far as he was concerned, *he* himself, had *no* problems.

+ killing*

Floyd's dreams presented during his diagnostic continued to feature the themes of hurt and destruction. In one dream "there was a big thing that broke through the window and *punched* him in the leg." In another dream "a terrible man came through a window and stuffed a *knife* into him."

+ closing down
upon
destructively*

Floyd revealed his concerns about murder with inappropriate reversal of affect as he told how he thought Khrushchev would bomb Boston in two months. With a big smile he elaborated how it would *kill* everyone around but him. Floyd also laughed inappropriately during psychological testing.

+ reversal of
affect*
+ kill*

His therapist pointed out to Floyd that "when hate goes into a child from a parent, it wants to come out some way or another," and asked how did it come out from him. Floyd then confided that he had joined in the activities of a gang who had "messed up" the neighborhood and had hurt property.

+ delinquency*

Sources of Stimulation
children's tactile and visual erogenous contacts with the adult body

1. Floyd spontaneously spoke of seeing girls and boys interacting sexually, but did not make clear the age of the participants.

− / + adult genital
erotic*

Behavioral Symptoms correlated with
children's tactile and visual erogenous contacts with the adult body

1. Floyd dreamed of carrying his penis around after it had been *cut* off.

+ biting/cutting*

Floyd stated that he had lots of terrible dreams. These dreams suggested that he had been exposed to adult genital erotic scenes, pictures or seductions: "a big thing broke *through the window*"; "a terrible man came *through the window* and stuffed a knife into him"; "a robber came and put a *poker through the window.*"

+ nightmares

Floyd
38

Stimulation-Symptom-and-Dream-Profile

	Separation Phobias	
	Night Terrors, Twilight States	
Sleep in Bed with Adult	Irrational Fears: Other	
	Irrational Tempers	
Adult Genital Erotic	Sexual Symptoms	
	+ Biting/Cutting, etc.	} *content of*
View Adult Coitus	Eyes	*dreams and*
	Fire	*symptoms*
	+ Learning Problems (levels 2 or 3, etc.)	
Punitive Yelling	+ Lying and Delinquency	
	+ Reversal of Affect	
+ Beatings	+ Closing Down Upon, Kill	} *content of*
	Falling	*dreams and*
		symptoms
	Excretory Symptoms and Dreams	
	Anal Masturbation	
Preoccupation with Child's BM	Enuresis	
	Illness, etc.	} *content of*
Anal Contacts	Pain	*dreams and*
	Death	*symptoms*
	Compulsions	

Case 39: George

According to the "intake account," eight-year-old George disrupted his class at school with his temper tantrums which occurred whenever he would make mistakes in his work. His teachers also complained that he was constantly found hitting his schoolmates. Yet he was known to cringe in school "as though he were afraid of being hit."

"Don't do this . . . don't do that . . . that's not good . . . that's not right . . . don't talk back to me" were George's parents' favorite words of communication with him. Anything counter to the parents' wishes aroused their wrath. Although their goal was perfection and social conformity, their interaction with George was negative and punitively controlling.

Sources of Stimulation:
adult punitive and excretory contacts with children

−/+ early deprivation

1. George was placed in a day care nursery from the age of nine months to four and a half years.

+ beatings*

2. The father frequently disciplined George by strapping him with an army belt. The parents reported that at times George would become black and blue from these beatings. George confirmed this report and then staged a scene with the play dolls to describe what typically went on in his home. In the play, the boy was beaten because he was looking at the wrong TV. The father called out, "Come and get your beating. . . . Come here so I can beat you."

Of note, during her own therapy hour, the mother took off her shoe to beat George's sister, age two, when the little girl lay on the floor of the social worker's room and began crying.

+ punitive yelling*

The parents would angrily scold and blame George (see introductory description).

Behavioral Symptoms correlated with
adult punitive and excretory contacts with children

+ negative behavior

+ learning (level 1)

1. The school report from George's principal read as follows: "The teachers are convinced that George's emotional instability is hindering his learning. Even on a very cold day he perspires freely when he gets in one of his states. His eyes get wild-looking. He starts screaming and crying out: 'I won't.' "

+ negative
  emotion

2. The school report went on to say: "Apparently George has said such nasty things to children about their mothers that they would not even repeat them to any of the staff."

+ freezing of
  affect

A dream George reported during his first diagnostic hour reflected freezing of affect as a central motif: "A monster, if he touched you, would make you stay still like you were *frozen*."

+ hurting

3. George's specialty was "pounding" other children, including the street bully. During his first diagnostic hour George explained how he provoked fights: "I tease people and then they bother me. I tease Jonas. I call him a shrimp and a midget and he gets mad."

Sources of Stimulation:
children's tactile and visual erogenous contacts with the adult body

No positive information was obtained with respect to erogenous stimulation.

Behavioral Symptoms correlated with
children's tactile and visual erogenous contacts with the adult body

+ irrational fears*

1. George was sometimes afraid of the dark and had bad dreams, his mother reported. George himself spoke about fears of thunder, a topic he referred to immediately after he had spoken of a mother doll yelling and a father doll beating someone.

+ irrational
  tempers*

2. Temper tantrums were one of the chief complaints from George's home and school at the time of his referral to the clinic. During his tantrums he would swear and "fly into a rage . . . with wild eyes." These rages would often begin when George claimed that somebody hit him.

+ sexual
  symptoms*

(+ closing down
  upon
  destructively*)

3. The school complained that George would look into the girls' bathroom. He also would "grab" a girl in school and rock with her. On one occasion a little girl was found lying on the floor in school while George was kicking her in the genital region. George, who had been belted black and blue by his father, now was taking his turn knocking a little girl black and blue. Unfortunately, his punitive behavior had become intermeshed with the discharge of sexual activity.

George
39

Stimulation-Symptom-and-Dream-Profile

		Separation Phobias	
		Night Terrors, Twilight States	
Sleep in Bed with Adult	+	Irrational Fears: Other	
	+	Irrational Tempers	
Adult Genital Erotic	+	Sexual Symptoms	
		Biting/Cutting, etc.	⎫ *content of*
View Adult Coitus		Eyes	⎬ *dreams and*
		Fire	⎭ *symptoms*
		Learning Problems (levels 2 or 3, etc.)	
+ Punitive Yelling		Lying and Delinquency	
		Reversal of Affect	
+ Beatings	+	Closing Down Upon, Kill	⎫ *content of* ⎬ *dreams and* ⎭ *symptoms*
		Falling	
		Excretory Symptoms and Dreams	
		Anal Masturbation	
Preoccupation with Child's BM		Enuresis	
		Illness, etc.	⎫ *content of*
Anal Contacts		Pain	⎬ *dreams and*
		Death	⎭ *symptoms*
		Compulsions	

Case 40: Hubert

The family had chosen Hubert to be the "defective" son upon whom they could discharge their negative emotion. Hubert's mother thought he was "retarded"; his father thought he was "slow and lazy"; while both his sisters bossed him and called him "stupid." At the age of sixteen, Hubert was finally referred for a diagnostic evaluation for a longstanding "learning" problem.

The mother and father presented their home life as harmonious and contented. According to their initial report, the parents were "mutually dependent" upon one another and found their marriage "gratifying." Only during the parents' therapy did the truth come out. The mother felt unloved by the father, whom she described as uncommunicative, unsupportive and withdrawn. The mother went on to report that at the age of eighteen she had suffered a depressive "breakdown." She also confided that the grandmother had been known for promiscuity and alcoholism. Now, Hubert's mother herself had recently become fed up with her own marriage and for a year's period had acted out by drinking heavily and becoming involved sexually with a married man.

Sources of Stimulation:
adult punitive and excretory contacts with children

+ early
  deprivation

1. The mother first described herself as being devoted to her children and recalled that Hubert was "a very good baby." Later, however, she stated that her daughter, one year older than Hubert, had been extremely ill during Hubert's first two years of life and most of her attention had been directed away from Hubert and toward this little girl. She recalled that Hubert as a baby sucked vigorously at the silk trimming of his baby blanket. Eventually he transferred the sucking to his pillow which he grasped when he went to bed. At the age of sixteen, Hubert was still sucking his thumb.

+ beatings*

2. Hubert's father made it clear he "wouldn't lay a hand on the kids" because he feared his own strength. Hubert's mother, therefore, disciplined the boy. Hubert indicated that he was very little when he got his worst spankings with a belt.

+ punitive
  yelling*

3. In turn, the mother complained that the father made Hubert nervous by *constantly* yelling at him for his laziness.

+ anal
  stimulation*

4. The mother "reproved" Hubert for soiling his diapers when he was three and four years old. At that time, the mother made "common use" of suppositories and enemas.

Behavioral Symptoms correlated with
adult punitive and excretory contacts with children

+ negative
behavior
(reversals)

1. "If you don't do this," the mother would threaten, "I'll break your arm." In return, Hubert made a point of doing the opposite of what his mother asked of him. "If my mother asks me to go to the store," Hubert explained, "I say I can't go right away. . . . When my mother wants my hair short I wear it long." Hubert often turned away from his mother's requests by pretending not to hear her.

+ learning*
(level 2)

The same situation was reactivated in school. In the third grade, when Hubert's teacher called him "stupid" in front of the class, Hubert thereupon "lost interest" in the class for the rest of the year and had to repeat the grade. Hubert also had repeated the second grade and at sixteen was just passing the eighth grade, this despite his possessing an average intelligence (full-scale Bellevue Wechsler score of 98).

Fortunately, the diagnostic interviews, which ended in a meeting consisting of Hubert, his parents and their therapists, served to help Hubert with his learning problem. It was pointed out to the entire family that not only was Hubert's intelligence normal but that he was rebelling against the whole family's devaluation of his abilities. Even before his subsequent year of therapy, the school reported that Hubert's schoolwork had markedly improved.

+ lying*

Another aspect of Hubert's negative behavior involved his confabulation at home and with his friends to build himself up, e.g., to let everyone know how good he was in football. His preoccupation with lying became intense enough to form the nucleus of a paranoid-like delusion in the making: Hubert described as one of his presenting problems a concern that the boys "talked behind my back" and had been saying that he was a *"liar."*

+ negative
emotion

2. Hubert's paranoid concerns that friends were talking *behind his back,* i.e., against him, clearly reflected a problem in negative emotion.

+ excretory
symptoms*

3. As a child, Hubert suffered from constipation.

In keeping with this history, Hubert would not take a bath for two weeks at a time. When he was first seen at the clinic his face was covered with impetigo, an infection with a predilection for dirt. Hubert picked at the dirty bandages on his face to make the messy disturbance worse.

+ non-organic
illness*
+ pains*

4. Hubert suffered from *severe headaches* which appeared when he "was asked to do something" and when his father got angry at him "which was often."

Of note, Hubert experienced his first seminal emission after he had been kicked in the testicles.[1]

Sources of Stimulation:
children's tactile and visual erogenous contacts with the adult body

−/+ sleeping in bed with adults* (only one occasion)

1. Hubert slept in bed with his mother on one occasion when he was six years old. More significantly, the father felt that Hubert at the age of sixteen was far too close to his mother physically. Hubert would sit on the arm of her chair; then "they would become physically too demonstrative."

+ adult nudity
−/+ adult genital erotic*

2. Hubert shared the *bath tub with his father until he was five years old.*

Behavioral Symptoms correlated with
children's tactile and visual erogenous contacts with the adult body

+ separation phobia*

1. Hubert displayed a school phobia when he was six. In contrast to his siblings who looked forward to entering school, he would cling to his mother and fought leaving her in the first grade. Hubert was described as always having been a "clinging child." In this connection he was fearful of hospitals and strange situations when he was little.

+ eyes*

2. Hubert suffered from an eye tic during which he would involuntarily blink and rub his eyes.

NOTES

1 Compare with case 34 of Barry who kicked a girl's genitals. In these cases sexuality was directly associated with hurting.

Hubert
40

Stimulation-Symptom-and-Dream-Profile

	+ Separation Phobias
	Night Terrors, Twilight States
Sleep in Bed with Adult	Irrational Fears: Other
	Irrational Tempers
Adult Genital Erotic	Sexual Symptoms
	Biting/Cutting, etc.
View Adult Coitus	+ Eyes
	Fire

content of dreams and symptoms

	+ Learning Problems (levels 2 or 3, etc.)
+ Punitive Yelling	+ Lying and Delinquency
	Reversal of Affect
+ Beatings	Closing Down Upon, Kill
	Falling

content of dreams and symptoms

	+ Excretory Symptoms and Dreams
	Anal Masturbation
Preoccupation with Child's BM	Enuresis
	+ Illness, etc.
+ Anal Contacts	+ Pain
	Death
	Compulsions

content of dreams and symptoms

Case 41: Irving

Irving's mother hit upon the label "minimal brain damage" to account for his long list of problems. At the age of eleven, Irving had trouble catching a baseball; he was not athletically inclined; he had "two personalities" in that he could be both docile and a "son of a gun"; he sucked his thumb and held onto a blanket; his expression she thought resembled that of a mongoloid; he was "impossibly negativistic and oppositional"; he displayed a severe learning problem. Psychological testing and a thorough medical workup revealed no signs of a neurological disturbance. His I.Q. score of 109 placed Irving's functioning within the normal range.

Sources of Stimulation:
adult punitive and excretory contacts with children

+ early
deprivation

1. Irving was an unwanted baby. When he was born, he had a collapsed lung and a "heart" condition. The mother was told there was "possible water on the brain" and the doctors wanted to check for brain damage. The mother was quite angry because the doctors kept her in suspense. To add to the upset, just before Irving's delivery, the father was hospitalized because of an erroneous diagnosis. What he thought was a heart condition involving a pain in the chest was later diagnosed as a duodenal ulcer.

When Irving was three months old, he developed pneumonia and was not expected to live. He was baptized by the priest and last rites were administered. It took him a full month to begin feeding normally; the parents considered all his developmental milestones to be slow.

The mother, overburdened by the extra care for Irving, became exhausted and suffered a mental breakdown when he was nine months old. She was hospitalized for nine days and was treated with a tranquilizer. By the time Irving was ten months old, he was "extremely nervous." He threw his food about and was generally hard to handle. Both parents concluded they had never derived any pleasure or joy from him.

+ punitive
yelling*

2. Irving's mother regularly lost "all self-control" when Irving would "get under her skin," which was most of the time. His parents continuously battled over him. The father felt he could no longer cope with the mother's fighting the boy. On the other hand, the mother claimed she could no longer put up with the father using Irving to vent *his* frightening, violent temper.

3. Irving's adolescent brother Cass, age fifteen, joined the family in using

163

+ beatings*
Irving for a whipping boy. Irving complained: "Cass won't stop hitting me. He is always picking on me. When he is mad he can't leave me alone. He takes it out on me." Whereas Cass hit with his fist, the father and mother used the strap. Irving said they hit him about every three weeks. He told his mother that her being upset was her own fault and claimed that she would strap him for nothing. However, Irving was most frightened by his father's loss of control.

+ adult
defecation
4. The mother and father regularly defecated in Irving's presence.

Behavioral Symptoms correlated with
adult punitive and excretory contacts with children

1. At home, Irving consistently dawdled, i.e., withheld and "balked" at the mother's every request. She described him as "totally negativistic and defiant."

+ enuresis*
Age eleven, he still would occasionally wet himself.

+ negative
behavior
Irving was equally negativistic at school and summarized one of his presenting problems: "I do not want to work in school." The teacher complained that he did "absolutely nothing for himself" and often refused to do his work. Sometimes he would simply sit on the classroom floor. At the time of his refer-

+ learning*
(level 2)
ral, Irving was repeating the fourth grade. His teacher wrote: "Irving tends to have a very short attention span. He seldom finishes his work or else takes a great deal of time completely out of proportion for the work assigned. His behavior leads to a growing antagonism with the other children."

+ falling*
2. During two separate diagnostic workups, Irving related a particular nightmare which troubled him: "I was on a bridge which was *falling* apart. Everybody went over it. There was a sign: 'Go at your own risk.' It was the highest bridge in the world. I *fell* off."

Sources of Stimulation:
children's tactile and visual erogenous contacts with the adult body

− / + sleeping in
bed with adult*
1. Eleven-year-old Irving still got into his father's bed about once a month.

2. He saw his mother, father and adolescent brother nude in the bathroom

+ adult nudity
and was often present while they urinated. He would also see his adolescent brother nude in the bedroom which they shared.

Behavioral Symptoms correlated with
children's tactile and visual erogenous contacts with the adult body

+ / − persistent
separation
phobia*
1. Irving often resisted going to school: he routinely dawdled while he was dressing; then if he were late he would try to stay at home to avoid the chance of being sent to the principal's office.

+ nightmares
2. During two diagnostic studies, Irving spoke of his nightmares about "some mad clown trying to get me" and about "falling off a bridge."

+ irrational
tempers*

Irving described his "principal problem": "When I do something wrong my mother gets too nerved up and I go crazy, then I don't know what I am saying."

Irving
41

Stimulation-Symptom-and-Dream-Profile

	+ Separation Phobias	
	Night Terrors, Twilight States	
Sleep in Bed with Adult	Irrational Fears: Other	
	+ Irrational Tempers	
Adult Genital Erotic	Sexual Symptoms	
	Biting/Cutting, etc.	⎫ *content of*
View Adult Coitus	Eyes	⎬ *dreams and*
	Fire	⎭ *symptoms*

	+ Learning Problems (levels 2 or 3, etc.)	
+ Punitive Yelling	Lying and Delinquency	
	Reversal of Affect	
+ Beatings	Closing Down Upon, Kill	⎫ *content of* ⎬ *dreams and*
	+ Falling	⎭ *symptoms*

	Excretory Symptoms and Dreams	
	Anal Masturbation	
Preoccupation with Child's BM	+ Enuresis	
	Illness, etc.	⎫ *content of*
Anal Contacts	Pain	⎬ *dreams and*
	Death	⎭ *symptoms*
	Compulsions	

Case 42: Jesse

Jesse, almost thirteen years of age, was attending a special school for children with learning problems. He had entered this school the preceding year because of his inability to do better than third-grade work in public school. Yet, on the Bellevue Intelligence test, Jesse earned a Full Scale I.Q. score of 101.

Of central concern to the diagnostic team was the mother's infantilization of this thirteen-year-old boy. She liked to tickle Jesse's feet, arms and neck when she put him to bed at night. It was she who brushed Jesse's teeth each morning and helped wash his "privates" and his "behind" in the bathtub to keep him clean. In this way, Jesse was constantly rewarded for passive surrender to his mother's ministrations and for pleasing his mother by remaining like a helpless infant. At the age of eight, he had just learned to dress himself and as yet could not tie his shoes.

Sources of Stimulation:
adult punitive and excretory contacts with children[1]

+ / – early
deprivation

1. Jesse was born seven months after conception and weighed only four pounds. The mother stated she was *depressed* at the time of his birth. He was slow in learning to talk.

+ beatings*

2. Jesse's mother answered the diagnostic questions as follows:

Question: Is your boy ever naughty? At such times what do you do to correct his behavior?

Answer: Spankings.

Question: Does your child get upset when he gets a spanking? Does he get resentful if you ever feel it is necessary to give him a strapping?

Answer: He gets very upset. Yes, he gets resentful. He can get evil.

Question: How often does he act up to the point that he needs a spanking?

Answer: A few times a week.

Question: What single method of spanking or strapping has proved most effective? a single swat? several? five to ten?

+ beatings*

Answer: *Several swats with a leather belt.*

Question: What were the circumstances of the worst punishment your boy ever had to receive? How was he punished?

Answer: He's broken windows and has been throwing things out of windows. *I'd give him a strapping.*

Question: What are the differences in your approach from that of your spouse?

Answer: He will beat him too. When he gives *a strapping, Jesse will later come out crying.*

Eventually, it became apparent that these casual references to strapping reflected the mother's extensive use of strapping as a means of disciplining Jesse.

+ punitive
yelling*

Question: Does your boy act up continually so that it is necessary to yell at him? Do you have to yell at him frequently? several times a month? several times a week? daily? constantly?

Answer: He can do a good job on me. Yes, I can yell at him several times a week.

Question: Are you upset by fights with your husband? Please explain. Does Jesse hear any of the fighting? Does he make any comments about it? How do you think he reacts to the upsets? Whose side does he take?

Answer: Yeah, I got upset New Year's night. *My husband was shaking me and I was hitting him.*

Of note, among his "presenting" problems, Jesse included, "I don't like people fighting all the time."

+ adult
preoccupation
with child's
BM*
+ adult
defecation

3. The mother helped wipe Jesse at the toilet until he was five or six years old.

At the age of thirteen, Jesse was still coming into the bathroom while his mother was defecating in the toilet. She explained, "He just turns his head. I say 'O.K.' and then he takes off. He's not embarrassed if he comes in while I'm having a bowel movement."

Behavioral Symptoms correlated with
adult punitive and excretory contacts with children

+ negative
behavior

+ learning*
(level 3)

1. Jesse's therapist concluded: "Jesse appears to have become to an excessive degree bound up and frozen by a world of destruction, severe punishment, and unpredictable behavior." Jesse's withholding and restriction contributed to his massive learning problem. When he was eight years old, with an I.Q. of 101, he had not been able to count beyond twelve. Contributing to Jesse's learning problem was his dislike of loud voices and noise. He explained "I don't like to be around a lot of kids for they make noise and throw erasers."

2. Jesse found it difficult to report any problem that bothered him. However, finally he stated: "When I see a cat or dog — I like a lot of animals — I

+ closing down upon destructively* (crush)

+ hurting

+ death* (ghosts)

+ excretory symptoms*

feel sorry for him for *a car might hit him* — and the car might not have cared."[2]

Yet Jesse liked to get into fights. When his mother was asked "How does your child like to show affection?" the mother explained "he likes to aggravate you and bother you; he will hit me a couple of times. He likes to get me and the kids upset." Of course, such behavior further provoked his being hit and hurt. The mother concluded "I think he likes spankings."

3. From the ages of three through five, Jesse experienced nightmares from which he would awake with visions of ghosts threatening him in the dark.

4. Jesse's withholdingness affected his capacity to defecate: he was able "to go" only once a week, even though his constipation resulted in a painful bowel movement. Jesse regularly defecated in his pants until he was seven. At the age of thirteen he still was troubled with frequent "accidents." "I go into the house and change if I have an accident. I'm embarrassed." Jesse explained: "Sometimes when I play football I have to go. One time I went in the street and got it all over me."

Sources of Stimulation:
children's tactile and visual erogenous contacts with the adult body

− / + sleeping in bed with adults* (frequency?)

1. Between the ages of three and five, Jesse would come into his mother's bed because of severe nightmares.

Behavioral Symptoms correlated with
children's tactile and visual erogenous contacts with the adult body

+ night terrors* (hallucinations)

1. Jesse's "terrible nightmares" culminated in "night terrors": even after he would awake, he would see things in the dark. In a panic he would call out about a ghost in the room, "It's there, it's there."

+ eyes* (reading problem)

2. Jesse's special reading teacher reported that despite Jesse's normal intelligence he still could not read words which they had been reviewing for six months.

NOTES

[1] Case material pertaining to "sources of stimulation" was acquired via the questionnaire form in Appendix 1 of the text.

[2] Jesse is like the animal who is smashed; the mother is like the car which smashes without caring.

Jesse
42

Stimulation-Symptom-and-Dream-Profile

	Separation Phobias
	+ Night Terrors, Twilight States
Sleep in Bed with Adult	Irrational Fears: Other
	Irrational Tempers
Adult Genital Erotic	Sexual Symptoms
	Biting/Cutting, etc.
View Adult Coitus	+ Eyes
	Fire

content of dreams and symptoms

	+ Learning Problems (levels 2 or 3, etc.)
+ Punitive Yelling	Lying and Delinquency
	Reversal of Affect
+ Beatings	+ Closing Down Upon, Kill
	Falling

content of dreams and symptoms

	+ Excretory Symptoms and Dreams
	Anal Masturbation
+ Preoccupation with Child's BM	Enuresis
	Illness, etc.
Anal Contacts	Pain
	+ Death
	Compulsions

content of dreams and symptoms

Case 43: Kevin

Kevin was a pathetic, thin, silent little boy of eight, with big sad eyes and thumb in mouth when his mother brought him for his first day of therapy. She had him all "dolled up" in a red, white and blue sailor suit so that he appeared like a trained monkey dressed for a circus exhibition. The school adjustment counselor had been struck by Kevin's forlorn restriction and inability to learn in class and felt that he was in dire need of therapy. Kevin was performing at a retarded level in school and was about to be placed in a class with the "retards" even though intelligence testing, when administered with utmost patience, revealed a performance in the superior range.

Sources of Stimulation:
adult punitive and excretory contacts with children

+ early
  deprivation

1. Kevin's mother, who as a young girl knew only a sordid life filled with poverty, screaming, beatings and sexual abuse, wanted one thing in life: to be beautiful, to have a beautiful home and to have a beautiful family living within it. All her efforts were directed toward these goals. She spent two hours each morning in front of the mirror while she made sure she was "perfectly" beautiful. She ran up enormous bills at the department stores in order to buy beautiful dresses, bills which her husband could not pay for from the meager salary he earned as a salesman in a music store. She endlessly purchased expensive furniture, rugs, drapes and accoutrements for the house. Often she would not allow her family to use her prized furniture for fear that it might be spoiled.

It is, therefore, understandable that the mother had little time to devote to Kevin when he was an infant. She was too preoccupied with the perfection of her appearance and that of her home. Furthermore, she was completely intolerant if in any way Kevin became messy. She would punish him for drooling, vomiting or defecating at the wrong time, or crying when she had "important" things to do. As Kevin grew up the mother became so punitive about any spots of dirt, urine or excrement, even in the bathroom, that both Kevin and his younger brother developed the habit of defecating and urinating outside of the house, on someone's lawn, or even in strangers' cars.

Neither could Kevin's mother enjoy feeding him when he was a baby. Usually Kevin's bottle was propped up in the crib for him to tackle as best he could.

+ beatings*

2-3. But the punishments and strappings which the parents gave Kevin in order to make him look and act "beautifully" were the worst part of his experience. He was strapped daily by both parents. The father, like his wife, wanted everything perfect, especially when he came home from a hard day's work. Therefore, the children were not to talk or make any noise at all at the table lest their activity spoil the peace and harmony of the home. Kevin and his brother would be screamed at as well as hit for the slightest infraction of parental law.

An example of the parents' capacity to vent their rage upon Kevin took place in his second year of life. Kevin had been playing with some black paint and had managed to get some of it on his face and upon the carpet of his room just as his mother entered. The mother, in her fury, pulled off Kevin's clothes, placed him in the bathtub and then poured turpentine all over his body to teach him a lesson and to make sure that all of the black paint was removed. Kevin never forgot this memory of his mother's rage and the turpentine burning his face, his eyes and mouth. Neither did he forget the daily beatings he had received from his father from earliest childhood.

+ punitive
yelling*

To add to the household disturbance, Kevin's father indulged in narcissistic rages not only at the children but also at his wife when she didn't exactly do his bidding, e.g., if his supper were not ready on time, if a certain food were missing from the menu or if his wife did not please him by immediately acceding to his sexual demands. As a result, Kevin's father screamed at his wife in front of his two children and frequently ended by physically abusing her. Several times he beat and bruised her so severely that she had to be taken to the hospital for emergency care.

− / + anal
stimulation* (only
one occasion)

4. Kevin recalled being given an enema as a little boy. In particular, he recalled his mother holding him down as she administered the enema.

Behavioral Symptoms correlated with
adult punitive and excretory contacts with children

+ negative
behavior

1. Kevin was withdrawn at home, at school and in therapy. His favorite occupation was sucking his thumb by himself or in front of the family TV.

It was so difficult to enable Kevin to talk or to express himself in any way during his therapy hours for the first three years of treatment, that the decision was made to remove him from the home and send him to a special boarding school.[1]

+ learning*
(level 3)

Kevin's negativism was reflected most clearly by his severe learning problem. In school he was functioning at a retarded level and it was only after Kevin's restriction was replaced by overt expressions of hate, defiance and sadism (see below) that his learning problem disappeared: at the age of eighteen Kevin achieved superior grades and was accepted for admission at several high-quality colleges.

When Kevin began to give up his restriction and his learning problems, his

+ delinquency*

negative behavior unfortunately became expressed for several years in delinquent opposition to authority and rules. In complete defiance of therapeutic
goals, he cheated the boys at school in gambling, lent money to them at exor-
bitant rates, stoned a neighbor's house, started indulging in alcohol, marijuana
and pornography, got kicked out of school and then secretly took a job with
law breakers, etc. Fortunately, Kevin finally gave up his delinquency, but only
after a full-fledged battle with his therapist.

+ negative
emotion

2. When Kevin came home from "prep school" for weekends, vacations and
summer recess, he continued to be seen in therapy once or twice a week. As the
years passed, his restriction was replaced by an ability to bring in his thoughts,
phantasies and dreams. These soon focused on one basic theme: dislike, hate
and destruction. No matter where one would turn in the recorded notations of
his hours, the same repeated theme of dislike and hate dominated his thinking.
To quote typical examples from Kevin's hours, he confided: "I used to *hate*
coming in. . . . I just *hated* coming in to therapy. . . . My friend loved to act
like *Hitler,* we *hated* Jews. . . . I always *hated* spiders. . . . I *find fault* with
everything that I *don't like.* . . . I find it so difficult to be nice to people after
I've *disliked* them. . . . Sandy was one of my closest friends but now I *hate*
him. . . . I *don't like* it when girls get dressed up. . . . I *don't like* the name
Bill. . . . I *don't like* criminals but I identify with them . . . the kids would *hate*
me because the proctor favored me. . . . Bill's roommate, I *can't stand* him;
he's a pest; he thinks we are his friends but we *hate* his guts; . . . this girl I met,
her father *hated* my family. . . . The teachers came to *hate* us because we were
militant . . . the only thing I *did not like* about Mr. R., he cheated on his girl.
. . . The first time I saw Nick I *hated* his guts: he had a *hate* problem. Nick
hated the janitors. . . . I dreamt about a Volkswagen. . . . I *hate* Volkswagens.
. . . I *couldn't stand* that kid Andy, the way he acted and the way he looked at
me with bulging eyes of *hate.* . . . I have this theory: if someone has the littlest
thing wrong, I *hate* the person . . . ," etc., etc., etc.

Interpretation did not stop this stream of hate and dislike. In vain, Kevin
and his therapist looked at the relation of his thoughts to the beatings and hate
he had received from his parents. Neither did education and sublimation stop
this flow of hate. With help, Kevin secured volunteer work at a local hospital
where he could help those who were afflicted and exposed to pain. Kevin also
got a volunteer job helping groups of retarded children. His work with these
children offered him one of the happiest summers he had ever experienced, yet
his obsession with hate continued.

+ freezing of
affect

Emotional negativism was also displayed in Kevin's marked freezing of affect; for Kevin never seemed angry during his therapy hours. His tone of voice
was always gentle, subdued and sad, in dramatic contrast to the content of his
therapeutic material and the school reports of his delinquent acting out.

+ closing down
upon
destructively*

3. Kevin recalled that as a child he tied his brother to a post and hit him;

+ pain* (needles)

at camp he once shot the brother with a BB gun. As a little child he "liked" getting needles. He "liked" throwing rocks at houses. He "loved" to act like Hitler. He also had thoughts of hurting himself to make his father feel badly for him. When he began to hang out with delinquent destructive children at public school, it was decided he should be in a corrective environment if he were to get help at all.

+ delinquency*

But his acting out continued surreptitiously at private school. He put a Nazi flag in his dormitory to upset the Jewish cleaning lady. He hung around kids who liked to beat up Jewish boys. He became friendly with a boy who pushed kids, kicked dogs and slashed tires. He was not upset when a boy threw a dog in the river and later burned an animal after pouring kerosene on it. It was unclear whether this latter incident was a reality or a daydream reflecting the early episode in his own life when his mother poured kerosene all over him.

+ torture
+ pain*

Kevin's sexual thoughts also were dominated by pain and hurt. For example, as a teenager he became preoccupied with thoughts of putting a glass rod in a penis and cracking the glass. He also was interested in stories similar to those reported by Freud's "Rat Man" — stories about victims' heads being trapped in a cage with rats.

+ closing down upon destructively* (crush)

+ killing*
+ falling*

Kevin's dreams at night directly focused upon these same themes involving destruction and being hurt, crushed or killed. For example, Kevin obsessively reported the following dreams: (a) "a boy was run over by a car"; (b) "a ruler started wars"; (c) "the god of wars"; (d) "men in German uniforms destroying everything"; (e) "this guy who got hit by a subway car"; (f) "this guy who told me I was to build a big army"; (g) "a person attacked by rats"; (h) "pushing my brother off a roof"; (i) "someone jumping out of a window"; (j) "my mother falling and my father falling as they were skiing"; (k) "someone dropped a boulder on the teacher"; (l) "Napoleon on a horse running over my brother."

+ excretory problems*

4. Kevin recalled that when he was first learning to use the toilet, he would sometimes stand up and have his bowel movement against the wall. He also recalled defecating in the bathtub as a child and being hit for it. At the age of eight he still had "accidents" in his pants. One time he "did it" in his pants while he was walking down the middle of the street; he seemed unconcerned that the excrement was dripping down the back of his leg.

Prior to therapy, Kevin and his brother would put excrement on sticks and "wing it" at houses, cars, mailboxes, etc. Sometimes they walked around with the excrement on the sticks in order to shock and frighten observers. "Everyone would want to run away."

On one occasion, Kevin recalled having a bowel movement on paper outside his home; he then doused the paper and feces with kerosene[2] and lit it on fire. As he tried to stamp out the fire he got the excrement all over his feet. Kevin also urged his little brother to defecate from a rooftop onto the path below.

Later in childhood, Kevin's voyeuristic sexual activity regularly involved the "rear end." At camp he busied himself looking up a boy's rectum and at school watched two children indulging in anal play. Another time, a boy stuck a finger into Kevin's rectum.

Sources of Stimulation:
children's tactile and visual erogenous contacts with the adult body

−/+sleeping in bed with adults*

1. Until his eighth year, when therapy began, Kevin and his brother liked to climb in bed with his father in order to read the Sunday funnies together.

+adult nudity

2. Prior to therapy Kevin had occasionally seen his parents without clothes.

Behavioral Symptoms correlated with
children's tactile and visual erogenous contacts with the adult body

+fire*

1. Kevin, it will be recalled, on one occasion defecated out of doors on a piece of newspaper, doused the paper with kerosene and lit it on fire.

+sexual symptoms*

For Kevin, all emotional discharge — fear, anger, separation anxiety, etc. — if present, was completely restricted and inhibited, except for his sexual preoccupations which became focused upon excretory body parts and functions.

NOTES

1 Even though Kevin's mother had completely stopped beating him, she continued to be controlling about his behavior. In addition, the father resisted therapy and sometimes insisted on a father's "rights" in the home if he saw fit to beat his children. It was hoped that at "prep school" Kevin could profit from "milieu" therapy and protection from his angry home environment.

2 Once again there appears a repetition of Kevin's early imprints of punishment during which he was covered with kerosene.

Kevin
43

Stimulation-Symptom-and-Dream-Profile

	Separation Phobias
	Night Terrors, Twilight States
Sleep in Bed with Adult	Irrational Fears: Other
	Irrational Tempers
Adult Genital Erotic	+ Sexual Symptoms
	Biting/Cutting, etc.
View Adult Coitus	Eyes
	+ Fire

Biting/Cutting, etc. ⎫ *content of*
Eyes   ⎬ *dreams and*
+ Fire   ⎭ *symptoms*

	+ Learning Problems (levels 2 or 3, etc.)
+ Punitive Yelling	+ Lying and Delinquency
	Reversal of Affect
+ Beatings	+ Closing Down Upon, Kill
	+ Falling

+ Closing Down Upon, Kill ⎫ *content of*
+ Falling   ⎬ *dreams and*
                           ⎭ *symptoms*

	+ Excretory Symptoms and Dreams
	Anal Masturbation
Preoccupation with Child's BM	Enuresis
	Illness, etc.
Anal Contacts	+ Pain
	Death
	Compulsions

+ Pain   ⎫ *content of*
Death   ⎬ *dreams and*
Compulsions ⎭ *symptoms*

Case 44: Leon

Leon's temper tantrums and defiance at home brought him and his mother to the clinic for a diagnostic evaluation when Leon was eight years old.

The diagnostic interviews as well as the next four years of therapy revealed the seriousness of the mother's own problems to which Leon was exposed.

The mother was engulfed by *negative emotion* and *negative behavior* as well as a drive to hurt, presumably because of her own past exposure to punishment stimulation. When Leon was two years old, the mother brought herself to a hospital emergency psychiatric service; she was terrified that she might kill herself or her children. When Leon's mother herself was a little child, her own brother died at the age of two years while he was being left in her care. Feelings in relation to this baby brother were reactivated during Leon's infancy and reached a peak of disturbance when Leon became two years old.

The mother experienced such feelings of worthlessness and badness that she could not tolerate any criticism. Rather she spent most of her free time venting her negative emotion upon those around her, especially upon her husband. Denigration of her husband accented her role as the self-sacrificing martyr of the family. She let others know that she was the one who "carried the burden of the family from every point of view down to having to buy my husband's own suits." In therapy, "the mother reviewed interminably the father's incompetency, his inadequacy as a wage earner, his refusal to take a stronger role as a parent." In front of Leon, the mother spoke of the stupidity of her husband's behavior in contrast to Leon's brightness. She would say to her husband, "Leon's problems are due to you because your son is more intelligent than you are." Then a few minutes later she would say to Leon, "I hate you, get dressed, go out, so I won't have to see you."

Even though Leon's father tried to be helpful he "never could win." For example, one Sunday the mother awoke late and discovered that her husband had washed the kitchen floor. She became very angry with him and said "Don't do woman's work." On another occasion she sent him to clean a storage closet and became infuriated when he complained that the shelves were cluttered with junk. He showed her a bottle of red liquid medicine and asked "Why do you keep this stuff?" The mother became so angry at her husband for talking to her this way that she picked up the bottle and threw it at him. She became terrified as the red medicine poured down his face.

With Leon, the mother often used an additional technique to increase her

176

importance: she infantilized him. When Leon was eleven years old she was still giving him his bath.

Sources of Stimulation:
adult punitive and excretory contacts with children

+ early
deprivation

1. The mother's pregnancy was not a happy one. She commented: "I gnawed inside from the moment I conceived until I delivered the baby." And her "troubles" continued after Leon's birth. A letter from the psychiatrist who treated her when Leon was two years old indicated that from the time of Leon's birth the mother suffered symptoms of depression, crying spells and weight loss. Her depression had become more and more intense during Leon's infancy until he approached the age of two.

Leon suffered from respiratory difficulties from early infancy and "couldn't breathe when a nipple was in his mouth." He, therefore, "developed difficulties around eating." At the age of three months, he had to undergo a tracheotomy to relieve his obstructed breathing. By fifteen months he had to have an adenoidectomy, an operation which had to be repeated three years later.

From the time Leon could crawl he was *hyperactive;* he would bang his head against the refrigerator and hurt himself. Also he would bite his forefinger until finally it became "misshapen."

+ anal
stimulation*

2. At the age of four, Leon was given suppositories by his mother for fecal withholding. The mother was so upset about Leon's bowel training that it was at this time that she first considered seeking psychiatric help for him.

+ beatings*

3. Leon's first memory was of being hit in the face with a stick. "It bled and it needed stitches." This was presumably a condensed screen memory based upon many similar memories. Leon indeed was exposed to much hitting throughout his life. His mother stated that the *only punishment that she had found effective with Leon was using a strap on him.* The strap often was used for inconsequential misdeeds, e.g., when Leon spilled soup and told his grandmother to quit yelling at him.

Leon's father also lost control, got angry and hit Leon for breaches of discipline. Leon felt his father hated him for it was always Leon, not his sister, whom the father scolded and hit.

+ punitive
yelling*

Leon constantly would find himself in the middle of his mother's noisy battles with his father, his grandmother, his uncle, etc. During family therapy, Leon finally commented that he was "tired of all the screaming and hollering at home."

Behavioral Symptoms correlated with
adult punitive and excretory contacts with children

+ lying*

1. During the intake interview, Leon's mother complained that Leon "cries whenever he gets upset about anything and lies all the time."

Leon did relatively well in grade school. However, his work became spotty and he occasionally flunked a subject. Because of the unevenness of his work, his teacher laughed when Leon expressed a wish to apply for entrance to the city's honor high school. Leon pulled up his grades to prove his teacher wrong and eventually was accepted at the honor high school. However, Leon, despite his ability, did not do well there and was not promoted.

+ learning*
(level 2)

2. Leon disliked public school, Sunday school, his therapist and himself. He once said during therapy "I'm the worst boy in the world in every way." But more frequently, like his mother, he took his anger out on others. When his therapist would not play basketball with him, he yelled "you're unfair. I can't stand it. I'm *never* coming back. I *don't* need you. You're always saying things that *upset* me. I'll get a nervous *breakdown* if I see you anymore." He went on to say that he *hated* his therapist and was going to see to it that the therapist's salary would be taken away. When the therapist later wanted to "work through" Leon's feelings regarding the therapist's plans to leave the clinic Leon responded "Good riddance!"

+ negative
emotion

3. The one dream which Leon reported during his diagnostic had to do with hurting: "I was playing basketball and I broke a window. The police were coming after me."

+ closing down
upon
destructively*

Leon directly expressed a wish to "kill" his mother and wished her "dead," especially when she wouldn't get him the things he wanted. Leon kept shouting during one temper tantrum "the rat killed the mother; the rat killed the mother."

+ killing*
+ death*

In addition, Leon was concerned hypochondriacally about his body health and he suffered from headaches. He claimed he did not want to go to school because he was afraid of getting *germs* there. As for the headaches, he demonstrated their manner of onset during his diagnostic visits. As he began telling how his mother hit him right on the mouth whenever he said the word "shit," he became very nervous and complained "I want to go. Now I've got a *headache.*" Somewhat later, Leon decided to tell his therapist his problems by staging a puppet play. As the "curtain" went up, and the therapist supportively clapped for a moment to show approval, Leon shouted "Don't clap. It gives me a *headache.*"

+ preoccupation
with illness*

+ pain* (and
aches)

4. Leon could not "move his bowels" in the toilet until he was five years old. When he was ready to have a bowel movement, he would scream for a diaper which his mother finally would give him.

+ excretory
symptoms*

Sources of Stimulation:
children's tactile and visual erogenous contacts with the adult body

1. At the age of eight, Leon was still *sleeping in bed between both parents* several times a week.

+ sleeping in bed
with adults*

2. Frequently in the mornings Leon would see his father unclothed.

+ adult nudity

Behavioral Symptoms correlated with
children's tactile and visual erogenous contacts with the adult body

+ separation
phobia*

1. Leon was terrified of going to school and tried to stay home for fear he would be exposed to "getting germs." When his family insisted upon his leaving home, Leon ended up late because "they" made him go.

Later, after bed-sharing had stopped, Leon did manage to go to camp and to enjoy himself there.

+ irrational fears*

2. Leon was not only afraid of germs; he was also afraid of the dark and of going to sleep alone (a presenting symptom). His pediatrician suggested a mild sedative to treat his agitation at night.

+ irrational
tempers*

3. Leon's tempers provided his primary referral symptom. His pediatrician thought that the prescribed sedative would help his tempers as well as his night fears. However, Leon's tempers continued unabated.[1] During one temper outburst, he violently threw a telephone at the bedroom wall. On another occasion, he scattered bread crumbs in his mother's bed.

+ sexual
symptoms*

4. The mother complained that Leon for years had a problem with masturbation. He masturbated constantly "from the time he was very small. This used to be very embarrassing because he would do it in public or anywhere." It didn't matter who was around. The mother would try to get him interested in "something else." If she found him masturbating in bed she'd get him up and "interest him in a game or something."

At the age of twelve and a half, Leon also was habitually rummaging through his sister's drawers and handling her personal clothing.

+ / − fire*

5. The mother had been concerned about Leon's playing with matches. She recalled that when he was "very young" Leon had held a whisk broom over an open gas flame.

NOTES

[1] Along with the mother's custom of continuing to bathe Leon in the bathtub.

Leon
44

Stimulation-Symptom-and-Dream-Profile

	+ Separation Phobias
	Night Terrors, Twilight States
+ Sleep in Bed with Adult	+ Irrational Fears: Other
	+ Irrational Tempers
Adult Genital Erotic	+ Sexual Symptoms
	Biting/Cutting, etc.
View Adult Coitus	Eyes
	+ Fire

Biting/Cutting, etc. } *content of*
Eyes } *dreams and*
+ Fire } *symptoms*

+ Learning Problems (levels 2 or 3, etc.)
+ Punitive Yelling   + Lying and Delinquency
                            Reversal of Affect
+ Beatings   + Closing Down Upon, Kill } *content of*
                            Falling   } *dreams and*
                                                       } *symptoms*

+ Excretory Symptoms and Dreams
                                   Anal Masturbation
Preoccupation with Child's BM   Enuresis
                                 + Illness, etc.   } *content of*
+ Anal Contacts   + Pain   } *dreams and*
                                 + Death   } *symptoms*
                                   Compulsions

Case 45: Malcolm

Malcolm's parents requested a diagnostic evaluation because of their intense fear of the "violence" Malcolm had been displaying since "very early childhood." Although the parents had not requested a diagnostic evaluation for Malcolm until he was ten, the mother claimed that it "just" seemed to her he had been "different" since birth. From that time on, he seemed to "reject" his mother and reach out to his father. By the time Malcolm was three months old, there was something "unnatural" about the way he did not look at her or respond to her when she went to the crib. Furthermore, from the time he was "eight months old onward it seemed that Malcolm had been intent upon killing the cat." Finally, when Malcolm was only two years old both parents locked their bedroom door for fear he would use a knife to "murder" them in their sleep.

Malcolm's diagnostic workup when he was ten and a half included a thorough neurological study including an electroencephalogram. The completely negative findings of this study disconcerted Malcolm's mother, who had persistently clung to the idea that there had always been something organically wrong with the child.

Actually, Malcolm, with an I.Q. of 118, had been an A student in school until the past year when his performance suddenly dropped sharply. And apparently it was this appearance of Malcolm's learning problem which precipitated the parents' decision to refer Malcolm for therapy. Malcolm's "violence" for a period of "ten years" apparently in itself had not concerned them enough to warrant their seeking therapy earlier. As might be surmised, Malcolm's mother later admitted during her own therapy that her fears of Malcolm's violence more appropriately pertained to her past fears of her own abusive father. She realized that when Malcolm exhibited a tantrum, she experienced the same feelings of fear and repulsion which she remembered having towards her father.

Sources of Stimulation:
adult punitive and excretory contacts with children

+ early
    deprivation

1. Malcolm's mother spoke of her own father's desertion when her younger brother was born. Many years later, at the time of Malcolm's birth, the mother again was faced with rejection, this time by her husband carrying on an affair with another woman. Confessing that her anger toward her husband and his mistress had been let out on the little baby, the mother divulged her guilt over

never having offered Malcolm love. She recalled that her breasts were so sore during his early infancy that *Malcolm was constantly hungry.* According to her story, it became necessary to introduce solid foods when he was only three weeks old. Since that time, Malcolm had severe problems about receiving food. At the time of his referral, there were few foods that he would eat; he would allow his mother to prepare almost nothing for him. At the age of ten, Malcolm was still repeating his early experiences of dissatisfaction with his mother's supply of food.

As Malcolm approached two years of age, he suffered additional painful traumas. For several months he had been suffering from ear infections which required repeated lancing. Eventually, it was necessary for Malcolm to be hospitalized. He was taken from his parents, put in a straitjacket because of his hysterical struggling and not allowed to see his family for three days.

2. According to the mother, Malcolm, at the age of two, threatened that if he were ever spanked again, he would knife his parents.

+ beatings*

Malcolm himself spoke of his mother using a belt on him and beating him so hard on the leg that he still bore a big scar. Even though his mother lost control easily, Malcolm was more scared of his father's beltings because the father "hits the hardest."

Among the incidents which warranted these beatings, Malcolm reported three examples. He was beaten when: (a) he did not eat his supper;[1] (b) he hit his brother; and (c) he tried to run away at the age of eight.

The father admitted "feeling terrible" about a beating he gave Malcolm a few months prior to Malcolm's referral. To make matters worse, Malcolm provoked one of his teachers to hit him with a ruler.

+ adult
   defecation

3. At the age of ten, Malcolm was still allowed to remain in the bathroom with his mother while she defecated.

Behavioral Symptoms correlated with
adult punitive and excretory contacts with children

+ negative
   behavior

1. Malcolm described his "first" problem: "They tell me to *study* and I *don't study.*" Later, he added, "The teacher will tell me to *get in line* and I *don't get in line.*" Malcolm's negativism affected his learning. Even though he had done very well in the second grade where his teacher had given him special projects because she felt he was so "gifted," yet he became extremely negative in the third grade. He refused to do his arithmetic on the basis that it was ridiculous; then he would concentrate on another subject instead. By the age of nine, Malcolm's learning was so disturbed that he was unable to do the simplest tasks in arithmetic or spelling.[2]

+ learning*
   (level 1; referral
   problem)

Restriction had been a factor which contributed to Malcolm's learning problem. Prior to the onset of his restriction Malcolm actually had been intellectually precocious. He used to cry because he could not read words when he was three. He picked out words to read when he was four and read sentences at five, yet when Malcolm reached nine the extent of "his reading became very constricted in range because he would only look at those books with happy endings."

−/+ lying*

At first, it appeared that Malcolm's learning problems were complemented by problems involving lying and deceit. The mother had claimed that Malcolm was quite a "con-artist," by which she implied that he lied about being beaten. However, during therapy it became clear that it was the mother, not Malcolm, who had been lying to conceal the past history of Malcolm's beatings.

+ negative
emotion

2. Malcolm's negative emotional reactions in school drove his teachers "out of their minds." He was reported to be "contemptuous," "sarcastic" and apparently a great threat to many teachers. He even complained about one teacher to the school principal and asserted that she should be fired because she was "incompetent." By the fourth grade Malcolm's antagonism began to be released upon his peers so that many children hated him.

3. Despite their claim that Malcolm was a "potential killer," Malcolm's parents could support their accusation only by reporting Malcolm's *threats* of harming them or his brother: the mother claimed she once saw Malcolm standing over his brother with a baseball bat and that she saved the brother by screaming from the window. She went on to say that as the brother escaped, Malcolm "smashed the bat to pieces" on a nearby rock. The parents also claimed that Malcolm threatened to kill his father after the father had belted him severely.

+ hurting

In school Malcolm did hurt other children, but not to the point of catastrophe. The teacher informed the parents that he was beating up other children. On the other hand, Malcolm was terrified of violence and hid under his bed if he were exposed to a violent radio or TV program.

+ death*

Even when he was very little, Malcolm was preoccupied with death. For example, he would place a dead bird in his baby blanket and then take the bird to his bed as though it were living. Malcolm's dreams reflected this same preoccupation with death. Within his first diagnostic hour he presented a dream about his "grandmother being run over by a car and killed."

+ killing*

Sources of Stimulation:
children's tactile and visual erogenous contacts with the adult body

−/+ sleeping in
bed with adults*

1-2. Malcolm at the age of ten and a half still "occasionally got into bed with both his parents for a half hour before his going to sleep." Bed-sharing was most often with his father. Malcolm confided that sometimes the father would be nude when they shared the bed together.[3]

+ adult genital
erotic*

+ adult nudity   Malcolm also saw his mother in the nude while she was taking a bath. Conversely, Malcolm would urinate in front of his mother while she was washing in the bathtub.

3. No direct information pertaining to observation of adult genital activity was obtained during this diagnostic. However, the parents did explain that for an extended period the whole family lived in one large room, a likely source for Malcolm's having seen intercourse.

Behavioral Symptoms correlated with
children's tactile and visual erogenous contacts with the adult body

−/+ persistent   1. A letter from Malcolm's school indicated that Malcolm "no longer wants
separation   to go to school."
phobia*

+ irrational fears*   2-3. Malcolm would hide under the bed in *terror* when he heard or saw a
+ nightmares   violent radio or TV program (see above). He also spoke of nightmares he had experienced. One such nightmare featured "a big red thing, as big as a chair. It had something to do with a wand and big teeth." Perhaps related to Malcolm's
+ biting/cutting*   preoccupation with teeth which can cut was his preoccupation with sharp knives
  (teeth)   and hatchets.

+ irrational   4. Malcolm's screaming, threatening tempers frightened both of his par-
  tempers*   ents. Such "fits" which Malcolm later "could not recall" were triggered not only by his parents' threats of punishment but also by "inconsequential" circumstances. For example, when the mother started to cook with onions, Malcolm would break out into "uncontrollable screaming."

5. In family therapy, the mother increasingly became aware of her disturbed feelings toward Malcolm. She reported a dramatic incident during which Malcolm accidentally started a fire in the rubbish can: a fire which threatened
+ fire*   him badly. The mother was able to face her own paralysis in responding to Malcolm's panic when she heard his screaming. Fortunately, her examination of these feelings of hatred toward Malcolm was followed by a "marked improvement" in her ability to feel some love and concern for him.

NOTES

1 Recall that Malcolm's failure to eat stemmed from early deprivation.
2 Malcolm was not left back. Fortunately, his learning problem was not deeply entrenched. Following a year of therapy, Malcolm once again became an "A" student.
3 One of the mother's chief complaints during her first diagnostic interview focused upon Malcolm "always having eyes for his father and not for herself." The mother expressed the wish to get Malcolm out of the house because Malcolm rather than herself was the object of the father's favoritism. Malcolm's sharing a bed with the nude father offered one erogenous source for the establishment of such an "inverse oedipal" struggle.

Malcolm
45

Stimulation-Symptom-and-Dream-Profile

	Separation Phobias	
	Night Terrors, Twilight States	
Sleep in Bed with Adult	+ Irrational Fears: Other	
	+ Irrational Tempers	
+ Adult Genital Erotic	Sexual Symptoms	
	+ Biting/Cutting, etc.	} content of
View Adult Coitus	Eyes	} dreams and
	+ Fire	} symptoms

	+ Learning Problems (levels 2 or 3, etc.)	
Punitive Yelling	Lying and Delinquency	
	Reversal of Affect	
+ Beatings	+ Closing Down Upon, Kill	} content of dreams and
	Falling	} symptoms

	Excretory Symptoms and Dreams	
	Anal Masturbation	
Preoccupation with Child's BM	Enuresis	
	Illness, etc.	} content of
Anal Contacts	Pain	} dreams and
	+ Death	} symptoms
	Compulsions	

Case 46: Nathan

Nathan, a nine-and-a-half-year-old boy with an I.Q. of 125 (Performance score 136, Verbal 110), was seen at the clinic for a diagnostic evaluation. His presenting problems were "aggression, sibling rivalry, and negativism."

Sources of Stimulation
adult punitive and excretory contacts with children

+ early deprivation (of empathic care)

1. Nathan was described as an "anxious baby who constantly cried and who first gave his parents a feeling of desperation and then exasperation when he resisted attempts to be loved and picked up. His parents used to drive him around in their car to try to calm him down, and when this was unsuccessful, his mother would resort to turning on the shower or vacuum to *drown out his cries*." The mother tried to breast-feed Nathan at first, but was too tense and had to substitute bottle feedings. Weaning took place at the age of one and a half when Nathan's brother was born. The parents "simply took the night bottle away from him and let him scream it out."

+ beatings*

2. Nathan was regularly strapped for misbehaving. His mother would hit him with her hand but the father would pull down Nathan's pants and use the strap on him. Unfortunately, the worst of Nathan's beatings began after the parents had consulted a psychologist who had diagnosed "sibling rivalry" as the central problem. Two different approaches were recommended to see which would be more helpful. The first approach was to be extremely permissive, fulfilling as much as possible the boy's need for love and attention. If that didn't help they were to shift and try *extreme* authority based upon punishment. Since application of the first method led to "absolute chaos," the parents soon resorted to the punitive approach with beatings. The father reported that this approach was creating better control in the house but that Nathan showed signs of becoming very frightened of him.

+ punitive yelling*

3. The father was distressed as he confessed how often he lost his temper with Nathan. He described himself as exploding, screaming and pounding his fists during his outbursts. At the end of the diagnostic interviews, Nathan confirmed this report: he drew a picture of his father screaming, with "hot air" blasting from his mouth.

+ anal stimulation*

4. At six months of age Nathan became impacted. Since enemas were unsuccessful, Nathan had to be "flushed" by a doctor.

+ adult
defecation

Nathan's parents often defecated in front of him. Nathan would be soaking in the bathtub while the parents came in to use the toilet.

Behavioral Symptoms
adult punitive and excretory contacts with children

+ negative
behavior

1. "Negativism" was a "face-sheet" presenting problem. In many matters such as taking precautions at dangerous street crossings, Nathan disobeyed all rules which the parents had tried to teach him. Likewise, when his father strapped him for exposing his penis to his brother, Nathan responded by doing it all the more. His father felt that Nathan enjoyed doing the opposite of what was requested and took a "delight in getting him angry." Nathan's beatings for fighting with his brother also resulted in only negative opposition. The father felt that "nothing got through to Nathan," patience, punishment or deprivation. Nathan's negative behavior also was expressed in his poor ability to get along with his peers. He was able to make friends only with two children who were much younger.[1]

+ negative
emotion

2. The marked instability of Nathan's self-esteem was reflected in his intense upsets when he did not get all A's in his school work. When asked during his diagnostic sessions what he didn't like about himself, Nathan replied "I don't like it when I make a mistake in school and don't get an A. Once I got a C in arithmetic, the next day I was sure to get an A."[2]

+ hurting

3. Nathan would consistently break and destroy his siblings' things: he would delight in their misery "without letting up from dawn to dusk." He also would side with children who were ganging up to beat another child. Nathan's preoccupation with hurting was reflected in his dreams. A nightmare he reported in his first interview focused upon destruction: "We were downtown and we had our car there and they were going to blow up the car because they were no good. I was close to the car and it blew up. I woke up screaming."

+ closing down
upon
destructively*
(destructive
explosiveness)

+ falling*

4. Nathan would attack his brother and push him hard enough to send him falling down the stairs.

Sources of Stimulation
children's tactile and visual erogenous contacts with the adult body

+ / – sleeping in
bed with adults*

1. Nathan was always a fitful sleeper. For many years this had driven him into bed with his parents. However, at the time of the diagnostic evaluation the parents were sending Nathan back to his own room.

(other close body
contacts)

2. Nathan at the age of nine and a half was still kissed on the lips by his father. The only time he was not kissed on the lips by him was when he "had a cold."

Nathan would sit on his father's or mother's lap while watching T.V. The father also would regularly wrestle with him. Nathan explained: "We get on top of each other; I get on top of him, he gets on top of me."[3]

+ adult nudity

3. Frequently while Nathan would be soaking himself in the bathtub, the father would expose his "big penis" to urinate.

Behavioral Symptoms
children's tactile and visual erogenous contacts with the adult body

− / + separation*[4]

1. It might be thought that Nathan would be glad to get away from his punitive home environment. In fact one of his favorite phantasies was to "get a Ford car and get to some quiet place away from all the yelling." However, his separation difficulties kept him from leaving home for even two weeks in the summer to go to camp.

+ irrational fears*

2. For four years Nathan was fearful of elevators. They reminded him of a hospital where he had stayed when he was little and where it had been necessary to remain overnight for the removal of a medal he had swallowed. Until the age of six, he would scream in terror if he had to go into any elevator.[5]

+ nightmares
+ night terrors*

At the age of three, he began to suffer persistent nightmares from which he would wake up crying. At the time of his diagnostic Nathan's nightmare of a car blowing up woke him up screaming. A series of Nathan's nightmares pertained to "a train whistle which would blow *louder* and *louder* until he would wake up crying," i.e., the nightmare involved auditory impressions which paralleled the punitive screaming of Nathan's father's voice becoming louder and louder.[6]

+ irrational
   tempers*

3. Nathan also gave vent to screaming temper tantrums. During one of these he pulled down and ripped his bedroom curtains.

+ sexual
   symptoms*

4. When Nathan wrestled with "the boys," including his brother, he would grab at their penises. The family was very distressed that they were completely unsuccessful in getting this behavior under control. The parents also complained that Nathan would try to kiss his sister on the mouth and would expose his penis to her as well as to his brother. Note: the father would kiss Nathan on the lips, get on top of him wrestling, pull his pants down, hit him on his bare buttocks and urinate in front of him. In turn, Nathan kissed his sister, wrestled sexually with his brother and exposed his penis in front of his siblings.

NOTES

1 One capacity which Nathan's negativism did not disrupt was learning: in school Nathan was a top A student.

2 There was a similarity between Nathan's need for all A's and Francis's (case 8) need for all A's. Both boys suffered from early deprivation with early feelings of helplessness. Both got very upset when they could not perfectly *compensate* for these helpless feelings by being *the* most competent in school. It is likely that for this reason Nathan would keep claiming to his parents that he was a genius.

3 Note the similarity of this case with that of Kolansky and Moore in which the beating and wrestling were both central themes (see synopsis of case 32 of Dick; see also case 78 of Larry and case 36 of Dominic).

4 Nathan displayed no separation phobic hysterics.

5 Fears of elevators also pertain to "closing down upon" and should be included above under that heading.

6 See case 100 of Ronny who would hear his father's punitive screaming voice echoing over and over again within his mind.

7 By error the following dream was not included in this case history and the ratings pertaining to +eyes and +bite were not included in the statistical investigation: "There was this land and it was all made of candy. I was walking around and *looking* at the things to *eat*. I don't know what happened for I woke up."

Nathan

46

Stimulation-Symptom-and-Dream-Profile

	Separation Phobias	
	+ Night Terrors, etc.	
+ Sleep in bed with Adult	+ Irrational Fears: Other	
	+ Irrational Tempers	
Adult-Genital-Erotic	+ Sexual Symptoms	
	Biting-Cutting, etc.	} *content of*
View Adult Coitus	Eyes	} *dreams and*
	Fire	} *symptoms*
	Learning Problems (levels 2 or 3 etc.)	
+ Punitive Yelling	Lying and Delinquency	
	Reversal of Affect	
+ Beatings	+ Closing-down-upon, kill	} *content of* } *dreams and*
	+ Falling	} *symptoms*
	Excretory Symptoms and dreams	
	Anal masturbation	
Preoccupation with Child's BM	Enuresis	
	Illness, etc.	} *content of*
+ Anal Contacts	Pain	} *dreams and*
	Death	} *symptoms*
	Compulsions	

Case 47: Otis

Otis had been a "B student" when he entered the seventh grade in junior high school and always had been considered a model pupil. Then in the seventh grade, his marks started going downhill to C's. By the eighth grade he was getting D's. At the age of fifteen, Otis was referred for diagnostic evaluation because he was completely failing the ninth grade — even though Otis still obtained a full-scale Bellevue Wechsler I.Q. score of 123.

+learning*
(referral
symptom)

In the ninth grade, Otis also became a disciplinary problem in school. As his marks steadily declined, he began to associate with an "undesirable group of recalcitrant boys."

Sources of Stimulation:
adult punitive and excretory contacts with children

+early
deprivation

1. Otis was described as "a very good natured baby" who was *left alone a great deal* because his twenty-one-month-old sister required much of the mother's attention. The family doctor suggested that Otis be fed on demand, with the result that Otis then would take most of his meals at night and would sleep much of the day. At this same time Otis became hyperactive.

+beatings*
+punitive
yelling*

2-3. Until Otis was ten years old he was beaten by his father. When the ten-year-old boy "became too big to handle," the father gave up his beatings but instead "blew up and attacked Otis with terrible verbal lashings." The verbal lashings became worse as the father reacted to the death of his sister and turned to alcohol.

−/+anal
stimulation*

4. Otis recalled having an enema when he was five years old.

Behavioral Symptoms correlated with
adult punitive and excretory contacts with children

+negative
behavior

1. Increasingly Otis expressed his negativism through opposition and became resistant to authority. He failed to do his class work; he failed to show up for football practice even though he had previously been an excellent sports enthusiast; and he broke rules by smoking in school.

+delinquency*

+freezing of
affect

Otis's lack of concern was directly reflected during his second diagnostic hour when he asserted "there's nothing to talk about. . . . I don't want to go away to school, I don't want any help."

190

+ negative
emotion

2. During the year preceding his referral, Otis had become increasingly *"surly* and *defiant"* at school to the point that he was "kicked off" the football team and was about to be suspended from school. Otis had become "allergic" to any authority telling him what *not* to do. At the end of his second diagnostic hour he described in detail how he hung around the area where a *"mean* cop" who *hated* kids was stationed. Otis would then "look for trouble," i.e., he was attracted to individuals who would treat him punitively.

+ hurting

3. Otis told how he got into fights with his peers and with his teacher: Otis went to "belt a boy in the mouth" when the boy "took his lunch." Then the teacher grabbed Otis and banged him against the blackboard.

+ killing*

At the age of fifteen Otis talked of being in a "kill your sister" club after a murder took place in town.

+ hurting

+ falling*

Otis was also consistently *accident-prone:* (a) At the age of *six,* Otis suffered a broken leg after he *jumped off* the bumper of a car (and *fell* to the ground); (b) at the age of seven, Otis had his eye hit when he and his friend were fencing with a mop handle; the blow eventuated in an abscess of his eye; (c) at the age of ten, Otis *fell* off a swing and broke his wrist. This accident occurred during an afternoon he had run away from home, after he had been threatened with a beating from his father; (d) at the age of thirteen, during a fist fight at camp, Otis got a serious cut over his eye requiring several stitches.

Sources of Stimulation:
children's tactile and visual erogenous contacts with the adult body

+ adult genital
erotic*

1. Otis negatively withheld all answers pertaining to sexual stimulation and sexual behavior. However, his parents reported that Otis, at the age of thirteen, attended a summer camp where he was exposed to viewing the homosexual practices of a number of the camp counselors.

Behavioral Symptoms correlated with
children's tactile and visual erogenous contacts with the adult body

+ irrational
tempers*1

1. Otis's "hot tempers" caused him to be disliked by the school athletic coaches.

− / + sexual
symptoms*

2. Just prior to his referral, Otis began to associate with a gang who dressed exhibitionistically in tight black pants.

+ eyes*

3. Otis seriously injured his eye on two occasions: once when he was seven and again at the time he witnessed the camp counselors' homosexual activities.

NOTES

[1] By error not included in the statistical evaluation.

Otis
47

Stimulation-Symptom-and-Dream-Profile

	Separation Phobias
	Night Terrors, Twilight States
Sleep in Bed with Adult	Irrational Fears: Other
	Irrational Tempers
+ Adult Genital Erotic	Sexual Symptoms
	Biting/Cutting, etc.
View Adult Coitus	+ Eyes
	Fire

Biting/Cutting, etc. } *content of dreams and symptoms*

	+ Learning Problems (levels 2 or 3, etc.)
+ Punitive Yelling	+ Lying and Delinquency
	Reversal of Affect
+ Beatings	+ Closing Down Upon, Kill
	+ Falling

Closing Down Upon, Kill } *content of dreams and symptoms*

	Excretory Symptoms and Dreams
	Anal Masturbation
Preoccupation with Child's BM	Enuresis
	Illness, etc.
Anal Contacts	Pain
	Death
	Compulsions

Illness, etc. } *content of dreams and symptoms*

Case 48: Paul

When Paul finally started therapy at the age of thirteen, he had been stuttering severely for several years. His referral problems also included isolation from his peers, lying and poor conduct in school. His mother had specific concerns about Paul's recent habit of stealing money from her purse and his long-standing interest in playing with matches.

Sources of Stimulation:
adult punitive and excretory contacts with children

+ early
deprivation of
empathic care

1. Feeding was an unhappy experience for Paul during his first two months of life: he suffered from colic necessitating his being placed upon a special meat diet. Toilet training was also a problem since the mother forced Paul to be bowel trained when he was only one year old.

During his early childhood Paul was kept from having any friends: his mother made him stay in the house away from other children because she felt the slum neighborhood was "too dangerous."

+ beatings*

2. The mother reported examples of her punitive attacks upon her son. On one occasion, Paul dumped out some hair tonic and then would not admit his error. The mother became so enraged at his withholding of "the truth" that she did something she had thought she "could never do": she took a belt and "accidentally" smashed his face with the buckle. She became alarmed when she saw "a drop of blood" on his temple.

Actually, the mother admitted that she felt "guilty" if she did not punish Paul for improper behavior. However, she felt she did go "too far" and agreed that her tempers were too explosive. One time she hurled a cup of hot coffee directly at him. The coffee missed him but splattered all over the draperies. Another time Paul was criticizing his brother and sister throughout the family meal. At first, she did not interfere "because" she had already punished him several times that day. However, his behavior finally became too much for her, whereupon she suddenly grabbed a pitcher of punch and poured it all over his head.

Paul's "first" memories were full of references to his mother hurting him: "When my sister was two I remember my mother slamming the door on my finger. . . . I remember when my mother got mad at me and pushed me on a slippery floor. I had to have twelve stitches."

193

The mother's punitive discharge upon her son directly reflected her own childhood experiences. She recalled that her own mother hung a whip directly over her bed to remind her that if she even slightly questioned her mother's authority she would be whipped. Sometimes she was also beaten with a cat-o-nine tails which her father had brought from "the old country."

However, Paul was even more upset over his father's beatings. When Paul was "bad" the mother was sure to report the details to the father, who then let Paul "have it." One time Paul's back bled from his father's fingernails. Paul stated that he was hit frequently until the age of twelve, the year prior to his beginning treatment.

+ punitive
yelling*

Paul complained about his mother's custom of blaming him for things *she* had done. He recalled, for example, an episode during his early childhood when his mother was driving the car, with him in the front and his baby brother in the back. During the ride, the mother suddenly jammed on her brakes with the result that the baby fell on the floor. The mother rather than blaming herself broke out in a raging tirade against Paul.

Behavioral Symptoms correlated with
adult punitive and excretory contacts with children

+ negative
behavior

1. Negative behavior disturbed Paul's life in many ways:

Isolation, i.e., withdrawal from peers, constituted a presenting problem. According to the intake interview with the mother, Paul had never been able to sustain any friendships. At home he stayed in his room and "pretty much" spent his time watching TV.

Withholding and restriction dominated Paul's relationship especially with authority figures. In Paul's own words "I just never tell my parents anything . . . *if I open my mouth* it would be all over for me; my mother would kill me." One is able, therefore, to understand Paul's primary presenting problem of stuttering involving both marked activation and also spasmodic withholding of opening his mouth to speak out his anger. His mother would become furious when Paul, in the middle of a thought would abruptly withhold communication, cut her off and become silent.This withholding of communication was not only evident at home. Paul's group therapy leader noted that Paul was "quite constricted and very reluctant to reveal his opinion of himself."

+ delinquency*

Negativism, in the form of opposition to social rules, appeared most directly in relation to authority figures, presumably a generalization of his reaction to his punitive parents. Paul stole candy from drugstores and money from purses; he indulged in petty cheating in school, smoked against permission and later became a heavy smoker of marijuana.

Paul not only indulged in doing the opposite of what his parents requested but also learned to cover up his opposition by lying. Paul's parents reinforced

+ lying*

his lying: they always punished him for telling the truth. Gradually, Paul's deception became quite involved. For example, when his parents forbade his going downtown alone at night to the movie theaters, Paul requested the telephone operator to ring back his number to check whether the phone was out of order. When the bell rang, Paul made sure his parents heard him "making plans" on the phone to go over to his friend's house. In this way, he became free to oppose his parents without punishment.

+ learning
  (level 1)

With such negativism, restriction, withholding and opposition to authority figures, it is not surprising that Paul developed a learning problem in school. At first he got A's and B's; then his marks went down to the C and D level. The school became convinced that he did not possess the mental capacity to follow the college program. Only after therapy did Paul once again display his ability to get satisfactory grades and to go on to college. However, even after his grades did improve, Paul spoke to his therapist about missing "the good old days" of negativism when he was cutting up in school and getting very poor marks.

+ reversal of
  affect*

2. Reversal of emotion hid Paul's reactions of grief and anger. In the third grade, Paul began to play the part of the class clown. Later in therapy, he revealed in a poem some of the feelings which had been covered up by his laughter. In the poem, "a child went out sledding and laughing while inside of himself he was stricken with grief."

+ hurting
+ closing down
  upon
  destructively*
  (crush)

3. Sometimes violent destructiveness would break through Paul's restriction. He was reported to have pushed a little girl into a dark room and to have slammed her fingers in the door.[1] Another time he exploded at a boy who had been teasing him and kicked the boy hard in the groin. The boy's parents threatened to sue for damages after their son had to be taken to the hospital.

Paul liked wrestling with his kid brother. The wrestling would end up with the kid brother getting his head banged on the floor or his arm twisted.

On one occasion Paul "split open" his kid brother's head with a rock so that the blood spurted out all over his face.[2] Paul shook with shock as he told his therapist of this incident. When his brother covered up Paul's part in the incident, Paul thought "He sticks up for me. What a kid brother! . . . after all the bad things I've done to him!"

+ closing down
  upon
  destructively*

Paul's problems involving frontal attack also were demonstrated by hallucinatory activity which appeared when he was delirious with a fever of 106°. The hallucinatory images (which sometimes came back to him on future occasions when he shut his eyes), Paul explained, "had to do with bricks coming at me."[3]

+ falling*

Sometimes Paul took his destructiveness out on himself. Once he got so mad at his mother's tirades that he "just had to leave the room" and hit the wall with his fist. On another occasion he *fell off* his bike and sustained a head injury requiring hospitalization.

+ preoccupation
  with illness*

+ pain* (and
  aches)

+ excretory
  symptoms*

4. For weeks, Paul complained of somatic pains and aches about which he wanted his therapist to reassure him. In response to his therapist's recommendations that these symptoms should be checked medically, Paul retorted: "Boy you really can get a fellow mad!"

5. At the age of fourteen, Paul still experienced a problem with soiling. (This matter was not investigated beyond his admitting the problem during his initial diagnostic interview.)

Sources of Stimulation:
children's tactile and visual erogenous contacts with the adult body

1. Paul slept constantly in the parents' room until the age of three, when his baby sister was born. He was then suddenly "kicked out" of the parents' room as his sister took his place.

+ / − sleeping in
bed with adults*

While he shared the parents' room, Paul regularly would crawl into his mother's bed.

− / + adult genital
erotic*

2. The following history suggests but does not confirm the possibility that Paul may have been exposed to adult genital erotic contacts:

a) The grandfather molested Paul's mother when she was four;

b) The grandfather molested Paul's sister when she was four;

c) Finally, it was feared that the grandfather had also molested Paul;

d) Paul remained in the parents' room until he was almost four with opportunities to observe his parents' intimacies.

Behavioral Symptoms correlated with
children's tactile and visual erogenous contacts with the adult body

+ separation
  phobia*

1. During the first weeks of nursery school when he was three or four, Paul was school phobic and vomited every day. The mother felt that this school-phobic reaction at times reappeared in modified form throughout his school history.

+ fire*

2-3. During a confession to his fellow members in group therapy, Paul reported: "I used to light matches when I was lonely and things were piling up." This statement conforms with the parents' referral complaint that over the years Paul never ceased playing with matches.

+ biting/cutting*

Paul also told his peers in group therapy how he once took a razor and purposefully cut his face with it.

NOTES

1 This behavior possibly may have derived from the mother's slamming the car door on Paul's fingers.

2 Repetition of the mother's hitting Paul's head with a strap buckle so as to draw blood?

3 Repetition of an image equivalent to that of his mother's cup of coffee directed at his face?

Paul
48

Stimulation-Symptom-and-Dream-Profile

	+ Separation Phobias
	Night Terrors, Twilight States
+ Sleep in Bed with Adult	Irrational Fears: Other
	Irrational Tempers
Adult Genital Erotic	Sexual Symptoms
	+ Biting/Cutting, etc. } *content of*
View Adult Coitus	Eyes } *dreams and*
	+ Fire } *symptoms*

	Learning Problems (levels 2 or 3, etc.)
+ Punitive Yelling	+ Lying and Delinquency
	+ Reversal of Affect
+ Beatings	+ Closing Down Upon, Kill } *content of* / *dreams and*
	+ Falling } *symptoms*

	+ Excretory Symptoms and Dreams
	Anal Masturbation
Preoccupation with Child's BM	Enuresis
	+ Illness, etc. } *content of*
Anal Contacts	+ Pain } *dreams and*
	Death } *symptoms*
	Compulsions

Case 49: Reed

Reed was thirteen and a half when finally he was brought to the clinic with complaints that he was "disruptive in school: he talked back to his teachers, was defiant and disrespectful to them, and fought with his peers." Reed also threatened to run away from home because he felt "picked on."

Actually, when Reed's mother was a teenager *she* had sought help at the same clinic for "withdrawn behavior, failing in school, and a feeling that someone was at her shoulder." Unfortunately, her parents had not allowed her to continue therapy after her first two or three visits. Her negative emotion, negative behavior and preoccupation with hurting eventually were acted out upon her son, Reed: she could see that her reaction toward Reed was "uniformly quite negative" no matter what Reed might be doing. She constantly threatened Reed. To his face she wished he had been run over by a car and killed. To make matters worse, Reed's father also threatened the boy with promises to "wreck" him and "kill" him.

The parents' negative emotions were also displayed more subtly. Both parents called Reed stupid and gave Reed's siblings permission to do the same. The parents also failed to trust Reed and in turn lied to him: they told him that they were bringing his favorite dog to a farm in the country and instead they had him killed. They also brought Reed to the clinic without informing him he was to talk to a psychiatrist.

The family's negativism was reflected in a free-for-all opposition to one another's attempts to discipline Reed. The mother felt free to attack Reed, but she opposed the father's attempts to punish him; then the grandmother who lived in the home contributed to the inconsistent and chaotic interactions by opposing the mother's disciplinary efforts. For example, when Reed stole, the grandmother hid the stolen article so that Reed would not receive a severe punishment from his mother.

Sources of Stimulation:
adult punitive and excretory contacts with children

+ beatings*

1. The mother could recall "only" two occasions when the father used the belt on Reed, even though he was constantly threatening to "do a job on him." Reed himself stated that his father strapped him severely when he was little. However, belt or no belt, Reed was hit frequently. The mother had gotten so frightened when the father attacked Reed, that she constantly got between the

two of them to protect Reed. Whenever Reed swore in the home he was beaten; yet when his sister swore she was simply told not to do it again.

+ punitive
yelling*

2. Likewise, Reed was "scolded severely" for touching his siblings' toys although the siblings were not reprimanded at all for doing the same to him. The mother admitted that it was not only the father who "went wild" yelling at the boy with threats to kill him. She was aware that she herself constantly screamed at him and nagged him. She frequently swore at Reed as she openly expressed her wishes that he would be killed. She knew she could not stand Reed around. She realized that it was she rather than Reed who might be the one in need of psychiatric help.

Often, the parents' screaming would not be directed at Reed but at one another. Still, Reed found his name tossed about in the middle of arguments.

Behavioral Symptoms correlated with
adult punitive and excretory contacts with children

+ negative
behavior
(turning away
from auditory
contact)

+ learning
(level 1)

1. "Talking to him is like talking to a brick wall," the mother complained: "It is impossible to communicate with Reed in any way that's meaningful." Reed turned a "deaf ear" upon his mother's words and in addition kept wishing that he could run away from his home. His opposition at home was transferred to life in school. Reed "defied" the teacher, "refused" to work and "refused" to obey the rules in class. No wonder Reed did not do well in school and suffered from a "learning problem." The school felt that Reed was more than capable of doing his work; he actually scored above grade level in reading.[1]

+ lying*
+ delinquency*

Still another manifestation of Reed's negative behavior was his custom of lying. For example, he would steal, then lie to his parents to avoid punishment.

+ negative
emotion

2. Reed listed his first two overall "problems" as: *I do not like* school" and *"I do not like* math."

+ reversal of
affect*

So, also, he did not like his family. However when it came to speaking of being maltreated, Reed could only smile. *With a big smile,* he told how his sister screamed at him. The sister's screaming would bring Reed's mother to the scene; then the mother too would yell at him. Again, *with a big smile* Reed told how he used to be disciplined by "getting the strap."

+ hurting

3. From the time he was a toddler, when he himself was being hit, Reed hit "the other kids." Reed told how currently he "beat up on" the kids and teachers.

+ killing*

Reed dreamed of killing. In the one dream he reported during his diagnostic, "Jack the giant-killer killed the giant." Associating to the dream, Reed told how he liked to go hunting and how his father had promised to buy him a gun.

Reed made friends with delinquent peers. He was attracted, for example, to a boy who was enthusiastic about the Nazis[2] and involved Reed in antagonistic behavior toward the Jewish school principal.

Sources of Stimulation:
children's tactile and visual erogenous contacts with the adult body

No positive findings reported.

Behavioral Symptoms correlated with
children's tactile and visual erogenous contacts with the adult body

No positive findings reported.

NOTES

[1] On his Bellevue Wechsler intelligence test Reed was placed in the average range of intellectual functioning with a full-scale score of 103.

A diagnostic study which Reed had undergone at another clinic several years earlier attributed Reed's learning problems to perceptual-motor "minimal brain damage." However, psychological testing during the current evaluation indicated no signs of neurological involvement. Reed's performance on the Bender Gestalt tests and the Graham Kendall Memory for Designs proved well within normal limits.

[2] Compare this history with that of Kevin, case 43. Kevin, who was continually punished, also identified with the Nazis and their hate for the Jews.

Reed
49

Stimulation-Symptom-and-Dream-Profile

Sleep in Bed with Adult

Adult Genital Erotic

View Adult Coitus

Separation Phobias
Night Terrors, Twilight States
Irrational Fears: Other
Irrational Tempers
Sexual Symptoms
Biting/Cutting, etc. ⎫ *content of*
Eyes   ⎬ *dreams and*
Fire   ⎭ *symptoms*

+ Punitive Yelling

+ Beatings

Learning Problems (levels 2 or 3, etc.)
+ Lying and Delinquency
+ Reversal of Affect
+ Closing Down Upon, Kill ⎫ *content of*
                          ⎬ *dreams and*
Falling   ⎭ *symptoms*

Preoccupation with Child's BM

Anal Contacts

Excretory Symptoms and Dreams
Anal Masturbation
Enuresis
Illness, etc. ⎫ *content of*
Pain   ⎬ *dreams and*
Death   ⎭ *symptoms*
Compulsions

Case 50: Sam

Sam was twelve years old when his parents finally sought psychiatric help for his long-standing problems. Sam had always been nervous, fidgety and hyperactive. He frequently displayed temper tantrums. For a long while he had been stealing from his mother's purse. Gradually he also began to steal from a neighbor and from his teacher. He used the money to "make friends" with a number of children. Sam's parents could not understand what had gone wrong. They pointed out that their other five children never got into trouble.

Sources of Stimulation:
adult punitive and excretory contacts with children

+ early
  deprivation

1. Sam's mother had gained thirty to forty pounds each time she had been pregnant. Therefore, during her pregnancy with Sam, she took dexedrine to keep from gaining weight again.

After delivery Sam proved "to be a very fussy baby." During his first few months at home he seemed very hungry and cried incessantly. By the age of one year he was weaned from the bottle but continued thumbsucking until the age of ten. From the time he was able to walk, Sam "hyperactively climbed all over the place." He took "great risks," fell a great deal and frequently hurt himself. The parents recalled that Sam as an infant was constantly trying to get out of the crib. They recalled *getting so angry at him* that "sometimes" they would *keep slapping him forcefully to make him stay down.*"[1] The parents had to bring Sam to the hospital frequently for his "falls."

+ beatings during
  infancy*

+ beatings*

2. When asked how she handled Sam's problems, the mother shrank back in her chair, then pointed to her husband and said to the intake worker: "I turn it over to him." The father then explained how he had belted Sam until one year prior to the referral, at which time he found that after his beatings Sam began to twitch, tic and wring his hands. The mother added that she felt Sam became "nervous" and markedly fearful of the father.

The beatings were repeatedly triggered by Sam's lying to his father even in the presence of incriminating evidence. The enraged father resorted to slapping Sam in the face or on the bared buttocks to stop the lying, but to no avail.

Behavioral Symptoms correlated with
adult punitive and excretory contacts with children

+ negative
  behavior
+ lying and
  delinquency*

1. Sam eventually did the *opposite* of everything his father most fervently wanted him to do: he *lied,* he smoked and he stole. His defiance to authority

was indicated by his referral symptom, his "petty delinquency." The more Sam was beaten by his father for misbehaving, the more he misbehaved.

+ learning*
(level 2)

Sam's negativism also began to invade his learning in school so that when his teacher told him to sit down he would remain standing up. He was left back in grade two. Thereafter, he earned satisfactory grades until his last report card which had been "most disturbing": D in math, D in history, D in geography, and B in reading.

+ tics

Sam's facial tics were precipitated by his father's beatings.

+ falling*

2. From the time of his infancy and throughout his childhood, Sam fell and hurt himself constantly. At the age of five years, he fell and gave himself a concussion.[2] On several other occasions, he required stitches on his head. Once Sam kept jumping on his bed until he managed to land on a steel fan which cut him between his legs and required eighteen stitches.

Sam's screen-like first memories had to do with his falling and hurting himself: "When I was four, me and my friend were racing toward a door. I got there first, and he *pushed me over the steps.* . . . When I used to live down the street there was a big ledge. I remember when I slid on my sled right *over the ledge.*"

+ closing down
upon
destructively*
+ delinquency*

Sam hurt others as well as himself. He recalled "fooling around" with his sister and hitting her with a wrench when he was seven years old; the sister required four or five stitches. Eventually, his destructive behavior took on an overtly delinquent cast. A short time before his diagnostic referral Sam had broken off the antennae of several cars and had torn a neighbor's kitchen apart.

+ freezing of
affect

3. Sam was "not afraid of anything," neither was he able to express compassion. He could show no signs of remorse after his acts of destruction.

+ reversal of
affect*

Additionally, Sam often displayed a reversal of affect when it came to anger, hate or harm. He smiled as he reported his first problem, "I am always mad at my sisters and brothers." Then he smiled as he told of hitting his sister with a wrench; and laughed as he explained how he had not been able to keep his sled and himself from going over a ledge.

Sources of Stimulation:
children's tactile and visual erogenous contacts with the adult body

− / + adult genital
erotic*

1. Sam stated that sometimes he saw his fourteen-year-old brother masturbating. No information was obtained as to whether or not the brother had reached sexual maturity.

Behavioral Symptoms correlated with
children's tactile and visual erogenous contacts with the adult body

+ biting/cutting*

1. Sam reported a dream of a "head chopped off by a guillotine." Symptomatically, he cut his thigh between his legs. The cut, deep and jagged, required

eighteen stitches.

+ irrational
tempers*

2. The mother complained that Sam was constantly having temper tantrums over the slightest disagreement or frustration, e.g., he would start stamping, yelling and whining if she brought him a different kind of toothpaste from the usual or if she asked him to change his clothes.

NOTES

1 This case parallels cases 52 and 55 with respect to a history of (a) an infant being repetitively hit for getting up in his crib, and (b) behavioral problems appearing later in life: delinquency, freezing of affect; cruelty and "psychopathic character."

2 Bender Gestalt testing revealed no signs of brain damage. Sam attained an average I.Q. score of 103.

Sam
50

Stimulation-Symptom-and-Dream-Profile

	Separation Phobias	
	Night Terrors, Twilight States	
Sleep in Bed with Adult	Irrational Fears: Other	
	+ Irrational Tempers	
Adult Genital Erotic	Sexual Symptoms	
	+ Biting/Cutting, etc.	*content of*
View Adult Coitus	Eyes	*dreams and*
	Fire	*symptoms*
	+ Learning Problems (levels 2 or 3, etc.)	
Punitive Yelling	+ Lying and Delinquency	
	+ Reversal of Affect	
+ Beatings	+ Closing Down Upon, Kill	*content of dreams and*
	+ Falling	*symptoms*
	Excretory Symptoms and Dreams	
	Anal Masturbation	
Preoccupation with Child's BM	Enuresis	
	Illness, etc.	*content of*
Anal Contacts	Pain	*dreams and*
	Death	*symptoms*
	Compulsions	

Case 51: Todd

Todd was first seen for diagnostic evaluation when he was thirteen. His school had referred him with the following complaints: "Todd is continuously in trouble; he runs out of school and goes home; starts fights in class and on trips; he is not dangerous but very disruptive." Todd would interrupt the class by his restlessness. On the other hand, Todd was described as a "perfect gentleman" in a one-to-one relationship.

Two years later, at the age of fifteen, Todd was brought back by the police for an evaluation of his seriously delinquent activities: he was charged with "breaking and entering" while robbing a store. He had also attempted to run over a policeman with his car.

Sources of Stimulation:
adult punitive and excretory contacts with children

+ early
deprivation

1. Todd's father drank a great deal, and when he was drunk beat Todd's mother. The father had felt very trapped by each of the mother's pregnancies and was "particularly violent" with her during such times.

The mother became pregnant with Todd two months after she had given birth to her first baby. At that time she was not only faced with the close spacing of her unwanted pregnancies and the father's violent beatings, but also with the onset of her own mother's death from tuberculosis. Because of her pregnancy she was forced to wait *outside* of the TB hospital where her mother was dying. She resented bitterly that she could not support her mother at such a critical time. Todd was born one month before his grandmother died. The mother began to cry as she told how she never had a chance to say goodbye to her own mother. She was very open in stating that she was extremely depressed for at least a year following Todd's birth and the grandmother's death. With tears streaming down her cheeks, the mother expressed her fear that Todd knew he was unwanted. She tried to explain that it wasn't that she didn't want *him,* it was simply that she was in no condition to have a baby. When the mother returned from her own mother's funeral, Todd, who was only one and a half months old, came down with the measles, followed by chicken pox and impetigo.

+ beatings*

2-3. Both the mother and Todd reported incidents from his early childhood when he would be physically abused by his father. The father, who was jealous of the mother, would interrogate Todd about the mother's visitors during the day. If Todd said "no one," he was beaten by the father. *The father would also put a hot iron on Todd's buttocks in order "to teach him" not to touch a hot iron and poured hot coffee on Todd and struck him with a broom when he had "poor table manners."* These sadistic attacks lasted until Todd was four years old, when the parents divorced. However, during Todd's first diagnostic evaluation, the mother withheld all reference to the sadistic treatment Todd actually had received during his first four years of life. Instead, she prattled on with a variety of innocuous statements as to the difficulties she had experienced in disciplining Todd: "We tried all kinds of controls and punishments but none were successful . . . we tried spankings, bribing, reasoning with him. . . . We finally gave up the idea of punishing him any more. . . . " Not until Todd's second diagnostic evaluation when he was fifteen did she admit the sadistic punitive stimulation which Todd had suffered.[1]

+ punitive
yelling* (and
violence)

Until he was four years old, Todd also was exposed to violent fights between his father and mother. The mother finally decided upon a divorce only after the father had beaten her severely in front of all the children, ripped off her clothes and locked her out of the home.

Then, when Todd was four, the mother married a man who at first appeared relatively kind and helpful. But by the time Todd was fifteen his mother and stepfather were fighting tempestuously. On one occasion when the stepfather was attempting to assault the mother, Todd intervened and threw his stepfather down the stairs.

+ adult
defecation

4. Todd and his brothers, all teenagers, regularly would be allowed to see the mother when she was defecating.

Behavioral Symptoms correlated with
adult punitive and excretory contacts with children

1. The parents complained that Todd was impervious to family rules. So was he *impervious to the rules of society*: both Todd and his parents remarked that his problem centered about his attraction to delinquent children.[2]

+ delinquency*

In keeping with this pattern, Todd found it easy to lie. The mother felt that Todd did his lying in order to protect himself from punishment.[3]

+ lying*

2. Despite his average intelligence, (Full Scale Bellevue Wechsler I.Q. 101), Todd did no schoolwork. Consequently, he struggled with a "learning problem." After each poor report card, he would seem to try a little harder for a short time but then returned to his slump. At the age of thirteen he was about to receive a "social promotion," even though he was failing in every one of his subjects.

+ learning*
(level 2)

3. Todd's first memory was of jumping off some trunks and falling in such a way that his hand went through a window and broke the window. Likewise, Todd associated to a picture he had drawn at the end of his first diagnostic

+ falling*
+ hurting

+ closing down
upon
destructively*

when he was thirteen years old: "There are bags full of *rocks* and they throw them at the windows and break them. The cops got them." Todd's picture of breaking windows was not too different from delinquent behavior he acted out two years later when he was brought to court for breaking into and entering a store.

+ closing down
upon
destructively*
+ death*
+ killing*
+ closing down
upon
destructively*
+ reversal of
affect*

Moreover, at the age of thirteen, he reported two dreams: "A guy *pierces* this picture and blood pours out"; and, "A monster was chasing me and got *locked in a coffin* with a vampire and I drove a *stake through his heart*." The murder in these dreams also was "acted out" two years later: he stole a car, then attempted to run down a policeman who was trying to stop him. He claimed that he would have liked to have had the opportunity to run down his brother.[4]

4. Todd smiled "inappropriately" as he spoke of his delinquent activities for which he had been brought to court.

Sources of Stimulation:
children's tactile and visual erogenous contacts with the adult body

+ sleeping in bed
with adults*

1. Todd, at the *age of thirteen, would sleep "in the middle" between his mother and father* a couple of times a month. He confided that when his father worked at night he would sleep all night in bed with his mother and his four-year-old sister.

+ adult nudity

2. He also showered with his adolescent brothers and scrubbed their backs.

Behavioral Symptoms correlated with
children's tactile and visual erogenous contacts with the adult body

+ biting/cutting*

1. Todd reported a dream of a *werewolf* who was tearing his head off.

NOTES

1 The need for guilty parents to cover up their abusive treatment of their child always needs to be kept in mind.

2 Todd's mother reinforced this problem by knowingly or unknowingly rewarding him for delinquency. She allowed him, for example, to steal from her purse and got upset not because he stole from her but because he sometimes took too much.

3 Recall, as a little child, Todd had been threatened with a thrashing unless he told what man had been visiting with his mother. He soon learned to offer confabulations to avoid the beatings.

4 If Todd, as a little child, was half-murdered with a burning hot iron, now as an adolescent he was taking *his* turn to murder. It appears that early emotional imprints of murder were being triggered during adolescence.

Todd
51

Stimulation-Symptom-and-Dream-Profile

	Separation Phobias	
	Night Terrors, Twilight States	
+ Sleep in Bed with Adult	Irrational Fears: Other	
	Irrational Tempers	
Adult Genital Erotic	Sexual Symptoms	
	+ Biting/Cutting, etc.	} *content of*
View Adult Coitus	Eyes	*dreams and*
	Fire	*symptoms*
	+ Learning Problems (levels 2 or 3, etc.)	
+ Punitive Yelling	+ Lying and Delinquency	
	+ Reversal of Affect	
+ Beatings	+ Closing Down Upon, Kill	} *content of* *dreams and*
	+ Falling	*symptoms*
	Excretory Symptoms and Dreams	
	Anal Masturbation	
Preoccupation with Child's BM	Enuresis	
	Illness, etc.	
Anal Contacts	Pain	} *content of*
	+ Death	*dreams and* *symptoms*
	Compulsions	

Case 52: Victor

Victor was diagnostically evaluated at the age of nine and again at twelve. In a state of desperation, the mother first reported Victor's destructiveness and his getting into trouble. When he was seven, Victor had set a fire and was badly burned. At nine he was again setting fires and was so disruptive at school he was about to be expelled.

Sources of Stimulation:
adult punitive and excretory contacts with children

+ early
  deprivation

1. Victor's mother and father married when they were very young. Their marriage was extremely difficult from the beginning. With the father unemployed most of the time, the mother deeply regretted her pregnancy with Victor. During the early months of the pregnancy, she spent much time crying. Following Victor's birth, she became "very depressed" and overwhelmed because Victor had "boils which required shots of penicillin every other day for six weeks" whereas his one-year-old sister had just broken her collarbone.

By the time Victor was ten months old his whole body was covered with ringworm. The parents were separated for a two-month period when Victor was fourteen months old. During this time Victor experienced a "mild epileptic convulsion." Several neurological investigations (including EEG studies), when Victor was eighteen months, two and three years old, revealed no organic pathology.

Shortly thereafter, the mother decided to leave Victor in the care of his father while she went out to work. The father, who himself had been abused and beaten as a child, in turn became an abusive parent who regularly beat Victor. For example, when Victor as an *eighteen-month-old* baby stubbornly *refused to lie down in his crib upon his father's bidding, the father kept repetitively pushing him down and hitting him uncontrollably* on and off for one hour.

+ beatings*

2. The beatings continued as Victor grew up. At the age of nine, Victor was still being strapped every other day. Victor complained of the unjust reasons for the beatings. For example, the father would hit him for coming home late, yet the father himself would come home at three in the morning.

The mother also hit Victor: until he was seven years old she disciplined him by hitting him with a shoe. The mother attempted to cover up the beatings by

209

explaining "We used to spank Victor but now we just send him to his room"; or "We tried giving him lots of attention but that didn't help."

+ punitive
yelling*

3. During the period when Victor was ten to eleven years of age, his parents fought with increasing violence. Finally, the father "went to pieces" and completely lost control of his temper. Following an episode during which he physically attacked his wife, he put himself in a local hospital for two days' observation. The parents finally separated permanently from one another after a final attempt at reconciliation had erupted into violent quarreling.

− / + adult
defecation

4. Victor's mother and grandmother uninhibitedly passed flatus during the day. The impression derived from Victor's reports suggested that this type of activity was more or less a family game.

Behavioral Symptoms correlated with
adult punitive and excretory contacts with children

+ negative
behavior
+ lying*

1. From the time he entered kindergarten, Victor *refused to obey anyone* in school. Likewise, he opposed his parents' authority at home. He swore at his teachers as well as at his mother. Victor lied when it came to admitting his misdeeds. He always blamed someone else.

+ learning*
(level 2)

Victor's opposition to authority was accompanied by a refusal to work. His goal in life was "to do nothing," a likely contribution to the etiology of his severe learning problem. He repeated the first grade twice and was unsure whether he would fail for the third time, this despite an adequate I.Q. of 91.

+ delinquency*

Following his diagnostic, Victor was sent to a residential school where he did well. Unfortunately, after a year, Victor returned home where his problems immediately reappeared in full force. At this time, Victor's opposition to authority became accelerated: Soon he joined "a bunch of tough kids" who made a practice of breaking into parked cars and running the motors.

+ freezing of
affect
+ reversal of
affect*

2. Victor *did not cry* at the age of seven when he burnt his leg so badly that his pants were seared to his leg.[1] Also, he *laughed* when his parents beat him. Consequently, no form of punishment "ever worked." The parents claimed they had tried "every method." The Family Service worker also noted that Victor displayed "a good deal of *inappropriate* affect" and that Victor would *laugh* as he told how he liked to see the *funny* frown on his mother's face when he got her upset.

3-4. Victor appeared ready either to murder himself or to murder others. It is possible that the "murder" reactions, which were charged during his infancy when he was brutally beaten for a full hour, eventually were reactivated and discharged upon others and upon himself. Victor was constantly "destructive"

+ hurting

and "in trouble." He hit his little sisters, he sprayed paint on the draperies, he continually provoked others to hurt him.

Victor, however, came still closer to murdering himself. When he rode his

+ falling*

bike recklessly through an intersection without looking, his mother took his bike away. But Victor would not be discouraged from his course of action: he borrowed a bike from a friend, then crashed into a curb, *fell* off and knocked himself unconscious. It was found that he had suffered a head concussion. Victor's sister pulled him out of the street.

+ falling*
+ killing*

This murderous self-destructiveness was reflected in the two dreams which Victor reported during his diagnostic visits: "I fell off a cliff"; and "someone killed me."

+ closing down
upon
destructively*
(crush)

But the most disturbing manifestation of Victor's need to hurt involved his almost killing his little sister one evening: Victor took a pillow and put it over the face of his younger sister.[2] He almost choked her to death before he let her go. The mother felt he didn't realize what he was doing since he became genuinely upset after she pointed out the danger of his behavior. On another occasion, however, Victor again came close to killing as he tried to hurl a huge rock at another boy.

− / + excretory
symptoms*

5. Victor's last words of his diagnostic pertained to his pleasure in passing flatus: "Me and my mother like to pass gas."

Sources of Stimulation:
children's tactile and visual erogenous contacts with the adult body

+ sleeping in bed
with adults*

1. Victor's first diagnostic workup when he was nine revealed that he would get restless and get into his mother's bed every night. Often he would sleep throughout the night between his mother and father. The mother complied with the clinic's recommendations for her to desist from sleeping with Victor. However, two and a half years later when he was again seen at the age of twelve, Victor was found to be regularly sleeping in bed with his grandmother.

− / + adult genital
erotic*

2. Even though he had once slept nightly with his parents, Victor said that he had never witnessed his parents copulating.

Behavioral Symptoms correlated with
children's tactile and visual erogenous contacts with the adult body

− / + separation
phobia*
(homesick not
phobic)

1. Victor cried for two weeks when he first went to public school. And despite his miserable life at home where he had known so much violence, Victor was markedly homesick at the age of twelve when he went away to a residential school. Finally, he threatened to run away if his mother returned him to the school for a second year. Therefore, the mother permitted Victor to return home even though his behavior had improved markedly at the residential school.

+ irrational
tempers*

2. A local school report stated "Victor does not adjust to his group; he is totally unable to control his temper; he angers easily and frequently, and swears at the nuns."

+ eyes*

3. One of Victor's first (screen) memories pertained to being accidentally hit in the eye: "My father and I were throwing boxes around and one hit me in the *eye*." In school, Victor performed especially poorly in reading.

+ fire*
+ burn*

4. At the age of seven, Victor set a fire which badly burned him. He remained in the hospital for a month for skin grafts on his leg. However, at the age of nine, he was again found setting fires. A neighbor saw him sitting in a parked car as he was tossing out lighted matches at a little girl.

NOTES

1 Even in this state, Victor's fear of punishment led to his negative insistence upon denying the truth: he claimed he had not set the fire and insisted he had caught some other boys responsible for the deed.

+ pain*
+ non-organic
  illness*

On the other hand, Victor could cry when he was not paralyzed with expectations of punishment. For example, Victor screamed with pain from an earache even though a physical examination by his physician revealed no organic basis for the disturbance.

2 It is possible that Victor's behavior was a repetition of his father's brutally pushing down upon him in his crib (see above).

Victor
52

Stimulation-Symptom-and-Dream-Profile

	Separation Phobias	
	Night Terrors, Twilight States	
+ Sleep in Bed with Adult	Irrational Fears: Other	
	+ Irrational Tempers	
Adult Genital Erotic	Sexual Symptoms	
	Biting/Cutting, etc.	} *content of*
View Adult Coitus	+ Eyes	} *dreams and*
	+ Fire	} *symptoms*
	+ Learning Problems (levels 2 or 3, etc.)	
+ Punitive Yelling	+ Lying and Delinquency	
	+ Reversal of Affect	
+ Beatings	+ Closing Down Upon, Kill	} *content of dreams and*
	+ Falling	} *symptoms*
	Excretory Symptoms and Dreams	
	Anal Masturbation	
Preoccupation with Child's BM	Enuresis	
	+ Illness, etc.	} *content of*
Anal Contacts	+ Pain	} *dreams and*
	Death	} *symptoms*
	Compulsions	

Case 53: Walter

The juvenile court referred Walter to the clinic for a diagnostic evaluation when he was sixteen and a half years old. Following a disagreement with his father who had slapped his face in front of his friends for a minor transgression, Walter had become involved in a car theft and had "taken off" for another state.

Despite an average intelligence (I.Q. 105), Walter suffered from a learning problem at school where he was repeating the tenth grade.

Sources of Stimulation:
adult punitive and excretory contacts with children

+ beatings*

1. The father, "like a wild man," had beaten Walter for many years. Even when Walter was sixteen, the father threatened to beat him with a hose. Therefore, when Walter stayed out with his friends until midnight, his father became furious and "smashed" him on the head. Walter still flinched whenever his father or, for that matter, any authoritarian figure came near him. The punitive treatment he received from his father was made all the worse by the father's extreme favoritism for Leo, Walter's brother. Walter finally made up his mind "He's not going to push me around like a little kid anymore."

Even though the mother ostensibly protested Walter's beatings, she was always the one who notified the father of his misdeeds. Each evening when the father arrived home she would greet him with her complaints and incite the father to beat the boy.

+ punitive
  yelling*

2. The mother and father constantly quarreled about Walter. The mother stated openly that the father was actually "emotionally disturbed" in the way he handled Walter. She "of course" did not approve of the father's losing control and screaming at Walter.

+ punitive bowel
  training

3. Bowel training was disturbed; it was associated with scoldings and spankings. When Walter was four or five years old the mother was still spanking him in her efforts to control his soiling.

Behavioral Symptoms correlated with
adult punitive and excretory contacts with children

+ excretory
  symptoms*
+ enuresis*

1. Not only did Walter still soil at the age of four or five, but after that he continued to have occasional "accidents" and wet his bed until he was ten or

213

eleven years old.

+ negative
emotion

+ reversal of
affect*

2. Walter felt that he was ugly and that nobody liked him. He walked with his head down so that nobody would notice his nose, which had been broken. On the other hand, he displayed some reversal of emotion whereby he covered up his upset in school by "horsing around" and playing the part of the class clown.

+ freezing of
affect

Most of the time Walter's emotion was frozen. For example, he had no feeling for the owner of the car he had stolen. He indicated during his diagnostic that it was because of a "stupid error" that he and his friend were caught with the stolen car. Reflecting this problem of inhibited, frozen emotion, Walter reported in a dream that he was "in the middle of an *iceberg*."

+ negative
behavior

3. Walter regularly opposed authority. Walter's father wanted him to get a diploma more than anything else, so Walter skipped school and "got in trouble." "It burns my father up . . . ," Walter noted, "I drive my father up a wall." Walter frequently solved his problems by withdrawing from authority figures. In addition to skipping school, he ran away from home on several occasions. His father accused him of being a "quitter." Considering his negativism it is not surprising that Walter was faced with school difficulties and a learning problem. At the time of his referral, he was repeating the tenth grade.

+ learning*
(level 2)

+ lying*

Walter learned to lie in school, i.e., to tell the opposite from reality in order to oppose authority yet at the same time to avoid punishment. However, as already noted, Walter was sent to a juvenile court for "taking off" for another state in a car which he had stolen.

+ delinquency*

+ hurting (self)

4. Walter was accident-prone and maneuvered himself into situations where he was hurt by others. (a) At the age of six, he broke his arm when a boy threw a stick at him while he was riding his bicycle. When he came home crying his mother paid no attention until she took off his jacket and saw a bone coming through the skin. (b) At the age of eleven he "busted" his nose when a boy gave him a push. (c) At the age of fourteen, while emptying a garbage can, Walter slipped on the ice and broke his leg. He was in pain a long time before a police cruiser finally picked him up and brought him to the hospital.

+ falling*

+ killing*

+ falling*

+ excretory
dream*
(swamp)

+ death* (casket)

Walter's sadomasochism was reflected in his dreams which were full of scenes of killing, falling and death. Walter reported them as follows: (a) "My brother gets *killed*." (b) "My friend gets *killed*." (c) "I was in the middle of an iceberg. I suddenly *fell* under it" (a likely source of death). (d) "My friend had a motor scooter and someone stole it. We were looking for it and went into a *swamp*. We saw it lying under a *bunch of junk*. We lifted up the stuff but instead of the scooter we saw a *casket*. The police drove after us. One of my friends took off. He showed the cops the *casket*. They charged him with *murder*." (e) In association to a final dream, Walter told about a friend of his brother's who died after touching a live antenna. The brother watched him being *buried*. "He must have felt awful."

Sources of Stimulation:
children's tactile and visual erogenous contacts with the adult body

− / + sleeping in bed with adults* (adolescent was only thirteen)

1. Walter did not share beds with any adults. However, until he was ten he slept in the same bed with his brother Leo, who was three years older. Walter elaborated on how he and Leo would wrestle together "and we would like to kill each other for pure fun."

Behavioral Symptoms correlated with
children's tactile and visual erogenous contacts with the adult body

+ persistent separation phobia*
+ / − irrational fears*

1. The mother described Walter as a "frightened boy" who did not want to be home alone at night.

2. When he was four, Walter would only use his own toilet. He was afraid to use his parents'. Other than this fear, the diagnostic revealed no history of specific phobias.

+ eyes* (dream content)

3. Walter dreamed (as already noted): "My friend had a motor scooter and someone stole it. We were *looking* for it and went into a swamp. We *saw* it lying under a bunch of junk. We lifted up the stuff but instead of the scooter we *saw* a casket."

− / + irrational tempers*

4. The mother also spoke of her concern about Walter's uncontrollable anger. Yet she did not give any specific examples of the anger. Instead, she elaborated upon his being accident-prone.

+ sexual symptoms*

Walter stated that when he was little, he looked like his handsome brother. However, when he broke his nose, he became self-conscious and upset about his appearance. Since the day a girl told him his nose was too big, he expressed shame about going out on dates.

Walter showed evidence of a masturbation problem. He reported that his mother would say to him: "What are you playing in your pocket for?" Walter denied any concerns about this behavior.

Walter
53

Stimulation-Symptom-and-Dream-Profile

	+ Separation Phobias	
	Night Terrors, Twilight States	
Sleep in Bed with Adult	+ Irrational Fears: Other	
	Irrational Tempers	
Adult Genital Erotic	+ Sexual Symptoms	
	Biting/Cutting, etc.	*content of*
View Adult Coitus	+ Eyes	*dreams and*
	Fire	*symptoms*

	+ Learning Problems (levels 2 or 3, etc.)	
+ Punitive Yelling	+ Lying and Delinquency	
	+ Reversal of Affect	
+ Beatings	+ Closing Down Upon, Kill	*content of dreams and*
	+ Falling	*symptoms*

	+ Excretory Symptoms and Dreams	
	Anal Masturbation	
Preoccupation with Child's BM	+ Enuresis	
	Illness, etc.	*content of*
Anal Contacts	Pain	*dreams and*
	+ Death	*symptoms*
	Compulsions	

Case 54: Abel

The father blamed Abel's problems upon a bicycle accident Abel had experienced when he was six or seven years old. Abel had fallen off his bicycle as he bumped into a car and was "knocked out for five hours." However, he never went to the hospital for a checkup. Since the accident, Abel claimed he had not been able to remember things.

When Abel was fourteen, his stepmother convinced the father to bring the boy to the clinic for a diagnostic evaluation. At that time Abel was not only failing in school but already had been placed on probation with the courts for attacking children and stealing their money.

Despite his accident, Abel earned a Full Scale score of 96 (Verbal 101, Performance 92) on his Wechsler Bellevue Intelligence Test. An electroencephalogram taken at the time of Abel's diagnostic study revealed no significant findings other than a suggestion of barbituate intake. This finding was in keeping with Abel's own report that he had already taken hallucinatory drugs such as hashish.

The parents' emphasis upon Abel's accident as a principal source for his delinquent behavior paralleled their efforts to make light of Abel's unsatisfactory home environment. His "real mother," a "bar maid," deserted the family when Abel was eleven and thereafter showed no interest in seeing the boy. Abel openly told his father "I know my mother doesn't love me and it doesn't bother me." However, it was after his mother's desertion that he first began stealing. Likewise, Abel's father and his stepmother both reacted without emotion when they finally admitted the father's beatings, which, on one occasion, had sent Abel fleeing to the clinic for protection. In answer to the clinic's pleas for the parents to control the beatings, Abel's stepmother responded that the father "always has acted that way and was not going to change."

Sources of Stimulation:
adult punitive and excretory contacts with children

beatings*
1. Abel's father had been brought up the "hard" way. As an adult he became a boxer who later suffered from ulcers, cancer and high blood pressure. He did not hesitate to beat his son. Abel reported that the father "used" to beat him a great deal; once the father gave him twenty-five lashes. Abel's effort to deny ongoing beatings failed when he came trembling to the clinic begging protection from his father's threats.

217

The stepmother too was accustomed to hitting Abel. Abel was particularly upset when she punched him in the face.

Beatings were administered for any kind of misbehavior, e.g., Abel was beaten for playing with his "dingy."

+ punitive
yelling*

2. Stepmother, father and Abel agreed on one thing: the parents were constantly fighting with one another. The stepmother claimed that since childhood she "never had any patience." The father admitted that he and his wife both easily "blew up" but "they didn't hold grudges" toward one another. Abel offerred as a presenting diagnostic problem "my mother and father argue too much. They are always fighting, screaming and slapping each other." Abel and his stepmother also battled constantly. At the time of the diagnostic, the stepmother felt her tempers with Abel were getting out of hand because she had become "nervous" about an impending operation.

Behavioral Symptoms correlated with
adult punitive and excretory contacts with children

+ negative
behavior

+ delinquency*

1. In stating why he had been sent to the clinic, Abel explained "I like to be the leader of the kids. I've been to court. I had been jumping a couple of kids and took $2.40 from them." Abel's opposition to his father and all other authority figures left him a delinquent. His father did not want him to smoke, so he smoked. His mother reinforced his opposition by giving him cigarettes. More seriously, his defiance to authority was reflected in his stealing, hitting his teacher, "rolling drunks."

+ lying*

With an opposition to authority figures in the external world, it was not surprising to find Abel's "internalized" social values were defective: he easily lied in order to oppose the law and at the same time avoid punishment.

+ learning*
(level 2)

With such opposition to authority figures, Abel did not succeed in school, this despite his average intelligence as indicated by his Bellevue Wechsler scores. His father complained that Abel's marks were "terrible." At the age of fourteen, Abel was reading on a third grade level and couldn't spell. His marks were usually D's and E's, although recently he had "improved" and got only two D's with the rest C's.

Abel's negativism in the presence of any discomfort also added to his learning problem. His father noted when Abel tried to fix something such as a radio, if he got stuck with it at any point, he wanted to give up even though others might offer him help. In reading, if he "got stuck" on a word, he refused to struggle with it but simply omitted it. The father described Abel as "giving up before trying."

+ freezing of
affect

2. Abel's freezing of emotion was reflected in his indifference towards his problems or towards his punitive environment at home (except when he was directly threatened by one of his father's beatings). For the most part he was

neither interested in help at the clinic nor in placement within a protective environment.

+ hurting

Abel confided another problem: "I like to get into fights. I fight a lot. Sometimes, I really want to hurt someone. I knocked ten teeth out of a boy's mouth." Abel's pleasure in hitting people was also displayed in school where he "gave it" to his teacher.

+ / – falling*

+ closing down upon destructively* (strangle)

It is not known whether Abel also took it out on himself e.g. by his bike accident during which he *fell* off his bike and smashed himself unconscious (see above). However, Abel's involvement with "hurting" and "being hurt" unquestionably was reflected within the two dreams he described during his brief diagnostic workup. Dream 1: "There was a snake in my bed. I ran around the house yelling, 'Get me a rock so I can *hit him* and *bust him* in the head.'" And, Dream 2: "A man was trying to *strangle me* and *stabbed me* in the arm and blood came."

Sources of Stimulation:
children's tactile and visual erogenous contacts with the adult body

+ adult nudity

1. Abel regularly saw his seventeen-year-old adolescent brother unclothed.

+ adult genital erotic*

2. From the time he was eleven, Abel saw a great many hard-core pornographic pictures of large penises being sucked and inserted into a partner's rectum.[1]

Behavioral Symptoms correlated with
children's tactile and visual erogenous contacts with the adult body

+ sleepwalking*

1-2. Abel claimed he dreamed repeatedly of snakes (see above). At night his anxiety erupted into sleepwalking. During this state, Abel would get dressed and walk outside, where he undressed again without knowing it.[2]

+ eyes* (reading problem)

3. In addition to a generalized learning problem, Abel particularly suffered from a specific *reading* problem. His reading level was approximately six years below the norm for his age.

+ sexual symptoms*

4. As noted, Abel would openly play with his "dingy," behavior which would induce his parents to give him a sound beating.

NOTES

[1] Note Abel's delinquency and stealing began at the age of eleven when his mother left and he began his indulgence in hard-core pornography.

[2] For a relation between fugue-like states and exposure to primal scenes see case 29, synopsis of Berta Bornstein's "Sonja."

Abel
54

Stimulation-Symptom-and-Dream-Profile

	Separation Phobias	
	+ Night Terrors, Twilight States	
Sleep in Bed with Adult	Irrational Fears: Other	
	Irrational Tempers	
+ Adult Genital Erotic	+ Sexual Symptoms	
	Biting/Cutting, etc.	⎫ *content of*
View Adult Coitus	+ Eyes	⎬ *dreams and*
	Fire	⎭ *symptoms*

	+ Learning Problems (levels 2 or 3, etc.)	
+ Punitive Yelling	+ Lying and Delinquency	
	Reversal of Affect	
+ Beatings	+ Closing Down Upon, Kill	⎫ *content of* ⎬ *dreams and*
	+ Falling	⎭ *symptoms*

	Excretory Symptoms and Dreams	
	Anal Masturbation	
Preoccupation with Child's BM	Enuresis	
	Illness, etc.	⎫ *content of*
Anal Contacts	Pain	⎬ *dreams and*
	Death	⎭ *symptoms*
	Compulsions	

Case 55: Bruno

Bruno, seven years old, lived with his mother, his ailing grandmother and his grandfather, all of whom attempted to discipline him. When Bruno was two and a half years old, his mother left his father. From that time on the mother worked daily and Bruno's care was left to his ailing grandmother. Bruno became hyperactive and enuretic and talked incessantly. He had no friends and cried a lot. The mother became desperate about Bruno's problems and had no idea what she should do to help her child.

Sources of Stimulation:
adult punitive and excretory contacts with children

+ early
deprivation

1. Because her marriage was full of discord, the mother was especially unhappy when she found she was pregnant with Bruno. Throughout the nine-month period of gestation she suffered from intense nausea. Following Bruno's birth she developed "spastic colitis" which lasted for several months. She described herself as being upset during this period and recalled her fear of social criticism and disapproval.

Bruno suffered from stomach pains during his infancy. His mother found she should have been heating his bottle but had discontinued doing this when he was six months old. She never went to a pediatrician to seek help for Bruno's discomfort because Bruno's father refused to spend the money necessary for the treatment. The mother explained that she did not know enough about an infant's needs for she also should have brought Bruno to the pediatrician for the care of a foot defect which caused him to trip whenever he tried to walk.

Bruno soon developed into a poor sleeper. This problem, presumably reflecting an early lack of comforting, still persisted at the time of his referral. In an effort to get himself to sleep at night, seven-year-old Bruno would have to talk to himself for hours at a time.

+ beatings*
(during
infancy)

To make matters worse, Bruno's father, a highly intelligent man, had been emotionally troubled since his own childhood. As a little boy, he had been sent to a psychiatrist because he had threatened to throw himself out of the window during a temper tantrum. The father, accustomed to having his own way, unfortunately could not stand Bruno's crying. Consequently, one night he became so upset when Bruno would not stop crying that he *took the baby by the neck and without restraint kept slamming Bruno's head against the wall*. The mother, who could put up with the father's tempers directed at herself, could not put up with such violence inflicted upon Bruno. She, therefore, finally proceeded to separate from Bruno's father.

+ punitive
yelling*

2. Prior to his parents' separation when he was two and a half years old, Bruno was exposed to his father's ill-tempered attacks upon the mother during which the father would threaten and hit her.

Following the parents' separation, Bruno and his mother lived with the maternal grandparents. The grandfather was described as a "very cold man who was impatient with children" and who the mother felt would hurt Bruno badly if ever allowed to hit the boy. The grandfather constantly *threatened* to hit the little boy though he never carried out his threat. Havoc resulted when everyone tried disciplining Bruno at the same time. Bruno's mother and grandmother never were able to get along well and particularly disagreed about handling Bruno's discipline. The grandmother would countermand the mother's decisions for Bruno's discipline, with the result that the mother and grandmother *constantly bickered* in front of him. Bruno found himself the center of these constant quarrels. The mother stated that no method of discipline seemed to work whether it involved taking away Bruno's privileges or spanking him.

+ anal
stimulation*

3. Bruno was constipated during infancy and early childhood. Because this constipation kept him from being trained, the mother resorted to the application of rectal suppositories.

Behavioral Symptoms correlated with
adult punitive and excretory contacts with children

+ enuresis*

1. Bruno wet his bed every night until, just prior to his diagnostic, he visited his father for two months.

2. Bruno's first (screen) memory pertained to the toilet: he recalled taking TV tubes and dropping them down the *toilet*.

+ excretory
symptoms*

Bruno's sexual play with two other boys focused upon the boys putting a stick into Bruno's rectum. Bruno claimed this did not hurt, rather it tickled so that he liked it. The two children took turns poking his rectum but he did not do it to them.

+ closing down
upon
destructively*
+ death*
+ negative
behavior
+ learning
(level 1)

3. After his first day's visit to the clinic, Bruno threatened his mother with a pen knife. At this time, the mother in a panic called her worker to report that Bruno was "very preoccupied with *death*."

4. The mother was aware that Bruno was displaying a disturbing stubbornness for several years prior to his diagnostic referral. However, it was only at the time of the diagnostic that he manifested a learning problem in school. The mother broke down in tears as she reported that Bruno was not doing at all well in school and in fact could do no work. Bruno complained that he did not like the school telling him what to do. He also suffered from a restrictive speech

disturbance with lisping. Two years of speech therapy had resulted in only "some improvement."

5. Even during the initial intake phone call, the mother expressed concern about Bruno's laughing when punished. She had just read an article which had said such behavior was a problem. The mother also had noticed that Bruno would smile a lot when there was nothing funny to smile about; he seemed to laugh for no reason. Bruno displayed a fixed smile when he arrived for his first diagnostic visit. At that time, he gave the impression of a fast talking, bouncy master of ceremonies who was looking for a laugh.

Sources of Stimulation:
children's tactile and visual erogenous contacts with the adult body

None reported by Bruno or by his mother.

Behavioral Symptoms correlated with
children's tactile and visual erogenous contacts with the adult body

1. Bruno spoke of once being frightened about a dream of a man under his bed.

2. The mother reported that Bruno had a bad temper, would cry, but was never destructive.

3. Bruno would tear his tie to shreds with his teeth.

4. Bruno masturbated "severely" as a small child, then stopped, but started up again six months before his referral. The mother added that he masturbated frequently in bed and while watching TV. She told him that it was "dirty" and not to do it. She also was concerned that occasionally he wanted to put on lipstick and nail polish.

Margin notes:

+ reversal of affect*

+ nightmares

+ temper tantrums*

+ biting*

+ sexual symptoms*

Bruno
55

Stimulation-Symptom-and-Dream-Profile

	Separation Phobias	
	Night Terrors, Twilight States	
Sleep in Bed with Adult	Irrational Fears: Other	
+	Irrational Tempers	
Adult Genital Erotic	+ Sexual Symptoms	
+	Biting/Cutting, etc.	} *content of*
View Adult Coitus	Eyes	} *dreams and*
	Fire	) *symptoms*

	Learning Problems (levels 2 or 3, etc.)	
+ Punitive Yelling	Lying and Delinquency	
+	Reversal of Affect	
+ Beatings	+ Closing Down Upon, Kill	} *content of* / *dreams and*
	Falling	) *symptoms*

	+ Excretory Symptoms and Dreams	
	Anal Masturbation	
Preoccupation with Child's BM	+ Enuresis	
	Illness, etc.	} *content of*
+ Anal Contacts	Pain	} *dreams and*
	+ Death	) *symptoms*
	Compulsions	

Case 56: Clinton

Clinton had not known that his grandfather had attempted suicide and that his grandmother succeeded in committing suicide prior to his diagnostic evaluation. His mother committed suicide several years after the diagnostic. This case therefore may reflect upon some stimulus factors prevalent within a suicidal setting.

Clinton, age ten, was seen for psychiatric evaluation because of his parents' concern about a number of his symptoms. Clinton had suffered from hyperactivity, thumb sucking and enuresis since infancy; recently his school work had deteriorated despite his high intelligence (I.Q. 134). Clinton was found cheating on exams in an effort to keep up his good grades.

Sources of Stimulation:
adult punitive and excretory contacts with children

+ early
deprivation

1. Clinton's mother tried to nurse him for his first three months. However, it was necessary for her to be out of the house a great deal in order to take care of an ailing aunt. At such times, a housekeeper fed Clinton a bottle. According to reports, "Clinton never had enough to eat. Ever since these days of early infancy, he had his thumb in his mouth."

When Clinton was three months old his mother deliberately became pregnant again. "I wanted to fulfill myself as a woman" she explained, "but I wanted to get it over with." Meanwhile, she spent increasingly long periods out of the house away from Clinton. The father became annoyed at being left with the responsibility of caring for Clinton as a baby.

By the age of four months, Clinton began head-rocking with intense screaming and *hyperactivity*. Two of Clinton's referral problems, his overactive thumb-sucking and his hyperactivity, were already established when Clinton was only four months old.

+ punitive
yelling*

2. Clinton's parents were extremely bright people who were outwardly charming and verbal. However, they fought violently with one another, often with their fists, without any regard for the presence of their children. "The parental fighting was chronic, impulsive, and uncontrolled from the very beginning of the marriage. . . . They screamed, raged, scratched and hit each other in their constant arguments." The situation worsened as the years went by, and Clinton's mother became alcoholic. She had begun drinking in order to calm

herself for dinner which always had been a noisy, raging free-for-all. Unfortunately, the mother's drinking increased to the extent that she began to pass out at all hours of the day. Frequently, Clinton and his brothers would be locked out of the house and would have to jimmy the window to gain entrance.

The parents expressed no manifest guilt or anxiety regarding their own behavior. For example, when the diagnostic team indicated that Clinton could make little progress in therapy unless the parents found a way to control their own outbursts of violence, each parent responded rather glibly about vague plans for separation if the situation didn't improve. However, the father had recently impregnated his wife against her will to prevent her from divorcing him.

+ beatings*   3. *As an infant and thereafter Clinton was hit and punched by the father* who himself had been beaten with sticks on his bared buttocks when he was little. The mother could not handle Clinton's subsequent disturbed behavior. Therefore, she too resorted to beating, yelling and neglecting him as modes of discipline.

+ adult   4. Clinton regularly was allowed to enter the bathroom while his mother or
  defecation   father were on the toilet.

Behavioral Symptoms correlated with
adult punitive and excretory contacts with children

1. Ten-year-old Clinton was able to offer only the following "two" problems about himself he would like to change: (a) "cleaning my room," (b) "I mess my room."

+ enuresis*   Clinton still wet his bed. Further inquiry revealed that he liked to poke his
+ excretory   finger into his little brother's "rear," then smell and eat the feces. He expressed
  symptoms*   no feeling about this being a problem.

+ negative   2. The parents stated that at home Clinton was openly defiant.
  behavior
+ learning*   In school, Clinton's capacity to learn began to deteriorate. Even though he
  (level 1; referral had been an A student in the past, at the time of his referral he was "not
  problem)   working up to capacity."

                      3. The school reported that Clinton was displaying periods of silliness and
+ reversal of   clowning, an affect reversal in the face of the unhappy fighting, yelling and
  affect*   beatings to which he was being exposed at home.

+ freezing of   Clinton demonstrated also a frozen inhibition of affect during his diagnos-
  affect   tic hours. For example, he stated that a prominent tic of his did not bother him
                      at all and demonstrated no interest whatsoever in getting help.

+ hurting   4. In nursery school Clinton used to swing out and "hit anything within reach, as if he were oblivious as to what was around." His mother decided he was suffering from "petit mal" attacks but never brought him to the neurologist "because there was nothing to be done in the way of treatment for brain damage anyway."

At home, throughout his life, Clinton was physically assaultive with his siblings and attacked them with obscene and abusive language. The mother complained that Clinton severely beat and "ruined" his younger brother.

+ killing*

Understandably, Clinton's one short answer to a diagnostic inquiry as to what might be some of his worries was: "A war might break out."

Sources of Stimulation:
children's tactile and visual erogenous contacts with the adult body

− / + sleeping in bed with adults* (only once)
+ adult nudity

1. Clinton recalled that once he slept between his father and mother. However this had never happened again.

2. At first Clinton stated that "occasionally" he saw his mother or father nude and volunteered that he freely entered the bathroom when his mother or father were urinating. However, by the end of his second and last diagnostic hour, Clinton confided, "When my mother gets very high she walks around without clothes. If you don't believe me, ask my father. She hits the kids and swears a lot too."[1]

Behavioral Symptoms correlated with
children's tactile and visual erogenous contacts with the adult body

+ irrational fears*

1. As noted, Clinton finally admitted a worry that "a war might break out."

+ irrational tempers*

2. Clinton would swing out and smash anything in reach while he was in nursery school.

+ eyes*

3. Clinton displayed a severe *eye tic*. He dreamed: "We *looked* up. There was a huge eagle pulling a huge aeroplane."

+ sexual symptoms*

4. Clinton played sexually with his little brother. The activities which he was able to report consisted of *watching* the brother *masturbate, poking* the brother in the rear with his finger, then smelling and eating the feces. Clearly Clinton's sexual activities were influenced by his interest in excrement.

NOTES

[1] At the beginning of his diagnostic, Clinton had claimed he had been beaten only once.

Clinton
56

Stimulation-Symptom-and-Dream-Profile

	Separation Phobias
	Night Terrors, Twilight States
Sleep in Bed with Adult	+ Irrational Fears: Other
	+ Irrational Tempers
Adult Genital Erotic	+ Sexual Symptoms
	Biting/Cutting, etc.
View Adult Coitus	+ Eyes
	Fire

$\left.\begin{array}{l} \\ \\ \end{array}\right\}$ *content of dreams and symptoms*

	+ Learning Problems (levels 2 or 3, etc.)
+ Punitive Yelling	Lying and Delinquency
	+ Reversal of Affect
+ Beatings	+ Closing Down Upon, Kill
	Falling

$\left.\begin{array}{l} \\ \\ \end{array}\right\}$ *content of dreams and symptoms*

	+ Excretory Symptoms and Dreams
	Anal Masturbation
Preoccupation with Child's BM	+ Enuresis
	Illness, etc.
Anal Contacts	Pain
	Death
	Compulsions

$\left.\begin{array}{l} \\ \\ \end{array}\right\}$ *content of dreams and symptoms*

Case 57: Douglas

Douglas was thirty-six years old when he started weekly psychotherapy in an attempt to collaborate with the treatment of his six-year-old son, Junior (see case 58) who was still refusing to use the toilet and was continuing to deposit feces in his pants.

Douglas was worried about pains in his heart, pains which his medical doctor diagnosed as psychosomatic in origin. He gradually began to realize these pains were related to his wife's angry, violent screaming which he would regularly provoke.

Sources of Stimulation:
adult punitive and excretory contacts with children

+ beatings*

1. The father of Douglas was a primitive man who knew only one way of teaching his son; this was by beatings. (a) Once he beat Douglas black and blue for stealing a chicken egg; (b) On another occasion he chased Douglas with a belt and then hit him till he "shit and peed" in his pants because Douglas had been noisy and had awakened him from his sleep; (c) He had been known to "hang out" with prostitutes; yet he would leave welts on nine-year-old Douglas's body to teach the boy not to look at a prostitute stationed in her window; (d) The worst beating occurred following Douglas's refusal to fight a neighborhood bully. The father, enraged that Doug wouldn't fight, chased him down the street while lashing at him with a whip. He did not stop his whipping until Douglas finally agreed to fight the boy.

Unfortunately, others joined the ranks of those who beat Douglas severely. His grandfather beat him with a long whip, his mother beat him with the branch of a tree and his teacher disciplined him by hoisting him out of the school window and dangling him by a belt in mid-air.

Behavioral Symptoms correlated with
adult punitive and excretory contacts with children

+ negative
behavior
+ negative
emotion

1-2. The rigidity of Douglas's negativism was revealed by his refusal to change in therapy. Therapeutic understanding, education and support did little to help him change his policy of being verbally abusive to his wife and refusing to be helpful to her. Douglas continued to call his wife "fatso," "pussy face," "a bad apple," "bitch," "stupid" and "old witch." When Douglas impregnated his wife a third time against her will, his response to her plight consisted of an

229

unconcerned "that's *your* problem."

Douglas was "allergic" to the word "No" and therefore found it impossible to say "No" to anyone including his children who consequently became wild and unmanageable. He also found it difficult to say "No" to his subordinates who + delinquency* constantly stole. In this way he became involved in delinquent activities.

+ excretory   3. The importance of excrement in Douglas's life was considerable:
  symptoms*

Anal intercourse was one of his favorite activities both before and after his marriage. Even though his wife was disturbed by anal penetration, it was diffi-cult for him to control his driven need for rectal intercourse.

Another manifestation of Douglas's attraction to excrement appeared in relation to his son Junior's toilet-training. When Junior was six years old, he was still being wiped by his father. With so much rewarding erogenous stimu-lation it is not surprising that Junior continued to soil as the years went by. There was every indication that Douglas would have continued to wipe Junior after Junior's eleventh birthday had it not been for the clinic's intervention and education.

+ death*   4. Douglas struggled with obsessional fears of *dying* to the point that he
+ obsessions*   could not concentrate on his work. During these episodes of fear, he developed
+ pain*   pains in his left chest, pains which closely reminded him of heart disease. Med-
+ non-organic   ical examinations indicated no signs of organic disturbance. Reassurance by his
  illness*   doctor provided little respite from his anxieties. Once his pains were so severe
                              he required hospitalization for several days. Douglas was aware that this preoc-
+ death*   cupation with illness and death haunted him from his ninth year when he had
                              been severely beaten for stealing an egg. It was during the same ninth year of
+ closing down   his life that he experienced an hallucination of a casket in the sky bearing his
  upon   father who actually was not to die until thirty years later.
  destructively*
  (casket)   **Sources of Stimulation:**
                              children's tactile and visual erogenous contacts with the adult body

+ adult nudity   1-2. When Douglas was five years old, his aunt *would take him into the*
+ adult genital   *shower with her, pick him up and rub him up and down upon her breasts.*
  erotic*   Douglas could remember his intense excitement during these activities.

Later, as a young adult, Douglas spent much time looking at hard-core pornographic pictures of fellatio and anal intercourse. The pornography re-
+ view adult   minded him of his childhood when he had witnessed his *parents in the act of*
  coitus*   *sexual intercourse.* He also recalled that at the age of eleven he and a friend
                              peeked through a hole in a wall to watch an adolescent boy and girl copulating.

Behavioral Symptoms correlated with
children's tactile and visual erogenous contacts with the adult body

+ hallucinatory   1. At the age of nine, it will be recalled, Douglas experienced an halluci-
  twilight state*   nation of a casket bearing his father who actually was still alive.

+ irrational fears*   2. Obsessional fears of illness and death often interfered with Douglas's capacity to attend to work.

+ sexual
  symptoms*   3. Douglas demanded sexual intercourse up to five times every night. It mattered not to him whether his wife was depressed, ill, angry or tired; he was driven to fellatio and sodomy; he was not to be stopped. Douglas could see a connection between (a) the excessive excitement he had encountered as a child when his aunt had used him in the shower to masturbate her breasts, and (b) his driven, compulsive sexuality which he directed toward his distraught wife during adulthood.

Douglas

57

Stimulation-Symptom-and-Dream-Profile

	Separation Phobias	
	+ Night Terrors, Twilight States	
Sleep in Bed with Adult	+ Irrational Fears: Other	
	Irrational Tempers	
+ Adult Genital Erotic	+ Sexual Symptoms	
	Biting/Cutting, etc.	} *content of*
+ View Adult Coitus	Eyes	} *dreams and*
	Fire	} *symptoms*
	Learning Problems (levels 2 or 3, etc.)	
Punitive Yelling	+ Lying and Delinquency	
	Reversal of Affect	
+ Beatings	+ Closing Down Upon, Kill	} *content of* } *dreams and*
	Falling	} *symptoms*
	+ Excretory Symptoms and Dreams	
	Anal Masturbation	
Preoccupation with Child's BM	Enuresis	
	+ Illness, etc.	} *content of*
Anal Contacts	+ Pain	} *dreams and*
	+ Death	} *symptoms*
	+ Compulsions	

Case 58: Douglas, Junior

Doug, Junior,[1] at the age of six refused to use the toilet and instead defecated in his pants. He rebelled generally against rules: he was described as "very rough to handle," defied his mother and was "in danger of hurting his sister."

Sources of Stimulation:
adult punitive and excretory contacts with children

−/+early
deprivation

1. The mother, a highly religious woman, was terrified that she had damaged Junior by trying to abort him during her pregnancy. Even though she was living with Junior's father at the time and married him within a year, she tried to put Junior up for adoption soon after his birth. For this reason, she did not attempt to nurse him. Once she finally did decide to keep Junior, however, the mother settled down to enjoying her son. Things then went "smoothly" and she described Junior as a wonderful baby and toddler until he was two and a half years old.

−/+beatings*

2. Both the mother and father, finding themselves ineffective in controlling Junior's rebellious behavior, would lose their tempers and explosively spank him. For a long period of time they continued hitting him despite advice from their therapists to discipline him in a less punitive way.

+punitive
yelling*

3. The household in which Junior lived echoed with constant bombardments of punitive screaming.

Since her own father was "an abusive, screaming man, who drank too much," the mother wanted "to be a lady," to be calm and to display good manners. She stated that she wanted a warm, harmonious household where the children could grow and learn and where there was courtesy and love[2] rather than screaming and hate. Yet she could not control herself from repeating the patterns of her parents. She and her husband felt they were destroying each other by their constant arguments. He persisted in calling her a "bad apple," "bitch," "fatso" and "pussy face" and accused her of being "a lousy sexual partner." She, in turn, continuously berated him for not being involved with the children, for being away so much, for not working together with her in disciplining Junior, for using bad language, for walking out on things, etc., etc. At the same time, she wished that her husband would stay away because she thought things became even more upset "with him around."

Junior's mother could see she yelled "for nothing." She knew she couldn't

232

tell the children to cease doing something without screaming at them. Often her husband would try to calm her in vain. She knew she was not a stupid woman but felt that she simply "could not cope." Fury was evident in her voice when she described how the children would not pick up their things or would not eat the good food she cooked. Her mood could change instantaneously and she could switch her controlled, calm voice to horrendous loud yelling, which made the situation worse, because then none of the children responded to her instructions. Junior's pushing and hitting his sister made her the wildest. When the sister built something out of blocks and Junior pushed her to take the blocks away, the mother "became furious beyond speech." She would yell "BE careful, don't HURT her, watch what you're doing, don't put YOUR FINGERS SO CLOSE TO HER FACE," etc.

As time went on the mother could see she let out on Junior some of the rage she felt toward her husband. She was enraged at her husband's sexual demands, one night after another, two, three, four, five times a night, whether she was depressed, angry or ill. Likewise, she was infuriated that when her husband had impregnated her again, he could do no more than tell her "That's your problem."

Most tragically, the mother, even with help from the clinic, could not use reward to replace her infuriated discharge of punishment. When her therapist recommended that she try rewards to help Junior learn to defecate into the toilet, she tried this suggestion on two successive occasions and found it worked. However, following this success, she became angry because "if he could do it for a reward *then* he could do it all the time"; thereupon she immediately discontinued rewarding him.

+ adult preoccupation with child's BM*

4. Both the mother and father still cleaned up all the excrement from Junior's buttocks when at the age of seven, he still defecated daily in his pants.

Behavioral Symptoms correlated with
adult punitive and excretory contacts with children

+ negative behavior

1-2. Junior's disobedience at home and in school, his opposition to authority, was referred to as a presenting problem. Equally prominent was his withholdingness. In therapy, he was almost totally unable to talk directly of his worries and difficulties. The best he could do was to tell stories about animals which reflected directly upon his primitive fears and problems.

+ learning (level 1)

Increasingly, Junior's negativism interfered with his ability to learn in school even though he was of average intelligence (he attained a WISC score of 107 and was felt to have higher potential). At first he required special help in learning to read; later it was even more difficult for him to keep up with his class.

+ negative behavior (turn away)

Turning away was another aspect of negative behavior which characterized Junior's life. One story after another involved this theme: "This is a story about a boy. It was Christmas Eve, and he *ran away* and he slept on the ground and he got to be freezing and he started shivering and then a fairy came and asked him his wish and his wish was he wanted to not live with his mother. . . . A zebra went to his mother and the mother said 'go away' and the mother kicked him into the gutter. . . . A skunk ran away . . . an elephant ran away . . . a cougar ran away . . . a turkey that ran away . . . a cow that ran away from the farmer . . . a squirrel that ran away . . . about a monkey and a donkey that ran away . . . about a cow and a horse that ran away . . . about caca, doo-doo that ran away into the toilet and was flushed in the toilet and couldn't get out . . ."[3]

3. Although Junior was a little angel at the clinic, his father and mother reflected that he often was "a devil" at home. For example, Junior had recently hit his little sister on the head with a shovel and then became dreadfully frightened. It is, therefore, not surprising to discover that his stories (but not his dreams) reflected a preoccupation with killing and death: "A zebra went to his mother and the mother said 'go away' and the mother kicked him into the gutter and he started dying[4] and he cried for his mother. And he *died*. He started praying and he *died* . . . a bear started to bite a man. And the man started to *die*. And he did not like the man. The man shot a gun and *killed* him. And he *died*. There was a bomb and then he *died* . . . a turtle . . . had to get bait. He ate an Indian and he *died*. And someone *stepped on him and he got bloody* . . . a lion met a tiger. And the tiger bit the lion. And the lion started to fight with the tiger and he *died* because he was shot . . . a llama found a crocodile *was bleeding* . . . a tiger had a friend leopard. And the leopard saw a wildcat. And the wildcat *killed* a baby cat . . . a turkey ran away into the forest. A hunter *shooted him* and took him home and ate him and took his eyes out and put a needle in him to *kill* him."

In line with the content of these stories, the mother indicated that Junior frequently threatened to open the door and jump out from their speeding car.

+ kill* (suicide)

+ excretory symptoms*

4. At the age of seven, after a year of therapy, Junior was still soiling. The social worker's notes described the situation as follows: "Junior is still not bowel trained. He is supposed to clean himself off and wash his pants, but frequently doesn't do anything at all or does a poor job. Several times, he has flushed his pants down the toilet; once he kept flooding the bathroom floor until the water leaked into the basement. In the winter he developed dry skin and the doctor told him to keep his hands out of the water. Therefore, the mother decided to clean him up. She said Junior does such a poor job he will stain the bathtub when he takes a bath. At times he squats down in the house or outside instead of using the bathroom. He doesn't soil at school as far as we know and does not soil at camp." When Junior was finally placed in a residential setting, his soiling completely stopped after a month.

Soiling was one problem which eventually Junior did discuss during his therapy hours. He ventured: "I hate doing it. I hate the smell. It stinks." He proceeded to speak of poking his finger into his rear end and sometimes putting some of the "doo-doo" in his mouth. This confession accompanied a reference to bees liking honey.[5] However, he was upset that he had gotten "doo-doo" into his mouth; "I don't like to eat it. It doesn't taste good. It tastes fart. I'm ashamed of it. I'm afraid I'm going to die."

+ anal
  masturbation*

+ death*

Sources of Stimulation:
children's tactile and visual erogenous contacts with the adult body

+ / – sleeping in
bed with adult*
(frequency?)

1. Prior to therapy, Junior would like to get in bed with his father. He would cry "Daddy I want to sleep with you" and would continue crying unless his father slept with him for the night.

+ adult nudity

2. Junior would watch his father "tinkle." He also would come in to watch the father shave in the nude.

+ / – adult genital
erotic*

3. A year or two prior to therapy the parents lived in very close quarters. The mother, therefore, was most concerned about the father's constant demands for sexual intercourse especially during the day, when supposedly the children were "napping" in the next room. She thought it likely that the children had peeked in at their activities or at least heard what was going on.

(+ / – view adult
coitis*)

Behavioral Symptoms correlated with
children's tactile and visual erogenous contacts with the adult body

+ irrational
  tempers*

1. Junior's temper regularly erupted at home. He screamed if his parents tried to discipline him by taking his privileges away. He screamed when his father could not immediately fix his bike. He screamed and kicked when he found his father sitting on the sofa with his sisters and was told not to push the sisters away.

+ / – irrational
fears*

2. Junior, as already noted, experienced fears of being poisoned by his feces. However, he was not preoccupied with these concerns.

+ sexual
  symptoms*

3. Junior was reported to have pushed part of a toy into his little sister's vagina. He had plenty of opportunity to carry out such activities since at the age of six, Junior still was taking baths with this younger sister.

– / + biting*

4. Junior presented no symptoms pertaining to flesh-biting but in his stories repeatedly referred to this topic: "a shark bit . . . a bear started to bite a man . . . a tiger bit the lion . . . the bobcat bit the baby tiger . . . the cougar bit the baby leopard, etc."

+ eyes*

5. Junior was troubled with a reading problem when he first started school.

Also, Junior "accidentally" hit his father in the eye[6] with a shoe.

Two of Junior's stories focused upon eyes: "A turkey ran away into the forest. A hunter shooted him and took him home and ate him and took his *eyes* out . . . a car ran over a dog and split his *eye* open."

−/+ fire*   6. Junior presented no symptoms involving fire. However, during therapy he frequently spoke of fire in an unusual way: He talked of his therapist's chair being on *fire*. . . . He poked into the radiator opening and asked whether it could catch *fire*. . . . He worried that maybe his family's automobile had caught on *fire* with his sisters in it. He put all the dolls in the doll house bathroom as he explained that the *bedroom* was on *fire*.

NOTES

1 Son of Douglas, case 57.
2 Compare this mother's reactions with those of Kevin's mother, case 43.
3 Despite these indications that Junior wanted to run away from home, he yearned to be home with his parents when he was later placed in a residential setting.
4 Since this content is presented in phantasy rather than as a component of symptoms or dreams, it has not been considered in relation to the overall statistical study.
5 In regard to anal masturbation and symptoms pertaining to bees, see also cases 77 and 100 of Kurt Junior and Ronny.
6 Compare with case 99 of Philip; case 100 of Ronny.

Douglas, Junior
58

Stimulation-Symptom-and-Dream-Profile

Separation Phobias
Night Terrors, Twilight States
+ Sleep in Bed with Adult   + Irrational Fears: Other
+ Irrational Tempers
+ Adult Genital Erotic   + Sexual Symptoms

	Biting/Cutting, etc.	*content of*
+ View Adult Coitus	+ Eyes	*dreams and*
	Fire	*symptoms*

Learning Problems (levels 2 or 3, etc.)
+ Punitive Yelling   Lying and Delinquency
Reversal of Affect

Beatings	+ Closing Down Upon, Kill	*content of* *dreams and*
	Falling	*symptoms*

+ Excretory Symptoms and Dreams
+ Anal Masturbation
+ Preoccupation with Child's BM   Enuresis

	Illness, etc.	*content of*
Anal Contacts	Pain	*dreams and*
	+ Death	*symptoms*
	Compulsions	

Case 59: Frank

Although eleven-year-old Frank attained a normal I.Q. score on his Belle-vue Wechsler Tests, Verbal I.Q. of 103, Performance of 96, total I.Q. 99, he displayed a learning problem at school. His mother was convinced that this problem was organic in origin and thought that he must have been afflicted with "St. Vitus Dance." She spoke of him as having been hyperactive as a baby and poorly coordinated. His initial efforts to walk, she felt, were characterized by the gait of a "drunken sailor."

Because of his "defectiveness," the mother felt "obliged" to *overprotect* Frank lest he be hurt or injured in some way. *She watched over his every move far more carefully than she did in the case of her other three children.* She reported that she also prayed more for Frank and did more for him than for any of the other children. Sometimes she felt as if he were her "only child."

With such indications that the mother was taking over her son's ego, it is not surprising that one of Frank's presenting symptoms was a pervasive passivity and lack of initiative.

Sources of Stimulation:
adult punitive and excretory contact with children

−/+ early
deprivation

1. Until the age of one year, Frank frequently spit up solid foods.

+ beatings*

2. The father was a highly explosive man when things did not go as he wished. During Frank's early childhood he would vent his tempers by strapping the little boy.

+ punitive
yelling*

3. The mother "used to" yell at Frank "all the time" because she was so "fearful" that he could not take care of himself. She added, "I made him a nervous wreck."

The father's continual yelling at the mother added to the noisy upset in the house. After his explosions, the father would attempt to "make up" by bringing home presents to the "kids."

−/+ anal
stimulation*

4. Frank reported that his twelve-year-old sister was continually constipated and given enemas. While he was offering this information, Frank became animated for the first time during his diagnostic interviews, an indication that possibly he may have been an excited spectator of these activities.

Behavioral Symptoms correlated with
adult punitive and excretory contacts with children

+ negative
  behavior

+ learning*
  (level 2; referral
  problem)

1. "Surface compliance, deeper defiance" described Frank's actions. In school he received A's for courteousness, yet did not do his work. Although Frank managed to pass his subjects, his teacher wanted him to repeat the grade because of his immaturity.

+ freezing of
  affect

Frank's restrictiveness appeared not only in school: it was pervasive. He could not react when the neighborhood children teased him. Similarly, when the father gave Frank's desk away to Frank's brother, Frank refused to speak up. His mother was angry that he was emotionally paralyzed in the face of insult and injury.

+ negative
  emotion

2. In school, Frank's politeness and conformity which earned him A's in conduct were balanced by his underlying hate for his teachers. Interestingly enough, it was *immediately* after his report of his sister's constipation and his mother's administering enemas to her that Frank erupted with a tirade of hate for one of the nuns in school: "She's mean . . . she makes me write a sentence a hundred times . . . she blames me . . . she fusses about wearing rubbers . . . she brings the kids' marks down . . . she talks about mortal sin and the evil of dirty talk. . . . One boy wrote a dirty word on a piece of paper and that was awful." One wonders if the nun did not serve as a convenient object of his inhibited rage activated by his mother's controlling behavior.

− / + excretory
symptoms*

3. Frank's first memories involved "a *black* stove," "*backing* into a screen" and "scribbles all over the wall," screen memories which contained fecal connotations (see Appendix 2, Table of Definitions).

+ closing down
  upon
  destructively*
+ falling*

+ hurting

4. Frank was plagued by accident-proneness. *He would run into the street* without looking, "throw himself with abandon into situations in which he was likely to get hurt" and was constantly getting himself banged up and bruised. He variously broke his arm, fell off his bike, ran into a wall and had to have stitches in his forehead.

Frank also was expert in inciting others to pick on him and fight with him. He would stubbornly and persistently provoke his father by coming to the dinner table every night with dirty hands. According to his mother the home was "peaceful" until Frank would walk in, whereupon he would immediately start fighting with his siblings. Frank would also provoke the neighborhood children to tease him, even though he was not able to stand up to them. His mother felt that he was frightened of fighting because if he broke loose, he might hurt somebody.

Sources of Stimulation:
children's tactile and visual erogenous contacts with the adult body

1. Although he was brought up under the influence of a strict Catholic doctrine which taught the sinfulness of carnal thoughts, Frank, at the age of

+ adult nudity   eleven, still saw his pubescent twelve-year-old sister, his father and his mother
                      naked as they walked around the house.

Behavioral Symptoms correlated with
children's tactile and visual erogenous contacts with the adult body

+ irrational fears*   1. Frank was phobic of spiders and bugs. He also suffered from bad dreams
+ nightmares   about witches. The dreams drove him to his mother's bed; however, his father,
                      in a fury, would send him out on these occasions.

Frank
59

Stimulation-Symptom-and-Dream-Profile

		Separation Phobias	
		Night Terrors, Twilight States	
Sleep in Bed with Adult	+	Irrational Fears: Other	
		Irrational Tempers	
Adult Genital Erotic		Sexual Symptoms	
		Biting/Cutting, etc.	*content of*
View Adult Coitus		Eyes	*dreams and*
		Fire	*symptoms*
	+	Learning Problems (levels 2 or 3, etc.)	
+ Punitive Yelling		Lying and Delinquency	
		Reversal of Affect	
+ Beatings	+	Closing Down Upon, Kill	*content of dreams and*
	+	Falling	*symptoms*
		Excretory Symptoms and Dreams	
		Anal Masturbation	
Preoccupation with Child's BM		Enuresis	
		Illness, etc.	*content of*
Anal Contacts		Pain	*dreams and*
		Death	*symptoms*
		Compulsions	

Case 60: Guy

Guy's mother sounded distraught when she called the child guidance clinic to ask for help about a "very acute" problem that was "getting increasingly out-of-hand." The source of her concern was the aggressiveness, hyperactivity, defiance and stubbornness of her five-and-a-half-year-old son, Guy, who repeatedly placed himself in dangerous situations. The mother noted, however, that "Guy was a bright, intelligent child with a great many interests and on many occasions was just an angel."

A report from a neurological specialist read as follows: Guy exhibited some "general symptoms, restlessness and hyperactivity, characteristic of mild neurological damage." The neurologist noted that: ". . . Guy had to ask about everything he saw and then go on to the next question before the answer to the first could be finished. He knew a lot verbally and was able to tell about the newest President and things of that nature to a surprising extent; it seemed his information and vocabulary were more like that of an eight-year-old than a five-year-old boy. . . . However, his outstretched hand evidenced a little choreo-athetosis. His hands were quite clumsy in holding a pencil and his work with a pencil was obviously far below his verbal activity. When he offered to print his surname he quite clearly started to curve a 'J' in a reverse direction, corrected his error and then printed fairly clearly. . . . His square was very poor for a child his age. It seems that his restlessness, his attention to detail and his spatial-perceptual difficulties point to brain injury, although there is obviously a great deal of defiance toward his mother in it too." Since electroencephalogram studies revealed normal findings, Guy's case was diagnosed as one of minimal brain disturbance.[1] Of note, on the form L-M of the Stanford Binet, Guy earned a Binet I.Q. score of 107.

Sources of Stimulation:
adult punitive and excretory contacts with children

+ early
deprivation

1. During her pregnancy, Guy's mother was "miserable, bothered, and uncomfortable." Shortly after conception her own father suddenly died, whereupon she became deeply depressed.

After Guy was delivered by caesarian section, the mother returned home to a husband who refused to be of help. She felt she was "forced to do more than she should." She also was frightened of her husband's hostility, "though he never attacked physically." In an attempt to improve their tense relationship,

241

she sought psychiatric help for both of them. However, Guy's father, who would only see a psychiatrist sporadically six or seven times over the year, reacted negatively to therapeutic intervention.

Furthermore, the father could do no better than "carp and denigrate his wife in front of people." He showed little concern for her when her labor pains started and even refused to take her to the hospital until he had taken his time to complete his morning shave.

The mother claimed that as an infant Guy was "an angel." "He ate well, slept well and seemed happy playing by himself even though he was active from the start." At the same time, she complained that following delivery Guy "was very stiff like a wooden baby" so that it had been impossible for her to get any rapport with him.

(+ falling*)

Soon after Guy arrived home he caught his head in the bars of his crib. Seven months later, after he had learned to climb out of his playpen, he repeatedly *fell out* and hurt himself. Neither parent seemed to be able to protect Guy nor able to quiet him by holding him securely or rocking him tenderly.[2]

When Guy was two years old, the parents used to lock him in his bedroom because he would not sleep.[3] Guy's response was to "rant and rave." The parents, however, felt that there was no other way of handling him.

+ beatings*

(+ enuresis*)

2. The father tried every possible kind of punishment to "bend Guy to his will" without success. He confessed that *he preferred strapping Guy for he was afraid he might really harm the boy if he hit him with his hand.* Many of his beatings were inflicted upon Guy for inconsequential misbehavior or for disturbances which more appropriately required helpful intervention. For example, Guy, at the age of four, did not want to return to day camp and would wet himself. The father handled the situation simply by beating him.

The father had been severely beaten when he was a child. In particular, he recalled being severely strapped by his father for playing hooky from school when he was Guy's age.

The father's sadism became all the more evident when he reported "the happy news" that the clinic's suggestion that he talk with Guy rather than beat him "had not worked at all." He opposed all suggestions to offer Guy psychotherapy for his problems and refused to consider any possibility of giving up his practice of teaching Guy right from wrong by beating him.

Sometimes the mother would have to stand between the father and Guy because she did not feel it right for such a big man to lose his temper so quickly with a little boy. However, the mother herself was accustomed to attacking Guy by hitting him with her fists.

+ punitive
yelling*

3. Guy continually asked his parents: did his father like spanking him? did his mother like screaming at him?

Behavioral Symptoms correlated with children
adult punitive and excretory contacts with children

+ negative
behavior
(opposites)

1. "When the policewoman at school told Guy to come across the street with the other school children he refused to come; then when she signaled for the automobiles to go ahead, he dashed out in front of them."

(reversals)

The question arises as to whether Guy's writing a "J" in reverse (thereby forming an "L"), and his writing an "L" in reverse (thereby forming a "J"), may have reflected his negative tendency to reverse and to do the opposite from what he was supposed to do.

Negatively refusing to listen was also a problem. "I put my hands over my ears," Guy explained, "and block my ears when I don't want to hear."

(+ withdrawal)

Guy also continually stayed away from nursery school in the afternoon; he did not return home until long after dark.

+ freezing of
emotion

2. During his diagnostic, Guy reported one of his *first* memories: "Sometimes when I was hurt, I would *not cry*."

+ reversal of
affect*

Likewise, Guy directly demonstrated a reversal of affect via an inappropriate silliness during his diagnostic interviews. His psychologist wrote: "By the end of his first hour, Guy acted not as silly and was more relaxed as he noted, 'I like it here, because you don't fuss too much.' " However, in his next interview, "Guy was extremely and inappropriately silly and remained that way; he acted 'fresh' and continually parroted my words."

+ killing*

3. Guy often *threatened to kill himself* but ended up laughing when his father asked what kind of weapon he would like to do it with. In reality, Guy constantly flirted with getting himself killed. His mother noted that Guy paid absolutely no attention to traffic on the street; he constantly ran in front of cars. She felt all she could do was "pray" that nothing would happen. To make matters worse, Guy on three occasions got into his father's car which was parked on an incline and then released the brake. One time the car picked up momentum as it rolled downhill toward a busy intersection. Guy managed to get out before the car smashed into a parked vehicle at the foot of the hill.[4] Guy said he *had* to do these things even though he knew he shouldn't; even his father recognized the driven quality of this behavior.

+ closing down
upon
destructively*

+ compulsions*

+ hurting
+ falling*

Frequently Guy did manage to hurt himself. He suffered a double fracture of his arm when he *fell* from the banister. (Recall Guy had frequently fallen out of his crib when he was a little child.) Once he "nearly severed his finger"; several times he got his head "busted open."

+ death*

Guy dreamed about a "skeleton and bones in the street: if you touched the bones twice it made you *die*."

With such concerns about dying, Guy understandably "went wild" when he was brought to the hospital for a tonsillectomy. The mother reported that even though Guy had been given an "absolutely enormous dose of ether," he still managed to get out of his crib on the way back from the operating room.

Guy's involvement with hurting, which was primarily directed toward himself, also became verbally directed towards his sisters who baby-sat with him. Once Guy threatened to pierce his sisters with an umbrella. This threat panicked them to the point that they were ready to call the police.[5]

Sources of Stimulation:
children's tactile and visual erogenous contacts with the adult body

+ adult nudity

1. Guy recalled watching his mother take a bath. He frequently saw his twelve-and-a-half-year-old sister nude. Occasionally Guy showered with his father.

+ kissing

2. Guy's father explained, "I don't feel guilty continuing to spank Guy because at the end of the day we *kiss* and make up." The father also spoke of Guy's liking to wrestle with him: "Guy's only pleasure is wanting to pin me down." When the two would start to wrestle, the father regularly "tickled him out of it."[6]

Behavioral Symptoms correlated with
children's tactile and visual erogenous contacts with the adult body

+ biting/cutting*

1. On one occasion Guy almost cut his finger off with a knife.

+ irrational
tempers*

2. The parents complained of Guy's "terrible temper tantrums": *"Nobody could do a thing with him."* [7]

NOTES

[1] This case therefore involved behavioral symptoms accompanying excessive punishment stimulation with or without a background of minimal brain dysfunction.

[2] The question arises as to whether Guy's hyperactivity from early infancy reflected the absence of such patterns of tranquilizing stimulation. See cases 19, 44, 47, 75, 76, 83, 86, regarding the relation of hyperactivity to early deprivation.

[3] The father also suffered from a sleep problem.

[4] Significantly, the parents did not lock the car after this incident and did not prevent Guy from trying to smash it up on two subsequent occasions.

[5] The parents also became "panicked" with feelings of desperation yet the father refused to get an adult to sit with the children on the few occasions the parents went out for an evening. Neither the advice of the diagnostic team nor the pleas of his wife could induce the father to protect the girls and protect Guy from such dangerous situations.

[6] This case involving the father's showering with Guy, kissing him, wrestling with him, beating him, demonstrates the same patterns of stimulation prominent in the history

of Nathan, case 46; see also the synopsis of Kolansky and Moore's Dick, case 32, regarding the dynamics of fathers who have homosexual problems of beating children and wrestling with them.

7 This case illustrates the need to treat not only the organic disturbances which may possibly be present but also to protect the patient from excessive punishment and/or erogenous stimulation. The more helpless the child, the more the need for protection from traumatic stimulation. Of note, Guy's parents' most disturbing deficits involved their *incapacity to protect* their boy: from falling out of his baby crib, from staying outside until after dark, from getting into an unlocked car three times and sending it rolling downhill or from continuing to be left home alone at night with his young sisters who were so frightened of him. The parents could offer Guy only beatings and screaming.

Guy

60

Stimulation-Symptom-and-Dream-Profile

Separation Phobias
Night Terrors, Twilight States
Sleep in Bed with Adult   Irrational Fears: Other
+ Irrational Tempers
Adult Genital Erotic   Sexual Symptoms
+ Biting/Cutting, etc.   } *content of*
View Adult Coitus   Eyes   } *dreams and*
Fire   } *symptoms*

Learning Problems (levels 2 or 3, etc.)
+ Punitive Yelling   Lying and Delinquency
+ Reversal of Affect
+ Beatings   + Closing Down Upon, Kill   } *content of* / *dreams and*
+ Falling   } *symptoms*

Excretory Symptoms and Dreams
Anal Masturbation
Preoccupation with Child's BM   + Enuresis
Illness, etc.   } *content of*
Anal Contacts   Pain   } *dreams and*
+ Death   } *symptoms*
+ Compulsions

Case 61: Henry

Eight-year-old Henry was referred to the clinic for a "behavior problem at school." By this time he had experienced a sad and disturbed life. Until he was five, Henry lived with his mother, a highly intelligent woman who gave up a college scholarship for a life of "pleasure" devoted to drugs, drinking and promiscuity. The mother, intensely attached to Henry, kept him always close to her. Offering him few controls, she permitted Henry to do and say anything he wished so that he learned little tolerance for being "crossed."

Then Henry's mother died following an attempted abortion when Henry was five. At that time, he was sent to his grandparents where his life suddenly became turned upside down. Over-permissiveness, exposure to drugs and sexual promiscuity were replaced by iron controls, restriction and beatings incurred for the slightest infraction of the grandparents' demands.

Source of Stimulation:
adult punitive and excretory contacts with children

+ early
deprivation

1. Henry's birth was traumatic. With his umbilical cord wrapped around his neck tightly, he required artificial resuscitation for fifteen minutes before he finally breathed spontaneously.[1]

Henry was "brought up" under "shaky" home conditions. At the age of two and a half, he was admitted to a hospital medical ward with the notation "mother was under the influence of alcohol, patient had received a scalp laceration from a blow of a hammer." Just prior to his mother's death, Henry, at the age of five, was once again brought to the hospital, this time for an abdominal pain. The attending surgeon wrote, "This is a *neglected child*, under the care of a neighbor; boy is suffering from poor hygiene; lying on the bed he plays with his genitalia with one hand while sucking his thumb of the other hand."

+ punitive yelling
and violence*

2. Henry retained many memories of violence in his mother's home. He recalled one of his mother's boyfriends "wrecking" his mother. He described, for example, the activities of his mother's boy friend, Mack: "Mack threw the alarm clock and got an axe and broke the windows when my mother tried to keep him out. It cost my mother about $200. I ran to get the police. Mack was going to wreck my mother. I got there just in time."

Later, in the new home, the grandmother and grandfather constantly argued with one another in addition to their castigating Henry.

246

+ beatings*

3. Henry's grandmother felt that her husband lost his self-control when he hit Henry. She, therefore, "insisted" on being present to try to stop him from such punishments. She questioned physical punishment yet she herself frequently resorted to belting Henry with a strap.

In Henry's words, "My grandfather beats with a strap, many times at a time. He hits me so hard I've had marks all over. He looks at me like he likes to beat. My grandmother does not beat me so much but she uses a belt too." Even when the grandfather reduced the frequency of his beatings, he still continued to threaten Henry with "disaster."

+ adult
  defecation

4. Henry was allowed in the bathroom while his grandfather attended to his toilet functions.

– / + anal
stimulation* (only
one occasion)

Also of possible significance, Henry was subjected to a digital exam of his rectum when he was brought to the hospital with an abdominal pain just prior to his mother's death.

Behavioral Symptoms correlated with
adult punitive and excretory contacts with children

+ negative
  behavior

1. Henry's teacher commented that Henry had difficulty staying in class when he felt negativistic. He suffered from a severe restrictive learning problem. At the age of nine with a *verbal* I.Q. of 104, Henry only attained second grade scores on his "word knowledge" and attained *first grade* scores on "word discrimination."

+ learning*
  (level 3)

+ lying*

Henry also displayed another form of negativism: a propensity to make up fibs, e.g., he stole, then presented reports opposite from reality so as to avoid punishment.

+ falling*

2. Henry's earliest memories all involved falling: (a) "I was crawling out of my bed and the bed *tipped over*"; (b) "I remember walking down the steps and I *fell*"; (c) "I was getting on a [toy] truck and my sister pulled it from under me and I *fell*. I hurt my back."

These early memories of being hurt, were re-enacted by Henry as he grew older. In the residential school where he was placed, Henry was adept *at provoking* counselors to attack him, knock him down and end up holding him on the couch, floor or bed. While Henry's part in instigating these battles was often forgotten, it was easy for an observer to become angry at the "brutal" counselors for manhandling a helpless boy.

+ killing*

Henry "tried" to *kill himself with a knife* while he was living with his mother. He also went through the motions of this activity when he was living in a residential school for children with emotional problems. On one occasion he threatened to jump out of the window as a form of suicide.

Henry was also ready to kill others. He was caught throwing rocks at a window from a rooftop. Finally, Henry was expelled from his residential school because he *threw a knife toward one of his peers*. This time the knife was thrust at another boy rather than himself. Actually, two years earlier, Henry had told his therapist a dream: "I was ready to kill this boy with a knife."[2]

+ / − excretory
symptoms*
− / + pain* (only
one occasion)

3. Henry suffered from some constipation. When, at the age of five, he was sent to the hospital emergency room, the attending physician's diagnosis was "abdominal pains (transient) due to constipation."

Henry also avoided bathing to the degree that others would complain of his body odor.

Sources of Stimulation:
children's tactile and visual erogenous contacts with the adult body

− / + sleeping in
bed with adults*
(frequency?)

1. Henry told how he slept in bed with his mother two days before she went to the hospital from which she never returned. He spoke also of Lilly, his mother's girl friend, who "landed drunk as could be" in Henry's bed.

+ adult nudity

2. Henry saw both his mother and Lilly without clothes. He recalled Lilly walking out of her room with only a towel around her waist with her breasts exposed, and on another occasion seeing his mother drunk and completely unclothed. As he spoke of seeing his mother's pubic hair, Henry added: "I couldn't take it any more so I ran away and didn't come back till twelve o'clock at night. I had a secret way to get in the house: my sister would let me up."

Henry was also exposed to seeing his mother's used menstrual pads. He thought it contained "shit with blood."

3. It is not known whether Henry directly observed his mother's or Lilly's sexual contacts with their numerous boyfriends or with one another when they were using alcohol or drugs. Henry did recall seeing Lilly kissing different men. He added "she was too friendly with the boys."

+ adult genital
erotic*

Henry was repeatedly exposed to pornographic pictures belonging to his mother and his aunt. He recalled pictures of naked men, naked women and "funny-book pictures" of both.

Behavioral Symptoms correlated with
children's tactile and visual erogenous contacts with the adult body

+ irrational
tempers*

1. Henry would swear, kick and yell with little impulse control when he didn't get his way. He offered his therapist a full-blown demonstration of these temper tantrums. His therapist noted, for example, "At the end of one of our sessions Henry decided that he was going to take home some toy soldiers from the therapy room. When I explained why he couldn't take them . . . he yelled 'I'm going to cut off your finger. You are supposed to let me take them home 'cause I said I want them.' " On another occasion, Henry stamped " 'Why did

you bring in these stupid girl's toys?' and began throwing them furiously on the floor."

+ sexual symptoms*

2. During Henry's referral to emergency OPD for an abdominal pain when he was five years old, he openly and compulsively masturbated.

Henry also recalled getting into his mother's high-heeled shoes and then running outside naked. He also liked to put on his mother's girdle.

+ fire*

3. During his first diagnostic hour, Henry presented a *dream* about fire: "My pants were on *fire*. They were drying on the stove. I got a hose and squirted it all over the window. Then it stopped."

This same theme of fire repetitively appeared within Henry's phantasies. To quote from his therapist's notes: "Henry took out a fire engine and said there was going to be a *fire* while he placed the father doll in bed. . . . On another occasion Henry asked for *matches* 'cause he wanted to *start a fire.*' . . . Once Henry yelled '*fire, fire, fire,* ding, ding, ding' and then commented that the father doll likes to fool around in bed all the time."

Unfortunately, Henry's prolonged neglect during his infancy, then five years of overpermissive sexualized living with his mother and five subsequent years of suppressive beatings by his grandparents laid the groundwork for the establishment of such a severe disturbance that it was not possible to control his many problems and it became necessary for the residential school to transfer him to another therapeutic setting.

NOTES

1 Henry was finally discharged in good condition. Later neurological studies, including an EEG when Henry was ten, revealed no signs of brain damage.

2 The dramatic parallel between Henry's dream and his behavior two years later suggests how a dream may function like an activated goal, channeling the course of future action.

Henry
61

Stimulation-Symptom-and-Dream-Profile

	Separation Phobias	
	Night Terrors, Twilight States	
Sleep in Bed with Adult	Irrational Fears: Other	
	+ Irrational Tempers	
+ Adult Genital Erotic	+ Sexual Symptoms	
	Biting/Cutting, etc.	} *content of*
View Adult Coitus	Eyes	} *dreams and*
	+ Fire	} *symptoms*
	+ Learning Problems (levels 2 or 3, etc.)	
+ Punitive Yelling	+ Lying and Delinquency	
	Reversal of Affect	
+ Beatings	+ Closing Down Upon, Kill	} *content of dreams and*
	+ Falling	} *symptoms*
	+ Excretory Symptoms and Dreams	
	Anal Masturbation	
Preoccupation with Child's BM	Enuresis	
	Illness, etc.	} *content of*
Anal Contacts	Pain	} *dreams and*
	Death	} *symptoms*
	Compulsions	

Case 62: Ian

Ian was seventeen when he attempted suicide by ingesting thirty to fifty tablets of aspirin. "Ian had become increasingly withdrawn and unable to function at home, in school, or in the world of peers. Outpatient therapy in the past had not been helpful."

Despite an I.Q. of 124, Ian had been unable to keep up with his four older "brilliant" siblings. His schoolwork had always been "poor"; he had no interest in sports. In general, he pictured himself doomed to failure.

Sources of Stimulation:
adult punitive and excretory contacts with children

+ early
  deprivation

1. Ian was born when his father was 48 and his mother 47. His mother felt that because of their age she and her husband did not have as much patience with him as they had had with their older children. Everyone in the family "brushed Ian off."

Ian became a lonely hyperactive baby. Reportedly, by the age of four he referred to himself as "Ian, alone against the world."

2. The father was said to have a "hot temper" and described himself as a "severe disciplinarian." He would insist that Ian eat all food placed before him at the table even though Ian was uncomfortably overweight.

+ beatings*

The father regularly beat Ian and his older brother. Beatings, according to the mother, became increasingly severe from the time Ian was six years old. A particularly upsetting episode occurred when Ian was ten. The father was resting in bed when Ian gave his mother a rather flip response to a request. Thereupon, the father took Ian's pants down and beat the boy with a belt. With shame Ian admitted that his father "had knocked the shit" out of him.

+ anal
  stimulation*

3. The father on a number of occasions administered enemas to Ian as an adolescent to alleviate his constipation. The parents noted that Ian had hated the procedure.

Behavioral Symptoms correlated with
adult punitive and excretory contacts with children

+ negative
  behavior
  (withdrawal)

1. Ian never enjoyed close friendships and was withdrawing more and more into the confines of his room. He expressed it this way: "I once had a friend

but he moved away. Now all I want is to be left alone."

+learning*
(referral
problem)

Ian withdrew in school also. One day he was expelled for falling asleep in class. In general, he irked many of his teachers by his lack of attention and by constantly turning away from the work at hand. He repeatedly failed to complete his assignments. It was no wonder that his schoolwork had been "poor."

+negative
thinking

Reflecting his intensely negative mode of thinking, Ian spoke of his image of man in the future, "Man will have *no* ears; *no* nails, his nails will *disappear* because they are remnants of claws; *no* teeth, his teeth also will *disappear*."

+negative
emotion

2. Ian's negative emotions were succinctly reflected by his report of his three main problems: (a) "I have problems with my courses and I *don't care* any more"; (b) "I *hate* spiders"; (c) "I *hate* people. They make promises that they don't keep. People alter themselves to make themselves more popular."

+hurting

3. Ian had been accident-prone for many years. His diagnostic record stated: "At camp, Ian's head was split open twice from rocks. One time one of his counselors knocked him out cold as punishment for freshness. When Ian played, he seemed to *fall down* and *sprain or strain* a limb. He has had a history of having to be X-rayed many times. The previous summer Ian displayed many burns on his arm from letting the wax from a burning candle pour down his arm." Of note, no sooner had Ian talked of his father's beatings than he recalled episodes when his head had been "split by rocks."

+falling*

+burn* (+fire*)
+closing down
upon
destructively*
+non-organic
illness*
+pain*

Ian developed *painful* headaches whenever he was exposed to pressure at home or school. His headaches interfered with his ability to concentrate.

+death*

Death was an area which greatly upset Ian. The year of his diagnostic referral, Ian had made a much better start in school, that is, until his teacher in physics suddenly died. Following this event, Ian seemed unable to resume any interest in academic study.

+killing*

Ian's death wishes were reflected by disturbing thoughts which he presented during his diagnostic. He mentioned that tuna fish were filled with mercury; eating them would *kill* us. He went on to speak of a compulsion to *kill* bugs, then once again expressed a wish to *kill* himself. Ian did ingest a bottle of aspirin during an actual suicide attempt.

+excretory
symptoms*

4. Ian suffered from constant constipation, a source for erogenous and painful anal-rectal stimulation.[1]

Sources of Stimulation:
children's tactile and visual erogenous contacts with the adult body

+adult nudity

1. From birth till age three, Ian slept in the same room as his sister (older than he by nine years); from the age of three to six years, he slept in the same room as his brother who was older by ten years; from the age of six to ten years, he slept in the same room as his father. He had been accustomed to

seeing each of them when they were dressing and undressing. Thus from the age of three, Ian continually saw the large bodies of his adolescent siblings or of his father, a possible source for impressing upon him that he alone in the family possessed a small and inadequate body.

Behavioral Symptoms correlated with
children's tactile and visual erogenous contacts with the adult body

+ irrational fears*

1. At the age of ten, Ian put his head under the covers because of his frightening thoughts of *robots*.[2] Under the covers, he would sweat with such terror that he could "hardly breathe."

During his elementary school years Ian developed numerous "phobias," among them fears of clouds and fears of the cellar. At night Ian insisted that all the doors of his bedroom and the doors of his closet be left open.

+ irrational tempers*

2. At the age of two, Ian demonstrated "mild" temper tantrums "at inconvenient times." Then, during three years of therapy when he was a young boy, Ian was urged to let out his angry feelings. Unfortunately, this approach eventuated in his "letting loose" not only in the therapy room where he would throw "things" around but also at home where he would recklessly "destroy things" in his room.

NOTES

1 Ian did not like showers and refrained from bathing. It is understandable, therefore, that he saw himself as "crappy" both inside and out, a basis for his identification with excrement and with the dirty bugs which he felt compelled to kill.

2 It was at the age of ten that Ian's father like a robot had "beaten the shit" out of him (see above under "beatings").

Ian
62

Stimulation-Symptom-and-Dream-Profile

	Separation Phobias	
	Night Terrors, Twilight States	
Sleep in Bed with Adult	+ Irrational Fears: Other	
	+ Irrational Tempers	
Adult Genital Erotic	Sexual Symptoms	
	Biting/Cutting, etc.	} *content of*
View Adult Coitus	Eyes	} *dreams and*
	+ Fire	} *symptoms*

	+ Learning Problems (levels 2 or 3, etc.)	
Punitive Yelling	Lying and Delinquency	
	Reversal of Affect	
+ Beatings	+ Closing Down Upon, Kill	} *content of* *dreams and*
	+ Falling	} *symptoms*

	+ Excretory Symptoms and Dreams	
	Anal Masturbation	
Preoccupation with Child's BM	Enuresis	
	+ Illness, etc.	} *content of*
+ Anal Contacts	+ Pain	} *dreams and*
	+ Death	} *symptoms*
	Compulsions	

Case 63: Julius

Julius was twelve years old at the time of his diagnostic evaluation. His referral note read: "Behavior problem in school; cannot accept discipline; some lying; running away; and threats of suicide." Greatly concerned that Julius might carry out his suicide threats, Julius's mother and her therapist questioned whether special placement outside of the home might be necessary.

Sources of Stimulation:
adult punitive and excretory contacts with children

−/+ early
deprivation

1. Between the ages of sixteen and eighteen months, Julius suffered from lead poisoning. Beyond this information, no material was available in relation to early deprivation other than Julius's first memory: "I was climbing on top of the counter to get something to eat."

2-3. Julius's mother had been sent to reform school when she was fourteen years old because she had attacked another girl with a knife. At reform school she was accused of pushing a matron down the stairs. She recalled seeing a psychiatrist who told her to "scream and pound the walls rather than hit out." It is, therefore, understandable that she saw her rage toward Julius as poten-

+ beatings*

tially murderous. She pointed out, "I could hurt or kill him." Sometimes she became so angry she smashed dishes against the wall. Until the clinic intervened, she "disciplined" Julius by beating him. Julius confided, "She hits me with a cord and a belt every couple of days. One time two months ago she beat me till the skin came off."

+ punitive
yelling*

The stepfather also beat Julius, usually on his "bare behind." However, according to Julius's mother, the stepfather did not go as far as she did. Frequently, he just "got upset and nervous and screamed and hollered." In answer to a diagnostic question, "What do you think are your problems that make you worried or scared or angry?" Julius stated, "When my *father always starts yelling he swears at me.*" Julius stated that he was not allowed to say the swear words. When his therapist listed a number of swear words, Julius admitted that his stepfather screamed at him with the words "shit" and "asshole."

+ beatings*

After being beaten violently *on his bare rear end*, Julius would look at his bruised flesh in the mirror: "My rear looked like two cups," he admitted, "lousy, like a ball *cut* in half; it was all swollen."

Behavioral Symptoms correlated with
adult punitive and excretory contacts with children

+ negative
  behavior
+ lying*

1. Three of Julius's referral problems highlighted negative behavior: (a) refusal to accept discipline in school (opposition to authority); (b) lying at school (stating opposite from reality); (c) running away from home.

In addition, Julius attended school irregularly; and according to the school report when he did attend "he was withdrawn, with no friends at all. He would sit and sulk unless the teacher gave him a lot of attention. If she succeeded in drawing him out, he performed well in reading and math but could 'put up with it' for only brief periods; then he would pick a fight and get put out of the room. . . . This pattern recurred day after day." Within the four years prior to referral, Julius's I.Q. fell from 115 to 92.

+ learning*
  (level 2)

+ freezing of
  affect

2. Julius appeared "affectless" during his diagnostic interviews. The psychologist who tested him wrote: "Julius is a thin child with a round full face. His face is very inexpressive, with a kind of blank stare at most times." Similarly, the diagnostic notes state: "Julius is a thin boy with back-bones protruding. He looks absolutely listless and affectless."

+ negative
  emotion

The emotion Julius did express was *dislike*. Julius complained to his mother that he didn't like his therapist. He complained that the therapist had used "swears" with him and treated him like a baby.[1]

+ killing* (self)

3. It was Julius's suicide threats and his aggressive attacks upon others which had precipitated his referral for diagnostic evaluation. Julius had also been found *jumping between rooftops* and *climbing* to dangerous positions high in *treetops* from which it was feared he would *fall*.

+ falling*

+ hurting

Julius not only endangered his own life but also threatened others. He beat up his sisters and liked to punch them in the chest. On one occasion he started to attack his mother with a kitchen knife. However, he did put it away when his mother told him to.

+ closing down
  upon
  destructively*

Sources of Stimulation:
children's tactile and visual erogenous contacts with the adult body

+ adult nudity
+ adult genital
  erotic*

1. According to his mother's reports, Julius had frequently come across hard-core pornographic magazines.

Behavioral Symptoms correlated with
children's tactile and visual erogenous contacts with the adult body

+ twilight states*

1. One night Julius awoke with the conviction that his shoes were suddenly "rising in the air"[2] and going around in circles. He assured me, "I saw it only once but it was real. Oh yes, it was."

NOTES

1 It turned out that not only his stepfather but both grandparents swore constantly in the house; yet Julius had been beaten for swearing. Julius continued to feel negatively about swearing even though his mother now supported her therapist's view that it would be better for him to let his hate out by a little swearing rather than by suicidal preoccupations.

2 The image of shoes *"rising in the air"* coincides with Julius's symptoms of *climbing dangerousiy high* in the trees as well as his *jumping* from rooftop to rooftop. If punishment overstimulation often eventuates in the *reversal of emotion*, Julius's symptoms pertaining to the image of *flying high* may reflect the reversal of a fear of *falling* (a typical fear among children who have been excessively punished). An omnipotent image of flying, reversing and countering fearful feelings of falling, is appropriately labeled *counter*-phobic.

Julius
63

Stimulation-Symptom-and-Dream-Profile

	Separation Phobias	
	+ Night Terrors, Twilight States	
Sleep in Bed with Adult	Irrational Fears: Other	
	Irrational Tempers	
+ Adult Genital Erotic	Sexual Symptoms	
	Biting/Cutting, etc.	*content of*
View Adult Coitus	Eyes	*dreams and*
	Fire	*symptoms*

	+ Learning Problems (levels 2 or 3, etc.)	
+ Punitive Yelling	+ Lying and Delinquency	
	Reversal of Affect	
+ Beatings	+ Closing Down Upon, Kill	*content of dreams and*
	+ Falling	*symptoms*

	Excretory Symptoms and Dreams	
	Anal Masturbation	
Preoccupation with Child's BM	Enuresis	
	Illness, etc.	*content of*
Anal Contacts	Pain	*dreams and*
	Death	*symptoms*
	Compulsions	

Case 64: Kristen

Kristen is a highly intelligent Scandinavian woman who has been in once-a-week psychotherapy for the past thirty years, from the age of eighteen to forty-eight. In addition to her honesty, Kristen has demonstrated the highest standards of conscience and integrity as well as a faithfulness to therapy. A winter blizzard would shut down the clinic, yet Kristen would be sure to arrive for her appointment. Initially she had been hospitalized and had received shock treatment for the "depressive phase of a manic-depressive condition with schizoid features." During her first therapeutic interview at the hospital, it took three hours and the offer of a cigarette before Kristen could say her first words: "Thank you."

Sources of Stimulation:
adult punitive and excretory contacts with children

+ / − early
deprivation

1. Kristen's first memory offered a clue to a history of early deprivation: she remembered being bathed in a basin of cold water.

During therapy, Kristen also experienced a dream of a baby left freezing in a crib while icy winds drifted in from the bedroom window.

+ beatings*

2. Kristen's childhood was dominated by her father's abusive sexualized beatings. These beatings would be triggered by Kristen's remaining too long in the bathroom with the door locked; her wasting water from the faucet; running water late at night when she was supposed to be sleeping; or talking back to her father and not listening to him. The beatings would begin with the father chasing Kristen wildly around the house, around tables and chairs, while he screamed, "You fucking bitch, I'll get you." The father and Kristen screamed so loudly at one another, the mother trembled for fear of what the neighbors would think. Usually the father cornered Kristen in the kitchen where, panting, he would press against her body and then strap her until she was ready to fall upon the floor.

The father's sadistic beatings were matched by his sadistic curses. He screamed that Kristen was so evil that she would be sure to burn in hell. He even induced a priest to lecture Kristen about her lack of respect for her elders and to inform her that she was the "worst girl who had ever lived in the world."

The mother, who was of the "old school," believed it was "not right" for her to interfere in any way with her husband's attacks upon Kristen.

+ excretory
stimulation

3. Even during Kristen's adolescence, the father regularly used the family bathroom in Kristen's presence. He would blow his nose into the basin, cough and spit out his sputum, urinate and defecate in front of her. Also, he left his feces in the toilet for her to inspect.

Behavioral Symptoms correlated with
adult punitive and excretory contacts with children

+ negative
behavior

1. Kristen's extreme negativism formed the core of her psychotic adjustment to life. Withdrawal, restriction, withholding and opposition made it impossible for her to "make it" in the world. At the age of eighteen she had to be hospitalized.

Withholding and *restriction* were activated to such a degree that during her first therapy session (as noted above) it took Kristen three hours to say her first word and this only after she was offered a cigarette. It took many months before her withholdingness could be even slightly modified. Her movements were restricted to the point that it took her over an hour to wash a single dinner plate. Shock treatment exerted no effect whatsoever.

Prior to her hospital admission Kristen would remain in the family bathroom for hours with the door locked while her enraged father would bang on the door in dire need to urinate or defecate.

(opposition)

Such unyielding rigidity, combined with her withholdingness and tendency to *counter the wishes of others* generated a most disturbing *control* problem, a problem which had a heyday when it came to commencing and terminating her therapy hours. For over a year Kristen was not able to talk during the first hour of her therapy. It became necessary to meet with her for one-and-a-half-hour sessions in order to gain any positive contact with her. Even then, in a controlling way, she would bring up the most urgent material during the last five minutes in an effort to prolong her interview. When it was time to talk, she would not talk, whereas, when it was time to stop talking, she would start talking. After she was discharged from the hospital she would come late for each appointment, i.e., she withheld her appearance just as long as she possibly could and still get away with it. And if Kristen arrived on time, she would manage to keep the therapist waiting by going to the "washroom" from which she would not emerge for half an hour or more, thus, in part, reproducing the scene of keeping herself locked in the bathroom while the father had to wait impatiently outside.

Despite her high ethical standards, Kristen's withholding-negativism was only slowly replaced by positive interactions as the years of therapy rolled by. Fortunately, once Kristen became dependent upon her therapy hour it was possible to present to her a flat rule that if she arrived even one minute after the time set for her appointment, she would not be reprimanded but therapy for that week would be cancelled. Kristen of course did at first arrive ninety seconds late, received sympathy and assurances and a moment or so of kindly conversation but was not seen until the following week. In this way it was possible to reduce her negative controlling behavior not only in therapy but also in the outside world. When Kristen was first discharged from the hospital, she continually arrived late at work, and consequently held no less than fourteen jobs over the period of a year. As she learned to be prompt for her therapy hours, she gradually learned to be prompt for her work. Yet it took almost ten years before she could control her negative behavior to the extent that she was able to retain a job for a full year's period. Even after fifteen years of therapy when Kristen had progressed to the point where she was putting herself through four years of college, she still found herself rigidly withholding studying for exams until the very last minute at which time she would become desperate lest she completely fail. With such negativism it was not surprising that she was faced with a severe learning problem at college, this despite the fact that as a child she had been an A student.[1]

+ learning (level 1)

+ negative behavior

Kristen referred to another aspect of her blatantly negative behavior: a compulsion to do the *opposite* of what she should be doing. Over and over again she repeated, "But if I did things *right* then it would seem *wrong*." Her confusion of "right" and "wrong" set the stage for *compulsive doubting*. When she thought something was "right," the *opposite* feeling soon overcame her and she assumed it might be "wrong."[2] Or, when she first thought something was "wrong," again the "negative," *opposite* feeling soon overcame her so that she then assumed it might be "right." When Kristen was required to make a decision, her negativism resulted in her not knowing which step to take and which step not to take.

+ freezing of emotion

2. At the time of her referral to the hospital, Kristen displayed a massive inhibition of emotion. All functions were inhibited, i.e. , depressed, to the extent that she routinely either slept or remained silent and inactive. If fear, anger or sexual feelings were potentially activated, the expression of such emotion was so inhibited that no signs of their presence could be detected. Although this "depressive" phase of Kristen's "manic-depressive" disorder did not respond to electroshock treatments, it gradually did respond to psychotherapy over a period of ten years. Then, unfortunately, following a suggestion that maybe now she would be able to profit by therapy sessions lasting an hour and a quarter each week in place of the customary hour-and-a-half sessions, Kristen went into a tailspin over the rejection. A "manic" phase of behavior was set in motion along with a course of severe alcoholism.[3]

+ reversal of affect*

Kristen's manic activity dramatically illustrated another aspect of negative emotion, i.e., *reversal of unpleasurable emotional states into pleasurable*. During her "manic phase," suddenly everything was going "wonderfully," people were "so nice," they liked to hear her "sing," they "admired" her. Kristen perseverated about "good news" and how this and that was "fantastic" and "fabulous." Meanwhile, in reality, she was going downhill and getting into trouble, fighting with the authorities, disobeying the rules, etc.

3. From childhood on, feces were of central importance to Kristen. The father's exposure of himself defecating and urinating in front of Kristen was reflected by her own fascination with related body parts and body products.

+ excretory symptoms*

Kristen made the bathroom her palace and the toilet her throne. She would remain there for hours while her enraged father, as already noted, clamored to get into the bathroom to relieve himself. She spent much time on the toilet, as she constantly would wipe herself until her "cleanliness" became a basis for anal masturbation. This anal masturbation became exacerbated as she would dig the toilet paper further into her rectum to make sure it was perfectly clean. This physical association of compulsive cleanliness with anal erogenous sources of pleasure and reward provided a physical basis for the establishment of cleanliness compulsions appearing in the midst of her need to live in dilapidated, disorderly surroundings. For example, when finally Kristen decided to wash her sweater she could not stop washing it in near-boiling water until it had shrunken to the size of doll's clothing. Likewise when she did decide to take a bath, and that was very infrequent, she scrubbed herself so vehemently in steaming hot water that she became concerned that she would rub off her skin.

(+ anal masturbation*)

+ obsessions and compulsions*

Kristen managed to settle upon other sources for anal-rectal stimulation. Withholding of feces together with overeating provided a basis for rectal extension and pressure. Kristen's efforts to "hold in" developed into widespread tic movements involving the tightening of her lips, closing of the eyelids and a shaking back and forth of her head in a "no-no" fashion. Such withholding resulted in fecal staining of Kristen's panties and in episodes of sudden expulsive soiling.[4]

+ tics
(+ eyes*)

Excrement itself provided a source for erogenous excitements. What Kristen could not discharge upon her father's exposed penis when he urinated and defecated in front of her throughout her childhood *and* adolescence, she finished upon his feces. The sexualized looking, touching and mouthing or smelling was in part discharged upon the feces which he would leave in the toilet. Kristen recalled putting her hand in the toilet and handling his excrement with the same excitement she would have felt if she had handled her father's penis. By association, the smell of excrement became sexually exciting to her, a basis for her compulsion to smell her father's stained underdrawers and then her own. Another example of Kristen's involvement with excrement-like messes occurred just prior to her hospitalization when she left her used menstrual pad on the floor in the corner of her closet. Weeks later, Kristen found the bloody pad crawling with maggots. Knowledge of these experiences sheds light upon the origin of a symptom which disturbed Kristen for many years to come: a horror and panic experienced in relation to bugs and vermin.[5]

+ hurting (and torture)

4. Kristen dreaded the punishments of hell because she had committed so many sins against her father. During the early days of therapy, no assurance

+ death*

that God always has been understood to be associated with kindness, love and forgiveness could convince her that she was not going to hell once she died.

+ killing*
(suicide)
+ falling*

+ closing down
upon
destructively*
(crush)
+ obsessions*

Other obsessive thoughts filled Kristen's mind. She struggled with worries about jumping to her death. These thoughts ran rampant when she would have to wait on a subway platform. She became terrified by a compulsion to jump off the platform in the path of an oncoming train that would crush her to her death. Likewise, suicidal thoughts of jumping to her death would overtake Kristen when she found herself upon a bridge high above an expanse of water. She pictured herself gasping for air and *choking* while sinking into such a watery grave. Even in the bathtub or shower Kristen was overcome by these thoughts of drowning and not being able to breathe.

On other occasions, Kristen came close to acting out her wish to be murdered. One year, when she was working as a secretary at a state prison she started to make dates with a criminal who had just been released on parole. Another time she indiscriminately picked up a man at a dance hall, landed in a hotel room with him, and then after a screaming bloody battle was raped.[6]

Sources of Stimulation:
children's tactile and visual erogenous contacts with the adult body

+ kissing

1. Even after Kristen had reached adolescence the father would often corner her in the basement, and seek affection from her by pressing his unshaven whiskers against her face, and then force kisses on her mouth.

Bed-sharing with the parents did not take place. However, Kristen did share a bed with her older sister until she was thirteen years old and the sister was fourteen. The parents recommended that the sisters sleep closely with their buttocks together in order to preserve their "heat" on cold winter nights.

+ adult nudity

2. Throughout her childhood *and* adolescence Kristen's parents took no precautions with respect to exposing her to their nudity, despite the fact that Kristen had been taught that thinking of the flesh was a sin. The mother dressed and undressed in front of Kristen in the dining room where it was "warm." The father walked around the house with only an undershirt on with his genitals displayed for the family to see. At meal times he would urinate into the toilet with the bathroom door open so that Kristen in the adjoining dining room would be exposed to watching him urinate with his elongated penis while she ate.

− / + view adult
coitus*

3. Kristen would regularly hear her parents in the act of sexual intercouse as she listened in the dark outside of the open door of the parental bedroom. Kristen remembered the mother's repetitive protestations accompanying the father's advances.

+ adult genital
erotic*

In addition, Kristen's father beat her as he panted and pressed his body close to her own body (see under "beatings").

Behavioral Symptoms correlated with
children's tactile and visual erogenous contacts with the adult body

−/+ separation
problems* (no
separation
phobias)

1. Even as an adult, Kristen found it extremely difficult to detach herself from the family, despite their physical and derisive mental cruelty. Only after long years of therapy could Kristen begin to substitute friends to replace a longing for her family. However, the factor of controlling others was more important to her than her actual *attachment*. For example, Kristen was not upset when she rejected her family and did not contact them for days even though she was very upset when members of her family rejected her in a similar fashion. In brief, she often did not mind separation as long as it was she who did the rejecting.

+ irrational
tempers*

2. The shrieking which went on between Kristen and her father elicited complaints from the neighbors. Then, at the time of her hospitalization, Kristen's anger stopped. Her rage remained frozen for ten years hence. Only during her subsequent "manic" episodes did her screaming rages once again disrupt the barriers of inhibited affect.

+ irrational fears*

Kristen suffered from "irrational" obsessive thoughts and phobic reactions which have already been mentioned. In particular, thoughts of bugs, vermin, death and hell sent her into a panic.

+ sexual
symptoms*

3. Kristen's sexual life was behaviorally extremely limited. There was a period when she began a splurge of picking up men who would then make overtures to her in an automobile. However, all sexual activity was so markedly associated with sin that the only way Kristen could approach sexual interaction was by staying awake for two days and nights prior to a "pick-up" so that she would end up asleep at the time her partner might try to contact her sexually. This acting out proved to reflect Kristen's negative need to upset her parents by her becoming pregnant, rather than her sexual wishes. For as soon as she was told that therapy would be terminated unless she kept strictly on "the pill," Kristen conformed by accepting birth control measures but then immediately stopped her sexual promiscuity.

Addendum

The symptomatic effects of punitive and excretory overstimulation: (a) negative behavior, (b) inhibition and reversal of emotion, (c) excremental preoccupations, and (d) problems having to do with torture, death and suicide, predominated in highly magnified fashion in Kristen's history. The question then arises as to whether the etiology of some psychotic disorders may stem from severest early deprivation, together with extreme punishment and extreme erogenous stimulation during the formative years.

Excessive early deprivation and abusive beatings during infancy and childhood would be in a position to provide *irreversible chemical reactions* within the punishment system circuits of the brain so as to create a picture of psychosis. Excessive sexual problems imposed upon such a disturbance would magnify the intensity of the psychotic breakdown. This formulation in turn is compatible with the finding that Kristen responded to a continuous course of treatment with lithium and Mellaril in conjunction with her psychotherapy to maintain marked and lasting improvements in her emotional health. At the present time she is holding a responsible position within a medical institution, enjoys a number of close friends, enjoys music and travel, and has shown no signs of any manic or depressive symptoms for the last fifteen years.

NOTES

1 It was only through sheer, stubborn determination that she managed to graduate from college at the age of thirty-five, an achievement which brought her much pleasure.

2 See synopsis of Freud's "Rat Man," case 87.

3 The alcoholism was controlled only five years later when I insisted that if we were to continue working in therapy together, it would be upon the basis that she join Alcoholics Anonymous. Not only did AA succeed in making possible Kristen's alcoholic abstinence over the past ten years but it also served as a first source for her forming social contacts and her finding a place she could call home.

4 Also note the relation between the physical activity of Kristen's *withholding* her urine and feces and the social activity of her *withholding* her speech.

5 Compare these findings with those of "Kurt Junior," case 77.

6 To Kristen's knowledge this was the one and only time she had submitted to sexual intercourse. In this way, Kristen finally completed a brutal version of sexual intercourse to which her father had introduced her when he pressed against her body and then beat her against the wall until she was ready to drop to the floor.

Kristen

64

Stimulation-Symptom-and-Dream-Profile

	Separation Phobias	
	Night Terrors, Twilight States	
Sleep in Bed with Adult	+ Irrational Fears: Other	
	+ Irrational Tempers	
+ Adult Genital Erotic	+ Sexual Symptoms	
	Biting/Cutting, etc.	*content of*
View Adult Coitus	+ Eyes	*dreams and*
	Fire	*symptoms*
	Learning Problems (levels 2 or 3, etc.)	
Punitive Yelling	Lying and Delinquency	
	+ Reversal of Affect	
+ Beatings	+ Closing Down Upon, Kill	*content of*
	+ Falling	*dreams and*
		symptoms
	+ Excretory Symptoms and Dreams	
	+ Anal Masturbation	
Preoccupation with Child's BM	Enuresis	
	Illness, etc.	*content of*
Anal Contacts	Pain	*dreams and*
	+ Death	*symptoms*
	+ Compulsions	

SECTION 3
Cases 65-86

Focus:

SYMPTOMS ASSOCIATED WITH CHILDREN'S EXPOSURES TO EROTIC AND PUNITIVE CONTACTS WITH ADULTS

Case 65: Albert

Albert, a 140-pound, chubby twelve-year-old boy had been labeled a "limited, disadvantaged youngster who is open, frank, and non-suspicious." In addition he was described as "incorrigible" at camp and "impossible" at school because of his refusal to obey orders. His inability to learn required his placement in a special class for "slow children." At the age of twelve, he was barely able to do second and third grade work and attained an I.Q. score of only 78.

Fortunately, Albert's "limitations" disappeared when he was given help and protection with respect to his exposure to punishment and sexual stimulation. Thirteen years later, he was accepted at graduate school upon graduating from college a top scholar and president of his class.[1]

Sources of Stimulation:
adult punitive and excretory contacts with children

−/+ early
deprivation

1. Albert's mother was sick and depressed at the time of his delivery. His father was unsupportive. The mother recalled that her depression continued throughout Albert's infancy. She felt too miserable to enjoy or play with Albert and his two-year-old sister. However, Albert slept and ate well without demanding much care. He developed normally and was walking and saying simple words when he was a year old. It is possible that much of this healthful development was related to the frequent presence of Albert's grandmother in the home.

+ punitive bowel
training (during
infancy)
+ beatings*

2. The mother whipped Albert when he was eight months old in order to toilet-train him. She felt this method was "successful" since Albert "never soiled" after the age of one year. Strapping as a method of discipline continued throughout Albert's childhood. The mother reported that at home she could control him easily with the strap but added she could not be present in school to control his behavior there in the same way. Actually, in school the principal was "compelled" to use the rattan on Albert.

Albert reported his father's beatings were worse than his mother's even though his mother would often beat him with a hose. During his second diagnostic hour, Albert tried to minimize his agitation over his beatings while noting that he was "too fat to be hurt." But he came into his next interview with tears running down his face, after being hit by his mother and being called "a dirty bastard." He begged the clinic to find a place for him outside his home, a move which was effected after the mother hit him with an iron rod. The mother claimed that she did "not feel badly about using the rod on him one bit"; he

266

needed more punishment.

+ punitive
yelling*

3. In a "towering rage," the mother periodically threatened to send Albert away. Additionally, until the parents' divorce two years prior to Albert's diagnostic, Albert was exposed to the parents' constant yelling and fighting. In fact the mother always thought of Albert's problems as starting at about the age of five, when he witnessed one of the worst parental battles.

Behavioral Symptoms correlated with
adult punitive and excretory contacts with children

+ negative
behavior

+ learning*
(level 3;
referral)

1. According to his social worker, "at school last year Albert spent full energy in defying the teachers. . . . He had never settled down in school nor done any work. Then with a new and more reasonable classroom teacher this year, he did respond by doing some work." With so much defiance, it is not surprising that Albert suffered from a severe learning problem. Albert was repeatedly "left back" in school and eventually was placed in a special class for non-learners. As has been noted, Albert was barely able to do second and third grade work when he was twelve years old. Only after he was helped to live away from home did his learning problem begin to clear.

+ reversal of
affect*

At camp, as at school, Albert's negative reaction to rules, orders and requests drove the counselors "bananas." The head counselor wrote: "Albert is a problem with everyone; but a slight improvement is being shown. I believe him to have intelligence if you can gain his attention." Other counselors complaining about lack of cooperation, described him as "incorrigible" and "a stone wall." At night he would not obey orders to be quiet after taps and kept his cabin in an uproar. He was described as giggling when he got frightened or anxious. His counselor concluded that Albert had to learn that "the world is not one continuous joke." Often Albert would end up running away after he had broken rules "once too often."

+ closing down
upon
destructively*
+ hurting
+ falling*

2. Albert dreamt "this guy *knocked down* our door and tried to use our phone. I *hit* him over the head."

In the real world, Albert would start fights "in a fun way." In school he would "jokingly" stick his foot out in the aisle to *trip* children. He would bully anyone regardless of their size. His mother felt he really didn't hurt others but provoked them to hurt him physically. By his unruliness and defiance, he did manage to incite his counselors and teachers to hit him.

+ falling*

To try to give a picture of what Albert was like, his mother described the following incident. Albert (age 12) suddenly *fell* in school and then acted as though he had seriously damaged his leg. The mother was called to the school and she and her son were taken to a hospital emergency room. By the time the doctor saw Albert at the hospital, the mother began to suspect that Albert was "faking" but said nothing either to him or to the doctor. Even though a complete examination revealed no pathology, the physician finally gave in to Albert's insistence that he was badly hurt and offered him some crutches. The emotional aspects of this complaint were confirmed the next day when Albert discarded his crutches.

+ non-organic illness* (hypochondriaisis)

+ excretory symptoms*

3. Albert was able to tell his therapist that he would smell his feces and occasionally would put the feces into his mouth. He was upset by these activities and did not know why he did such things. His preoccupation with eating feces is of particular interest because he had been whipped at the age of eight months for soiling and forced to become bowel trained at that early time. Of note, at the age of twelve, Albert still suffered from constipation. His constipated bowel movements hurt his rectum and were accompanied by passing of blood in his stool.

Sources of Stimulation:
children's visual and tactile erogenous contacts with the adult body

− / + sleeping in bed with adults* (only occasionally)

+ adult nudity

1. Albert would sleep periodically with his mother when he was nine years old. When this stopped, he slept in the same bed with his two younger brothers "because they were scared."

2-3. *Age ten*, Albert, weighing approximately *130 pounds*, still shared *baths with his father*.[2] The baths stopped only because the parents became divorced and the father permanently left home.

+ adult genital erotic* (+ view adult coitus*)

In a hallway of his housing project, Albert witnessed a teenager and his girlfriend in the act of sexual intercourse. Upon offering this information, Albert asked "Why are daddy seeds green?" and then told how the boy *totally exposed his penis as he had an emission in front of Albert*.

Behavioral Symptoms correlated with
children's tactile and visual erogenous contacts with the adult body

+ / − irrational fears*
+ eyes*

1-2. Albert talked of his fears of being crazy as he told of a recent dream: "The guy sprayed his gun in our faces and we went *blind*."[3] He also reported dreaming: "I was sleeping in my mother's room and I *looked out* the window and *saw* a turkey."

+ sexual symptoms*

3. Albert's eating of his own feces was precipitated by his exposure to viewing the teenager's erect penis. The possibility arises that sexualized looking, touching and mouthing, which was activated by this visual erotic exposure to the teenager's erect penis, was in turn secretly discharged upon a body-related object of similar size and shape, i.e., Albert's own feces.

+ fire*

4. During his diagnostic interviews, Albert was beset with fears that his "big battery at home might set a fire." He admitted that he played with fire in the cellar and then related phantasies about skin burning so that it becomes red

like blood. At this point, he confided how sometimes blood came out when he played with his penis.

NOTES

[1] An indication that he possessed an I.Q. capacity within the normal or superior range.

[2] See case 66 of Bernard.

[3] Note the equivalence of this dream image with that of the penis ejaculating in front of Albert's eyes.

Albert

65

Stimulation-Symptom-and-Dream-Profile

	Separation Phobias	
	Night Terrors, Twilight States	
Sleep in Bed with Adult	+ Irrational Fears: Other	
	Irrational Tempers	
+ Adult Genital Erotic	+ Sexual Symptoms	
	Biting/Cutting, etc.	} *content of*
+ View Adult Coitus	+ Eyes	} *dreams and*
	+ Fire	} *symptoms*
	+ Learning Problems (levels 2 or 3, etc.)	
+ Punitive Yelling	Lying and Delinquency	
	+ Reversal of Affect	
+ Beatings	+ Closing Down Upon, Kill	} *content of dreams and*
	+ Falling	} *symptoms*
	+ Excretory Symptoms and Dreams	
	Anal Masturbation	
Preoccupation with Child's BM	Enuresis	
	+ Illness, etc.	} *content of*
Anal Contacts	Pain	} *dreams and*
	Death	} *symptoms*
	Compulsions	

Case 66: Bernard

The fear that her 160-pound, eleven-year-old son, Bernard, might become a criminal brought Mrs. B in a panic to the clinic. Bernard, she reported, had sliced a bedspread with a knife, cut up his own shoes, took money from his father and put ink on the wallpaper. To make things worse, although Bernard had an I.Q. of 118, he just wasn't making it in school; he was a "good" boy but could not learn at all.

The mother, who had no friends of her own, used her boy Bernard as a companion. He was the most important person in the house to her. She would take great pleasure going through the woods with him while they "searched for beautiful wild flowers."

Mrs. B had been brought up by a father who without mercy or restraint beat her brothers with a long belt. Her mother used to stand behind her father as he kept up the beatings. Mrs. B recalled that she would get sick watching on these occasions. She herself was "only" hit with a switch for certain misdeeds such as talking back to her elders or calling an older relative by a first name. It is therefore not surprising that Mrs. B, who sought to lead a "gentle" and "lovely" life with her son, constantly experienced dreams of accidents befalling Bernard, dreams of finding him in the river, of his being run over, of his being in a hospital while she would be looking and looking and not being able to locate him. In her latest dream, Bernard had fallen through the ice and skin divers who were looking for him were only able to retrieve his little red hat. In turn, she never let Bernard alone in the bathroom when he was taking a bath for she was always afraid that something might happen to him.

Sources of Stimulation:
children's tactile and visual erogenous contacts with the adult body

+ sleeping in bed with adults*

1. The mother would lie down in bed with Bernard when he would regularly wake up with bad dreams and would stay with him for the remainder of the night. According to her account, bed-sharing had tapered off a year or two prior to his referral to the clinic; yet Bernard reported to his therapist that the bed-sharing was continuing: "My father sometimes kicks my mother out of the bed . . . he wouldn't let her in so she comes and sleeps in my bed. Sometimes I don't even know it . . . she comes in during the night, and I wake up and she's there." The mother encouraged still other forms of body contact with Bernard.

270

When, for example, the mother would be angry and argue with her husband, Bernard would be encouraged to put his arm around her and stroke her arm as he sat beside her on the couch. At other times, mother and son would indulge in hugging one another. She explained that Bernard's sadness had driven her to keep him very close to her and to give him constant assurance by hugging him.

+ adult nudity
+ adult genital erotic*
+ view adult coitus*

2. The *father and Bernard were still taking baths together* even though the boy was already *eleven years old and weighed 160 pounds*. Bernard particularly did not like it when the two of them were in the bathtub together[1] (where they were placed in unavoidably close contact with one another) and the father would insist upon "cleaning" him. Bernard also reported having *viewed his father on top of his mother in bed*.

Behavioral Symptoms correlated with
children's tactile and visual erogenous contacts with the adult body

+ separation phobia*

1. Bernard had not liked the idea of starting school, this despite his mother's repetitive efforts to let him know what a privilege it was for him to attend classes. Bernard responded, "Oh no, you have to stay, you don't love me if you leave me." And later, after his first day of school, Bernard complained over and over that it was "not a nice thing to do to the baby boy." Bernard's separation problem during his first school year necessitated the mother's getting the principal's permission for Bernard's sister to ride with him in the kindergarten bus.

Typical of school-phobic children, at the age of eight, Bernard demonstrated nausea in the morning prior to leaving for school. In this regard, Bernard's mother noted that he was never happy anywhere except in his own home. She gave an example of Bernard's going with his sister to "an aunt's beautiful vacation home on 200 acres in New Hampshire"; he was terribly lonely and cried all night long so that his father had to drive up the next day to bring him home.

+ nightmares

+ night terrors*

2. Bernard's continual nightmares would awaken him sweating and crying. He would dream about being chased by something bigger than he and about a man trying to push him off a cliff. Sometimes Bernard would talk out in his sleep, crying over and over again, "Don't let them touch me, don't let them touch me." Bernard's mother decided at these times to comfort him by "sharing his pillow."

+ night terrors* (hallucination)

Bernard's night terrors sometimes intruded into his waking life in the form of hallucinatory-like or delusionary preoccupations about a man who appeared with a big black hat and a long black coat.

3. Bernard's report of being in the bathtub with his father ran as follows: "When I take a bath I try to get out before he does. I'm afraid to look. . . . My father came in this morning and turned on the bright lights. I couldn't stand

+ eyes*

the light. . . . It was so bright I *couldn't see*." Several years later, Bernard developed an *eye tic* after he witnessed a nineteen-year-old boy masturbate.

+ cutting*

4. The theme of chopping and cutting formed the nucleus of Bernard's "bizarre" presenting problems: "he *cut* the bedspreads, he *cut* up his sneakers, he *cut* all the shoelaces in his mother's shoes, he *cut* the plastic clothes-line with the hedge-clippers."

Just prior to telling his therapist about being pressed close to his father in the bathtub, Bernard referred four times to *chopping* wood with his father. The intensity of such primitive reactions involving *cutting* was reflected later by *"hallucinatory" thoughts*, during which an "inner voice" told him: *"cut* that chair — *cut* that chair."

Of note, when Bernard was eight and a half, he was hospitalized for a circumcision. Following this he developed a mouth tic. The presence of the *mouth tic*, together with twitching fingers, led the neurologists to diagnose Bernard's case as "St. Vitus Dance." However, organic factors soon were ruled out and the emotional origin of his symptoms recognized. It was at this time that psychiatric help was first recommended.

+ fire*

5. Bernard set the curtains on fire. Afterwards he cried, saying he didn't know why he did these things. At the time of his referral, Bernard still could not keep from playing with matches. Also, at the age of ten he had turned on a false fire alarm at school. "It was a terrible experience; the principal and police lieutenant and two captains from the fire department were on the boy's back, grilling him about why he had done it." Bernard dreamed: "The radar is up in the sky and when it came down the house caught on fire. The fire engine put it out."

+ hallucinatory
   twilight state*

+ burn*

Bernard's preoccupations with fire, like his preoccupations with cutting (see above), became expressed in a hallucinatory form. Thus, his mother told how one day she noticed a large melted plastic area on the portable TV she had given Bernard. On being questioned, Bernard said that "the voice inside him [presumably feelings from his primitive brain] told him to see if it would burn."

Sources of Stimulation:
adult punitive and excretory contacts with children

+ early
   deprivation

1. Since infancy Bernard rocked in bed and banged his head against the pillow. These classic symptoms suggest that Bernard suffered from deficiencies in early infant care. The mother reported that he began the head-banging very early, i.e., since the age of four months. When he was old enough to sit up he would rhythmically bang against the chair, sometimes as long as an hour at a stretch. The mother's reaction was noteworthy in that she would let him continue to bang himself to see how long it was before he tired.

(early severe
 punishment)

One of Bernard's earliest memories (or "memories" told to him) involved his father heating his bottle while Bernard kept screaming. The father became so angry he shook little Bernard in a rage.

+ beatings*

2. Bernard was strapped by his mother at times e.g. when he stole $20 from his father's wallet. A more serious source for physical punishment stemmed from the father's "violent" attacks. The mother said that she closed herself in her room when her husband spanked Bernard. She said that (from the days her brother had been beaten violently by *her* father), the idea of the punishment made her sick. Now, when her husband was through beating Bernard, her son would come to her. He would not cry until she comforted him.

+ punitive
  yelling*

3. When Bernard came to the table without having "properly washed," the father would holler, rant and rave. Both the mother and the father would end up "choking" and could not eat. Then, Bernard would cry, rock and bang his head severely throughout the night.

Behavioral Symptoms correlated with
adult punitive and excretory contacts with children

+ non-organic
  illness*
+ pain*
+ hurting
+ closing down
  upon
  destructively*
  (crush)

1. From the ages of six to eight, Bernard would become nauseated in school and at the age of ten would develop headaches.

2. As a little boy Bernard would destroy toys by smashing them with a hammer. More serious, he was accident-prone and twice was knocked down by cars. Bernard also spoke of burning his cat. He pointed out: "It was better to kill him than to leave him in the gutter." It was not known whether Bernard was referring to phantasy or to fact.

+ dying*
+ falling*

Bernard's nightmares and night terrors focused upon related concerns. In one nightmare, a motor boat turned over accidently and a boy was dying.[2] In another nightmare, a boy was being pushed off a cliff.

+ negative
  behavior

3. When Bernard was scolded for coming to the table with dirty hands, he continually would do the *opposite* of what he was asked. His sister scolded Bernard while begging him to obey so that such scenes would be averted, but he would not obey.

+ learning*
  (level 3)

4. Bernard's negativism interfered with his ability to learn. As his restriction increased over the years, his I.Q. fell from 118 to 99 to 87. In school, he had to spend two years in each class before he received a social promotion.

+ lying*

5. Bernard lied to his mother about his schoolwork. On other occasions, he would lie to her when she demanded that he defend himself with other children: Bernard would claim that he hit someone back when he really didn't. He would also lie to cover up petty stealing.

+ reversal of
  affect*

6. Bernard would get his class in a turmoil by getting other children to laugh at the teacher. The inappropriateness of Bernard's humor became evident

when he would look up at his teacher and beam happily at her while she was calling him down for his poor school performance.

NOTES

[1] See also cases 65, Albert; 78, Larry; and 97, Martin.

[2] This should read: "a boy got wrecked." Therefore, "+dying*" is incorrect. The error was discovered too late to be corrected in the final computer calculations.

Bernard
66

Stimulation-Symptom-and-Dream-Profile

	+ Separation Phobias
	+ Night Terrors, Twilight States
+ Sleep in Bed with Adult	Irrational Fears: Other
	Irrational Tempers
+ Adult Genital Erotic	Sexual Symptoms
	+ Biting/Cutting, etc. } content of
+ View Adult Coitus	+ Eyes } dreams and
	+ Fire } symptoms
	+ Learning Problems (levels 2 or 3, etc.)
+ Punitive Yelling	+ Lying and Delinquency
	+ Reversal of Affect
+ Beatings	+ Closing Down Upon, Kill } content of
	+ Falling } dreams and } symptoms
	Excretory Symptoms and Dreams
	Anal Masturbation
Preoccupation with Child's BM	Enuresis
	+ Illness, etc. } content of
Anal Contacts	+ Pain } dreams and
	+ Death } symptoms
	Compulsions

Case 67: Clifford

Clifford, age seven, was referred for therapy because of his difficult home situation.

Cliff was almost ecstatic about beginning therapy. His brother had already started his therapy a year earlier and had told Cliff of the drinks and cookies and presents he had received from his therapist. Now Cliff could not wait to receive even more than his brother.

During the preceding year, his mother had been hospitalized after a suicidal threat. Upon her release from the hospital, she lived away from her family. Meanwhile Cliff and his eight-year-old brother, Mel, were placed in the care of their father who left them for long hours while he was at work. Both Cliff and Mel were uncooperative with their father's efforts to deal with them when he was home. Cliff's and his brother's presenting problems involved "diffculties listening to authority" and "inaccessible feelings."

Sources of Stimulation:
adult punitive and excretory contacts with children

+ early
deprivation

1. Cliff was not wanted. His delivery was difficult and necessitated a separation from his mother for two weeks. Returning home, his mother suffered from a postpartum depression requiring a month's hospitalization and electroshock treatments. Since the father at this time would not take care of Cliff or his brother, the children were placed in a foster home for four months.

Cliff's return home to his mother was followed by neglect and abuse. He was found at the age of two and a half in an "appalling condition." The social agency's record reported that he was dirty, had lost weight and was covered by bruises and scratches. His mother had admitted "going after" Cliff for defying her "deliberately" by messing his pants, saying "no," etc. She would lose control, then hit, scratch, punch, kick or bite him. He was, therefore, again placed in a foster home for another six months until he was three.

+ beatings*

2. Beatings were administered by Cliff's father as well as by his mother. The father employed a belt to beat him. "He beats me with my pants on," Cliff explained, "he also takes my pants off to beat me."

+ adult
defecation

3. The father defecated exhibitionistically out of doors in front of his children. Cliff spoke of his father's "big black hole": "it's the boom part . . . my

father's bum is so big . . . he did doo-doo outside and I would see his shit come out, little lumps."

Behavioral Symptoms correlated with
adult punitive and excretory contacts with children

+ negative
  behavior

1. Cliff's *defiance* to his father's authority and his inability to cooperate at home were the focus of the father's chief complaints and were listed as Cliff's presenting problems at the time of his referral.

Cliff's thought associations to a dream confirmed his proclivity for negative behavior. ". . . I ate fruit when I wasn't supposed to. . . . I was told not to touch the stove and I touched the stove."

2. What Cliff could not complete upon his father's exposed "big black hole" and feces, he completed upon his own. He played with "doo-doo" on the bed, for which his mother and father would hit him on the buttocks. In addition,

+ excretory
  symptoms*
  (+ anal
  masturbation*)

Cliff confided: "I stick my finger in my bum . . . it's smushy. . . . I do it almost every day. . . . I get my finger way up and it stings." To no avail, his therapist tried to help Cliff set up a goal to control "the pokies." Despite the therapist's efforts to help him see that this type of activity starts all kinds of worries and problems, Cliff could display no anxiety or concern over this behavior. Also,

+ enuresis*

Cliff at the age of seven still wet his bed.

+ negative
  emotion

3. The degree to which Cliff perseverated in his references to *the kids not liking him* suggested that he was prone to react with paranoid attitudes. His opening words during his first diagnostic hour reflected these feelings: "Someone called me *bad names* and beat me up at camp . . . someone took my baseball cap and threw it on a tree . . . this kid blamed something on me. He blamed me for spilling the applesauce. . . ," etc., etc.

During his first diagnostic hour, Cliff also presented a dream which featured negative emotion: "I was a little midget as big as my sneaker. *I stuck my tongue out.*"

+ reversal of
  affect*

Cliff demonstrated inappropriate affect as he joyfully told his problems. One would have thought he was telling an adventure story rather than the history of his problems. Even the last words of his diagnostic, "I think I'm going crazy," were spoken without any concern in his voice. Despite his highly trau-

+ killing*
+ closing down
  upon
  destructively*
  (crush)
+ falling*

matic history, he was aware of no fears or anxiety.

Cliff dreamed of "*killing gigantula.*" He also dreamed of walking into a passing car. During his associations to these dreams, he spoke of splitting his head open at camp and drew attention to his tendency to fall: "every time I *fall* I say 'fucken idiot,' 'fuck you,' 'fucken bitch.'"

Sources of Stimulation:
children's tactile and visual erogenous contacts with the adult body

+ sleeping in bed
with adults*

1. Cliff asserted that he used to get in bed between his mother and father. "About twice a week" when he was seven he still got in bed with the father and stayed there all night.

+ adult nudity

2. Cliff first shied away from answering questions as to whether his family made a big fuss when he saw anyone without clothes. However, finally he related "I laugh. I saw my mother when she was getting undressed in my room. . . . I saw her vagina. . . . I call it a 'dark, hairy cave.'. . . I saw my father's dink. . . . He has a big long dink — it would go all the way up here. It would go all across the room. It has a little hole in it. It hangs down. . . . It sometimes goes up." "Last year Daddy's dink was sticking way up and he would sprinkle into the toilet."

+ adult genital
erotic*

3. Cliff described seeing his father tickling his mother's "boobs." He also described hard-core pornographic photos in his father's collection. Among the pictures, he spoke of one in which "a man was licking another man's dink."

Actually the father possessed boxes and boxes of these pictures, pictures with which he found it very difficult to part. Despite the therapist's explanation that pictures such as of nude men ejaculating would activate many disturbed symptoms within his children's minds and would stimulate them to act out homosexually, the father could get rid of only a few pictures each day by burning them in the fireplace.

Behavioral Symptoms correlated with
children's tactile and visual erogenous contacts with the adult body

+ sexual
symptoms*

1. When Cliff was asked whether he had any worries about his "poking" the rear end (see above), he answered "Oh don't you *know*, they call it 'sex' and 'stripping.' My brother, Mel, taught it to me and so did my friend, Ringo. I don't let Mel poke me in the rear but I poke his. . . . We dance around when we strip. . . . Mel pee-peed in my mouth. . . . I felt like fainting. I thought it would hurt me. My father spanked Mel for peeing in my mouth.[1] A year ago, a teenage boy did it to Mel. The big boy stuck his dink in my brother's mouth and he also stuck it in my brother's rear."

+ fire*

+ biting/cutting*
(throat)

+ burn*

2. No sooner had Cliff finished speaking of these sexual activities than he suddenly put a big stick between his legs and talked of squirting a big *fire* hose. Actually, at the beginning of his diagnostic sessions, when asked what he thought his problems were, Cliff answered, "Matches and smoking cigarettes . . . I light them. Matches is a problem for it's naughty. The thing could puff up and could go down your *throat*.[2] You could *burn* your finger. . . . I burned my finger: My mother was lighting up the stove for supper, then into the stove went my finger."[3]

NOTES

[1] Here the father activated this behavior by allowing his children to be exposed to his pornographic pictures, then punished the children for discharging their excitement with one another.

[2] See Berta Bornstein's case of "Sonja," case 29.

[3] What Clifford could not finish on his mother's "hairy cave" and upon his father's hardcore porno pictures (see above), he finished on her oven and on his own rectum via anal masturbation .

Clifford
67

Stimulation-Symptom-and-Dream-Profile

	Separation Phobias	
	Night Terrors, Twilight States	
+ Sleep in Bed with Adult	Irrational Fears: Other	
	Irrational Tempers	
+ Adult Genital Erotic	+ Sexual Symptoms	
	+ Biting/Cutting, etc.	} *content of*
View Adult Coitus	Eyes	*dreams and*
	+ Fire	*symptoms*
	Learning Problems (levels 2 or 3, etc.)	
Punitive Yelling	Lying and Delinquency	
	+ Reversal of Affect	
+ Beatings	+ Closing Down Upon, Kill	} *content of* *dreams and*
	+ Falling	*symptoms*
	+ Excretory Symptoms and Dreams	
	+ Anal Masturbation	
Preoccupation with Child's BM	+ Enuresis	
	Illness, etc.	} *content of*
Anal Contacts	Pain	*dreams and*
	Death	*symptoms*
	Compulsions	

Case 68: Synopsis of Edith Buxbaum's "Poldi"

Poldi was ten years old when he began his therapy with Dr. Buxbaum at the Vienna Psychoanalytic Clinic. Poldi recently had been suspended from school because of his exhibitionistic masturbation (*Psychoanalytic Quarterly*, 1935, p. 161-89).

Poldi, Dr. Buxbaum notes, "was a well-proportioned boy, large and very strong for his age" but his face was frequently distorted by tic-like twitching movements involving blinking of the eyes, wrinkling of the nose and jerking of the mouth and hands. "He would hop from one foot to the other, at the same time opening and closing his hands convulsively and bringing his arms together, first in front, then in back." These movements perceptibly increased at times of emotional excitement (p. 161).

Dr. Buxbaum considered the possibility of an organic basis for Poldi's twitching symptoms as well as for his display of a limited intelligence (p. 162). The medical report indicated that Poldi might have suffered from an "encephalitis" when he was two years old and that a "cerebral defect" might have been responsible for the symptoms (p. 162). Poldi was subjected to a thorough neurological workup which revealed no organic findings though the possibility of organicity was not excluded (p. 161). The emotional basis for Poldi's symptoms was suggested by (a) the negative neurological findings, and (b) the complete resolution of Poldi's exhibitionistic masturbatory symptoms during therapy. However, with the improvement of Poldi's symptoms, the parents removed Poldi from therapy before his tic-like reactions had been resolved (p. 184, 189). Whether or not some hidden organic disturbance might have been present to account for his tics, it became evident that Poldi's neurotic symptoms responded well to Dr. Buxbaum's therapy which dealt with Poldi's exposure to excessive sexual and punishment stimulation.

Sources of Stimulation:
children's tactile and visual erogenous contacts with the adult body

+ adult genital
erotic*

+ view adult
coitus*

1-2. Poldi's mother, who "could never free herself from the thought that she had married beneath her, had developed a strong sexual aversion to her husband" and resisted his sexual advances (p. 164-65). Consequently, on frequent occasions, Poldi's father "forced her to have intercourse with him. Poldi slept in the parents' bedroom and was often witness to these scenes" (p. 164-165). Poldi and his mother both reported *Poldi's observations of his parents as*

279

they indulged in fellatio (p. 173). In therapy, Poldi re-enacted some of these scenes as he played the violin with interruptions consisting of "snorts, grunts, deep groans" whereupon "he became intensely excited sexually, grew red in the face and made unmistakable coitus-like movements" (p. 170).

Behavioral Symptoms correlated with
children's tactile and visual erogenous contacts with the adult body

+ separation
phobia*
+ irrational fears*

1-2. "Poldi was tormented by constant anxiety which made it impossible for him to be alone even for a short time" (p. 161). At night he was frightened of the dark (p. 178).

+ sexual
symptoms*

3. Poldi's referral for therapy had been precipitated by his excessive and exhibitionistic masturbation for which he had been suspended from school (p. 161). His sexual preoccupations were also displayed both at home and at his therapist's office. Not only did the mother report that Poldi had been genitally aggressive to her and had fondled her breasts (p. 176, 183) but when Dr. Buxbaum spoke to him about the behavior, Poldi in turn tried to act sexually with Dr. Buxbaum (p. 176). One day he came into the therapy room with his trousers open and then exhibited his penis (p. 174). Dr. Buxbaum helped Poldi so that his masturbation could be discharged in private and not in public (p. 177).

+ eyes*

4. Poldi, as noted, suffered from a severe eye tic (p. 161).

− / + biting/
cutting*

5. During one therapeutic hour, Poldi "suddenly stiffened, became very pale, and sprang up with a cry: 'I am a monster.' He flew aggressively at Dr. Buxbaum . . . and then repeatedly threw his knife so that the point stuck in the floor." At each thrust he named a different part of her body and ended with threats of cutting her "arse," after which Poldi exclaimed, *"Now you are all cut to pieces"* (p. 174). However, Poldi evidenced neither symptoms nor dreams pertaining to biting or cutting.

Sources of Stimulation:
adult punitive and excretory contacts with children

+ beatings*

1. Poldi's father "had hoped that his son would reach the goal he himself had been unable to attain and, therefore, could not forgive the child for a limited intelligence and poor scholastic record. He studied with his son, which was torture for both of them, and according to the mother he often beat Poldi for his stupidity" (p. 165). In turn, the father stated that Poldi's mother often had furiously beaten the boy because of Poldi's restless behavior (p. 165). "Each parent would only admit that the other beat the child and each accused the other of 'whipping him silly.' They both reported that upon a teacher's advice the beatings had been stopped *except* 'now and then' " (p. 165). Actually, Dr. Buxbaum had to threaten that she would break off therapy if the parents continued to beat Poldi. The father then finally did abandon this form of punishment (p. 168).

Behavioral Symptoms correlated with
adult punitive and excretory contacts with children

+ negative
   (inhibited)
   behavior
− / + learning
(limited
intelligence?)

+ freezing of
   emotion
+ negative
   emotion

+ reversal of
   affect*
   (pleasure from
   beatings)
+ destruction*
   (violent)

+ delinquency*
+ compulsions*

1. "When Poldi came to analysis he was completely intimidated and was unable to say a word" (p. 166). In school "arithmetic was particularly difficult for him." Only with the help of his fingers could the ten-year-old boy add or subtract "and even then he made mistakes" (p. 161).

2. Poldi complained to his parents that his analyst was trying to talk him into believing that he was angry at his father for *beating him*. He complained that she was crazy: "he *wasn't angry* at his father at all." In therapy, Poldi's inhibited hate for his father was let loose upon Dr. Buxbaum once Poldi realized he could express himself without punishment. " 'You often talk to me like an old fishwife,' he spat, 'you're a Buxbaum that is shit on. You can go to the devil you damn old witch' " (p. 167).

3. Poldi demanded in play that Dr. Buxbaum beat him and massacre him. When she refused he begged her "at least to tickle him" (p. 175).

More seriously, Poldi tried to hurt himself while in therapy, then impulsively tried to destroy all Dr. Buxbaum's possessions (p. 169).

4. Poldi developed a compulsion to steal (p. 179). "As his exhibitionism increased, his stealing came increasingly to the fore" (p. 180). "At the climax of his exhibitionism . . . he stole quite openly [from Dr. Buxbaum] and put the stolen objects into the [fly] opening of his trousers" (p. 181).

Buxbaum's "Poldi"
68

Stimulation-Symptom-and-Dream-Profile

	+ Separation Phobias
	Night Terrors, Twilight States
Sleep in Bed with Adult	+ Irrational Fears: Other
	Irrational Tempers
+ Adult Genital Erotic	+ Sexual Symptoms
	Biting/Cutting, etc. ⎫ *content of*
+ View Adult Coitus	+ Eyes ⎬ *dreams and*
	Fire ⎭ *symptoms*

	Learning Problems (levels 2 or 3, etc.)
Punitive Yelling	+ Lying and Delinquency
	+ Reversal of Affect
+ Beatings	+ Closing Down Upon, Kill ⎫ *content of*
	⎬ *dreams and*
	Falling ⎭ *symptoms*

	Excretory Symptoms and Dreams
	Anal Masturbation
Preoccupation with Child's BM	Enuresis
	Illness, etc. ⎫ *content of*
Anal Contacts	Pain ⎬ *dreams and*
	Death ⎭ *symptoms*
	+ Compulsions

Case 69: Dwight

Dwight was a friendly, outgoing, little six-year-old boy who despite his hyperactivity and poor attention span tested 112 on the Bellevue Wechsler. However, the school staff was thoroughly disturbed by his sexual behavior: Dwight, at the age of six, could not be stopped from his sexual activities with both girls and boys in the classroom coat closet. In addition, Dwight displayed a variety of tics including rolling of his eyes, shaking his head back and forth and grunting "uh." At school he found it difficult to control himself and frequently became excited and wild.

A neurological workup at the Children's Hospital ruled out the possibility of an organic basis for Dwight's symptoms.

Sources of Stimulation:
adult punitive and excretory contacts with children

+ early
deprivation

1. Accurate information regarding Dwight's care during his first year of life was not available. However, the likelihood that Dwight suffered from early deprivation was reflected by his habit of *rocking* in bed during infancy. At the age of six, Dwight still maintained this habit when he would awaken upset at night.

Dwight's first screen memory also suggests early rejections: "When I was born, my mommy wanted to kill me but she didn't. She thought I was ugly but I said 'ga-ga' so she kissed me."

+ punitive bowel
training

2. The mother hit Dwight with a brush in order to bowel-train him.

+ beatings*

3. The mother's boyfriend, Alex, later to become Dwight's stepfather, would wildly hit Dwight; he threw Dwight around and hit him on the jaw. Dwight would sometimes be left bleeding.

The mother would also hit Dwight with a strap or a brush and would slap him on the mouth. Even after the clinic stressed the importance of not beating Dwight if he were to have a chance to get over his symptoms, the mother remained ambivalent about the beatings. Dwight retorted, "She still says she don't care what the doctor says, she's going to hit."

+ punitive
yelling*

4. As in so many similar cases, Dwight's mother would get the stepfather Alex to yell at him and punish him. Dwight confided, "She likes Alex to yell at me. Alex blows up at me and smashes me in the jaw."

283

Dwight was also exposed to fighting and yelling going on "all night" between his "parents": "Alex and my mother fuss every night. Alex pushes my mother; she bled right there [as he pointed to his leg]. She looked like she were going to fall dead on the floor, but she didn't."

Behavioral Symptoms correlated with
adult punitive and excretory contacts with children

+ closing down upon destructively* (crush)
+ death*
+ fears*

1. Dwight's dreams reflected his preoccupation with people being run over and hurt. One dream was about "my mommy. She goes by a traink [train] and she got *runned over*, and it took her neck off." A second dream had to do with "Dracula," who was coming to take his mommy away. Dwight developed fears of the dead, i.e., fears of ghosts in the dark haunting his room.

+ falling*

2. While he was in the process of telling his therapist about his beatings, Dwight suddenly experienced a feeling that "the sky was *falling* off."

+ excretory symptoms*
+ anal masturbation*

3. Dwight became involved with poking his finger into his rectum and the rectum of Marc his boyfriend. "I put my hand to my bottom and I take caci out and put it in my mouth. It tastes terrible, like chalk. . . . Marc calls it 'dookie.' He likes me to put my finger in his rear. I did it to him. He wanted me to do it. . . . Marc stuck his finger up my rear. I felt like I was dying."

+ negative behavior
+ lying*
+ learning* (level 2)

4. Dwight drove his mother "crazy" by doing the opposite of what she requested. He jumped on his mother's couch, put on the TV at 6:00 A.M., refused to take his bath at the appropriate time, etc. He responded to his mother's punishments by lying[1] and becoming increasingly restricted. Concomitantly Dwight developed a learning problem entailing a drop in his I.Q. score from 112 to 93 within a period of four years.

Sources of Stimulation:
children's tactile and visual erogenous contacts with the adult body

− / + sleeping in bed with adults* (slept only occasionally with an adult)

1. Dwight would watch TV while he rested in bed between his mother and his stepfather, Alex. When he was little, Dwight sometimes slept all night in bed with his mother.

Close body contact between Alex and Dwight also occurred when the two would indulge in mutual wrestling bouts. Often they would keep up the wrestling for as much as three hours.

+ adult nudity

2. Dwight explained, "I see my mother and Alex both naked. My mother's ding-dong is tucked in." In consideration of Dwight's oversexualized behavior, the mother was advised not to appear nude in front of him. Unfortunately, she was unable to follow these recommendations.

+ adult genital erotic* (+ view adult coitus*)

3. Dwight told how he *saw Alex take all his mother's clothes off, squeeze her neck, and then stick his "ding-dong" into his mummy's mouth.* Dwight heard

Alex tell his mother, "I want to take a picture of inside your butt," then took pictures of her with all her clothes off and showed it to everybody. Dwight pathetically protested, "That gets me very mad. I just wish that God was there."

Behavioral Symptoms correlated with
children's tactile and visual erogenous contacts with the adult body

+ sexual
symptoms*

1. The severity of Dwight's driven sexual acting out in school led his teacher to insist that he immediately receive help for his emotional problems. As already noted, he could not be restrained from both homosexual and heterosexual activities in the classroom coat closet.

Once Dwight understood that he was allowed in therapy to talk about anything "in the whole world" as long as his discussions could help him with his problems, Dwight was able to disclose some details about his sexual activities. He told about his girl friend Betsy: "I play with her and we sleep together. . . . I put my hands down by her crack. All the time she says, 'Put your dink in my mouth.'" At this point, Dwight started smelling the desk and described an orgastic feeling: "a light came on all over me and I changed into Captain Marvel."

+ biting/cutting*

2. During his first diagnostic hour, Dwight reported a bad dream about "Dracula going to *bite* my mommy and I think he's going to take her away."

+ eyes*

3. A severe eye tic was one of Dwight's referral symptoms. Dwight's tic became evident during his diagnostic interviews: his *eye* would roll up toward the top of his head while he *sucked* his tongue. The severity of this symptom caused the family to be concerned that he might be suffering from epilepsy.[2]

+ twilight states*

4. In response to his intense exposure to both punitive and erotic stimulation, Dwight displayed feelings of "un-realness." At one point during the diagnostic evaluation, Dwight suddenly quivered and said: "Now I think I'm dreaming. I think *you are not real*,[3] like you're made out of water and you would go away and there's no one in the world and God's not there and the sky falls off."

+ separation
phobia*

5. At camp, Dwight cried daily for his mother and insisted upon phoning her because of his fears that she might have died.

NOTES

[1] For example, the camp report stated that Dwight fabricated a great deal.

[2] With therapy, only traces of these tics remained.

[3] See synopsis of Selma Fraiberg's "Sally," case 23, referring to Sally's panic: "Mommy, I'm not me."

Dwight
69

Stimulation-Symptom-and-Dream-Profile

	+ Separation Phobias
	+ Night Terrors, Twilight States
Sleep in Bed with Adult	+ Irrational Fears: Other
	Irrational Tempers
+ Adult Genital Erotic	+ Sexual Symptoms
	+ Biting/Cutting, etc.
+ View Adult Coitus	+ Eyes
	Fire

$\left.\begin{array}{l}\\ \\ \end{array}\right\}$ *content of dreams and symptoms*

	+ Learning Problems (levels 2 or 3, etc.)
+ Punitive Yelling	+ Lying and Delinquency
	Reversal of Affect
+ Beatings	+ Closing Down Upon, Kill
	+ Falling

$\left.\begin{array}{l}\\ \\ \end{array}\right\}$ *content of dreams and symptoms*

	+ Excretory Symptoms and Dreams
	+ Anal Masturbation
Preoccupation with Child's BM	Enuresis
	Illness, etc.
Anal Contacts	Pain
	+ Death
	Compulsions

$\left.\begin{array}{l}\\ \\ \end{array}\right\}$ *content of dreams and symptoms*

Case 70: Elsie

The nursery school director referred four-year-old Elsie for treatment of her temper tantrums and crying. Elsie was considered by the school staff to be the most difficult child in the center to manage.

Elsie talked so frequently about sex in school that mothers of other children were becoming increasingly upset. One mother had already withdrawn her child from the center because of Elsie.

At the time of her referral, Elsie's mother and father were experiencing serious marital problems. The mother was sexually cold and would try to discourage the father's sexual advances. Thereupon he would sit depressed in a dark room by himself or would masturbate in his closet with the use of a "girlie" calendar. Two years later, the parents separated, the father to seek another wife, the mother to live with a lesbian friend.

Sources of Stimulation:
children's tactile and visual erogenous contacts with the adult body

+ sleeping in bed with adults*

1. In the morning Elsie frequently slept in bed between her mother and father. Elsie would also like to get in bed together with her aunt and her grandmother.

Elsie was exposed to other sources of erogenous tactile contacts: the mother would (publicly) kiss Elsie lingeringly on the mouth and had to be remonstrated by the school director: "You don't *kiss* a daughter *like that* or hold her *that way.*"

+ adult nudity

2. Elsie was exposed intimately to viewing the nudity of both her parents. She spoke of her father's "pee-pee" as ugly. She took baths with her mother and was very much aware of her mother's pubic hair. On one occasion, Elsie was particularly disturbed when she noticed that her mother's pubic hair was blood-stained. Elsie also spoke of her mother's big lips and big legs.

+ adult genital erotic*
(+ view adult coitus*)

3. Elsie described *seeing her mother and father doing "pussy" and "nasty"* (intercourse) together and demonstrated with the mother and father dolls how her parents kissed each other's genitals.

Eventually, it was found out that the *mother masturbated in front of Elsie:* Elsie watched the mother wiggling funny on the floor while exposing and "poking" her vagina.[1]

The question arose as to whether the father also had direct sexual contact with Elsie. She reported that he would put his finger in her vagina and then "hit her there." It was uncertain whether the father simply had been applying some salve to Elsie's vagina as a treatment for vaginal bleeding (see below).

Behavioral Symptoms correlated with
children's tactile and visual erogenous contacts with the adult body

+ persistent separation phobia*

1. Elsie was school phobic to the point that she choked and vomited when she was forced to go to school. Elsie's mother reported that as a child she, too, suffered from a full-blown school phobia so that it had been necessary for her own mother to sit with her day after day in school.[2]

+ hysterical states* (conversion symptoms)

2. Elsie would suddenly say "my legs won't work." Thereupon, she would allow her legs to collapse and would insist upon being helped or carried to a chair. Medical examination revealed no organic basis for this symptomatic behavior.

+ irrational tempers*

3. Elsie's presenting problem, her temper hysterics repeatedly taking place in school, were duplicated during her therapy hours. She would roll back and forth on the floor or on her therapist's desk, slide off chairs, while she thrashed and yelled. These fits of temper could be stopped just as easily as they started. If Elsie's attention were turned to a new topic she could "pull out" of her rage immediately.

+ sexual symptoms*

4. Elsie's masturbation was excessive to the degree that it resulted in vaginal bleeding. Unfortunately, the salve which the physician prescribed was applied to her vagina by both her mother and father. It thus became a source for even further stimulation.

Elsie also acted out sexually with other children at the nursery school to the extent that mothers began to complain. She spent as much time as possible near the school toilets, where she exposed herself and became involved with "poking" the vaginas of other girls.

+ biting/cutting*

5. Elsie reported biting a little girl in her nursery school. She also presented a dream about flesh being devoured: "A monster had *eaten me up* and took me to his other monster and *ate me* up again." In another dream, "A monster *bit* me. He made bumps and my mommy took it off. There were bumps on my face because he *bit*." And following reference to seeing her father's "ugly" genitals, Elsie presented a dream about "ugly grapes, pretty grapes *to eat*; and it's very good to eat." Considering Elsie's preoccupation with thoughts of biting and eating flesh, it is not surprising that she suffered from spells of nausea and vomiting.

During therapy Elsie reported phantasies focused upon biting and cutting. For example, "Elsie put the *scissors* in her mouth. Later, she put the scissors to her genital area; then she drew a picture of a 'pee-pee' and put her mouth to it.

Later, she pretended to *eat up* her therapist as she busied herself *cutting* paper. As she cut paper she said 'it's a dinky; it's a big one; it's my father's.' Following this play she wanted to eat up the mother and father dolls as she had them kiss." Months later, the same kind of thoughts perseverated: "he *bit* the gun; he took it away . . . the mother and father dolls are taking their clothes off and he *bites* her arm . . . the little girl wants to eat mummy up in her privates. . . . I'll *cut* it off [as Elsie drew a picture of a 'dinky']; I'll eat it. . . . I want to punch you in the mouth. I want to punch you in the *teeth*. . . . There was a lion but he didn't *bite*. . . . I'll take Dr. ___'s penis off. . . . The snake *bites* [draws a snake]. . . . I'll *cut* Janice's hair off."[3]

+ eyes*

6. Elsie dreamt of a "man with green *eyes* and his *eyes* turned red into a fish." In response to this dream Elsie freely associated "Be nice to me, I want a penis. If I get a penis, I'd be a boy."

During a subsequent hour when her therapist gave Elsie a stuffed animal, Elsie complained: "but it has bad *eyes*." Later, she expressed the feeling that the teddy bear's *eyes* were staring.

Sources of Stimulation:
adult punitive and excretory contacts with children

+ early
deprivation

1. Unfortunately, Elsie's mother suffered a deprived childhood within a fatherless family of six children. When she married, she was determined to establish a *clean*, well-regulated house. In order to gain a "good life" she and her husband bought a house which could not be paid for without Elsie's mother going to work and boarding out Elsie from the age of six months to her fourth year. Elsie was moved from one day care center to another.[4] At least two of these "centers" were overcrowded with insufficient supervision and staff-to-child ratios ranging from one-to-ten to one-to-fifty. In the latter home, Elsie developed "very bad" eczema. When Elsie did return home, she was still neglected. The mother was so busy keeping her house clean she had little time to read or play with Elsie. The mother did not even like Elsie's learning to crawl since she might get her dress dirty.[5,6]

+ beatings*

2. Elsie's mother hit her routinely, sometimes with a brush or a shoe.

+ adult
defecation

3. Elsie sometimes saw her father on the toilet while he was defecating. She also reported finding his feces in the unflushed toilet.

Behavioral Symptoms correlated with
adult punitive and excretory contacts with children

+ enuresis*
+ excretory
symptoms*

1. Elsie wet her bed until she was four years old. Also, she was able to confide that she had put "doo-doo" in her mouth and that it tasted "nasty." Before she could tell about her own coprophagia, she presented her phantasies that her father ate "doo-doo," her mother ate "doo-doo" and so did "a little

girl." She presented these thoughts repeatedly in association to her memories of seeing her father's penis and her mother's vagina. For example, reference to seeing her mother's privates was followed by thoughts of "eating mommy up in her privates" and of "eating her 'poo-poo.' " Eventually, Elsie confided that she often would poke her finger into her own rectum,[7] then extricate some feces which she would smear and put into her mouth.

(+ anal masturbation*)

The mother's exposure of her vagina while masturbating in front of Elsie would be expected to have activated the looking, touching and mouthing sexual forepleasure reactions to the mother's vagina and its contents. Possibly Elsie discharged upon her rectum the touching and poking sexual forepleasure responses which initially had been activated in relation to the mother's vagina.

+ negative behavior

2. Only one example of symptomatic negative behavior appeared within Elsie's history. In response to her mother's punishments, Elsie displayed perfect table manners at home. However, once she arrived at nursery school she did the opposite: she ate with her fingers and purposefully smeared food on her hands, face and clothing.

+ falling*

3. Elsie's presenting symptom, her temper tantrums, were accompanied by her *falling* upon the floor where she would kick and scream. One of Elsie's therapists noted that she "seems to lose her balance and moves as if loss of balance is imminent."[8]

NOTES

[1] A possible source of this behavior was the mother's history of sleeping with the maternal grandmother throughout childhood and adolescence. As she matured the mother had been overcome by an urge to masturbate while sharing her own mother's bed. See synopsis of Marjorie Sprince's "Debby," case 96, under heading "bed-sharing."

[2] Recall that Elsie's mother slept in bed with the grandmother during her childhood and throughout adolescence. History was repeating itself.

[3] This material could lead to a diagnosis of "psychosis," "inadequate personality," "ego defect," *or* it could lead to the conclusion that Elsie was being so erotically stimulated by exposure to parental intercourse and her mother's exhibitionistic masturbation that her primitive brain reactions were charging and discharging out of control.

[4] Of significance, during her first diagnostic hour, Elsie described her "presenting problem" by referring to a "little girl who was sad because *her mommy got lost.*"

[5] Compare this history with that of Kevin (case 43) whose mother decided to compensate for the sordidness of her childhood by an absorption with making herself and her house beautiful at any cost.

[6] All in all, these incidents reflect Harlow's findings that chimpanzee mothers subjected to infantile deprivation themselves, have difficulty in giving emotionally to their own infants. In the present case, lack of early positive affect apparently resulted in disturbed infant and child care even though Elsie's mother attempted to compensate for her past defective life by striving for beauty and perfection in the home. (See Harlow,

H., *American Psychologist*, 1958, Vol. 13, p. 673.)

[7] In order to help Elsie with this driven anal masturbatory behavior, her therapist gave her a big pink teddy bear and expressed to her the hope that when she felt lonely and wanted to do "pokies" she could hold on tight to her teddy bear. If she could do that it would help her a lot in getting over her worries and problems.

[8] Medical checkups revealed no organic sources for these falling spells. Compare with case 77 of Kurt Junior.

Elsie

70

Stimulation-Symptom-and-Dream-Profile

	+ Separation Phobias	
	+ Night Terrors, Twilight States	
+ Sleep in Bed with Adult	Irrational Fears: Other	
	+ Irrational Tempers	
+ Adult Genital Erotic	+ Sexual Symptoms	
	+ Biting/Cutting, etc.	} *content of*
+ View Adult Coitus	+ Eyes	} *dreams and*
	Fire	} *symptoms*
	Learning Problems (levels 2 or 3, etc.)	
Punitive Yelling	Lying and Delinquency	
	Reversal of Affect	
+ Beatings	Closing Down Upon, Kill	} *content of* / *dreams and*
	+ Falling	} *symptoms*
	+ Excretory Symptoms and Dreams	
	+ Anal Masturbation	
Preoccupation with Child's BM	+ Enuresis	
	Illness, etc.	} *content of*
Anal Contacts	Pain	} *dreams and*
	Death	} *symptoms*
	Compulsions	

Case 71: Flossie

Flossie was six years old when her kindergarten teacher referred her for a diagnostic evaluation because of her strange behavior in school. First she would be withdrawn; then, the next moment, she would be aggressive or start hugging and kissing. Flossie could not pay attention in class nor could she take care of her belongings.

Sources of Stimulation:
children's tactile and visual erogenous contacts with the adult body

+ sleeping in bed with adults*

1. At the time of her referral Flossie was sleeping nearly every night with either her two-year-old brother or her mother. Before her parents had been divorced, Flossie liked to sleep with her father. She noted that her father wore no clothes to bed and "snored all night."

+ adult nudity

2. Flossie would see her father in the nude as he showered. She explained that he never pulled the shower curtain nor shut the door to the bathroom. The mother would yell at him, "Shut that door!" but he refused.

+ adult genital erotic*
+ view adult coitus*

3. Even though her mother and father were separated, Flossie reported that her father still came over to do "nasty" with the mother. Flossie elaborated how one night she saw them take their clothes off; then her mother tried to put on her pajamas but before she could, the father did "nasty" with her. Another time when Flossie knocked on the bedroom door, her mother opened the door and there was her father standing "with his pee-pee sticking way out."

Behavioral Symptoms correlated with
children's tactile and visual erogenous contacts with the adult body

+ irrational fears*

1. At night Flossie would be possessed with illusions that her doll, which had been hung on the wall, was an Indian looming at her in the dark. She would panic with the thought that the Indian would take a bow and arrow and poke her in the eye or stomach. At other times, the doll, in the dark, would appear to be her brother. When the doll was removed from the wall, she became even more frightened. These fears of the dark drove Flossie into her mother's room.

+ eyes*
+ biting/cutting/ stomach*

+ sexual symptoms*

2. Flossie admitted to her mother that she and her little brother kissed on the lips and then her brother would bite her lip. While in her mother's bed, Flossie also tried to touch the mother's "titties," pinch her "titties," and pinch her between the legs. Every time she tried these activities her mother would give

292

her a beating.

Flossie also acted out sexually at school. She would pull up her skirts and run after the boys who were at a loss as to what to do.

Sources of Stimulation:
adult punitive and excretory contacts with children

− / + early
deprivation

1. During her first year of life, Flossie ate and slept "poorly."

+ beatings*

2. Flossie's mother believed that beatings were an essential part of bringing up children "the right way." No amount of explanation could convince her that this method of controlling children was harmful. Flossie's mother insisted that Flossie's therapist did not understand her ethnic group's goals to achieve perfect behavior "and that was that." She was not going to give up the beatings. Actually, the mother's own father had beaten her severely when she was a child. She had been so frightened of him that she had slept with a knife under her pillow. On one occasion, he chased her with a hammer. As is typical of child abuse cases, Flossie's mother, without knowing the reason, was meting out to Flossie what had been inflicted upon her. Flossie's mother would kick Flossie with a shoe so hard that she left a red mark on the child's leg. She would also use a belt to "give it to" Flossie and her little two-year-old brother.

Flossie also witnessed her father beating her mother "black and blue."

+ punitive
yelling*

3. The mother yelled at Flossie throughout the day "git out there . . . git in there . . . stop that." But the loudest yelling in Flossie's home went on between her mother and father, who fought and argued in front of the children. Flossie reported that they fought mostly at night. In front of Flossie, they would yell at each other: "fuck you" and "you mother fucker."

Behavioral Symptoms correlated with
adult punitive and excretory contacts with children

+ excretory
symptoms*
(coprophagia)

1. Flossie played with her "dookey" (excrement); it was "hot and gushy and mushy." She confided, "When I play with dookey and my brother plays with dookey, then we get in trouble and my mother takes the belt and beats us." Flossie would also get excrement in her mouth: "It tastes terrible," she complained, "It isn't good for me. . . . I felt so terrible when I got it in my mouth. My mother smelled something so she whipped me and took me to Children's Hospital."

+ freezing of
affect
+ reversal of
affect*
+ hurting

2. Flossie's withdrawn behavior in kindergarten was a presenting chief complaint. Flossie's therapist noted "Flossie would often come into my office with a *fixed grin* on her face, wide-eyed and frozen."

3. Flossie confided: "I wish I was the mother so I could beat my mummy." Also in reality Flossie was very much a little sadist. She would kick her little

two-year-old brother, then run to her parents and complain that he had hit her. Her mother would encourage Flossie to hit her brother back. Flossie would then slap the boy in the face.

+ death*
+ closing down
  upon
  destructively*
  (crush)

Flossie's introductory material during her diagnostic focused upon the theme of crushing and death. When asked what she thought her *problems* might be, she went on to say, "I worry about my dog Pixie because he *died* and he's in heaven. He went under a car that ran over him. The dogs used to beat him up in the bushes."[1]

+ hurting

Unfortunately, Flossie violently acted out her destructiveness just after positive plans were being made to terminate therapy. A "smash-bang" fight between her father and mother triggered Flossie's regression in school: Flossie all but destroyed one classroom as she vented her fury by slashing pictures and hitting other children in the face.[2]

NOTES

[1] All of this may have referred to simple facts, just as manifest content of dreams regularly reflect the residues of recent events. However, it is significant that Flossie chose to report her "problems" as centered upon a creature being hurt, beaten up and killed. Certainly these words by themselves give an excellent clue to the sadistic beatings (with consequent fears of death) to which Flossie had been exposed. The opening words of Flossie's second hour of her diagnostic once again focused upon the theme of death: she noted once again her dog was *dead* while her very next association pertained to her mother *hitting* the children.

[2] Just as she had been hit in the face by her mother.

Flossie
71

Stimulation-Symptom-and-Dream-Profile

	Separation Phobias	
	Night Terrors, Twilight States	
+ Sleep in Bed with Adult	+ Irrational Fears: Other	
	Irrational Tempers	
+ Adult Genital Erotic	+ Sexual Symptoms	
	+ Biting/Cutting, etc.	} content of
+ View Adult Coitus	+ Eyes	} dreams and
	Fire	} symptoms

	Learning Problems (levels 2 or 3, etc.)	
+ Punitive Yelling	Lying and Delinquency	
	+ Reversal of Affect	
+ Beatings	+ Closing Down Upon, Kill	} content of
	Falling	} dreams and symptoms

	+ Excretory Symptoms and Dreams	
	Anal Masturbation	
Preoccupation with Child's BM	Enuresis	
	Illness, etc.	} content of
Anal Contacts	Pain	} dreams and
	+ Death	} symptoms
	Compulsions	

Case 72: Gene

Gene appeared to be a friendly, sturdy, little five-year-old boy who willingly took his therapist's hand as they walked to the office for his first diagnostic hour. Once the nature of helping him with his worries was structured, he sat quietly during the full hour as he told his problems. He had a winning way, with a round face full of expression, his eyes focused directly on his therapist.

The above details regarding Gene's appearance contrast markedly with his presenting symptoms and even more so with some of the detailed information which was disclosed during his diagnostic interviews.

Gene was brought to the clinic because of his disturbed behavior at home where he had been cutting bedspreads, drapes and his parents' prized furniture. He had also urinated and defecated on the rugs and scribbled "all over the house."

Sources of Stimulation:
children's tactile and visual erogenous contacts with the adult body

−/+ sleeping in
bed with adults*

1. The parents separated when Gene was only eight months old. Gene lived alone with his mother from that time until he was four. Though Gene had his own room and bed, the mother "once in a while" would wake up mornings to find him in her bed.

The mother then married Gene's "new" father, whereupon Gene found another bed to share: his stepfather brought four children from his previous marriage with him into his new home. Gene liked to get in bed with the oldest of these children, Susie, age thirteen. That this bed-sharing probably was highly sexualized is suggested by the finding that (a) Susie had recently been taken to the police station after distributing a note with extremely "vulgar" language; (b) Susie was accustomed to going about the home scantily clad in a sheer nightgown.

Gene was exposed to other forms of tactile erogenous stimulation: the mother admitted that there was a time when Gene could *not keep his hands off her*. The stepfather agreed that Gene and his mother were far too close physically.

2. At first Gene denied that he ever saw any adults unclothed. However, he was able to answer the therapist's question as to how the body of a woman and man differ: he explained that a lady has a lot of hair "down there" near her

296

+ adult nudity

legs. When it was pointed out to him that someplace he must have seen a lady with hair "down there," Gene "suddenly" remembered that he had seen his mother without her clothes. His mother independently confirmed this report as she told her worker how Gene had been in a "stage," from the age of three on, of trying to see her undressed. When she was in the bathtub, he would decide he needed to go to the bathroom. Furthermore, Gene got a good look at his mother and adolescent sister as they paraded about the house in their transparent gowns, and one night Gene saw *his mother and stepfather in the nude "making out" on the living-room couch*. The mother pointed out that she "quickly" covered up.

+ adult genital
    erotic*

3. How much Gene saw of his mother's and stepfather's sexual activities on the living-room couch is uncertain. However, it was certain that, at the age of two and a half, Gene had visited his own father and had watched the father and the father's girl friend copulating. Gene had discovered his *father and friends* high on marijuana and *unabashed about having sexual intercourse in front of the child*. The father also had offered Gene some of the "pot." Gene was able to report these events in graphic detail to his grandmother, who for a long time was afraid to let Gene's mother know what had happened.

+ view adult
    coitus*

Of note, when Gene's parents were urged not to "make out" in front of Gene so as not to activate further his sexual feelings and his jealousy, both parents smiled with an expression of amazement. They indicated they didn't know how they could possibly manage to limit their natural impulses to that degree.

Behavioral Symptoms correlated with
children's tactile and visual erogenous contacts with the adult body

− / + separation
hysterics*

1. Gene demonstrated no evidence of panic when he was separated from his mother. However, his relation to his mother resembled that of a possessive husband rather than a son. He would say to his mother, for example: "Let's you and me leave and be just us together again." Similarly, he did not like it when anybody came near his mother and he became very irritated and jealous when his stepfather put an arm around her.

+ nightmares

2. According to the mother's report, "Gene used to dream every night about frightening animals."

3. Gene did not give vent to screaming temper tantrums even though he did demonstrate his temper in the form of soiling, cutting and scribbling all over the house.

+ sexual
    symptoms*

4. Gene masturbated compulsively and continually. This behavior first appeared at the age of two and a half following his observation of his father copulating with his girl friend.

Gene also would urinate in an exhibitionistic way, as though he were imitating sexual intercourse. He urinated into a paper bag, "which had a hole in it with a bunch of junk," and he urinated on the bag before he took it out "for the trashman." As Gene spoke of this material during his diagnostic hour, he spread his legs apart and revealed a hole in his crotch through which his penis was exposed.

+ biting/cutting*

5. Gene's presenting problem consisted of his cutting bedspreads, drapes and furniture. Actually, before he carried out this behavior, he would bring scissors and knives to his mother so that she would keep him from using them. However, when his mother did take the scissors and knives away from him he would resort to ripping and cutting with a fork.

+ fire*

6. At home, Gene kept talking about matches and insisted that his mother teach him how to light fires. Finally, he stole a big box of matches. His mother was terrified that he would set the house on fire.

Sources of Stimulation:
adult punitive and excretory contacts with children

+ early
deprivation

1. After Gene was born, the mother could not eat or sleep. Her weight went down to ninety-three pounds. She stated she collapsed from exhaustion and that many times she had thoughts of suicide. Gene soon became involved with head-banging. Then, when Gene was six months old, he fell off a dressing table. Apparently, his mother did not offer the protection which would have prevented the accident.

+ beatings*

2. Gene's mother remembered how as a child she hated her own brother. On one occasion, she tried to stuff leaves up his nose and another time *she tried "putting blankets over his face."* At the time of Gene's referral, his mother reported dreaming every night of ways to kill her children. In line with this information, Gene disclosed with much detail how his mother had tried to strangle him. Gene looked pale as he told how he couldn't breathe when his mother put her hands around his throat. He was petrified that the clinic would tell his mother about this confession and then he did not know what she might do to him next. He begged, "don't you dare tell her," but did not ask if he could live in another home.

Gene also described how his mother hit him with a strap while his stepfather only used his hand. With some resistance his mother admitted to using physical abuse as a means of punishment for Gene. She stated that his behavior was so out of control that she "couldn't help it." The stepfather also ashamedly admitted he threatened Gene that he "would put him through the wall" if Gene did not behave.

+ punitive
yelling*

3. Since their marriage, one year before the clinic referral, Gene's mother and stepfather fought continuously. On two occasions, the mother got a black

eye. On three separate occasions, the mother and Gene packed up to leave the house.

+ adult
defecation

4. Gene would see his mother when she sat on the toilet to defecate.

Behavioral Symptoms correlated with
adult punitive and excretory contacts with children

+ negative
behavior

1. The mother stated that Gene shut himself in his closet for three days straight to punish himself. She did not see any connection between this behavior and her own method of having punished him once by keeping him in his room for three days.

+ freezing of
affect

2. The mother was surprised to find that Gene "acts like his punishment never happened, no matter how much he's punished." After the mother spanked him across her lap, she felt "scared" when she noticed he didn't cry at all but merely stared at her.

+ enuresis*
+ excretory
symptoms*
(soiling)
+ hurting
+ reversal of
affect*
+ closing down
upon
destructively*
+ death*

3. Soiling, both urination and defecation in inappropriate places, was one of Gene's presenting problems. He would do "pee-pee" on the floor. He would refuse to go to the bathroom and then would deliberately defecate on the rug.

4. When Gene was two and a half, he began to want to be hit. He would tell his mother, "Hit me harder." This wish that he — a poor little fellow be hit developed into a wish for *other "poor little fellows" to be hit*. Gene told his therapist, "I throw rocks. I punch Billy. He lives down the street. I kick him. There's only one person I want to make die: Billy. He's a poor little boy who sits in the street."[1]

+ killing*

Gene also expressed the wish to kill himself[2] and to be dead. He poignantly told his mother: "Why did God put me on earth? He should take me away." Unfortunately once again, Gene's wish — this time a wish to die — became converted into a wish for other poor little creatures to die: Gene tried to kill one of the mother's little kittens and succeeded in killing another one. He put enough detergent in the kitten's food to kill the little animal. Later he was caught trying to flush the other kittens down the toilet. Here one can observe, in the making, a process whereby child abuse is learned and thereby handed down one generation to another.

NOTES

[1] At this point, his therapist tried to help Gene to see how he was acting like his mother and tried to structure a goal for Gene so that he would not have to be mean like her. Following this plea, Gene said: "I don't want to go, I like you."

[2] Gene dreamed: "I was staying in the car my Lincoln Continental and me and my sister was in it and I was starting the motor. I put the motor on; I took the keys. I drove

+ / – falling* (the
   wheelchair)
+ eyes* ("see" in
   dreams)

down the hill. This man in a wheelchair was rolling down the hill. Then my mother came out. She *saw* the car wasn't there. She *saw* it wasn't there. Then the car came down the hill. She ran down and told me to give her the keys." Compare this dream with the actual behavior of "Guy" who also had been exposed to the most severe beatings and who actually did set his father's car rolling down a hill (case 60).

Gene
72

Stimulation-Symptom-and-Dream-Profile

	Separation Phobias	
	Night Terrors, Twilight States	
Sleep in Bed with Adult	Irrational Fears: Other	
	Irrational Tempers	
+ Adult Genital Erotic	+ Sexual Symptoms	
	+ Biting/Cutting, etc.	} *content of*
+ View Adult Coitus	+ Eyes	*dreams and*
	+ Fire	*symptoms*
	Learning Problems (levels 2 or 3, etc.)	
+ Punitive Yelling	Lying and Delinquency	
	+ Reversal of Affect	
+ Beatings	+ Closing Down Upon, Kill	} *content of dreams and*
	+ Falling	*symptoms*
	+ Excretory Symptoms and Dreams	
	Anal Masturbation	
Preoccupation with Child's BM	+ Enuresis	
	Illness, etc.	} *content of*
Anal Contacts	Pain	*dreams and*
	+ Death	*symptoms*
	Compulsions	

Case 73: Hoagy

Hoagy was a sturdy, outgoing, thirteen-year-old boy who struck his teacher and hit the neighborhood children. In contrast to his "tough" behavior in public, Hoagy often secretly comforted himself by sucking his thumb.

Hoagy was crippled by a massive learning problem. He attained only a 71 Full-Scale WISC score with a verbal I.Q. of 79, yet he could read complex texts dealing with his special topic of interest: the classification, habits and care of snakes. During his diagnostic hours and follow-up therapy, he demonstrated strong intellectual capabilities. He was able, for example, to use abstract reasoning to associate freely to his dreams and to respond constructively to therapeutic understanding and help.

Sources of Stimulation:
adult punitive and excretory contacts with children

+ beatings*

1. His mother genuinely cared for Hoagy, as indicated by her complete willingness to follow whatever recommendations the clinic had to offer. However, prior to therapy she had disciplined him regularly by *beating him with a strap, a broom, a bat, a switch and a thin electrical cord* and would scream "I'll beat the shit out of you." Fortunately, Hoagy's mother responded excellently to therapeutic advice and ceased beating him once she understood how children could be emotionally harmed by being beaten.

Hoagy's parents fought violently with one another until they were divorced when Hoagy was nine years old. The father, for example, on one occasion stabbed the mother in the head with a knife. Eventually it became necessary for the mother to flee for her life and take her children to live with relatives. Finally, the mother procured a court order requiring that the father be hospitalized for his emotional disturbance.

The father also hit Hoagy. He often would take off his shoe to discipline Hoagy for some inconsequential mistake, this despite his attempts to protect Hoagy from the mother's beatings.

Behavioral Symptoms correlated with
adult punitive and excretory contacts with children

+ negative behavior (forgetting, opposition)

1. Hoagy most vehemently denied that he had been beaten. At first he denied that his mother had ever hit him, until finally his mother, together with

301

her worker, assured Hoagy that she had severely belted him to deal with his difficult behavior. Even when Hoagy could admit that his mother did beat him, it soon became evident that he "forgot" what he had done to prompt the beatings.[1]

Hoagy regularly would "forget" to bring home articles his mother had ordered at the store. Likewise, he would forget to come back home on time. In such ways he would manage to do the opposite from his mother's requests.

−/+learning*
(level 3, I.Q.
capacity?)

But Hoagy's negativism displayed itself most dramatically in relation to learning. He read what he wanted to read − i.e., about snakes or football. Otherwise, he could not read at all and refused to do his work in school. The school found it necessary to place Hoagy in a special class with children who were retarded.

+freezing of
affect
+reversal of
affect*

2. Hoagy's feelings toward his mother for her cruel whippings remained frozen. Hoagy also displayed a reversal of affect when he set a living room couch on fire. Instead of experiencing panic when the fire spread out of control and burned his fingers, Hoagy laughed with expressions of glee (see below).

+enuresis*
+excretory
symptoms*
(+anal
masturbation*)

3. Both Hoagy and his brother, two years younger, wet their beds. Additionally, the two boys had anal sexual contact, with Hoagy putting his "pinky" into his brother's rear and vice versa. At times, Hoagy would put his finger into his own anus.

+killing*

4. When Hoagy was nine years old, his mother took her children and ran away from the father. Immediately thereafter, Hoagy *killed* a cat, despite his special love of animals.

And as Hoagy's mother hurt him, so Hoagy felt justified in hurting other children. One day he told his therapist: "I hate this boy. I can't cope with him. He tells me one thing and tells his friends another. I almost killed him. I shoved

+delinquency*

my two fingers down his throat. I gave him what he deserved." Again Hoagy told how he "half-murdered" another boy: "the boy tapped me on the shoulder. I went after him. I hit him laying on the ground. His eyes were all bleeding." These descriptions were not stories: the neighborhood was in an uproar about Hoagy's brutality.

Hoagy's capacity to hurt burst through his passive restrictive withdrawal in school. He ended up hitting his teacher, although he *never* hit his mother who had beaten him so severely. Hoagy explained "If anyone touched me, I'd go hysterical.[2] When they touched me the heat would go down my arm and I'd smack 'em. They suspended me because I hit the teacher by mistake. I didn't mean to hit him. I threw my arms up so quick."

Hoagy's dreams reflected his preoccupation with killing, poison, falling and death. He related two dreams:

+closing down
upon
destructively*

(a) "This dog was *hanging from a rope*. Some man pulled him up. He was moving around and trying to get down." Hoagy's *associations* led him to talk about "this lady who *killed* dogs with a *poison* spray on the grass so that the dogs wouldn't go to the bathroom on the lawn. The dogs licked the grass and *died*. One dog was *dead* with maggots." Hoagy associated further to the dogs hanging: "The dog would *fall* if you let him go. He would *die*. He would *fall* on the cement."

+ falling*

(b) "I'm way up on a roof or something. All of a sudden I *fall*." This dream coincided with an early screen memory of Hoagy's *falling* off his bike.

+ death*

Hoagy acted out some of his self-destructive preoccupations. For example, he started smoking marijuana which made him feel as though he were *dead*. Hoagy trembled with fear as he told his therapist that he almost *jumped out of a window* while he was "on pot." As he had looked out a window, he entertained the thoughts that the window did not look real and experienced the urge to check by jumping through it. He realized how close he had been to *death*.[3]

Sources of Stimulation:
children's tactile and visual erogenous contacts with the adult body

1. Hoagy liked to get in bed with his eleven-year-old brother. When they were in bed together, he liked to "lie under" the brother.

+ adult nudity

2. Hoagy, *age thirteen,* was accustomed to seeing all adults in his family (his mother, his mother's boyfriend and his teenage sisters) completely nude.[4] Hoagy also frequently came across his sister's used sanitary napkins which were carelessly left out in the open.

+ adult genital erotic*
(+ view adult coitus*)

3. When he was nine years old, Hoagy *saw his mother and father copulating*. At the time, he recalled seeing his father's erect penis. In relation to this information, Hoagy added that he was *not able to stop reading hard-core pornographic magazines showing "stuff — it's called sperm — coming out of the pee-pee hole."* Actually Hoagy could recall seeing pornographic pictures as far back as his sixth year when he was exposed to a picture of "a man lying on top of a woman . . . she was sucking his dink." As he spoke of these pictures, Hoagy became visibly anxious and indicated he needed to be excused a minute to go to the toilet. Hoagy also witnessed the "live" sexual activities of a number of adolescent boys doing "that stuff" with a girl and with one another.

Behavioral Symptoms correlated with
children's tactile and visual erogenous contacts with the adult body

+ irrational fears*

1. Hoagy recalled that when he was little, he was *terrified* at night that a fire truck would crash into the house. At such times, he would go into his mother's room and sleep with her. He also recalled fears about "a guy who went chopping people's heads off in a movie."

At night, Hoagy also experienced fears of "pictures" on the wall. His mother promised to put a bunk bed against the wall to alleviate his fear.

+ sexual
symptoms*

2. Hoagy directly acted out sexually with his brother and with himself. He "poked" into his brother's rear and the brother "poked" into his. He also lay under his brother in bed while they both experienced erections.

With himself, Hoagy became involved in duplicating the pornographic pictures he had seen: he began masturbating while looking at himself nude in the mirror. In this way, he completed on himself the sexual excitement which had been associated with pictures of a man's penis ejaculating. Such forms of sexual gratification provided Hoagy not only a *discharge* of sexual excitement but also additional sexual *charge* via visual erogenous stimulation. His orgasms during these visual contacts provided a further source for the male body image becoming conditionally associated with intense sexual emotion.

Hoagy also discharged his excited sexual emotion upon a neighborhood boy: As noted, Hoagy grabbed this boy and shoved his fingers forcefully down his throat. In Hoagy's words "I almost killed him. It was so warm, like feeling a girl." The boy's father came over to Hoagy's house in a state of rage because the back of his son's throat had been ripped sore and raw; he demanded that Hoagy be kept off the neighborhood streets.

+ biting/cutting*

3. In one of his dreams: "*Dogs* were *attacking*"[5] Hoagy. Hoagy's associations to another dream led him to speak of a vicious dog which growled, jumped and *bit*. Hoagy also entertained fears about "a guy who went *chopping* people's heads off."

+ eyes*

4. Hoagy's disturbed thoughts while he was smoking marijauna included delusions about eyes. Hoagy reported: "The clock would play *eyes* on me and so would my teacher; whenever *I blinked my eyes* he would blink his, too."[6]

+ fire*

5. When Hoagy was little he was phobic about "fire trucks crashing into the house." Later these fearful thoughts came close to being realized when Hoagy *set a fire* in the home. Hoagy and his little brother set the living room couch on fire: "We lit a fire. We wanted to examine it. We thought it would light up like a light bulb. We took a broom into the fire. We burnt our fingers. We threw a broom on the couch and the whole couch went up on fire. We thought it was funny. The whole place was catching fire."

NOTES

[1] Perhaps the beatings resulted in inhibition of the *memory* of the misbehavior rather than an inhibition of the misbehavior itself, i.e., in life we often manage to forget our most discomforting memories.

[2] Language of this sort would seem to reflect an I.Q. higher than 71.

3 Fortunately, Hoagy was able to realize the harmfulness of his intake of marijuana and eventually managed to stop using the drug.

4 Of note, Hoagy's direct association to his presentation of this information was: "I like snakes. I love snakes."

5 Presumably with their teeth.

6 Also one of Hoagy's most destructive fights with a neighborhood boy involved hitting the boy's *eyes* (see above). "The boy lay on the ground, his eyes all bleeding." Compare this *attack* upon the *eyes* with similar behavior evidenced by Philip and by Ronny, cases 99 and 100, who also were exposed to exceedingly intense sexual stimulation. In these cases, "penetration" of the eye by a penis was duplicated via a "penetration" of the eye with a fist, stick or arrow.

Hoagy

73

Stimulation-Symptom-and-Dream-Profile

	Separation Phobias	
	Night Terrors, Twilight States	
Sleep in Bed with Adult	+ Irrational Fears: Other	
	Irrational Tempers	
+ Adult Genital Erotic	+ Sexual Symptoms	
	+ Biting/Cutting, etc.	⎫ *content of*
+ View Adult Coitus	+ Eyes	⎬ *dreams and*
	+ Fire	⎭ *symptoms*
	Learning Problems (levels 2 or 3, etc.)	
Punitive Yelling	+ Lying and Delinquency	
	+ Reversal of Affect	
+ Beatings	+ Closing Down Upon, Kill	⎫ *content of* ⎬ *dreams and*
	+ Falling	⎭ *symptoms*
	+ Excretory Symptoms and Dreams	
	+ Anal Masturbation	
Preoccupation with Child's BM	+ Enuresis	
	Illness, etc.	⎫ *content of*
Anal Contacts	Pain	⎬ *dreams and*
	+ Death	⎭ *symptoms*
	Compulsions	

Case 74: Irwin

Irwin, an eight-year-old boy with average intelligence, suffered from an overwhelming learning problem. He repeated the first grade and was about to repeat the second. Reading and writing were practically impossible for him. He hated school but was reported by his teacher to be "one of the nicest and meekest little boys in the classroom."

Sources of Stimulation:
adult punitive and excretory contacts with children

+ early
deprivation

1. Irwin was "pushed aside as a baby and was never given the attention he needed." The mother, whose own mother had been hospitalized for a manic-depressive psychosis, openly expressed her distaste for being married and having to care for her children. In line with a history of early deprivation, Irwin, like his mother, was asthmatic.

From the age of three to five, Irwin was hospitalized frequently for his asthma. It was necessary to tie him down in order to administer his oxygen therapy. His father recalled Irwin's crying, fighting the restraints and begging "Dad, untie me!"

+ beatings*

2. In Irwin's *first memory, he was hit by his mother* for spilling his milk. He added that his mother still hit him on the face and pulled his hair, while his father disciplined him by thrashing him with a belt.

Irwin also witnessed his father drunkenly beating his mother. On one occasion, the father threw the mother down their stairs.

+ punitive
yelling*

3. When Irwin would watch his father striking his mother, the father would blast out at him. The mother felt that Irwin was unjustly used as the scapegoat during these upsetting scenes and would blame the father for yelling at "poor Irwin."

Several of Irwin's early screen memories focused upon his parents fighting and yelling. He explained: "At night I'd stay awake [while] my father and mother yelled at each other." He recalled the time his father yelled "Look at all that shit," to which his mother yelled back: "It's not mine; it's the kids'."

Irwin also remembered a typical scene when his mother screamed at him. In Irwin's words: "I called my brother a bitch and my mother told me not to swear, but I got so mad I could not help it; then she said 'Don't swear again or I'll knock the shit out of you.'"

306

Behavioral Symptoms correlated with
adult punitive and excretory contacts with children

+ negative
behavior

1. Irwin always did as he was told in school. However, his teacher concluded that most of Irwin's compliance was due to his "overly restrictive nature." The degree of this passive restriction was noted by another teacher who reported: "Early in the year I gave Irwin an assignment, and then went over to work with another student. About ten minutes later I looked up and noticed Irwin sitting peacefully at his desk yet to have made a mark on his paper. When I asked him what the trouble was, he answered with perfect equanimity 'I don't have a pencil.' 'Oh' I said and gave him one, whereupon the assignment was completed." With such frozen passivity, it was no wonder that Irwin was struggling with a severe learning problem which required that he be placed in a special class for children with learning problems.

+ learning*
(level 2)

A tendency to write in the *opposite* direction, i.e., to reverse his numbers and letters, exacerbated Irwin's learning problem. His teacher in the second grade complained: "in arithmetic, Irwin constantly reverses the numbers '3,' '6,' and '9.' Also he confuses 'b' and 'd' in the printed alphabet."[1]

+ lying*

Still another expression of Irwin's negativism was his emphasis upon the opposite of the truth: lying. Irwin's therapist pointed out with reference to Irwin's history of "being beaten," that "when hate goes in, it wants to come out." The therapist then asked Irwin how hate came out from him. In answer to this question Irwin then explained: "*I start lying.* My mother says *'Don't look* at TV' *so I look* at it and then I *say 'I wasn't* looking.' "

+ negative
emotion

2. Irwin's dislike of school was a chief complaint. Often he expressed the "*I don't care" attitude.*

+ freezing of
affect

Freezing of affect became particularly evident at times when Irwin was subjected to physical injury. When he burned his hand, for example, he was quite neglectful of it. He said, simply and without feeling, that it would get better soon and that "hurts never last long."

+ reversal of
affect*

3. Irwin not only reacted inadequately to being hurt but also reported with glee how he enjoyed showing the school children the dead skin of his burnt hand and watching their reactions of revulsion. In a similar vein Irwin spoke with pleasure of how the children had carried on with screams while they were getting their medical "shots."

+ falling*
+ closing down
upon
destructively*
(crush)
(quicksand)
+ killing*

4. The two dreams which Irwin recalled during his diagnostic hour dealt with falling: "My brother *fell* in a big hole with a lot of *quicksand* in it," and, "When my father and I were at the top of a hill, there were big monsters which were going to *push us down.*"

In reality, Irwin "accidentally" killed his pet gerbil with his "powerful air gun."

+ enuresis*

5. Irwin would wet the bed "occasionally" until he was eight years old. After that he would wet himself nightly at the beginning of the school year.

+ excretory
symptoms*
(anal sex play)

Irwin confided that he and his brother stuck pencils into his sister's anus. His sister would say: "Now it's my turn."[2]

Sources of Stimulation:
children's tactile and visual erogenous contacts with the adult body

− / + sleeping in
bed with adults*
(not weekly)

1. When Irwin was scared, he would crawl into bed with his father. This happened about "once every five weeks." Sometimes he slept in bed between his mother and father.

+ adult nudity

2. In the bathroom, Irwin would see both of his parents without clothes. Additionally, Irwin would spend the day with his father at a men's club where the men, completely exposed, would sunbathe nude.

+ adult genital
erotic*

3. Irwin and his siblings would sneak in to see his mother's hard-core *pornographic pictures of adult homosexual and heterosexual activities.*

Behavioral Symptoms correlated with
children's tactile and visual erogenous contacts with the adult body

1. Most of the time Irwin was silent and emotionless without any display of anger. However, his mother reported that at home he was a perfectionist, and that if *anything* went wrong with an object with which he was playing, he

+ irrational
tempers*

would go into a mad rage and become destructive. On one occasion Irwin took a kite down to the beach on a windy day. The string broke on the kite but he was able to rescue it. When he brought the kite home he ended up in a wild tantrum over the string breaking and started tearing the kite apart.

2. As noted, Irwin, his brother and his sister poked sticks into each other's

+ sexual
symptoms*

rectums: perhaps a reflection of the activities they had viewed in their mother's hard-core pornographic pictures.

+ eyes* (reading
problem)

In school, Irwin did especially poorly in *reading* and writing.

3. Irwin and his brother would play with matches in the basement of their

+ fire*

home. On one occasion, they built a small doll's house which they then burned. The boys supposedly put the fire out then went outside to play. However, they had not put the fire out completely, and since the boys did not run for help, their own home eventually was completely demolished.

For several years, Irwin continued to play with matches and fire. Once he and his brother made a fire "too large" for their fireplace and caused substantial smoke damage to their home. Also, at camp, Irwin and his friends built large bonfires. On one occasion, they decided to throw aerosol cans into the fire and then waited for the cans to explode.

NOTES

1 Some specialists at this point would emphasize minimal brain damage as the source for Irwin's learning problems. However, such a theory is contradicted by the fact that with long-term psychotherapy, *Irwin's learning problem was completely alleviated.* Irwin's reversals reflected the findings of this study: that one way the brain can react to punitive overstimulation is to predispose the child to do the opposite, i.e., reverse ongoing behavior.

2 The association between pain and pleasure during anal play provided a basis whereby pain in general became capable of eliciting pleasure and therefore became rewarding.

Irwin
74

Stimulation-Symptom-and-Dream-Profile

	Separation Phobias	
	Night Terrors, Twilight States	
Sleep in Bed with Adult	Irrational Fears: Other	
	+ Irrational Tempers	
+ Adult Genital Erotic	+ Sexual Symptoms	
	Biting/Cutting, etc.	} *content of*
View Adult Coitus	+ Eyes	} *dreams and*
	+ Fire	} *symptoms*

	+ Learning Problems (levels 2 or 3, etc.)	
+ Punitive Yelling	+ Lying and Delinquency	
	+ Reversal of Affect	
+ Beatings	+ Closing Down Upon, Kill	} *content of dreams and*
	+ Falling	} *symptoms*

	+ Excretory Symptoms and Dreams	
	Anal Masturbation	
Preoccupation with Child's BM	+ Enuresis	
	Illness, etc.	} *content of*
Anal Contacts	Pain	} *dreams and*
	Death	} *symptoms*
	Compulsions	

Case 75: Synopsis of Selma Fraiberg's "Roger"

Roger was four years old when he began his analysis with Selma Fraiberg (Journal of the American Psychoanalytic Association, Vol. 10, 1962, p. 338-67). His parents were reduced to complete helplessness by Roger's behavior. Roger was "obstinate, negative, and relentlessly goading. He would seize upon any trivial point to challenge his parents and finally provoke them to anger and spanking. . . . His parents described destructive orgies in which he would run about the house in a giddy fashion . . . smashing objects and giggling in a peculiar joyless way. . . . In the chaos of Roger's four-year-old personality no one had been able to catch a glimpse of an extraordinary intelligence that revealed itself after better integration of his personality was achieved" (p. 339-40).

Sources of Stimulation:
children's tactile and visual erogenous contacts with the adult body

−/+ sleeping in
bed with adults*
(frequency?)
+ adult nudity

1. Roger "confided with much giggling that he would sometimes get up at night and get into his mother's bed" (p. 342).

2. Obsessive interest in observing his mother's and sister's genitalia was accompanied by anxiety of such intensity that it precipitated frequent episodes of depersonalization. Sometimes Roger would clutch his penis during periods of preoccupation with his mother's genitalia (p. 345).

+ adult genital
erotic*
(+ view adult
coitus*)

3. Roger had also been exposed to *viewing his parents' coital activities* (p. 358-59).

Behavioral Symptoms correlated with
children's tactile and visual erogenous contacts with the adult body

+ eyes* (dream)

1. Roger dreamed of being at a *movie* lost in the dark.

+ sexual
symptoms*

2. Roger and his sister, Judy, indulged in sexual play in bed together. The sister, outspoken in her wish to appropriate Roger's penis and make it her own, would grab it "half playfully, half maliciously" (p. 349). In turn, Roger compulsively masturbated anally with phantasies of being a girl (p. 362). Roger "looked surprised at himself" as he told Mrs. Fraiberg " 'I wish I could have a little penis like a girl. . . . I don't know why I said that. I just said it' " (p. 354).

+ night terrors*
+ irrational fears*

3. Roger experienced terror dreams involving cutting, chopping (p. 344, 362) and robbers (p. 362). He also was afraid at night, e.g., when he experienced fears that there were robbers in the house and fears that a man was

310

chasing him (p. 343).

+biting/cutting*

4. In one terror dream "a radio announcer said in a loud voice 'all the boys are going to have their a-s-s *cut off.'* Then Roger was scared and began to run away" and then woke up (p. 362). In a recurrent dream, he feared that a "faceless man . . . would *cut off his penis* with a butcher knife" (p. 344). Still another dream was reported by Roger to be "*all chopped up* in little pieces" (p. 352).

+conversion
symptoms*
(twilight dream-
like state)

Roger also displayed hysterical conversion symptoms involving wishes to cut off his foot. He would suddenly cry out in pain " 'my foot hurts; my foot hurts.' " At such times, he would then hug his foot in misery while he perseverated, " 'I wish I could cut it off so that it wouldn't hurt and if I didn't have it then it couldn't hurt. It would be nice not to have a foot. *Cut off* both of them' "[1] (p. 354-55).

+irrational
tempers*

5. Roger would wildly kick doors during his temper tantrums (p. 340).

Sources of Stimulation:
adult punitive and excretory contacts with children

+early
deprivation and
punishment

1. Roger's parents dated their conflicts with him to the period after his first birthday when they were contemplating a divorce. At that time, Roger became an unwanted baby whose presence kept the parents from attaining their divorce. "When the mother's hostility toward her husband was at its height, the little boy became the object of a good measure of her destructive feelings . . ." (p. 340). To make matters worse, the mother could not tolerate Roger's heightened activity which emerged during this period (p. 340).

+punitive bowel
training

2. Soon there began a contest between mother and child *over bowel-training,* a contest which continued until Roger was nearly four (p. 341).

+yelling* and
violence

3. Roger and his sister also "were witnesses to the verbal battles between the parents." At night the children "could easily overhear the parents' quarrels in the bedroom next to the room they shared." Roger frequently watched *his mother's destructive rages.* On one occasion in his presence, she literally smashed a piece of furniture to bits (p. 340).

+beatings*

"The parents found no effective means of discipline for Roger. He was *spanked often in parental rage and helplessness.* . . . Roger's father found himself 'impelled against his better judgment'[2] to strike Roger with physical force" (p. 341).

During the early weeks of treatment, Mrs. Fraiberg helped Roger's parents understand that one of the motives of Roger's behavior was the "relentless provocation of punishment." Mrs. Fraiberg "enlisted their cooperation in giving up the spankings and . . . discussed other means of discipline. Much time was devoted to re-education of the parents" so as to strengthen "the positive ties to the child and enable the parents to employ . . . more effective discipline" based upon gentle "parental approval and disapproval" rather than punitive force (p. 342).

Behavioral Symptoms correlated with
adult punitive and excretory contacts with children

+ excretory
symptoms*

1. "Roger . . . soiled until he was nearly four years old. . . . His mother had been completely unsuccessful in trying to train him" (p. 361). To her chagrin "he left little deposits of feces around the house" (p. 364).

+ falling*

+ excretory
symptoms*

+ excretory
dream*
(brown food)

+ anal
masturbation*

By the age of four, Roger was "afraid of the noise of the toilet and afraid of falling in" (p. 362). Later, he reported a terror dream about a "witch and a toilet" (p. 360). In another dream, Roger was "in a movie[3] — lost in the dark — trying to find his way to the candy counter. Then he was eating a chocolate bar [reminding him of a BM], the round kind with nuts in it" (p. 361).

But Roger's most prominent excretory symptom appeared in the form of anal masturbation which Roger's mother reported to Mrs. Fraiberg. Roger was actually relieved when his mother offered him controls by reporting to Mrs. Fraiberg her concern regarding the persistence of the anal masturbation[4] (p. 362).

+ pain* (nails)

2. When Roger finally became able to express his upset feelings, he began to talk of a disturbing daydream. A look of misery came over his face as he forced himself to say: " 'In the daydream, I have a *stick and it . . . it . . . has nails* at the end of it . . . to poke the g-i-r-l with' " (p. 353). At the same time, Roger dreamed of *witches:*

a. " 'There was a witch with Judy and it seemed they were fighting on one side against me and my boyfriends on the other [side]. Then in the next scene, Judy and my mother and my father were trying to dissolve a powder that would make a mask like a witch's' " (p. 348).

+ pain* (needle,
pin)

b. " 'The witch has a *needle* or a *pin* or something and she dropped it on the floor. I was going to reach for it when Judy grabbed it and gave it to the witch' " (p. 349).

+ closing down
upon
destructively*

3. Roger's dreams also presented evidence of his preoccupations with destruction and killing. After one of his "witch" dreams, he associated:[5] " 'Witches could kill you. . . . That must be what I'm afraid of' " (p. 352). Later, Roger dreamed he was "coasting on a sled down a steep hill with Tumpis [his teddy bear] sitting in front of him. They *crashed into a tree.* The next thing he knew, they landed on a big toboggan and went coasting down on this one" (p. 356-57).

+ closing down
upon
destructively*

Reactions pertaining to destruction also involved Roger's waking life. He indulged in "destructive orgies" during which he would smash objects (p. 340). These orgies were at first repeated during his therapy hours. On one occasion, Mrs. Fraiberg reflected that Roger suddenly "was off on one of his destructive orgies [of] breaking crayons, pencils, doll furniture, everything at hand."

+ reversal of affect*

4. During these destructive bouts in Mrs. Fraiberg's office, "there was only the pixie Roger *gleefully* destroying objects" (p. 343). Likewise, at home when Roger would run about the house, kicking doors and smashing objects, he "*giggled* in a peculiarly joyless way" with no signs of remorse (p. 340).

+ freezing of affect

Actually, "a good part of the three and a half years of Roger's analysis was devoted to analysis of his defenses against affect" (p. 347). Roger, for example, would talk affectlessly of his fears that someone could steal his penis and then added: " 'Don't you think I'm doing good today? I'm surprised myself how good I can think when I don't try to. Now we're getting connectors' " (p. 353). In turn, Mrs. Fraiberg answered that Roger was working well "but there was one very important connection that he hadn't seen: '*Where were the feelings* that would go with all this? If a boy were so afraid of such terrible things, we would expect to see the *feelings,* too.' Roger took this in soberly"[6] (p. 352-53).

+ negative behavior

5. A referral complaint: Roger reduced his parents to "complete helplessness in coping with his behavior problems: he was *obstinate, negative* and relentlessly goading" (p. 339-40). To quote Mrs. Fraiberg: "Roger was suddenly struck by the fact that everything his mother asked him to do made him want to do the opposite" (p. 354). This negativism became evident during his initial therapeutic sessions with Mrs. Fraiberg, who noted: "Roger presented a special problem. He could relate only through negating strenuously. . . . When I invited him into my office at the beginning of the session, he would refuse obstinately. If I quietly ignored him and entered my office alone . . . he would come barging in triumphantly five or ten minutes later" (p. 341). Reflecting Roger's indulgence in negativism, he developed a game of disguising and *reversing* numbers[7] (p. 350).

Fortunately, Roger's psychotic-like behavior disorder responded well to Mrs. Fraiberg's therapeutic efforts toward helping Roger and his family to discontinue overstimulation and to "talk out" rather than "act out" disturbed feelings. Subsequent to the termination of Roger's analysis, Mrs. Fraiberg was able to note: "I was able to follow Roger's progress for five years while I remained in the same city. . . . He had become a gratifying child to his parents and presented no problems that they could not handle themselves during these years. His schoolwork was excellent and his precocity and joy in learning delighted his parents and his teachers" (p. 364-65).

NOTES

[1] What might sound like "nonsense" makes much sense in terms of Roger's sexual overexcitation of his penis subsequent to his viewing his parents copulating. Some pains

in his foot must have triggered the emotions associated with the painful tensions he had experienced in his penis.

2 The father's *dissatisfaction* with himself for hitting Roger may have been one of the factors which contributed to the eventual therapeutic success of this case.

(+ eyes* in dream)

3 Dream of "movie" = "eyes."

4 The cumulative findings derived from the 100 Case Study suggest that the frequency of anal masturbation is increased among children exposed to violent yelling and screaming (see also cases 58, 77 and 100 of Douglas Junior, Kurt Junior and Ronny).

5 Mrs. Fraiberg taught Roger to analyze his dreams through what she and Roger called "The What Pops Into Your Mind Game" (p. 348).

6 Fortunately, with Mrs. Fraiberg's interpretations, Roger *was* able to bring to the surface his feelings of misery.

7 Of note, during one of his therapy hours Roger playfully reversed the age of a girl toward whom he had intense sexual feelings (p. 350).

Fraiberg's "Roger"
75

Stimulation-Symptom-and-Dream-Profile

	Separation Phobias	
	+ Night Terrors, Twilight States	
Sleep in Bed with Adult	+ Irrational Fears: Other	
	+ Irrational Tempers	
+ Adult Genital Erotic	+ Sexual Symptoms	
	+ Biting/Cutting, etc.	} *content of*
+ View Adult Coitus	+ Eyes	*dreams and*
	Fire	*symptoms*
	Learning Problems (levels 2 or 3, etc.)	
+ Punitive Yelling	Lying and Delinquency	
	+ Reversal of Affect	
+ Beatings	+ Closing Down Upon, Kill	} *content of*
		dreams and
	+ Falling	*symptoms*
	+ Excretory Symptoms and Dreams	
	+ Anal Masturbation	
Preoccupation with Child's BM	Enuresis	
	Illness, etc.	} *content of*
Anal Contacts	+ Pain	*dreams and*
	Death	*symptoms*
	Compulsions	

Case 76: Jerry

The mother had been extremely concerned about Jerry's persistent hyperactivity and had been unsuccessfully seeking psychiatric help for over a year. Jerry's habit of beating his dog also worried his mother. Since he was very attached to the little animal, Jerry's cruelty seemed all the more puzzling. Finally, at the age of four, Jerry started psychotherapy.

Sources of Stimulation:
adult punitive and excretory contacts with children

+ early
deprivation

+ hyperactivity

1. During her pregnancy, the mother took an overdose of Librium as a "suicidal gesture" in an effort to get people to notice her. Jerry at the age of six months was left in a foster home of ten children while his mother went back to work. Two months later, he returned home where his grandmother and aunt were placed in charge of him. By the time Jerry was about a year old, he would bang his head on anything hard, the floor, the sink, etc. Eventually, the head-banging ceased, only to be replaced by his incessant "running around like crazy," a symptom which still continued at the time of his referral.

+ punitive
yelling* (and
hitting)

+ beatings*

2. The mother was deserted by her own father when she was two. From that time on she easily flew into tantrums, threw things at her antagonists, and got her own way by terrorizing her family. Prior to therapy, she continued to give vent to this same kind of behavior in dealing with her son, Jerry. Daily he would be subjected to her tantrums. When his response in any way was the least bit frustrating to her, she would scream, swear and beat him; she would also strike him on the face. She tried talking to him, but it did "no good." Fortunately, Jerry's attendance at nursery school provided him with some respite from the upsets in his home.

Behavioral Symptoms correlated with
adult punitive and excretory contacts with children

+ enuresis*
+ excretory
symptoms*

(+ anal
masturbation*)

1. Jerry wet himself until he was four years old. He also failed to wipe himself effectively following defecation, a likely cause for anal itching. The itching led to anal scratching and poking. Jerry confided it felt good to put his finger in his "poopie hole." "Sometimes," he also played in the toilet with his feces.

+ negative
  behavior

2. According to his mother's report: "Even though Jerry had a fantastic memory and was able to tell you when he did something wrong, yet he continued to repeat the wrong behavior over and over again."

+ negative
  emotion

3. Jerry easily displayed "dislike" and "hate." He fought his therapist by screaming profanities, behavior which mimicked his behavior with his mother and with other children.

+ closing down
  upon
  destructively*
  (strangle)
+ killing*
+ hurting

4. Jerry was adept in evoking attacks upon himself, especially from his mother. He spontaneously related how he liked to trap her and make her explode. Of even more concern, Jerry spoke directly of wishes to *strangle* himself. In relation to strangling, Jerry dreamed that a snake was *coiling* around his neck. To *kill* it, Jerry had to stab it with a knife.

Jerry also liked to hurt others. He hit his dog in the face,[1] pulled his hair, threw things at him. Jerry also hit a child on the head with a pool ball simply because the boy did not want to play with him.

+ preoccupation
  with illness*

+ death*

This tendency to hurt others contributed to Jerry's fears that his destructive wishes might someday be realized. He overreacted to sickness and to death. He feared he was responsible when his mother came down with appendicitis. Likewise, he went into a tailspin of anxiety and regression with night terrors and tempers when his school principal suddenly died.

+ death*
+ closing down
  upon
  destructively*
+ hurting

Jerry related the following dreams: "This haunted house it was scary; there were *ghosts* and spiders in the house. Two *skeletons*[2] came and *strapped me down*. I rolled on my side like this. I broke the straps and *hit* them. A skeleton[2] was going to *hurt* me. I was being *shot* by a man with a mask. I woke up my mother and she *shot* the man."

Sources of Stimulation:
children's tactile and visual erogenous contacts with the adult body

+ sleeping in bed
  with adults*

1. Jerry was sharing his mother's room and bed when he first started therapy; periodically he was continuing to do so a year later. Jerry showed his therapist how close he slept next to his mother by putting two of his fingers directly in contact with one another. All the explanations as to how Jerry's emotional health would improve if he could have his own bed and room were offered in vain: neither Jerry nor his mother would at first give up this form of gratification. Only after Jerry's second therapist assured the mother that Jerry's problems would *never* improve unless he slept in his own bed was a change finally effected.

+ adult nudity

2. Jerry saw his mother in the bathroom while she was completely nude. Sometimes, he would see her when she was on the toilet. On other occasions he would see her when she got out from her bath; he even liked to pinch her on the "rear" at such times. Jerry was particularly aware of his mother's pubic hair and entertained vivid phantasies of pulling at it.

Jerry also spoke of seeing his uncle's penis and compared it to a giant hot dog. In relation to seeing his uncle urinate, Jerry commented that the uncle's penis "sure looked yuky."

+ adult genital erotic*
(+ view adult coitus*)

3. Jerry eventually was given his own room and bed. But unfortunately, this move did not result in an end to stimulation. Jerry confided to his therapist how he sneaked out of his bed and opened the door to his mother's room "a tiny crack," just enough to look at his mother and her boyfriend copulating in bed. Viewing the boyfriend's penis particularly disturbed Jerry to the extent that Jerry wanted to cut it off. In a panic he told his therapist "It gets me all mixed up. I can't stand it. I feel like I'm going crazy."

Behavioral Symptoms correlated with
children's tactile and visual erogenous contacts with the adult body

+ nightmares
+ night terrors*

1. Jerry suffered from nightmares about cuts, skeletons and killing. On one occasion, his mother was awakened by his screaming in his sleep while his body remained stiff with tension. It took his mother a long time to awaken him and calm him down.

+ conversion symptom* (twilight, dream-like state)
+ separation phobia* (and hysterics)
+ irrational tempers*

Jerry displayed evidence of a conversion symptom: while he was talking to his therapist about "dinks" and "bums," Jerry suddenly stopped and cried out as he sat motionless "I'm paralyzed."

2-3. Jerry often refused to separate from his mother at the clinic so that his therapist would have to carry him back to the office. At such times, Jerry would rage for a half hour or more. Each time the therapist questioned him about his self-control with respect to staying in his own bed, his screaming would intensify. Jerry would shout at the top of his voice "Shut up you fucker. I don't want to hear." He would twist and thrash his body and kick. When his therapist tried to reassure him by holding him gently, Jerry would pinch and scratch or vigorously bang his head back into his therapist's chin. Then he would turn red and moan for his mommy.

In general, Jerry's temper was triggered whenever he did not get his way at home or during his therapy sessions. His therapist noted, for example, that when Jerry could not immediately get candy from his therapist, Jerry threatened to kick the desk and file cabinet. He admitted he had done the same thing at home. He discussed how he hurt his ankle during one tantrum and showed his front tooth which he had chipped by biting the handle of a locked cabinet which wouldn't open.

+ sexual symptoms*

4. At the age of six, Jerry was compulsively acting out homosexually with a neighborhood boy. Jerry's words: "I play with Roy. I fiddle with his dink and I suck on it too." As Jerry in a panic confided these secrets, he began to complain of a "ringing"[3] noise in his ears.

+ biting/cutting*

5. At the age of six, Jerry was reported to have bitten his boyfriend and

on another occasion bit his therapist's finger.

Problems involved with biting were paralleled by nightmares about *cutting*. Jerry dreamed, "A skeleton was going to *cut* my hand off," and, "Two skeletons came and strapped me down. They covered my eyes and mouth with a cloth. They took off my pajamas. They had a big *knife* and held it here" [over pelvis]. In association to the dream, Jerry spoke of his dentist who took out his *tooth*.

Jerry also expressed the conscious wish to *cut off* his mother's boyfriend's penis but feared retaliation.

"Cutting" not only permeated Jerry's *nightmares* and *daydreams* but intruded also into Jerry's daily *behavior*: Jerry was adept in "accidentally" getting himself cut. Thus, the social service report read as follows: "In the past year, Jerry has made three trips to the emergency room with a *cut* foot, a *cut* finger, a *cut* on his side, and then a *cut* near his eye."

+eyes*   6. Jerry cut himself near his eye. He also entertained irrational fears that his mother might come into his room at night and scratch his *eyes* out. Likewise, in one dream already noted, "Two skeletons covered my *eyes and mouth* with a cloth. . . . "

−/+fire*   7. Jerry presented no symptoms or dreams involving fire. However, he presented a number of disturbing phantasies involving fire. For example, no sooner had he related how he had seen a neighborhood boy showing off his penis than Jerry began to complain about the heat in the office. He thereupon became afraid that the temperature would go so high it would melt everything, kill everyone and set the whole building on *fire*.[4] Likewise, when Jerry was telling how he was "sucking another boy's dink," he went on to elaborate: "His dink poked right up through me, it felt like I was catching on *fire*."

NOTES

[1] Recall Jerry's mother hitting *him* in the face.

[2] *Parental screaming, anal masturbation* and a preoccupation with *skeletons* and *death* also predominate in case 77 of Kurt Junior.

[3] Compare with cases 69, 77 and 100 of Dwight, Kurt Junior and Ronny.

[4] It would appear that Jerry was referring to his own very hot bodily feelings that accompany vascular dilatation during sexual excitement. Compare with case 30 of Terry.

Jerry
76

Stimulation-Symptom-and-Dream-Profile

	+ Separation Phobias	
	+ Night Terrors, Twilight States	
+ Sleep in Bed with Adult	Irrational Fears: Other	
	+ Irrational Tempers	
+ Adult Genital Erotic	+ Sexual Symptoms	
	+ Biting/Cutting, etc.	*content of*
+ View Adult Coitus	+ Eyes	*dreams and*
	Fire	*symptoms*
	Learning Problems (levels 2 or 3, etc.)	
+ Punitive Yelling	Lying and Delinquency	
	Reversal of Affect	
+ Beatings	+ Closing Down Upon, Kill	*content of dreams and*
	Falling	*symptoms*
	+ Excretory Symptoms and Dreams	
	+ Anal Masturbation	
Preoccupation with Child's BM	+ Enuresis	
	+ Illness, etc.	*content of*
Anal Contacts	Pain	*dreams and*
	+ Death	*symptoms*
	Compulsions	

Case 77: Kurt Junior

Kurt Junior, the son of Kurt Senior (case 85), was four years old when his nursery school insisted that he receive psychotherapeutic help for his disorderly, disorganized, provocative behavior.

The following brief extracts from his two diagnostic hours highlight Kurt's disturbed state at the time of his referral.[1] Of significance was the presence of key words reflecting erogenous and punishment overstimulation. The prominence of the key-word imagery was not diminished by its occurrence within a "psychotic" rather than neurotic or normal conversation. First, in response to his therapist's question as to what were his worries, Kurt answered, "I still can't *read*. There are X-rays in my *eyes*. I have X-rays in my *eyes*. When the *eye* comes over here then I climb up for X-ray. Ah-ha, it points to the floor where we went." Later Kurt went on to report: "I have a *skeleton* inside my body. If the bone is *destroyed*, all the *teeth* will come loose and will *fall* off. I look at food and look at how I grow up. . . . I *fell*. . . . I was born and first I turned into Kurt. Then you came to this office. Dr. Y is his name and my mother doesn't have a *penis*. Something comes out of her *botsie*. She has a thing with some fur on it. I've got a long tie. Mom and dad bought it for me. . . . Daddy's work company has a chair with some wheels on it like Dr. Y's. . . . I'm going to grow up and be a man. . . . If a girl were *trapped* in a glass, she would be staying there; she wouldn't get out. And if someone *cuts* the rope from the glass, it will come up. . . . If a shadow was a *skeleton* it would scare me terrible. If they shot each other, they'd be *dead*. The sniper would *cut his head off* and would come up from his body. . . . My sister tried to *choke* me. She tried to get milk out of my *throat* . . . an elephant's mouth is short. Mr. Duby says they use *poison* for prevention. They were *dead*. If they're *poison,* you got to keep them locked up. . . . Sometimes you feel like a coffee cake, because you like to eat it. . . . If a boy scout *went over a cliff* his car would go over and *crash.*"

As will be reviewed in detail, each of the above italicized expressions statistically relates to children's erotic or punitive or excretory stimulus contacts with adults. Kurt's expressions therefore provided a meaningful form of communicating significant information despite their jumbled appearance. It soon became apparent that the "nonsensical" appearance of Kurt's initial communications derived from the degree to which Kurt, like Erna Furman's "Carol" (see case 84) was overwhelmed by adult genital erotic contacts at so young an age. Once the parents were able to discontinue exposing Kurt to hard-core pornography together with their own nudity, and once Kurt was afforded an opportunity to be helped with his upset feelings about scenes of adult masturbation, fellatio and sodomy, his "dream-like" way of communicating became replaced by "rational" forms of speech.

Sources of Stimulation:
children's tactile and visual erogenous contacts with the adult body

− / + sleeping in bed with adults* (only occasionally) + adult nudity

1. Prior to his referral when he was four, Kurt occasionally liked to get in bed with his mother and to cuddle with her.

2. Kurt would see both of his parents in the nude, especially in the bathroom where they tended to their toilet functions and where Kurt sometimes took baths with his father. Kurt's description of his mother's body reflected his detailed observation of her "privates." "She has a thing with some fur on it and something comes out of her botsie."

+ adult genital erotic* (+ view adult coitus*)

3. Prior to therapy, Kurt was repeatedly exposed to his father's graphically detailed, hard-core home *pornographic movies[2] which included scenes of a man masturbating a big penis "sticking up to the ceiling" as well as close-ups of adults indulging in fellatio and anal intercourse.* [3]

Behavioral Symptoms correlated with
children's tactile and visual erogenous contacts with the adult body

+ irrational fears*

1. Kurt was panicked by flushing toilets and their associated noise. Even as he described his fears, he broke out crying "Help, Help, Help!" Kurt also expressed fears of the dark, fears of bees and fears of skeletons. Sometimes, his experience of fear was accompanied by his hearing a ringing in his head like someone shouting far away.[4]

+ hysterical twilight state*

+ sexual symptoms*

2. Kurt liked doing "pokies" with his younger sister, Sally. The sister was the active member who poked a finger into Kurt's rear end. This was a difficult activity to get under control despite both Kurt's and his therapist's efforts to set limits. Kurt would also land beneath his sister during repeated wrestling contacts.

+ eyes*

3. Kurt's opening statement of his problem has already been quoted: "There are X-rays in my *eyes*. I have X-rays[5] in my eyes. When the eye comes over here, then I must climb up for X-ray." This kind of reference to eyes reappeared over a period of many months. For example, early in therapy Kurt rambled on: "I hit the people with my *eye* and I made them into a skeleton. Under water I hold my nose. Oh, he's got *eyes*." "Eyes" also figured in one of Kurt's bad

+ biting/cutting/ mouth*

dreams involving "squirting on the lady's *eyes* and on her *mouth* and she grew a big, big beard."[6]

− / + fire*

4. Kurt demonstrated no symptoms pertaining to fire. However, no sooner had he begun to refer to pornographic observation of an adult masturbating than he began to talk directly about a fire.

Sources of Stimulation:
adult punitive and excretory contacts with children

+ beatings*

1. Prior to therapy, both parents regularly used a belt to strap this frail little four-year-old boy. During his last years of therapy when he became capable of communicating rationally, Kurt explained that his daddy's belt hurt the most and would make him "cry and cry." Many of the spankings would be administered because Kurt "wouldn't listen" or wouldn't take care of his room. Kurt also reported: "My mother hits me through the wall when I do not make my bed." The mother punished Kurt for not taking care of his room even though she herself would go through periods of not being able to perform her own housework.

+ punitive
yelling*

2. In Kurt's words: "When mother gets mad she yells and yells and yells and yells; my mommy and daddy fight so much; she yells at him, 'Don't give me no fuckin' shit' [yet she forbade Kurt to swear]. . . . She yells at us like crazy and we can't hit her." When Kurt complained to his mother about her yelling she went wild, shook him and screamed, "I'll show you what being yelled at is like." Even during the third year of therapy, Kurt reported, "Mother was throwing a mental fit after I came home from therapy. It was exactly like doomsday, 'Yap, yap, yap'; she makes you do the floors and clean the room and ya gotta answer, 'yes mam, yes mam, yes mam.' . . . Today mother and dad yelled at us so much, I couldn't stand it. I tried not to think of running away from home. She yells at me like a hurricane." It was not surprising that Kurt confided, "Ever since I can remember, I heard ringing in my ear," a hallucinatory reaction.

+ anal
stimulation*

3. Throughout Kurt's infancy, his mother jiggled a thermometer in his rear end "to help him go to the toilet." In addition, she figured that the only way to teach Kurt how to defecate in the toilet was for him to watch herself and her husband while they defecated.

Behavioral Symptoms correlated with
adult punitive and excretory contacts with children

+ negative
behavior

1. In the "civil war" which raged at home, the mother yelled at Kurt and hit him, while in return, he fought back by doing the opposite from what he was told. The "civil war" in this way perpetuated itself like a vicious cycle.

Unfortunately, Kurt's intense negativism interfered with his progress in therapy. For example, despite his therapist's explanation as to how he would get over many of his sad problems if he could stop wrestling with his sister, Sally, or doing "pokies," Kurt did the opposite from what was recommended.

+ reversal of
emotion*

2. Kurt's pervasive nonsense and silliness, a reversal of his fear, anger and depression, drove his parents "crazy." It equally alienated him from children at school and in the neighborhood. He would babble on his nonsense: "Pardon

me, before you die may I have your autograph. . . . If I knew you were coming, I'd have baked a cake" (giggle, giggle, etc., etc.).

It was of interest that one day during his third year of therapy when his therapist finally succeeded in blocking his silliness, Kurt directly revealed terrifying thoughts of skeletons under his chair (see below).

+ excretory
symptoms*

3. Kurt often did not wipe himself after defecation. The remnant feces soiled his undershorts and irritated his anal region. He was troubled by the stinging sensations of the raw and irritated skin on his "botsie." At first, he referred to the "caci" on his behind as "itchy bugs." He explained: "Itchy bugs are caci. They itch in the tail. They're itching all the time. Here's the dangerous part of the itchy bugs: they're like bumble bees and they *sting.*" He described the "ass hole" as a bumble bee hive with all the bees around; that the "farts" are like the bees buzzing — "bzz, bzz."[7]

+ pain*

With such involvement with "caci" it is not surprising that Kurt was terrified of losing his "caci" down the toilet. His irrational terror of the flushing toilet was a presenting problem; so was his fear that he could go down the toilet like "caci." One day Kurt even tried to climb into the toilet bowl to see if this could happen but instead found that his foot "got stuck" in it.

+ excretory
symptoms*

Kurt's "itchies" in turn led to continued anal scratching and "pokies" into his rectum. Unfortunately, despite the irritation associated with this activity, its erogenous and pleasurable aspects eventuated in its becoming an anal masturbatory habit which was difficult to control.

(+ anal
masturbation*)

Educational guidance to some extent helped Kurt control his soiling. He was taught how better to wipe himself and to use talcum powder on the chafed skin so as to prevent irritation and itching. Yet anal masturbation continued and then became replaced by anal "pokies" with his sister, Sally. Both of these children who had been charged up under the impact of pornographic stimulation at home discharged their excitement together. Sally became the active partner and Kurt the passive recipient of the anal "pokies." Unfortunately, Kurt's social behavior paralleled the physical. When physically "the pokies" were at their worst, then socially he became an impossible "stinky itch" who drove the kids and his family "out of their minds," e.g., by provocative negativism and silliness.

The therapist clarified for Kurt the relation between his physical anal behavior and his unhappy social problems while pointing out that a big step in his getting over his worries would be working together so that he wouldn't have to do the "pokies." Kurt tried hard and was so proud when he could control himself. Then he would come in shouting to his therapist, "What do you think, I didn't do any pokies this week!" However, his "pokies" would reappear at times when his mother's screaming was at its worst, much like a child who had sucked its thumb returns to this habit when exposed to a barrage of anger and upset.

+ death*
(skeletons,
poison)

+ hallucination*

+ falling*

+ closing down
upon
destructively*
(crush)

4. Kurt perseverated with references to *skeletons* which, in turn, he associated with thoughts of death. "A skeleton" according to Kurt, "is when you drink *poison* and *die.*" The skeletons appeared within his dreams as well as his phantasies and semi-delusions. For example, on one occasion, he exclaimed, "I'm scared sitting on this chair; there's a skeleton under the chair and the skeleton has a finger going right up my rear. I always thought there was one under my bed. I'm even afraid of it in school; oh, now I hear a sound in my head."[8] In one set of associations via a "make-believe story," Kurt told how "skeletons hided in a dark secret cave; they *hurted* me and sticked me inside."

In life, Kurt actually was prone to being hurt. At the time of his referral, he was said to be suffering from some "rare disease" which made him lose his balance and *fall.* Kurt constantly displayed episodes of falling during his first year of therapy. He would suddenly fall over in the hallway, in the therapy room, off chairs, off the desk, while sitting, while standing, etc. Fortunately, the diagnosis of a rare neurological disease involving permanent brain damage was ruled out. As the parents learned to stop strapping Kurt, his falling symptoms gradually ceased.

Only during the last year of therapy could Kurt begin directly to express his wish to hurt himself and to be dead: "My mother and father make me so angry, I want to crush myself. . . . I'm so angry, I can't stand it. . . . Mommy is so mean I want to be dead and turn into a ghost."

NOTES

[1] These statements appeared along with more rational conversations.

[2] See case 85 presenting the history of Kurt's father who was exposed to pornographic pictures taken of his own mother.

[3] Following the onset of therapy the parents were able to put an end to excessive sexual arousal of their children.

[4] See cases 69, 76 and 100 of Dwight, Jerry and Ronny.

[5] Another patient drew a picture of X-rays radiating to the eyes at a time when he disclosed information about sleeping in bed with his nude father during the night and going down under the covers early in the morning to investigate the father's erect penis.

[6] "Squirting . . . on her mouth . . . and she grew a big, big beard," suggests the father's fellatio movies to which Kurt had been exposed. See an almost identical dream of Albert (case 65) who had been exposed to viewing a teenage boy ejaculating.

[7] The bee sting also reminded Kurt of the sting he felt when his mother whacked him on the shoulder.

[8] Compare this case with that of Ronny, case 100. Both children had been exposed to beatings and to overwhelming punitive yelling as well as to flagrant adult sexuality. Likewise, both children identically developed problems involving (a) anal masturbation, (b) bee phobias, (c) hallucinatory noises, and (d) bouts of uncontrollable hostile

silliness. Regarding a relation of hallucinations to anal masturbation, see also cases 30, 69, 76 of Terry, Dwight, and Jerry. Incidentally, the connection between anal sexual stimulation and auditory hallucinations were noted in the 16th century by Johann Weyer (Zilboorg, 1941: p. 225).

Kurt Junior
77

Stimulation-Symptom-and-Dream-Profile

	Separation Phobias
	+ Night Terrors, Twilight States
Sleep in Bed with Adult	+ Irrational Fears: Other
	Irrational Tempers
+ Adult Genital Erotic	+ Sexual Symptoms
	+ Biting/Cutting, etc. } *content of*
+ View Adult Coitus	+ Eyes } *dreams and*
	Fire } *symptoms*

	Learning Problems (levels 2 or 3, etc.)
+ Punitive Yelling	Lying and Delinquency
	+ Reversal of Affect
+ Beatings	+ Closing Down Upon, Kill } *content of / dreams and*
	+ Falling } *symptoms*

	+ Excretory Symptoms and Dreams
	+ Anal Masturbation
Preoccupation with Child's BM	Enuresis
	Illness, etc. } *content of*
+ Anal Contacts	+ Pain } *dreams and*
	+ Death } *symptoms*
	Compulsions

Case 78: Larry

After repeating kindergarten, Larry, at the age of eight, was about to be left back in the first grade. "His attention span was limited; he was easily distracted; he seemed unable to focus on the tasks at school." In the presence of his teachers, Larry was usually quiet and polite. The question as to whether he was emotionally disturbed or intellectually limited began to arise because of his poor academic functioning.

On the Bellevue Wechsler, however, Larry attained an I.Q. score of 99 (Verbal I.Q. 90, Performance I.Q. 108).

Source of Stimulation:
adult punitive and excretory contacts with children

+ early
  deprivation

1. Larry's mother was two months pregnant when she and Larry's father married. The father was extremely upset to be trapped into a "forced" wedding rather than a "proper" one. Additionally, both the paternal and maternal grandparents vigorously opposed the wedding.

During her pregnancy, the mother was depressed. She was lethargic and nauseated, and disappointed that her husband had suggested she have an abortion. During her pregnancy and the first year of Larry's life, the father consistently accused her of entrapping him. In turn, the mother accused him of never wanting to marry her in the first place.

Larry's father "hated" babies. He could "not stand the smell of Larry's dirty diapers." He could "not stand babies crying." And even though Larry was described as basically a good baby who slept and ate well, the father became enraged when Larry did cry. On one occasion, he *slammed little Larry so hard in his crib* that the bottom of the crib fell out. At the time of this incident, Larry was only six months old.

+ beatings*

2. The father admitted that from that time on he continued to beat the boy. There was always an excuse which justified the beatings. For example, the father stated he could not stand lying. It made no difference to him whether it was a severe or white lie that was discovered; he would lose all control and explode with fury.

The mother also strapped the boy. She recalled that when Larry started first grade she was very upset about the teacher's daily complaints of Larry's aggressiveness. One day the mother spanked him so hard that Larry grabbed

326

the belt and started to beat her. After a struggle the mother got the strap back. Since that time she "tried" not to beat him because he became so frightened.

+ punitive yelling*

3. The mother confided that she was too impatient. She felt that she yelled at Larry even more than she spanked. His father, each morning, continually hollered at him. As Larry talked about the parents yelling at him, he suddenly began to stutter.

+ feces in face

4. At the age of five Larry defecated in bed and tried to hide the soiled linen in his mother's hamper. The mother, upon discovering the mess, pushed the feces into Larry's face.

+ punitive bowel training

Larry recalled also being beaten with a shoe or a strap when he had an accident in his pants. The beating "felt like a rock crushing you." Both parents, without guilt, indicated that they also spanked Larry for wetting his bed.

Behavioral Symptoms correlated with
adult punitive and excretory contacts with children

+ negative behavior

1. Larry wondered "I don't know why, but I always *forget* to brush my teeth." This thought followed directly upon Larry's telling how, after a beating, his father would say "Try to be good next time." Larry's capacity to "forget" and then do the opposite from what was requested was reflected by his mother's comment: "Larry is forgetful, slow, and subtly resistive one way or another. However, he is never fresh or argumentative."

Likewise, the school reported no behavior problem evidenced by this very polite boy. On the other hand, Larry offered endless excuses for *withdrawing* from any efforts to *work*. He would do tasks *only if he enjoyed* what he was doing. He was considered an "uptight" boy. It is not, therefore, surprising that at the age of eight, Larry was about to repeat the first grade.

+ learning* (level 2)

+ lying*

Larry reported the *opposite* of the truth to avoid further punishment. In addition to lying at home, he tried to "con" his teachers in school.

+ killing*
+ falling*
+ death* (skeleton)

2-3. Larry presented the following two dreams: (a) "I was watching this guy *kill* a lady. I ran and ran and ran. The guy saw me and I ran into the bushes. I tripped and *fell*. He got me. He was going to pull a trigger"; and (b) "The house next door was a school. I went down into the cellar. There was a dead *skeleton* in the chair. The *skeleton* chased me. He caught me on top of a roof and threw me over" (once again there appears the image of *falling*). In the world of reality, Larry acted out these reactions pertaining to falling: the school complained that Larry was in the habit of tripping children.

+ excretory symptoms*
+ enuresis*

4. Larry reported having had a bowel movement in his bed and wetting his bed in defiance of his mother's warnings.

Sources of Stimulation:
children's tactile and visual erogenous contacts with the adult body

−/+ sleeping in bed with adult* (frequency?)

1. On many occasions, Larry spent the night with his mother in bed, especially when his father was away.

+ adult nudity

2. Larry confided "when I go into my mother's bedroom I have on no clothes and my mother has no clothes. . . . She says to me, 'Stay out; you should not come in without knocking,' but I come in anyway."

+ adult genital erotic*

Larry was accustomed to seeing the father naked. The father would take baths with Larry. On one occasion when they took a bath together Larry placed his feet up upon his father's penis. The father, in turn, put his legs around Larry's thighs. When on other occasions Larry bumped into his father's "dinky," the father would say: "That's not nice."

(sexualized wrestling with adults)

3. At one point in therapy, Larry announced "Do you know what? I kiss my mother all the time. . . . Mother and I have good times"; then he added "Me and my father have good times too. My father wrestles with me. He lays on the bed on top of me until I say 'I'm dead.' My father is very heavy and sometimes I have a lot of trouble breathing when he's on top of me." At this point in the interview Larry suddenly panicked and had to run to the bathroom to have a bowel movement.

+ adult genital erotic*

(+ view adult coitus*)

4. Larry remembered going into his parents' room at night when their door was not closed and seeing his father in bed wriggling on top of his mother and whispering "I love you." Larry remarked about all that "hair" his father had and "such a big arm."

Behavioral Symptoms correlated with
children's tactile and visual erogenous contacts with the adult body

+ irrational fears*

1. Larry, frightened at night, wandered alone through the halls of the house. Then he would wander into his parents' bedroom, stand by his father's bureau and call out "Mama, I'm scared."[1] He would be especially worried by the light from outside reflecting upon his parents' ceiling.

+ eyes*

2. Larry dreamed of being *on top of a gun*[2] and of "someone who was *looking* at me, *staring*. He pointed a gun at me. It was a play gun."[3]

In his learning Larry suffered particularly from a reading problem. In school, reading was his poorest subject.

+ / − biting*

3. Larry reported that he had numerous dreams about owls. [4]

+ / − irrational tempers*

4. When he was two years old, Larry displayed temper tantrums during which he would "spill and throw things." However, these tempers which were punished by his mother, eventually became no longer apparent.

+ sexual
symptoms*

+ learning*
(level 3)

Epilogue: Larry was seen diagnostically once again when he was fifteen years old. He had unfortunately been sent to an overpermissive residential treatment center where he indulged in homosexual behavior with other adolescent boys. Unfortunately, also, Larry then returned to his home where beatings were continued. With the continuance of beatings at home inciting his negativism, Larry's learning problem became increasingly grave. At the age of fifteen, he was still reading on a fourth grade level. His verbal intelligence quotient had fallen from 90 to 80. The effects of punitive and erotic primitive stimulation were overshadowing and disrupting the dominance of higher cognitive functions.

NOTES

[1] Compare with Selma Fraiberg's case 23 of little "Sally."

[2] Larry had put his feet on top of his father's "play gun." Later the father was on top of him.

+ eyes* (dream
content)

[3] Larry also had an uncertain dream: "I was rocketing to Mars, I *saw* Indians and cowboys."

[4] The owl is known as a bird of prey with prominent eyes and pointed beak.

Larry
78

Stimulation-Symptom-and-Dream-Profile

	Separation Phobias	
	Night Terrors, Twilight States	
Sleep in Bed with Adult	+ Irrational Fears: Other	
	+ Irrational Tempers	
+ Adult Genital Erotic	+ Sexual Symptoms	
	+ Biting/Cutting, etc.	} *content of*
+ View Adult Coitus	+ Eyes	} *dreams and*
	Fire	} *symptoms*
	+ Learning Problems (levels 2 or 3, etc.)	
+ Punitive Yelling	+ Lying and Delinquency	
	Reversal of Affect	
+ Beatings	+ Closing Down Upon, Kill	} *content of dreams and*
	+ Falling	} *symptoms*
	+ Excretory Symptoms and Dreams	
	Anal Masturbation	
Preoccupation with Child's BM	+ Enuresis	
	Illness, etc.	} *content of*
Anal Contacts	Pain ~	} *dreams and*
	+ Death	} *symptoms*
	Compulsions	

Case 79: Murray

Murray, age fifteen, with an I.Q. of 107, was brought by his parents for diagnostic evaluation with the following complaints: "Murray's academic performance has been satisfactory. However, he has shown great difficulty in getting on with his peers. He is aggressive and destructive with other children though he is primarily a follower. He steals newspapers and cigarettes, lies, resists authority, swears, and is fresh." A psychiatrist who interviewed him when he was four years old thought Murray might have "craved punishment to get attention."

Murray's mother and father made "a lovely" appearance at the time they requested help for their son. The intake worker wrote, "Mother is a warm woman, looks much younger than father who appears somewhat depressed. Their marriage appears to be stable with no lack of communication between them. The parents nevertheless admit that fights and disagreements do occur between them."

A full diagnostic workup revealed that the parents' reference to "some fights and disagreements" was clearly an understatement. Violence was commonplace in Murray's home and it was eventually disclosed that the father, who regularly became drunk, was "vicious, angry, and assaultive towards the family." On one occasion, he ordered neighbors to leave the house because "he planned to kill his wife and there would be blood all over the place." The police were called but, before they arrived, the father had chased his wife with a butcher knife. On another occasion the father choked the mother into unconsciousness. A year later, the father himself was found unconscious after an apparent "suicide attempt" from large doses of pills and heavy drinking. The mother thereupon secured a legal separation, but the separation lasted only five months. Actually the mother had wanted to leave the father when Murray was a year old, but her mother, fearful of a scandal, talked her out of it.

Sources of Stimulation:
adult punitive and excretory contacts with children

+ early
  deprivation

1. The mother stated that "Murray was babied the longest" of all her children and she just could not understand why he had been upset when he was little. However, this image of the mother giving Murray so much attention during his infancy must be matched with the parents' picture of their marriage as "warm" and "communicative." Actually, she must have been highly upset and

330

distracted during Murray's first year of life since the father had driven her to seek an immediate divorce from him. In any case, Murray soon showed multiple signs of early deprivation. He failed to thrive and at the age of four and a half, he weighed only twenty-seven pounds. Additionally, from early infancy Murray was *hyperactive*[1] to the extent that his parents from the beginning reacted bitterly about his behavior. It is not surprising that Murray reacted with a depression when he was hospitalized at four and a half for scarlet fever. At that time, he failed to recognize his parents when they came to visit.

+ beatings*

2. In keeping with the pretense of gentility which the parents affected during their intake interview, the father first explained how he would punish Murray by sending him to bed. However, during the diagnostic interviews the father soon admitted that punishments included "plenty of lickings" carried out with a strap on the behind. At still another time the father let slip "I get tired of punishing Murray every night!" and complained about Murray causing much of the parents' marital discord. The mother added that punishment just was the only way of controlling Murray. Once she had become so angry at him that she threw her shoe directly at him. Murray himself indicated that his father hit the hardest with his belt but that his mother was worse because she was accustomed to hit him so often.

+ punitive
yelling*

3. As Murray began speaking of having been belted, he suddenly burst out with accounts of the violence in his home. He told how his father had been hospitalized three times for wild outbreaks at home. Murray would wake up at night to hear his father and mother yelling at one another with mutual accusations of infidelity. Drinking would precipitate the father's explosions during which he would threaten the whole family. Since Murray was his father's "favorite," the father alternately acted one moment "like a pal" to him then suddenly vented his rage with screaming threats that he would kill Murray.

+ adult
defecation

4. The mother was accustomed to sit on the toilet defecating while fifteen-year-old Murray would be washing himself in the tub nearby. The mother would tease him by saying, "Turn around now dear." Conversely, she would bathe in the tub while Murray performed his bowel movements.

Behavioral Symptoms correlated with
adult punitive and excretory contacts with children

+ enuresis*

1. Murray wet his pants until he was eight years old. Anal problems, however, did not become apparent until he became an adult (see below).

+ negative
behavior

+ lying*

2. Murray's negative behavior to all controlling authority figures formed the nucleus of his presenting symptoms. The parents reported, "Murray steals, lies; he resents authority and is fresh." The mother complained of Murray's "lying his way out of situations." She deplored his continuing to do the opposite from what he was told, despite her punishments. In school Murray infuriated his teachers by a "defiant" attitude. He talked incessantly and refused to do any

+ delinquency* homework.[2] The mother also was concerned that he associated with a delinquent gang which defied social rules by smoking, stealing and getting into trouble with the police.

+ negative
emotion

3. In school, Murray acted "bored" and "apathetic" and did not hesitate to
walk away while his teacher was in the middle of talking to him.

Murray's negative emotions also surfaced when he was with his gang. Murray confided that not only did he get the kids in the gang *against* him but also
that he liked to control "the gang" by setting one member *against* another.

+ hurting
+ closing down
upon
destructively*

4. At the early age of two and a half, Murray pushed a door key down his
baby brother's throat.

During his latency years, Murray was so effective in setting other children
against himself, including the tough members of his gang, that he became terrified of going to school for fear the boys would hurt him. Murray provoked
the boys at school to *put a rope around his throat.* It appeared that Murray was
getting himself involved in situations which ended up with his being choked the
way his father had choked his mother.

+ closing down
upon
destructively*
(strangle)

Still later, as a young man who returned to the clinic for a visit ten years
after his diagnostic evaluation, Murray reported that he was living with another
man homosexually and had been regularly submitting to anal intercourse. Most
tragic, at that time, he became consumed with lurid paranoid delusions. He was
convinced that the Mafia had planted a poison *bomb* into his bowels and pleaded
that his therapist immediately get a surgeon to remove the *bomb*, otherwise he
definitely would die within twenty-four hours. Of note, as a child, Murray
dreamed that there was a "monster under the *back* porch of a man." The "back
porch of a man" suggests the protrusion of the buttocks.

+ excretory
symptoms*
+ preoccupation
with illness*
+ death*
+ excretory
dream*

Sources of Stimulation:
children's tactile and visual erogenous contacts with the adult body

+ adult nudity

1. The mother, as already noted, would allow fifteen-year-old Murray into
the bathroom while she bathed.

(+ / – view adult
coitus*)

2. As a young child, Murray went to drive-in movies with his father and
the father's mistress. Murray would sit in the front seat while the father "made
out in the back with his woman." Murray said there were things that happened
which he never could tell his mother.

+ adult genital
erotic*

Then when Murray was five or six years old he was *seduced by an adult
male baby-sitter. He was led to go under the covers and to place the man's penis
into his mouth.*

Behavioral Symptoms correlated with
children's tactile and visual erogenous contacts with the adult body

+ biting/cutting*

1. Murray dreamt of a monster under the back porch of a man who had
his finger cut off.

+ irrational
tempers*

2. Murray's temper frequently erupted in school. On one occasion when his mother was called to school because of his provocativeness, the teacher spoke to Murray and the mother together: Murray apologized and said he would try to behave. However, as he left the room, he slammed the door so hard that the glass rattled in the windowpane.

+ sexual
symptoms*

3. At the age of twelve or thirteen Murray was accused of molesting two girls in school. On one occasion he exposed himself in class. When questioned about the exposure, Murray denied its import, claiming he was just zipping up his pants. His mother noted that Murray did have a bad habit of forgetting regularly to zip up his pants. Actually, the year before, Murray had exposed himself to his four-year-old sister, put his hands down in her panties and asked her to fondle his penis. Murray also displayed signs of wanting to impersonate a girl. When his mother found him with bright nail polish on his nails, he explained that he had been putting it on his little sister's nails and it "accidentally" got on him.

+ irrational fears*

At the age of fifteen, Murray helplessly began acting out homosexually with one of his teenage boyfriends much against his conscious wishes. The acting out began when he and the boyfriend went down to the basement of his house where they looked at pictures of nude women. Under the guise of heterosexual interest in the pictures, Murray and his friend experienced emissions together. During his adulthood, Murray finally accepted a homosexual adjustment with an emphasis upon anal intercourse. Concomitantly, he was beset with fears that the Mafia had placed poison bombs in his bowels. Soon these fears reached delusional proportions.

+ fire*

4. Of note, at the age of five, after he had submitted to fellatio at the hands of a male baby-sitter, Murray threatened to set his grandparents' house on fire. Several months later he actually did set the back door of the house aflame.

NOTES

1 There occurs the question as to whether early deprivation may serve as a primary source for the establishment of children's hyperactivity commencing during infancy.

2 Surprisingly enough Murray "functioned on a par" with his class, having received five B's and one C on his report card.

Murray
79

Stimulation-Symptom-and-Dream-Profile

	Separation Phobias
	Night Terrors, Twilight States
Sleep in Bed with Adult	+ Irrational Fears: Other
	+ Irrational Tempers
+ Adult Genital Erotic	+ Sexual Symptoms
	+ Biting/Cutting, etc. ⎫ *content of*
+ View Adult Coitus	Eyes ⎬ *dreams and*
	+ Fire ⎭ *symptoms*

	Learning Problems (levels 2 or 3, etc.)
+ Punitive Yelling	+ Lying and Delinquency
	Reversal of Affect
+ Beatings	+ Closing Down Upon, Kill ⎫ *content of*
	⎬ *dreams and*
	Falling ⎭ *symptoms*

	+ Excretory Symptoms and Dreams
	Anal Masturbation
Preoccupation with Child's BM	+ Enuresis
	+ Illness, etc. ⎫ *content of*
Anal Contacts	Pain ⎬ *dreams and*
	+ Death ⎭ *symptoms*
	Compulsions

Case 80: Nicholas

Nicky was an undernourished, anorexic, six-year-old boy referred for psychotherapy by his pediatrician with a diagnosis of "physical and emotional immaturity" and infantile speech. During his visits to the clinic Nicky impressed the staff with his pathetic hyperactivity: at first he was "all over the place." He dashed away from his therapist, ran down the corridors to and from his sessions, knocked on office doors, threw a container of blocks across the office, hit the therapist with a stick, attempted to glue together Bender Gestalt cards and chalked the elevators as well as the chairs and walls in the waiting room.

Sources of Stimulation:
adult punitive and excretory contacts with children

1. After Nicky's birth, the mother was ill but soon went back to work. She recalled being depressed, weepy and withdrawn but did not feel her state was more serious than the periods of depression she had experienced in the past.

+ early
deprivation
From the time of earliest infancy, Nicky suffered from a feeding problem. At birth, he weighed only four pounds and had to remain in the hospital an extra week for special care. He had difficulty sucking, spit up a good deal and held food in his mouth. Then, when Nicky was seven months old, the pediatrician became concerned because he was gaining too much weight and advised the mother to stop giving him pablum. After the mother complied with this recommendation, Nicky "never seemed to enjoy food again" and insisted upon holding food in his mouth.[1]

+ beatings*
2. Nicky aggravated his mother by talking back to her until she would swat him with a ruler. At the time of Nicky's referral, the father claimed he had *ceased* striking Nicky physically: an indication that at one time he *had* been accustomed to striking him. The father admitted that he did continue to threaten the boy with violence.

To complicate the picture, Nicky would see his father beating up his mother, especially when the father would come home after heavily drinking.

+ punitive
yelling*
3. However, yelling rather than beating was the primary problem in Nicky's family. The father recognized that Nicky was afraid of him and that yelling at the boy did not help the situation. He realized he was re-enacting his own fearful experiences with his own excessively strict father. Yet he could not keep himself from exploding.

335

Furthermore, the relation between Nicky's parents was a negative one. Their mutual social and sexual life was distressingly unfulfilled. Negativism, finding fault, scolding and blaming were the only ways they could relate to one another. Yelling would alternate with periods of silence during which they would become emotionally withdrawn. Unfortunately, Nicky found himself in the middle of these parental battles. Sometimes the father became so furious that he ended up pounding the walls in the bedroom. The degree of punitive yelling in the house was reflected by Nicky's becoming upset over any loud noise in the house; e.g., if he heard his parents laughing he would immediately call out, "Don't fight, don't fight."

+ adult
defecation

4. The father while on the toilet would request Nicky to bring him the evening paper. Nicky, therefore, would frequently be present in the bathroom when his father was defecating.

Behavorial Symptoms correlated with
adult punitive and excretory contacts with children

+ negative
behavior

1. At home, Nicky was accustomed to doing the opposite of what he was asked to do, e.g., he went outside when he was asked to remain at home, he talked back when he was asked to be quiet, etc.

+ reversal of
affect*

2. When Nicky's therapist spoke to him directly about recent parental quarrels and family problems, Nicky explained that these scenes did not upset him. Instead they made him laugh.

+ / – falling*

3. His therapist was struck by Nicky's frequent references "to people falling off bikes, falling off trucks, and getting hurt." Then, at camp he was reported to have had a severe fall, even though a few months previously he had undergone an operation for a hernia and had been warned to be careful about injuring himself.

Sources of Stimulation:
children's tactile and visual erogenous contacts with the adult body

+ sleeping in bed
with adults*

1. Despite the mother's effort to hide her close physical contacts with Nicky, it gradually became apparent that he was in fact sleeping in bed with his mother on a regular basis. Bed-sharing finally was stopped during Nicky's first year of therapy and he was extremely proud of his own efforts to work with his therapist to control the problem. On several occasions, he greeted his therapist with an announcement that he hadn't slept in his mother's bed "all week!"

+ adult nudity

2. Nicky was regularly exposed to seeing his parents nude and to observing his parents, particularly his father, urinating. When talking about being in the bathroom with his nude father, mother and sister, Nicky exclaimed, "Now, that's what I call a problem!" Nicky would also see his mother nude when she was getting undressed before retiring.

+ adult genital
erotic*

3. *Through a hole in the bathroom door, Nicky, on several occasions, secretly watched his father masturbating.*

Behavioral symptoms correlated with
children's tactile and visual erogenous contacts with the adult body

+ irrational fears*

1. Nicky expressed fears of "robbers on the trolley" and men "breaking out of the state prison." He also displayed excessive concern that something might happen to his father during a snowstorm and constantly sought reassurance that he would be all right.

+ irrational
tempers*
+ sexual
symptoms*

2. Nicky displayed periods of smashing, throwing and breaking things.

3. Nicky was continually preoccupied with thoughts of his penis breaking. As he unlatched the handle of a cap gun during a therapy hour he exclaimed "it's like ripping off someone's dinkie." Or as he broke an aeroplane model he said "it's like breaking a dink." His hours were replete with phrases such as "suck your dink," "eat my dink." Also, as he would smell and taste Coke, he would state the drink to be urine.

+ / − biting/
cutting*

Nicky would talk about cutting his penis when he became involved in cutting paper or dividing clay. And one day when his therapist asked him how she could help him, he responded: "Cut off my dink." At home, Nicky "made believe" to his grandmother that he had *cut* his finger off with a pair of scissors.

+ fire*

4. Nicky and a friend were caught setting two fires. The police also found them setting off a fire alarm. In therapy, Nicky went on and on talking of fires and concluded: "I have one problem: I really love fires. I love to go and see them." In the office, Nicky would eagerly listen for the sound of fire sirens. Sometimes his therapist felt he was blocking her out when he was caught up in his own world of daydreaming about fire.

NOTES

1 Unfortunately, these eating problems still were present at the time of Nicky's referral for therapy and became a source of severe conflict between him and his father. The father felt so strongly that his son should stop dawdling with his food he would keep Nicky at the table for as much as an extra hour to make him finish his food or to force Nicky to swallow the food he was holding in his mouth. Since the mother opposed the father's methods in handling Nicky's eating problem, this problem stemming from infancy became a source not only for Nicky being scolded and punished, but also for the mother and father fighting with one another in front of him.

Nicholas
80

Stimulation-Symptom-and-Dream-Profile

	Separation Phobias
	Night Terrors, Twilight States
+ Sleep in Bed with Adult	+ Irrational Fears: Other
	+ Irrational Tempers
+ Adult Genital Erotic	+ Sexual Symptoms
	+ Biting/Cutting, etc. ⎫ *content of*
View Adult Coitus	Eyes ⎬ *dreams and*
	+ Fire ⎭ *symptoms*

	Learning Problems (levels 2 or 3, etc.)
+ Punitive Yelling	Lying and Delinquency
	+ Reversal of Affect
+ Beatings	Closing Down Upon, Kill ⎫ *content of* ⎬ *dreams and*
	+ Falling ⎭ *symptoms*

	Excretory Symptoms and Dreams
	Anal Masturbation
Preoccupation with Child's BM	Enuresis
	Illness, etc. ⎫ *content of*
Anal Contacts	Pain ⎬ *dreams and*
	Death ⎭ *symptoms*
	Compulsions

Case 81: Ozzie

Ozzie and a friend were molested by a strange man who, at gunpoint, forced them into his car. The man masturbated in front of the two boys and then threatened to kill them if they ever told. At the time, Ozzie was five years old. Ozzie's mother, because of her concern, brought him to a psychiatric clinic. Unfortunately, she was assured the boy would be all right and that therapy was not necessary.

Three years later Ozzie was brought to the clinic because he had developed a severe learning problem. His mother noted that prior to being molested Ozzie had been learning well: when he had begun kindergarten he could write his first name and knew colors. After "that experience" he could no longer remember these accomplishments. Often he withdrew from contact with his surroundings and for a time thereafter he was terrified of going to and from school.

Sources of Stimulation:
children's tactile and visual erogenous contacts with the adult body

+ sleeping in bed with adults*

1. Ozzie slept between his parents frequently until he was seven years old.

+ adult nudity

2. Ozzie saw his sister, age thirteen, without clothes. He also saw his mother and father undressed and remarked about seeing their pubic hair. The bathroom was the scene for much of Ozzie's close visual contact with his parents' bodies: he explained that he would watch his mother and his father doing their "pee-pee." Also the father and Ozzie would wash close together in the shower.

+ adult genital erotic*

3. As noted, the child-molester masturbated in front of Ozzie and his friend as they both were held captive in a car.

Behavioral Symptoms correlated with
children's tactile and visual erogenous contacts with the adult body

+ sexual symptoms*

1. Ozzie complained that when he heard his mother and father "fucking," then his penis moved around and he felt like joining them and fucking someone, too.

+ eyes*

2. Shortly after Ozzie told his therapist about the exhibitionist who masturbated in front of him, he complained about his eyes: "When I look at a book I can't read," he explained: "My eyes burn and get shiny." Ozzie's behavior reflected a specific reading problem which accompanied his overall restrictive learning difficulties.

339

3. The dream Ozzie reported during his second diagnostic hour focused upon a big giant brown spider which came in with fire on him. The spider had *hairs* and long legs. Ozzie directly associated to this dream as he went on to say

+ biting/cutting*

that he was afraid the spider was going to crawl on him and *bite* him and then was going to walk on its head and bite his friend.

In line with these preoccupations with biting, Ozzie perseverated at home about "people's heads being *cut* off." Even though Ozzie's mother had been negligent about attending her clinic appointments, the irrationality of Ozzie's comments about cutting brought her in for her appointment in a state of real concern.

+ irrational
tempers*

4. One of Ozzie's problems at home was his repetitive temper tantrums. His mother said she never was able to determine exactly what caused them. Later when Ozzie was admitted to a residential school, he would display wild tempers during which he swore at his teacher, kicked at the doors and punched wildly. These tempers usually were triggered when attention was bestowed upon others rather than upon himself. He told his therapist, for example, he would tear the place apart if his therapist ever saw anyone else for therapy.

+ twilight state*

5. Ozzie frequently phased out in class, to the point that he would fall asleep. On one occasion he fell asleep while standing up.[1]

+ fire*

6. Ozzie's nightmare about the spider biting also involved fire. In the dream the "big giant spider came in with *fire* on him. The giant spider came and *burned* the house down." Ozzie associated to this dream by telling how he had a friend who gave him money for firecrackers and how he liked to light them. Then he confided, "I stopped lighting firecrackers but now I light fires. I set the grass on fire and the firemen had to come to put it out."[2]

Sources of Stimulation:
adult punitive and excretory contacts with children

+ / − early
deprivation

1. When Ozzie was an infant his father accused his mother of being an unfit mother to Ozzie because she let him cry prior to feeding. At the age of one and a half years Ozzie started tearing his sheets apart and would often make strange noises which were very loud.

+ punitive
yelling*

2. Ozzie's father fought violently with Ozzie's mother and many times beat her in front of the children. Ozzie's mother described herself as being impatient, "cross and irritable," especially during periods when, unknown to the children, she tried to commit suicide. Ozzie explained "I call my mother a jerk because she yells at me."

+ beatings*

3. Ozzie reported as one of his earliest memories an occasion when his father had gone wild and hit him with a belt for breaking the window of a "guy's car." However, beatings apparently did not become frequent in Ozzie's life until the second year of therapy when his mother remarried. Ozzie's new

father had been beaten himself during childhood and had been sent to reform school; he had left reform school feeling "thankful" for beatings and convinced that "kids need strappings." He proceeded to belt Ozzie regularly and resented the clinic's attempts to stop him. The clinic became concerned that Ozzie was being abused.

+ adult
defecation

4. Ozzie was allowed in the bathroom while his mother defecated. He noticed that often she did not flush the toilet and that her bowel movement "looked like bugs."

Behavioral Symptoms correlated with
adult punitive and excretory contacts with children

+ excretory*
(dream of
brown)
+ learning*
(level 2)

1. Ozzie dreamed of a *brown* spider (see above).

2. Ozzie demonstrated a marked restriction in his capacity to learn following his contact with the exhibitionist. According to Ozzie, his mind was so preoccupied with this man and with his fears of being kidnapped and attacked by him, he found it impossible to concentrate in school — i.e., part of Ozzie's learning problem was related to the activation of excessively disruptive phantasies with which he was preoccupied during his waking life.

Although Ozzie had been more than a satisfactory student prior to his encounter with the exhibitionist, his work thereafter deteriorated and it became necessary for him to be placed into a special class for slow learners (see introduction).

+ reversal of
affect*

3. Reversal of affect became evident during his second year of therapy: when he heard that his mother might have cancer he yelled, "What else, what else?" and then broke out *laughing*.

+ hurting

Ozzie constantly started fights and picked on other children in school.

+ falling*

Of more serious import, during the period when his stepfather was regularly beating him, Ozzie would run out in front of stopped cars and say, "Hit me," or would say, "Let me jump," as he stood at the top of a long flight of stairs. Ozzie told his therapist he wished he could break his arm or leg.

+ closing down
upon
destructively*
(strangle)
+ death*
(skeleton)
+ killing*

A dream Ozzie reported during his first diagnostic hour reflected his preoccupations with his being hurt and his hurting others: "A monster *strangled* me. There was a *skeleton*. The monster was *killing people*."

NOTES

[1] See case 85, Kurt Senior, for a study of "narcolepsy" which responded to psychotherapy geared to control sexual overstimulation.

2 At this point Ozzie must have felt relieved that someone was trying to understand and help him, for he went on to say, "Can I go to this school? I like it here."

Ozzie
81

Stimulation-Symptom-and-Dream-Profile

	Separation Phobias
	+ Night Terrors, Twilight States
+ Sleep in Bed with Adult	Irrational Fears: Other
	+ Irrational Tempers
+ Adult Genital Erotic	+ Sexual Symptoms
	+ Biting/Cutting, etc. } *content of*
View Adult Coitus	+ Eyes } *dreams and*
	+ Fire } *symptoms*
	+ Learning Problems (levels 2 or 3, etc.)
+ Punitive Yelling	Lying and Delinquency
	+ Reversal of Affect
+ Beatings	+ Closing Down Upon, Kill } *content of dreams and*
	+ Falling } *symptoms*
	+ Excretory Symptoms and Dreams
	Anal Masturbation
Preoccupation with Child's BM	Enuresis
	Illness, etc. } *content of*
Anal Contacts	Pain } *dreams and*
	+ Death } *symptoms*
	Compulsions

Case 82: Perry

Perry was a bright ten-year-old boy with a verbal I.Q. of 130. Perry lived most of his life with his grandmother and grandfather. His mother had deserted him when he was a few days old. His father, who would visit him regularly each week, died when Perry was eight years old. In vain his grandmother contacted one agency after another in search of help for him. She felt he had a "dual personality": half of the time he was thoughtful, kind and cheerful, while at other times he was just the opposite: defiant, provocative and destructive. Despite his high I.Q. he was "not learning well in school where he disrupted his class with aggressive behavior toward the other children."

Sources of Stimulation:
children's tactile and visual erogenous contacts with the adult body

+ / – sleeping in bed with adults*

1. Perry shared his grandparents' bed from the time he was one until he was three years old. Otherwise, with respect to bed-sharing or exposure to family nudity, etc., there were no incidents to be reported. The grandparents had brought Perry up "puritanically."

+ adult genital erotic*

2. On several occasions, *a group of adolescent boys masturbated directly in front of Perry*. The first time this happened, Perry was five years old. At the age of ten, Perry still "hung out" with older adolescents.

Behavioral Symptoms correlated with
children's tactile and visual erogenous contacts with the adult body

+ irrational tempers*

1. Perry reported, "My first problem is the worst — my temper." His therapist praised Perry for being so honest in telling his problems so directly. Perry then went on to say "I take it out on everybody. . . . I pick fights. . . . I keep on fighting." In turn his grandmother described Perry as being irrational at times: sometimes during his temper tantrums he tore his clothes and broke articles for no reason she could fathom.

+ nightmare

2. Perry reported a nightmare about a "funny looking man who died and came back . . . his hand . . . everybody tried to *chop* it off and kill him."[1]

+ biting/cutting*

3. The cutting-chopping theme appearing in Perry's nightmares, also intruded pathologically into his waking life. For example, Perry complained to his grandmother that the boys tried to *cut* him with a razor. Actually the school

343

found the razor on Perry's person. Similarly, as the grandmother reported during the intake interview, Perry took his grandfather's knife and his grandmother's scissors and was found trying to *cut* his bedroom rug.[2]

+ fire*

4. At the time that Perry was cutting his bedroom rug he also lit matches under the living-room mantel. Actually Perry had already succeeded in lighting several dangerous fires. When he was five he set a fire in the basement (it was when he was five that he witnessed the adolescent boys masturbating in the basement). Later he and his friends set a whole garage on fire.

Sources of Stimulation:
adult punitive and excretory contacts with children

−/+ early
deprivation

1. At birth Perry was deserted by his mother. For the first twelve months of his life he lived with a foster family.

+ beatings*

2. Perry's father was very strict and could not tolerate any misbehavior on Perry's part. *For the slightest infraction of discipline he would beat Perry to the point of "half-killing" him.* Once when the school called the father regarding Perry's misbehavior, the father arrived, laid Perry across a desk and beat him with a ruler in front of everyone in the third grade. His grandmother also would hit him "with all her might." She felt that beatings were "no good" for a child but she saw no other way to control Perry's bad temper. One time she felt so badly after beating him that she had to go to the doctor for her "nerves."

Behavioral Symptoms correlated with
adult punitive and excretory contacts with children

+ negative
behavior

1. The grandmother, who loved Perry and wanted so much to get psychiatric help for him, could not understand why sometimes he became stubborn and "just wouldn't do anything."

When Perry was asked during his diagnostic interviews what his problems were, he answered: "I just sit in my seat when the teacher *tells me to do something* and I do *nothing*." It is not surprising that despite his high I.Q., he was not learning well. He had learned adequately in kindergarten and first grade but by the second grade "he showed no desire to learn" and would not do his homework. Actually this increasing difficulty in learning upset Perry to the point that he tried to compensate by trying to "be perfect." However, he only ended up making mistakes and expressing his rage by throwing crayons across the classroom.

+ learning*
(level 1; referral
problem)

Perry's negative behavior increased still further in the third grade: he began to lie, became more disruptive in class and was not able to keep any friends.

+ lying*

+ negative
emotion

2. One Friday Perry came home with one hundred percent in every paper. His grandmother was so pleased she "just beamed all over her face." She said to Perry "see if you try you can do it." In return he answered, "I know but I

don't like school, and I don't want to go to school, and I'm not going to go."
Similarly when his grandmother spoke to Perry about seeing a psychiatrist to
talk his problems over, Perry retorted: "I'm not going to see anyone, why do I
need to see anyone, I don't have a problem." Yet when he "pulled out" of his
negative moods, Perry did admit he had problems.

+ hurting

3. More striking than his negative behavior or negative emotion was Perry's
involvement with hurting, hitting and pain. According to his grandmother: (a)
he provoked other children by poking them until they knocked him down; (b)
he destroyed his toys and tore them apart; (c) he would come to his grandmother and ask her if she would whip him. She could not understand how he
would take pleasure in being whipped. (d) He took pleasure in sticking pins in
his hand and forehead.

+ reversal of
affect*
+ pain*

+ falling*
+ closing down
upon
destructively*
(strangle)

According to Perry's own report during his first diagnostic visit: (a) he often
hurt himself, e.g., he would climb trees and then would fall from the high
branches; (b) he *tied* a belt around his cat's neck and swung the cat around until
he almost killed it; (c) he and his friends threw rocks at a "cop's" car until the
"cops" stopped them and took their names. Perry added: "I'm a trouble maker.
I get in fights and I get the worst of it." (d) As if to dramatize this statement
Perry claimed he wanted to be just like John Dillinger in the movies: John got
sent to prison and beat up all the guys in prison. He used machine guns and
robbed banks. (e) Perry dreamed of a man who *died* and came back. Everybody

+ death*
+ killing*
+ excretory*
(dream of
brown)

tried to *kill* him: "a funny looking man who *died* and came back. All you could
see was a brown glove. Everybody tried to kill his hand and chop[3] it off."

Fortunately, by the time his diagnostic evaluation was completed, Perry
demonstrated that he *did* want to get over his problems and would be willing to
go to a special residential school if that would help him. At least for the time
being, he decided he had changed his mind about wanting to be John Dillinger.

NOTES

[1] See synopsis of Margaret Gerard's Robert, case 28.
[2] See cases 66 and 72 of Bernard and of Gene.
[3] See above re "biting/cutting."

Perry
82

Stimulation-Symptom-and-Dream-Profile

	Separation Phobias
	Night Terrors, Twilight States
+ Sleep in Bed with Adult	Irrational Fears: Other
	+ Irrational Tempers
+ Adult Genital Erotic	Sexual Symptoms
	+ Biting/Cutting, etc.
View Adult Coitus	Eyes
	+ Fire

⎫ *content of*
⎬ *dreams and*
⎭ *symptoms*

	+ Learning Problems (levels 2 or 3, etc.)
Punitive Yelling	+ Lying and Delinquency
	+ Reversal of Affect
+ Beatings	+ Closing Down Upon, Kill
	+ Falling

⎫ *content of*
⎬ *dreams and*
⎭ *symptoms*

	+ Excretory Symptoms and Dreams
	Anal Masturbation
Preoccupation with Child's BM	Enuresis
	Illness, etc.
Anal Contacts	+ Pain
	+ Death
	Compulsions

⎫ *content of*
⎬ *dreams and*
⎭ *symptoms*

Case 83: Ricky

The school psychologist claimed that Ricky was the "sickest child" she had ever seen. The referral note read: "This five and a half year old boy is provocative, destructive; he lies; he is preoccupied with blood and death; he suffers from insecurity." Psychological testing revealed that Ricky obtained a Verbal I.Q. score of 100 and a Performance I.Q. of 75 on the Bellevue Wechsler.

Sources of Stimulation:
adult punitive and excretory contacts with children

+ early
deprivation

1. The mother was extremely unhappy during her pregnancy with Ricky. During the entire nine-month gestation period she gained only one pound. Her husband had "taken off" for six months once he had been informed of the pregnancy. She then tried to work but finally gave up and applied for welfare relief. She could not eat, her blood pressure was up and she tried to avoid thinking about her condition with the hope that it might magically terminate itself. Sometimes she thought she would be lucky if the baby happened to die at birth.

The mother was in labor intermittently for a week. At that time, she reflected rather sadly that "labor stopped because she didn't want the baby." During this period of false labor her thoughts were suicidal; then she worried that her other children would be taken away from her because her thoughts were so "abnormal."

Shortly after Ricky's birth, his father returned to live in the home. But his return brought new problems, for the mother soon became pregnant again, only to hemorrhage and spontaneously abort four months later. She then became even more depressed and developed a lasting hatred for Ricky's father. In turn, the father frequently reacted to her with violent anger.

As an infant, Ricky did not sleep "as much as other babies" and became *hyperactive*. By the time he was two, he had displayed numerous upsets which were like severe temper tantrums during which he would turn blue. The doctor had said these attacks might be epileptic but indicated that Ricky was not yet old enough for a brain test.[1]

2. Ricky's mother, who had been herself exposed to extreme punishments as a teenager at boarding school, was afraid of injuring her children seriously. She once beat Ricky's sister so severely the child would have been killed had the

mother not succeeded in stopping herself by walking out of the house. She had already beaten the child black and blue.

+ beatings*

The mother also punished Ricky *in "every way" she could* from the time he was an infant. When he was three years old, she tried making him kneel in a corner and put his hands behind his back because beatings did not help. Sometimes she would *"crack him* on the behind *every hour on the hour."*

When Ricky referred to these beatings, he told how sometimes his mother *hit him so hard he felt he would break.* Ricky also spoke of two men who in turn became his "new fathers." One of them named Art beat Ricky with a big black belt.

Behavioral Symptoms correlated with
adult punitive and excretory contacts with children

+ negative
  behavior

1. Ricky refused to obey rules in school and, punishment or no punishment, he regularly disobeyed his mother's orders.

+ lying*

Ricky also regularly lied to his mother. This symptom was prominent enough to have been discussed during the intake interview.

+ negative
  emotion

2. In school, Ricky "found out children's faults" and then called the children names. At home, he expressed hatred for his sisters.

+ freezing of
  affect

Freezing of affect was particularly evident during his beatings: his mother complained that he would show no response whatsoever to the punishments.

+ closing down
  upon
  destructively*

3. Ricky's referral problems pertained to his destructiveness and preoccupation with blood and death. "Ricky didn't like windows unless they were broken" his mother explained. Recently at the age of five and a half, he had *broken a store window.* He also was accustomed to *throwing* rocks at big children.

+ killing *

The school psychologist who tested Ricky reported that if he had been big enough he would have tried to *kill* her. Ricky also wished his sisters dead. He threatened his mother that if she had any more babies he would *kill* them.

At the beginning of his first diagnostic hour, Ricky responded in a confused way to the question "what were his problems": (a) "Look at me *kill*; someone *shot* me there. I saw a *bullet* in here. I grabbed a boy's gun and *shot* him," and

+ death*

(b) "My mother says Ricky is *dead."*

Sources of Stimulation:
children's tactile and visual erogenous contacts with the adult body

− / + sleeping in
bed with adults*
(occasionally)

1. Ricky confided that sometimes he slept between his mother and her boy friend, Zeke.

+ adult nudity
+ adult genital
  erotic*

2-3. In the bathroom, Ricky was induced to *tickle Zeke's large penis.* As Ricky relayed this information, he started to make the family doll in his hands do wriggling movements. He then added how Zeke would tickle him on his feet and stomach and bum and how Zeke would tickle his sister on the feet.

Ricky told how Zeke had "nasty" books of people without clothes and began to talk faster and faster as his reference to the pornography led him to talk of "titties being *chopped* off" and "caca coming out of the bum."

Behavioral Symptoms correlated with
children's tactile and visual erogenous contacts with the adult body

− / + irrational
fears*
+ eyes*

1. Ricky "jumped terribly" when he was disturbed in his sleep.

2. He expressed the following bizarre thoughts: "When I close my left *eye* I get stabbed in the *eye* like this . . . if it were a triangle, I would turn into a witch."

+ biting/cutting*

3. Ricky reported one dream: "I put one of my things there like that and *cut* the paper. I was *cutting* it. I *cut* it off. I got going and going; it got longer and longer. I got to the end and *cut* it right off."

+ sexual
symptoms*

4. The mother reported that Ricky had been involved in "considerable" sex play.

+ fire*

5. She also reported that Ricky had already set several fires.

NOTES

[1] No signs of epilepsy appeared thereafter. Medical examination and psychological testing at the time of Ricky's diagnostic evaluation revealed no indications of a neurological disturbance.

Ricky
83

Stimulation-Symptom-and-Dream-Profile

	Separation Phobias	
	Night Terrors, Twilight States	
Sleep in Bed with Adult	Irrational Fears: Other	
	Irrational Tempers	
+ Adult Genital Erotic	+ Sexual Symptoms	
	+ Biting/Cutting, etc.	} *content of*
View Adult Coitus	+ Eyes	} *dreams and*
	+ Fire	} *symptoms*

	Learning Problems (levels 2 or 3, etc.)	
Punitive Yelling	+ Lying and Delinquency	
	Reversal of Affect	
+ Beatings	+ Closing Down Upon, Kill	} *content of dreams and*
	Falling	} *symptoms*

	Excretory Symptoms and Dreams	
	Anal Masturbation	
Preoccupation with Child's BM	Enuresis	
	Illness, etc.	} *content of*
Anal Contacts	Pain	} *dreams and*
	+ Death	} *symptoms*
	Compulsions	

Case 84: Synopsis of Erna Furman's "Carol"

When, at the age of three, Carol began psychoanalysis with Erna Furman, she might easily have been labeled an incurable psychotic. Often her face and body would become "rigid, tense, and distorted" as she "stared in an intense blank fashion" or "rigidly danced around on her tiptoes, showing tremendous overall excitement. At such times she talked excitedly to herself or to others." Typical of her nonsense-talk is the following quote recorded in her nursery school classroom as she handed two wooden blocks to the teacher with "much dancing and waving of her hands: 'You hold this, then eat it — perfume. Feels good, it's an airplane' " (*Psychoanalytic Study of the Child*, Vol. XI, 1956, p. 312).

Sources of Stimulation:
children's tactile and visual erogenous contacts with the adult body

−/+ sleeping in
bed with adults*
(resting)
+ adult nudity

1. Carol occasionally came into her parents' bed in the morning (p. 315).

2. "At home, the parents would dress, bathe, and use the toilet in front of her" (p. 315).

+ view adult
coitus*

3. "Carol observed much sensual behavior between the parents" which the "father demanded as reassurance against his anxieties" (p. 315). Additionally, on occasion Carol peeked from her bedroom door into the living room to watch her parents in the act of fellatio and other sexual activities (p. 319, 329). (This report was confirmed by her parents.)

+ adult genital
erotic*

Carol was exposed to yet even more intense sexual stimulation. Her Uncle Jay, the father's brother, sought psychiatric help at the University Hospital Clinic because of his compulsive thoughts about performing perverse oral sexual acts with little girls (p. 320). The parents had "known that this uncle had often indulged in stimulating games with Carol" (p. 320). This uncle finally seduced Carol to perform fellatio. After horrendous nightmares which terminated in her vomiting, Carol was able first to act out the seduction in therapy and then talk of it in minute detail (p. 327-28): "Carol began to play with a large lipstick which she wanted to stuff into her therapist's mouth saying at a pitch of excitement 'you just open your mouth nicely honey. You'll be okay.' " Carol next "pushed the lipstick into her own mouth, gagged and in panic gurgled 'I can't talk, I can't talk.' [When] Carol was reassured that . . . now nobody was really doing this to her, she shouted out 'He put it in, and I bit it . . . and he got so mad at me! And I mustn't tell, I mustn't tell!' She was able to identify her Uncle

351

Jay and described having lain down with her legs apart while he touched and tickled her and inserted his penis into her mouth" (p. 327-28).

Behavioral Symptoms correlated with
children's tactile and visual erogenous contacts with the adult body

+ irrational fears*

1. To quote Mrs. Furman (p. 313): Carol was "ridden with innumerable fears to such an extent that shortly before her admission to the nursery, her mother had to allow her to stay in bed for several days because Carol was so afraid of stepping out, as well as afraid of every object, person and activity." In this connection, Carol was terrified of anything that made a noise and would react to it by covering her eyes and refusing to look in the direction of the noise (p. 320).

+ nightmares

Carol, in particular, was troubled by a persistent dog phobia (p. 330) and experienced nightmares about dogs. In one nightmare "a big dog sat on top of her" . . . "with his big fingers and with his knife . . . he poked holes into her all over . . . he poked her in the legs and belly, in her genitals, and finally in her eyes." At this point, Carol woke up vomiting (p. 327).

+ irrational
tempers*

2. When she was frustrated by an adult, Carol would react with screaming fits (p. 313). She also would wave her hands excitedly as an expression of wild anger: as Carol improved, "her excited waving of her arms turned into hitting her thighs, then into tentatively hitting the therapist, and finally into verbal aggression" (p. 317).

+ sexual
symptoms*

3. In nursery school, Carol "would suddenly throw off her clothes and roll on the floor." Occasionally these activities were accompanied by masturbation and attempts to "insert objects into her genital area" (p. 313).

4. Carol would bite children at the nursery school (p. 313). She would also *bite* inedible objects: toys, pencils, tassels of venetian blinds, until they sometimes cracked (p. 327).

+ biting/cutting/
stomach*

Biting, cutting and stomach concerns appeared in relation to Carol's nightmares. She woke up with a distressed *stomach* and *vomited*[1] after a nightmare of a dog who poked holes into her, and "she experienced a nightmare about several dogs in cages so that they could not *bite*" (p. 327). Also, concerns about cutting were reflected during waking hours by an incapacitating terror when it came to cutting paper. At such times, Carol would repeat to herself: "I mustn't *cut* all of it" (p. 318).

+ eyes*
+ hysterical
twilight state*
(conversion
symptoms)
(+ non-organic
illness*)

5. Carol "would pick up toys and hold them close to her face while staring at them, yet could not comprehend what she saw" (p. 317). Her apparent *partial blindness* motivated her family to insist that Carol have an eye examination. No organic visual handicaps were found (p. 317). On one occasion, when Carol was bringing up memories of watching her parents in the act of intercourse (and just prior to her staging an intercourse scene herself) Carol actually *could not see*

objects in the room, not even the therapist (p. 329).

"Eyes" also figured in Carol's nightmare within which "a big big dog . . . started poking her in the legs and belly, in her genitals, and finally in her eyes" (p. 327).

Sources of Stimulation:
adult punitive and excretory contacts with children

+ early
deprivation

1. Carol was exposed to early deprivation, especially in relation to feeding. "It was hard to find the right formula for her; she was always a poor eater. . . During her second year Carol did not feed herself . . . and the mother spoon-fed her with little success." In association with this failure-to-thrive syndrome of early deprivation, Carol did a good deal of *head-banging* during her first fourteen months[2] (p. 315).

+ hitting

2. The father's relation to Carol was very tense and inconsistent; at times he hugged and kissed her, at other times he suddenly and impulsively spanked her. Carol "was terrified of him although she provoked him to [such] exciting interplays" (p. 314).

+ hurting

Uncle Jay not only acted out sexually with this little three-year-old girl, but hurt her during the process. Apparently, Carol choked violently as he pushed his penis into her little mouth. At the same time, he "got mad" at her and threatened her to keep her from telling about his delinquent behavior (p. 327-28).

Behavioral Symptoms correlated with
adult punitive and excretory contacts with children

+ negative
behavior

+ negative
perception

1. Carol suffered from restriction of ego activities. At the time of her referral "she could not dress herself, she could not handle play material, she could not even open a door . . ." (p. 316). During the early phases of therapy, Carol's reactions of negation also interfered with her perception of reality. For example, she could not hear, even though "she would repeatedly ask 'Who is it? What's his name?' " Likewise at that time she could not even "acknowledge the existence of her baby sister" (p. 316).

+ freezing of
affect

2. Carol presented a frozen appearance at the time of her referral for therapy and "quite often . . . she would stare in an intense, *blank* fashion" (p. 312).

+ falling*

+ hurting

3. One of Carol's all-encompassing fears during the first two years of therapy was her fear of *falling down* and being *hurt*. It was because of her fear of being hurt that she refused to attempt the simplest task (p. 318). This same fear was reflected during Carol's therapy when she expressed her uncertainty as to whether the trees, snow, rain, sun or shadows *hurt* and when she refused to cut paper because in revenge she might be hurt (p. 318).

+ excretory
symptoms*

4. On several occasions Carol soiled (p. 322). Also "Carol had wanted to eat dirty substances as well as her own bodily products, and if not allowed to do so . . . refused to eat altogether" (p. 322).

+ compulsions*

Possibly in this connection as well as in relation to her fellatio experience with Uncle Jay, Carol developed a spitting compulsion: "For a while, she had to spit so compulsively that she would spread out a sheet of paper in the closet and [then] spit and spit" (p. 331).

+ death*

5. During one period of therapy Carol also expressed fears of death (p. 323).

Of note, psychoanalysis demonstrated that Carol was not incurably psychotic. With the institution of controls and empathic understanding of her disturbed reactions to memories of sexual overstimulation, she progressed to the point that she was able to function like any "normal" child: "In the first grade the new teacher found Carol very cooperative, socially accepted, and eager to do good work" (p. 335).

NOTES

1 In the light of her traumatic fellatio experience with her uncle and her fears about her primitively activated wishes to bite and devour his penis, Carol's nonsense garble quoted from her presenting symptoms became very meaningful. Her garble: " 'you *hold* this, then *eat* it — perfume. Feels good; it's an airplane' " appears to relate directly to the uncle's request for Carol to *hold* his penis and *eat* it (p. 312). (No wonder Carol suffered from stomachaches.) The uncle might lightly have added that his penis "was a toy to play with like an airplane — It feels good."

2 The relation between early *"oral" deprivation* and biting and cutting symptoms such as Carol demonstrated needs to be investigated statistically. A finding of a positive relation between early deprivation and biting concerns would not rule out a positive relation between sexual stimulation and biting concerns. Rather such independent stimulus sources for priming the same reaction would be expected to operate conjointly.

Furman's "Carol"
84

Stimulation-Symptom-and-Dream-Profile

	Separation Phobias	
	+ Night Terrors, Twilight States	
Sleep in Bed with Adult	+ Irrational Fears: Other	
	+ Irrational Tempers	
+ Adult Genital Erotic	+ Sexual Symptoms	
	+ Biting/Cutting, etc.	} *content of*
+ View Adult Coitus	+ Eyes	} *dreams and*
	Fire	} *symptoms*

	Learning Problems (levels 2 or 3, etc.)	
Punitive Yelling	Lying and Delinquency	
	Reversal of Affect	
Beatings	Closing Down Upon, Kill	} *content of* / *dreams and*
	+ Falling	} *symptoms*

	+ Excretory Symptoms and Dreams	
	Anal Masturbation	
Preoccupation with Child's BM	Enuresis	
	+ Illness, etc.	} *content of*
Anal Contacts	Pain	} *dreams and*
	+ Death	} *symptoms*
	+ Compulsions	

Case 85: Kurt Senior

Kurt entered therapy at the age of twenty-three in order to cooperate with the treatment of his children, Kurt Junior and Sally, ages three and four (see case 77 of Kurt Junior). Both children were referred because of their "disorderly" hyperactivity at nursery school from which they were expelled.

Kurt admitted that he needed help with his marital situation. He was extremely upset that his wife routinely refused him sexual gratification. He and his wife became angry at each other's lack of empathy and care. They "got even" with one another by withholding care all the more. Kurt's wife often would not cook or clean the house, or cater to him in any way; in return Kurt refused to paint the walls, repair the cabinets or buy some decent furniture for the home.

Kurt suffered from narcolepsy and would involuntarily fall asleep at inappropriate times.

Sources of Stimulation:
children's tactile and visual erogenous contacts with the adult body

+ adult nudity

1. Kurt, his brother and his sister slept in the same room until he was twelve years of age and the sister was fifteen. At that time, he began sharing a room with his father who would parade around nude in front of the boy.

Actually at a much earlier date, his father had blatantly exposed Kurt to adult nudity: at the age of seven or eight, for example, Kurt would see the nude pictures the father took of Kurt's seventeen-year-old uncle.

+ adult genital erotic*

2. But the father's preoccupation with stimulating Kurt sexually extended beyond such "tame" exhibitionistic activities: the following information was gradually pieced together over Kurt's four-year course of therapy:

(a) His father took nude pictures of his mother practicing fellatio upon the uncle. These pictures then were left in the house where Kurt and his friends were free to see them.

(b) Kurt, age seven, was inveigled to stimulate the father's penis to the point of erection. Then, when Kurt reached adolescence, his father encouraged Kurt's homosexuality by explaining to him that isolated masturbation was a sin because it "wasted semen," while there was nothing wrong with group masturbation among males.

(c) By the time Kurt was seventeen, his father had succeeded in using him as an object for fellatio. These practices went on during the period of a year until Kurt left home for the service.

(+ view adult
coitus*)

But adult genital erotic stimulation resulted not only from Kurt's father's activities. When Kurt was a little boy of four or five, he witnessed his mother practicing fellatio upon one of her boyfriends. Also, already noted, Kurt, as a child, was permitted to see pictures of his mother acting out sexually with his seventeen-year-old uncle. These memories were painful for Kurt to remember and difficult for him to report.

Behavioral Symptoms correlated with
children's tactile and visual erogenous contacts with the adult body

− / + separation
phobia*
+ irrational fears*

1. Even in his late teens, Kurt would cry when he was left home alone.

2. As a child, Kurt suffered from fears of enclosed places and drowning. His reactions in small enclosed rooms still disturbed him at the time of his referral.

+ sexual
symptoms*

3. Kurt was beset by numerous sexual disturbances:

(a) He was upset that something compelled him to be a Peeping Tom. During his childhood, he would go outside and try to peep through the bathroom window in order to watch his sister bathe or to watch her on the toilet. Later, during his married life, he was driven to peek with his binoculars into neighbors' windows. However, as an adult, his primary preoccupation centered upon viewing within his home hard-core pornographic movies and photographs demonstrating all the polymorphous perverse varieties of sexual activity. Additionally, Kurt was preoccupied with viewing his sexual activities with his wife in the mirror.

(b) Kurt was a compulsive masturbator all his life. He could not recall a day when he had not practiced his onanism.

(c) Kurt was so preoccupied with his penis and pictures of penises that sexual forepleasure looking-touching-and-mouthing was activated in relation to his own penis. Being double-jointed, he became involved with self-fellatio. At the same time, his primary complaint during therapy was his obsessional need for his wife to practice fellatio upon him. He was enraged when she would not regularly comply with these wishes.[1]

Kurt's sexual symptoms not only involved driven preoccupation with sexual forepleasures: additionally, he suffered chronically from inadequate sexual fulfillment in the form of premature ejaculation.

(d) Kurt's disturbed sexual life affected his little children: he callously exposed the children to his pornographic movies, a repetition of his own early overstimulation and one source for the psychotic deterioration of his four-year-old son's behavior (see case 77).

+ eyes* (reading)

4. Kurt did not know how to spell when he was in the second grade and intensely disliked reading. He would fall asleep every time he began to read. Even at the time of his referral for therapy, Kurt did not approve of reading books: books, he felt, had a "stifling" effect upon him.

+ biting/cutting*
+ fire*

5. As a child, Kurt liked catching possums, *cutting* them up or setting them on *fire*.

In addition, as children, he and his friend used lighter fluid to set rabbits on fire. He would watch the burning animals fleeing through the woods. On one occasion, a burning animal accidentally set his house on fire.

Even as an adult when Kurt was in the service, he persisted in setting living creatures on fire: he enjoyed long hours on guard duty in the tropics because he had an opportunity to entrap scorpions and spiders in the flames of his cigarette lighter.

A nightmare Kurt experienced reflected his absorption with fire: "my wife and I were eating each other out; we were in a place supposed to be our home; the house caught *fire* and I could stand on the bed and look out all over the place: everything looked *burnt*."

Sources of Stimulation:
adult punitive and excretory contacts with children

+ beatings*

1. Kurt was belted by both his father and mother. His father used to strap him nightly and would say that a spanking every night was good for children because "it eased their tensions." He would say, "the more kids cry with the belt, the less they'll piss."

Kurt's mother also hit him with a leather belt to make him stay quiet. A particularly cruel incident took place when Kurt was still very little: he had just come across his mother performing fellatio upon one of her boyfriends. The mother, instead of being empathic and helpful, grabbed a belt and beat Kurt severely.

+ anal
   stimulation*

2. At the age of seven or eight, Kurt came down with pinworms, a steady source for anal erotic stimulation. Shortly thereafter, he managed to put his hands into some infected cat excrement left under the porch of his house. This led to his coming down with the "creeping eruption" which infected his anal orifice after he had scratched the area with his contaminated fingers.

Behavioral Symptoms correlated with
adult punitive and excretory contacts with children

+ negative
   behavior

1. "Withholding" was a presenting problem for Kurt as an adult. As noted, he found himself in the middle of a battle of negativism with his wife. He

refused to paint the walls; he refused to put up the cabinets and bookcases, even though he was a master painter and carpenter. He refused to take his wife out for a meal or to buy her gifts. In return the wife refused to greet him when he came home from work, refused to cook and often left the children to his care. Prior to therapy, Kurt was unable to play with his children, to read to them or to take them out on excursions. Likewise, Kurt required therapeutic help to deal with his negativism at work. He would arrive late, quarrel with his superiors, and had found himself on the brink of being fired.

Kurt explained that until he was eighteen, he wanted to be a smart person and become a "consultant" or a "scientist" and to sit behind a desk. Then he added, "I've always done the opposite."[2] But despite an I.Q. in the superior range, Kurt as a child had just managed to pass in school.

+ freezing of affect
+ reversal of affect*

2. Kurt presented many examples of frozen affect. During his childhood, for example, he was not able to cry or to express any upset when he found his favorite dog murdered with a bullet through the eye. Later in life, when his wife screamed at him or tried to hit him, he would either *laugh* or fall asleep.

+ twilight states*

The most dramatic evidence of his freezing of affect was Kurt's presenting symptom: narcolepsy, a symptom involving massive inhibition of affect to the point of somnolence. The psychogenic origin of this disturbance was reflected by its response to psychotherapy: after three years of therapy, Kurt became free of narcolepsy (and no longer required medication for the condition). Kurt's associative material offered insight into the meaning of his narcoleptic episodes of sleep. He commented: "When my mother got through *beating* me, I wished my mother was *dead*. Ever since then I loved being *asleep* under the covers: it's like the whole world then is shut out."

+ hurting
+ falling*

+ closing down upon destructively* (crush)
+ killing*

3. Kurt's material was replete with references to episodes involving falling and being hurt ever since he was little. Over and over again it looked as though he were trying to kill himself. Kurt, for example, reported: "When I was a kid I *fell* off the back of a truck and landed on my head. My sister yelled to the driver to stop the truck; otherwise I would have been squashed. . . . We used to jump out of the second-story window. We were going to fly. . . . I went *straight down*. . . . [another time] I *fell* in a hole on our back porch. . . . I *fell* into a swamp. . . . I *fell* under the spikes of a hay machine and almost got killed. . . . When I was a kid, we played in the school yard. I ran out in the street to get the ball. If they didn't yell to me to *fall* down I would have been run over and killed. . . . One time I *flipped* on my bicycle and tore my scrotum open. .

+ closing down upon destructively* (crush)

. . We used to ride our bikes and *jump off* the hills. It was dangerous. We could have killed ourselves. . . . Once I ran my bike right in front of a car. The lady was afraid she had hurt me and took me home. . . . When I was a teenager I got in a motorcycle accident. I was going 90 miles an hour; a dog came out in front of me; I hit the dog and slid down. . . . Honest to truth I keep thinking

+ falling*

of *falling* off a cliff. . . ." Kurt presented a dream which reflected this same image: "I was walking down a narrow roof with a rolling top. My foot *slipped*, I slipped. The peak of the house turned into a cliff, my wife was on the peak trying to balance herself. I said *'don't fall, don't fall.'* "

If children's symptoms often are a reflection of their parents' problems, it is not surprising to find that a presenting problem of Kurt's four-year-old son at the time of referral for psychotherapy was a long-term psychosomatic symptom[3] of losing his balance and *falling*.

In line with his capacity to fall and to hurt himself, there also emerged from under Kurt's easy-going exterior an involvement with sadism. His sadistic pleasure in dousing animals with lighter fluid and setting them on fire will be recalled. Also, Kurt's dreams were often sadistic: "I was watching a movie about kids getting *killed* and my wife and I were the only ones left in the family; our children *died*; everyone was sitting around crying." During his last year of therapy, Kurt concluded that his biggest problem was his sadism. He added: "If someone were treating my kids like I do, I admit I'd belt them."[4]

+ killing*
+ dying*

NOTES

1 Significantly, Kurt's symptoms, including narcolepsy (see below) cleared only after he was helped to eliminate his indulgence in pornography, mirror gazing and fellatio with his wife and himself. These activities, involving an accent on looking at and mouthing the penis, continually amounted to thinly disguised homosexual activity. His sexual life perpetuated his original relation with his father: the fellatio which his father had practiced upon Kurt, Kurt now completed with his wife or with himself.

2 Fortunately, Kurt's negativism was not rigidly established. He reached out and worked most positively in therapy with the result that he made many advances at work, became one of the most popular technicians in his company and began college evening courses.

3 A symptom which cleared completely during psychotherapy (see case 77).

4 Despite the strikingly pathological material which appeared in the summary of Kurt's history, a true picture of his life also requires reference to some exceptionally healthy aspects of his behavior during his years of therapy (a) Kurt and his wife were deeply faithful to one another — even though their life circumstances and their primitive drives worked in an opposite direction; (b) they held no secrets from one another and confided in each other the most intimate details of their past and present life; (c) Kurt and his wife were able to apply the knowledge they had gained from therapy toward their third child, a boy, who was born at the time of their referral: this child was not exposed to bed-sharing, adult nudity, pornographic or adult genital erotic stimulation; neither was he yelled at nor hit. The results were most rewarding: the little boy at three became remarkably positive. When requests were made of him, he complied with a smile, so differently from his two siblings who had been brought up in the opposite fashion. Emotionally, he was sensitive and responsive so that he was easily motivated to correct misbehavior on his part. This new little child influenced the household for the better: if his parents began to argue he would start crying until, from remorse, the parents finally would try to communicate with a civil tongue.

Kurt Senior
85

Stimulation-Symptom-and-Dream-Profile

	Separation Phobias
	+ Night Terrors, Twilight States
Sleep in Bed with Adult	+ Irrational Fears: Other
	Irrational Tempers
+ Adult Genital Erotic	+ Sexual Symptoms
	+ Biting/Cutting, etc. ⎫ *content of*
+ View Adult Coitus	+ Eyes ⎬ *dreams and*
	+ Fire ⎭ *symptoms*

	Learning Problems (levels 2 or 3, etc.)
Punitive Yelling	Lying and Delinquency
	+ Reversal of Affect
+ Beatings	+ Closing Down Upon, Kill ⎫ *content of* ⎬ *dreams and*
	+ Falling ⎭ *symptoms*

	Excretory Symptoms and Dreams
	Anal Masturbation
Preoccupation with Child's BM	Enuresis
	Illness, etc. ⎫ *content of*
+ Anal Contacts	Pain ⎬ *dreams and*
	+ Death ⎭ *symptoms*
	Compulsions

Case 86: Stewart

For five years prior to his referral, and unbeknown to his mother, Stewart, age thirteen, had been his father's sexual partner. The father had been caught seducing a neighbor's son. This boy then "spilled the beans" about the father's activities with him and with Stewart. Stewart's father admitted his "wrong-doing" and sought psychiatric help. He pleaded for understanding: his mother had been a prostitute; he had been placed in an orphanage and had led a very deprived life; his sexual activities with Stewart began when Stewart's mother was admitted to a sanatorium where she remained over a year's period for "depression." The father would come home to his children at night only to feed them, put them to bed and then night after night listen to them falling asleep crying for their mother.

Sources of Stimulation:
adult punitive and excretory contacts with children

+ early
deprivation

1. Six months after Stewart's mother married she had a miscarriage. She felt that the miscarriage would not have taken place had it not been for her husband's constant sexual demands during her pregnancy. The husband, who had been exposed to his mother's prostitution, apparently was not in a position to limit his driven sexuality even when his wife again became pregnant with Stewart. Therefore, when Stewart was born, the mother was tired and angry. The father continued with his excessive sexual demands but offered no help to his wife while she tried to care for the baby. The mother soon could not tolerate the father *or* the baby. By the age of four months, Stewart would scream every night supposedly with "colic." His mother honestly stated that she always rejected him and never had been able to enjoy him. Stewart became a *hyperactive* child. Even when he entered school, he could not sit still; rather he would leave his desk during classroom lectures to walk around the classroom.

+ punitive
yelling* and
violence

2. Stewart's father blamed himself and his wife for Stewart's problems. He openly explained that he and Stewart's mother quarrelled constantly over money and sex in front of the boy. The father pointed out that in the middle of his sexual battles with his wife, she would often go into Stewart's room to escape from him while he pursued her. By the time Stewart was eight years old the mother was so upset she was afraid she would kill herself or her children. It was at this time that she was hospitalized for a year and received electroshock treatments for her "depression."

362

+ beatings*

3. The mother used the strap on Stewart "occasionally" since this was the "only" way she could get him to obey. However, she began to notice that this made him "quite hysterical." Therefore, she eventually stopped the beatings even though she continued to slap Stewart's face. On the other hand, Stewart's father clung to a conviction that Stewart often would "not settle down" unless he had a good thrashing. He explained that he frequently dealt with Stewart "gently" but insisted upon the value of his severe strappings which he administered "at the proper time." On one occasion, he even threatened Stewart with a knife.

Behavioral Symptoms correlated with
adult punitive and excretory contacts with children

+ lying*
+ negative behavior
+ learning* (level 3)

1. Stewart's mother complained that Stewart "lied and would not obey anyone." She recalled that he would "answer back" even when he was a little boy and that his opposition had grown increasingly severe. It is, therefore, understandable that Stewart's schoolwork, which had always been poor, finally seriously deteriorated: Stewart twice repeated the sixth grade.

+ reversal of affect*
+ freezing of emotion

2. The school counselor spoke of Stewart's "foolish grin" and noted how Stewart would "laugh raucously at inappropriate times." Similarly, during his diagnostic hours, Stewart grinned as he told a story about everybody being killed in a new war. Stewart expressed no concern over his disturbed behavior. It is, therefore, not surprising that he demonstrated no wish for help with his problems.

+ killing*

3. Stewart remembered a "dream" about war: "War was declared because of Berlin, and as a result everybody on earth was *killed* except me and my friend."

In the world of reality, Stewart actually *threatened* both his sister and his father *with a knife*. In school his violence erupted directly: when "two kids" in school began teasing him, he *slugged* one so strongly that he *feared he had killed him*. There also was a strong suspicion that it was Stewart who had been responsible for a *bomb threat* which had seriously disturbed the school authorities.

Sources of Stimulation:
children's tactile and visual erogenous contacts with the adult body

+ adult nudity
+ adult genital erotic*

1-2. Stewart used to take showers with his father. It was in the shower that Stewart's sexual looking progressed to sexual touching and mouthing activities with his father. Fellatio and masturbatory activity between father and son began when Stewart was eight. These practices continued for five years until the father's pedophile activities finally were exposed by neighbors.

Stewart was also exposed to hard-core pornographic pictures obtained from an adolescent boy. Sharing of the pictures with this boy eventually culminated in Stewart's watching the adolescent youth masturbate in front of him to the point of emission. Stewart himself was sexually immature.

Behavioral Symptoms correlated with
children's tactile and visual erogenous contacts with the adult body

+ irrational fears*   1. Stewart expressed fears of a war and fears that the H-bomb would bring destruction to everyone.

+ irrational   2. Stewart exploded into violent tempers at home. When his parents would not allow him to drive a car, he tore the telephone from the wall.
   tempers*

+ eyes* (reading   3. Stewart, who was placed in the "slow group" in school, was said to be doing particularly poorly in reading.
   problem)

+ biting/cutting*   4. Confabulating repeatedly, Stewart told how his grandfather met death in the *jaws (teeth)* of uncaged lions. He also mentioned that his father had found an *amputated (cut)* finger which had been carelessly thrown away in an operating room.

+ sexual   5. The neighborhood "was up in arms": Stewart was attempting to expose himself to little girls and to molest them. He was also trying to pick up adult men as sexual partners and was fired from an after-school job for soliciting such sexual contacts. Meanwhile in school Stewart was found on his hands and knees sensuously licking the classroom floor.
   symptoms*

Stewart
86

Stimulation-Symptom-and-Dream-Profile

	Separation Phobias	
	Night Terrors, Twilight States	
Sleep in Bed with Adult	+ Irrational Fears: Other	
	+ Irrational Tempers	
+ Adult Genital Erotic	+ Sexual Symptoms	
	+ Biting/Cutting, etc.	} *content of*
View Adult Coitus	+ Eyes	*dreams and*
	Fire	*symptoms*
	+ Learning Problems (levels 2 or 3, etc.)	
+ Punitive Yelling	+ Lying and Delinquency	
	+ Reversal of Affect	
+ Beatings	+ Closing Down Upon, Kill	} *content of* *dreams and*
	Falling	*symptoms*
	Excretory Symptoms and Dreams	
	Anal Masturbation	
Preoccupation with Child's BM	Enuresis	
	Illness, etc.	} *content of*
Anal Contacts	Pain	*dreams and*
	Death	*symptoms*
	Compulsions	

SECTION 4
CASES 87-100

Focus:

SYMPTOMS ASSOCIATED WITH CHILDREN'S EXPOSURES TO ANAL AND FECAL STIMULATION

Case 87: Synopsis of Freud's "Rat Man"

Freud's "Notes Upon a Case of Obsessional Neurosis" first published in 1909 (Standard Edition, Vol. X, 1955, p. 155-318) presents in detail the history of a young man suffering severely from "*fears* that something might happen to two people of whom he was very fond — his father and a lady whom he admired. Besides this, he was aware of *compulsive* impulses — such as an impulse, for instance, to *cut* his *throat* with a razor; and further he produced (disturbing) *prohibitions*, sometimes in connection with quite unimportant things. He had wasted years . . . in fighting against these ideas of his, and in this way had lost much ground in the course of life" (p. 158). Since one of this patient's most disturbing thoughts pertained to rats, he became known in analytic circles by the name of "The Rat Man." Within the following presentation, the patient will simply be referred to as "R" for "Rat Man," although Freud once called him "Paul" (p. 161).

Sources of Stimulation:
children's tactile and visual erogenous contacts with the adult body

1. When "R" was six or seven years old he was still sleeping in his parents' room (p. 161).

+ adult nudity

2. At the age of four, five and six he was still allowed to go to the Baths with his governess and sisters and recalled the intense excitement with which he waited "for the governess to undress and get into the water" (p. 160-61).

+ adult genital erotic*

3. At the age of four, "R" was exposed to his first intense sexual encounter. A description of the episode was recorded in his own words: "We had a very pretty young governess called Fraulein Peter. One evening she was lying on the sofa lightly dressed, and reading. I was lying beside her, and begged her to let me creep under her skirt. She told me I might, so long as I said nothing to any one about it. She had very little on and I fingered her genitals and the lower part of her body which struck me as very queer. After this I was left with a burning and tormenting curiosity to see the female body" (p. 160).

A year or two later, "R" reported additional erogenous contacts with another governess, Fraulein Lina: "I remember a scene . . . we were sitting together one evening — the governess, the cook, another servant girl, myself, and my brother who was eighteen months younger than me. The young women were talking, and I suddenly became aware of Fraulein Lina saying, 'It could be done with the little one; but Paul [the patient] is too clumsy, he would be sure to

366

miss it.' I did not understand clearly what was meant but I felt the slight and began to cry. Lina comforted me and told how a girl who had done something of the kind with a little boy she was in charge of, had been put in prison for several months. I do not believe she actually did anything wrong with me but I took a great many liberties with her. When I got into her bed I used to uncover her and touch her and she made no objections" (p. 161).

− / + sleeping in bed with adults*

Behavioral Symptoms correlated with
children's tactile and visual erogenous contacts with the adult body

+ irrational fears*

1. "R" suffered from fears that something might happen to two people of whom he was very fond: his father and his lady friend (p. 158). As a young man he was obsessed with the fear that "something dreadful would happen" (p. 163).

+ irrational tempers*

2. "R's" temper was *so wild* when he was approximately four years old (at the time he was under the care of his governess) that his father was led to exclaim, "The child will be either a great man or a great criminal" (p. 205; see also, under "beatings").

+ sexual symptoms*

3. By the time he was six, erections were disturbing "R" to the point that he complained about them to his mother (p. 161-62). However, his sexual impulses, overactivated during childhood, became restricted and "stunted" in adulthood (p. 158).

Not only was "R's" heterosexual adjustment far from satisfactory at the time of his seeking therapy but signs of homosexual conflicts in his adult life appeared also. Following his father's death, for example, he used to phantasize that his father was returning to the home through the front door which "R" would make a point to leave open late at night. While he was preoccupied with this phantasy he would expose his penis and proceed to look at it in the mirror. In this way he focused sexually upon the male body within the mirror as well as with thoughts of exposing himself to his father (p. 204).

+ biting/cutting*

4. According to his mother's reports, "R" at the age of four (when he was being exposed to contacts with his nurse's naked body) was beaten for *biting* someone (p. 160, 206). Subsequently, one of his most disturbing complaints at the time he sought help from Freud was his compulsive impulse to *cut* his throat with a razor (p. 158, 187).

+ eyes*

5. Sometime before he was eight years old, "R" loaded his toy gun with a ramrod and told his brother that "if he looked up the barrel he would see something." Then while his brother was looking in, "R" pulled the trigger. The brother fortunately was hit only "on the forehead and not hurt" but "R's" goal had been *to hit him in the eye.* Shortly afterwards, "R" was quite beside himself and threw himself on the ground while asking himself how he ever could have done such a thing (p. 184).

It is not surprising that one of "R's" two recorded dreams was involved with the eyes. In the dream "R" saw Freud's daughter in front of him with two patches of dung instead of eyes (p. 200).

Sources of Stimulation:
adult punitive and excretory contacts with children

+ anal
stimulation*

1. For many years during his childhood "R" suffered from a constant irritation from a worm infestation of his anal orifice. The activity of the worms lodged in his anal region and the accompanying itching provided a basis for an erogenous but torturous masturbatory stimulation of his anus (p. 213).

Another source of anal and excretory stimulation occurring during his sixth year involved "R's" repeated exposure to viewing his nurse's buttocks as she expressed pus from abscesses of her buttocks (p. 161).

+ beatings*

2. The father, who could be hasty and violent, occasionally brought down the most severe retribution upon his children when they were young and naughty (p. 201). "R" recalled that "his father had had a passionate temper and *sometimes in his violence had not known where to stop*" (p. 205, 209). On one occasion during his fourth year, "R's" reaction to his father's beating was so intense that his father never beat him again even though the father continued the practice of beating "R's" brothers and sisters (p. 206).

Behavioral Symptoms correlated with
adult punitive and excretory contacts with children

+ excretory*
(dream content)

1. One of "R's" two recorded dreams[1] focused upon excrement. In this dream "R" saw Freud's daughter in front of him with two patches of *dung* instead of eyes (p. 200).

+ excretory
symptoms*

"R's" focus upon the bowel and excrement, however, was reflected most dramatically by his principal symptom: his endless and repetitive obsessive thoughts about rats boring into the rectum of a living subject. This unbearable symptom had been set in motion by information reported to "R" by a cruel army officer who had "repeatedly defended the employment of corporal punishment." The officer had described to "R" an Oriental form of punishment according to which rats were encouraged to bore their way into the victim's anus. "R's" preoccupation with this account included images of the rats boring into his girl friend's rectum and into his father's rectum (p. 166-67).

2. Following his final beating at the age of four, "R" became extremely afraid of blows. "From that time on he was a coward" (p. 206).

(restriction)
+ learning*
(level 2)

Restrictiveness and withdrawal became a problem, so that despite his innate intelligence, he developed an obstinate incapacity for work which caused him "to postpone the completion of his education for years" (p. 199). Only after his father's death when his direct defiance to his father began to erupt did he once again begin to work and study (p. 204). In sum, "R's" negative withdrawal was manifested through a disturbing learning problem.

Negativism interfered with "R's" life in other pathological ways. He was exhausted by his obsessive compulsive activities during which he struggled to oppose his negative reactions (i.e., during which he attempted to negate his negativism). For example, "he used to make up prayers for himself which took up more and more time and eventually lasted for an hour and a half. The reason for this was that he found that something always inserted itself into his pious phrases and turned them into their *opposite*. If he said, 'May God protect him' an evil spirit would hurriedly insinuate a '*not*.' On one occasion, the idea occurred to him of cursing instead, for in that case, he thought, the *contrary* word would be sure to creep in" (p. 193).

+ obsessions and   Complementing such useless, compulsive demands he put upon himself,
compulsions*   "R" became obsessed with an exhaustive series of petty prohibitions. For ex-
                   ample, when he experienced a wish to see certain young women unclothed he
                   would be faced with a prohibition that if he saw them naked his father might
+ death*   die (p. 162). Or in response to an inner command that he pay back so and so
                   some money, he was confronted by a negative, opposing prohibition or "sanc-
                   tion" that he was *not* to pay back the money or punishment would ensue, etc.,
                   etc., etc., etc. (p. 168). In sum, the random intrusion of negative reversals of
                   orders associated with punishment played havoc with his life.

+ freezing of   3. Any feelings of *rage* for his father were totally inhibited and suppressed
affect   even though affectless thoughts about hurting and murdering his father (see
                   below) continually came to "R's" mind.[2] Other evidences of disturbed emotional
+ reversal of   affects appeared in the form of pleasure in the presence of misfortune. In one
affect*   dream, Freud's mother had died. "R" was anxious to offer his condolences but
                   was afraid that in doing so he might break into an impertinent *laugh* as he had
                   done on similar occasions in the past. He preferred therefore to leave a condol-
                   ence card with "p.c." (pour condoler) on it, but as he was writing this down,
                   the letters turned into "p.f." (pour feliciter: to congratulate). In an appendant
                   footnote, Freud suggests that this dream elucidates the occurrence of "*laughter*
                   which so often occurs on *mournful occasions* and which therefore has been
                   regarded as an unaccountable phenomenon" (p. 193).

+ killing* (self)   4. References to horror, torment, suicide and death repeatedly character-
                   ized "R's" symptoms. "R" was obsessed with suicidal thoughts. He was tor-
                   mented by thoughts of cutting his throat with a razor (p. 158). On other
+ falling*   occasions, as he stood near the *edge of a precipice* he was confronted with
+ obsessions*   internal commands to *jump*, i.e., to an inevitable *death* (p. 188). These maso-
                   chistic thoughts were complemented by sadistic "criminal impulses" (p. 159) and
+ hurting   fears that harm might come to those whom he loved, e.g., his lady friend or his
                   father (p. 158). After his father had died he became tormented with the thought
+ death*   that he should have been with his father at the time he was dying (p. 174) and

was aghast that he might have wished his father's death in order to inherit some money (p. 179). Other obsessive sadistic thoughts and fears counter to his high standards and ideals were directed toward his lady friend: a wish crossed his mind that his lady friend might not recover from an *illness* and would have to be *permanently sick* in bed (p. 194), or thoughts plagued him that he should have removed a stone from the road along which his lady friend's carriage was to drive; his negligence, he was sure, would result in her carriage coming to grief and she herself perhaps being hurt (p. 191).

+ preoccupation with illness*

"R's" absorption with horror, torture and pain (as well as with the bowels and excrement) was demonstrated most dramatically by his obsession with the cruel captain's account of rats boring into a man's rectum. The details of this Oriental form of punishment emphasized in every way horror, disgust and pain, i.e., the victim was *tied down* with the cord *pressing down* upon him to the point of helplessness, a pot with rats was then turned upside down on his buttocks so that they were induced to bore and gnaw their way into his anus (p. 165-67).[3]

+ pain*
+ obsession*

+ closing down upon destructively*

NOTES

[1] This is the same dream which equally focused upon the eye. See above marginal notation: + eyes*.

[2] The marked *inhibition of appropriate affect* in this case led Freud to the observation that, in obsessive-compulsive cases such as "R's," memory is not repressed as among hysterics, but rather the memory remains deprived of its affect. "What remains in consciousness is nothing but its ideational content which is perfectly colourless and is judged to be unimportant" (p. 196).

[3] This preoccupation which at first may appear to be complete nonsense becomes understandable if one keeps in mind that the account of rats boring into the rectum was in some ways equivalent to the patient's emotional memories of (a) worms boring into his rectum (p. 213) and (b) his finger boring into the deep recesses of his nurse's genitalia (p. 160). Unfortunately, the account of the rats must have served to reactivate tormenting but *highly erogenous and pleasurable* emotional reactions, a source for reinforcing the repetition of the ongoing thoughts.

Freud's Rat Man
87

Stimulation-Symptom-and-Dream-Profile

	Separation Phobias	
	Night Terrors, Twilight States	
Sleep in Bed with Adult	+ Irrational Fears: Other	
	+ Irrational Tempers	
+ Adult Genital Erotic	+ Sexual Symptoms	
	+ Biting/Cutting, etc.	*content of*
View Adult Coitus	+ Eyes	*dreams and*
	Fire	*symptoms*
	+ Learning Problems (levels 2 or 3, etc.)	
Punitive Yelling	Lying and Delinquency	
	+ Reversal of Affect	
+ Beatings	+ Closing Down Upon, Kill	*content of dreams and*
	+ Falling	*symptoms*
	+ Excretory Symptoms and Dreams	
	Anal Masturbation	
Preoccupation with Child's BM	Enuresis	
	+ Illness, etc.	*content of*
+ Anal Contacts	+ Pain	*dreams and*
	+ Death	*symptoms*
	+ Compulsions	

Case 88: Synopsis of Nancy Spiegel's "Nora"

"Nora, a pretty girl of nineteen, came into treatment not only because she felt 'empty' and could not do anything, but primarily because of her agitation about what she considered to be excessive masturbation. It was while Nora reproached herself for her masturbation" that she casually made reference to her almost life-long fetishistic involvement with shoe strings (*Psychoanalytic Study of the Child*, Vol. XXII, 1967, p. 404). At the age of two and a half, Nora "took her first shoe string from her mother's brown shoe" (p. 404). Eventually she would take a shoe lace from the shoes of other females and would proceed to gaze at the shoe lace and finger it. A shoe lace to touch and to hold became an essential part of her living: without her shoe lace, Nora felt she had "nothing" and was "nothing" (p. 405).

Sources of Stimulation:
adult punitive and excretory contacts with children

+ early
deprivation

1. For two weeks after Nora's birth the mother was afraid to touch Nora for fear of dropping her (p. 409).[1]

+ anal
stimulation*

2. When Nora was eight months old, two events took place: (a) Nora was weaned from the breast,[2] and (b) years of enema irrigations were instituted (p. 408, 409).

As Nora became older she not only continued to receive enemas but she also "asked" for them. *As far back as Nora could recall she would start the process by screaming with "abdominal cramps."* The mother would then talk on the phone with the grandfather about her plans for giving Nora enemas. Nora "would watch the telephone cord and at once think of water flowing out of a tube. She felt like 'exploding,' but also wanted to press tight to hold in. Right after the call, her mother would speak two cue words: 'Hurry, hurry.' These made Nora slow up immediately. She quickly squeezed her legs together and experienced a feeling of 'wetness.' The words 'hurry, hurry' were repeated" (p. 408-09). Thereupon Nora proceeded to submit docilely for her enema. "Her accounts focused on the following points: her mother was invisibly standing behind her; she had something long in her hand" (evidently the enema tube). Nora "screamed in anticipation of the enema. She maintained her father was always present. . . . She was sure mother also gave her father enemas."

Then at the age of eight years, Nora took "steps in the direction of health" and "refused to permit her mother to give her enemas any more. She screamed until the mother desisted, and from then on never was given another enema" (p. 414).

Behavioral Symptoms correlated with
adult punitive and excretory contacts with children

+ enuresis*

1. One of Nora's first memories was of "wetting herself all over and re-maining seated in a puddle till a teacher picked her up" (p. 410).

+ excretory symptoms*

When she was six, Nora indulged in homosexual activities with other girls. She recalled an occasion when she begged the girls to give her an enema. The girls, "incredulous and derisive, ran away from her" (p. 414).

+ anal masturbation*

During her adolescence, Nora was disturbed by compulsive anal mastur-bation (p. 405-06).

Nora also practiced an anal sexual ritual during which "stark naked, she placed herself in a prone position, on her knees, with her buttocks raised up. . . . She then either tugged at her breasts or fingered her anus" (p. 406).

Even when Nora later in life became involved in heterosexual activities with a young man, she limited her sexual relations with him to anal intercourse (p. 416).

+ preoccupation with illness*

+ pains*

2. Nora's hypochondriacal absorption with her painful abdominal cramps has already been mentioned as prevalent during the "enema" years. It was Nora's abdominal pains which precipitated the administration of her enema treatments (p. 408).

+ obsessions*

Additionally, Nora displayed sadistic preoccupations. For example, during her shoe lace ritual, Nora was *obsessively preoccupied* with a phantasy about going on a trip with a young man, a mother and the mother's little son. There then occurred "*a bad accident* in which the mother was injured and bloody" (p.

+ death*
+ closing down upon destructively* (strangle)
+ closing down upon destructively*
+ negative behavior (withholding)
+ learning (level 1)

406). Nora returned only to find the mother *dead*. Nora also entertained phan-tasies of *strangling* an infant with an umbilical cord (p. 417).[3]

Nora directly acted out some of her sadistic phantasies when she was a child. For example, when she became sexually involved with a group of girls who made fun of her for wanting an enema, she took revenge by throwing stones at the girls' heads to see them bleed (p. 414).

3. Nora was "rarely on time, being either too late or too early" and re-sponding "by holding back from what was to be done" (p. 420). It is no surprise that Nora suffered from a learning problem. She complained of not being able to work, read or think (p. 407).

+ negative emotion

4. Nora harped upon her negative feelings about herself. As has already been noted, she complained of being nothing and having nothing (unless this emotional feeling were reversed by contact with her fetishistic brown shoe

string). She felt she was stupid and was obsessed with feelings of emptiness (where "emptiness" refers to an experience that "nothing" is there, no feeling, no sensation) (p. 405, 407).

At the age of nine, Nora, immobilized by her rituals, broke down weeping and screaming. Her parents, alarmed at Nora's inability to give up her symptoms, finally placed her in a mental hospital for a brief stay. Here a massive reversal of emotion set in: from a "stupid," "bad," "empty," "nothing" she suddenly became a "supergirl." Here she developed a temporary delusion that "the children on the ward lifted her up on a table and gazed at her in wonder while they called her 'angel' " (p. 415).

+ reversal of
affect*

Sources of Stimulation:
children's tactile and visual erogenous contacts with the adult body

+ adult nudity

1. Nora's father and mother practiced casual nudity in her presence (p. 414). Nora was preoccupied with the mother's huge breasts which contrasted so markedly with her own lack of breast development (p. 412). Furthermore, until Nora was two and a half years old, her grandfather would arrange to have Nora *share the bathtub with him. Thereupon, he would fondle her in a provocative way* (p. 410).[4]

+ adult genital
erotic*

Behavioral Symptoms correlated with
children's tactile and visual erogenous contacts with the adult body

+ separation
fears*

1. Nora "suffered from severe separation anxieties when her mother placed her in nursery school" (p. 410).

+ irrational fears*

2. At about the age of five, "a new symptom appeared: fright. Nora was afraid of spiders, noises in the parental bedroom, and especially [thoughts] of her mother doing 'terrible' things to her father. The dark frightened her and she had to have a light on" (p. 412).

More typically, Nora was continually beset by fears of being empty and being "nothing" (p. 416).

+ irrational
tempers*

3. It was because of Nora's ceaseless weeping and *screaming* that the parents eventually resorted to placing her in a mental hospital (p. 415).

+ sexual
symptoms*

4. At the age of six, Nora acted out homosexually (see above). Attaching herself to little girls, she "stroked and fondled them. If they acknowledged her, she became submissive to them" (p. 414).

At the age of twelve and a half, Nora "took up with . . . *a group of very tough girls* who dolled her up. They made her a decoy for nighthaul drivers. . . . Her father found out about these excursions and intercepted her with the accusation that she was a slut."[5] Closely allied with such sexual activity was Nora's driven compulsion to steal at this time. The stealing focused upon sweaters of "girls who she fancied had breasts like her mother's" (p. 416).[6]

+ biting/cutting*   5. One of Nora's ritualistic compulsions included *lip-biting* (p. 412) and one of her phobias involved spiders (which *bite*).

+ eyes*   6. Nora's shoe string ritual required that her *eyes* be *wide* open, unblinking and fixed upon a blank part of a wall (p. 405-06). Within a second ritual *"she squeezed her eyes* shut till they stung" (p. 406).

Nora's upset over her eyes for a period disturbed her capacity to read: "as soon as she used her mind to read, her *eyes* betrayed her: they itched, blurred,[7] burned, shut, or fell asleep" (p. 408).[8]

NOTES

[1] Possibly, a failure to touch Nora during her first two weeks of life provided a basis for her imprinted-like attachments to inanimate rather than to animate objects and thereby account for her fetishistic preoccupations.

[2] It was at this same time that the mother first observed Nora twisting and staring "unblinkingly" at a beaded string (p. 410), a possible precursor of Nora's fetishistic fingering and staring at shoe strings.

[3] Recall the mother had been afraid to touch Nora the first two weeks of Nora's life, for fear she would harm her.

[4] It was at this time that Nora began her rituals with shoe laces from her mother's shoes (p. 404). Nora would *stare at the shoe lace* as she might have *wanted to stare at the grandfather's penis and genital hair*, i.e., there is a possible displacement of the look-touch sexual reactions from the grandfather's penis to the strand of string much like a strand of hair.

Of note, when Nora was some twenty years old, one of her boyfriends paraded nude with penis erect in front of her (p. 421). It was at this time that Nora allowed herself to become consciously aware of the adult penis. She reported " 'I stood frozen stiff, I had to look . . . and I was horrified at my own fright' " (p. 421). It was directly following this experience that Nora gave up her string fetishism. Nora admitted that prior to this time she had pictured a penis as being like an enema tube, pendulous and flexible (p. 421).

Thus, the string fixation, which began at the age of eight months when Nora was weaned from the mother's breast (p. 409-10), developed into a shoe string ritual when Nora was intimately involved with the sight of the *grandfather's penis*. Possibly Nora discharged upon her *string* the staring and touching reactions which had been associated with her mother's breast, her grandfather's penis and the mother's penis-like enema tube.

[5] Once again, the parents and grandparent can charge the child's "sexual batteries" by lax nudity and seduction, *but* when the child acts out, it is all her fault; she is a "slut."

[6] The sexual *look-grasp* reactions which were charged by the sight of the mother's large breasts possibly were discharged upon the sweaters of girls with large breasts. If Nora could not grab at big breasts and have them for her own, she could grab the sweaters lodging the big breasts.

[7] Compare these eye symptoms with those displayed by Ozzie, case 81.

[8] A relation between erotic visual overstimulation and narcolepsy is evidenced in case 85 of Kurt Senior. See also case 81 of Ozzie.

Spiegel's "Nora"
88

Stimulation-Symptom-and-Dream-Profile

	+ Separation Phobias	
	Night Terrors, Twilight States	
Sleep in Bed with Adult	+ Irrational Fears: Other	
	+ Irrational Tempers	
+ Adult Genital Erotic	+ Sexual Symptoms	
	+ Biting/Cutting, etc.	} *content of*
View Adult Coitus	+ Eyes	} *dreams and*
	Fire	} *symptoms*

	Learning Problems (levels 2 or 3, etc.)	
Punitive Yelling	Lying and Delinquency	
	+ Reversal of Affect	
Beatings	+ Closing Down Upon, Kill	} *content of dreams and*
	Falling	} *symptoms*

	+ Excretory Symptoms and Dreams	
	+ Anal Masturbation	
Preoccupation with Child's BM	+ Enuresis	
	+ Illness, etc.	} *content of*
+ Anal Contacts	+ Pain	} *dreams and*
	+ Death	} *symptoms*
	+ Compulsions	

Case 89: Talbot

When their ten-year-old son, Tal, was referred to the clinic, Mr. and Mrs. B thought there was "something wrong with his head." Despite an I.Q. of 92, Tal was functioning as a "mental retard in school," a reason for his having been brought initially to be tested at an institution for the retarded. The family was perplexed when they were informed of the completely negative findings revealed by a neurological workup.

Tal's "absolute lack of respect for authority" also worried his mother. According to her report, Tal would do "absolutely" nothing his parents asked him to do.

Of note, when Tal was five or six years old, a particularly disturbing event took place in his life: Tal was to have a tonsillectomy, but the doctor suggested that he not be told anything about the operation or the hospital. When they did reach the hospital, the doctor told Tal that he would be going to see "the babies." Then the doctor told the mother to leave and go home. The mother remembered seeing Tal left sitting on his bed and crying. When she returned that night, Tal could only say that he thought she had left him for ever and ever. Later, Tal told how "they" had tied his ankles and wrists in order to keep him under control.

Also of significance, Tal's father's life and thoughts frequently focused upon death. (a) The father frequently spoke of the large number of men whom he saw killed during World War II; (b) he loved to take Tal hunting and then skin the dead animals in front of the boy; (c) he himself appeared to be close to death on two occasions when he hemorrhaged from a stomach ulcer and passed blood from his mouth.

Tal was especially unprepared for dealing with such traumatic situations because he was pathologically infantilized by his mother. At the age of ten and a half, Tal was still being bathed by his mother.

Sources of Stimulation:
adult punitive and excretory contacts with children

1. When Tal's mother was three years old, she was placed in an orphan asylum. Later, she was taken into a family where she earned her keep by helping care for a young foster child. She never again was permitted to see her own mother. Then, while she was in the hospital at the time of Tal's birth, she received a report that her mother had just died.

+ / – early
deprivation

In light of her own deprivation, it is likely that Tal's mother was not in a position to give abundant "supplies" to Tal during his infancy. Confirming this formulation was the additional diagnostic finding that the mother could remember nothing of Tal's developmental history.[1]

+ anal
 stimulation*

2. From four to seven years of age, Tal regularly received enemas from his mother and father for pinworms. Apparently, he no sooner recovered from one case of the "worms" than he became reinfected. According to his mother, Tal "picked up worms most anywhere." Thus, he was exposed to repetitive anal stimulation in two ways: from pinworm infestation of his perianal membranes and from the enemas he received during treatment. Tal was able to tell how his father held him down during these procedures while his mother shoved the enema tube into his rectum. Tal recalled wildly kicking and spitting while his parents held him down.[2] He also remembered "messing" all over the bathroom after one of his enemas.

Of note, the father would encourage Tal to be interested in excrement, e.g., by telling him that if you put rabbit dung on your hands, it will make them strong, and if you put horse manure on your arms they, too, will become strong.

+ beatings*

3. The records reported only one statement pertaining to a history of Tal's being beaten, but this statement of the mother's worker was unequivocal: "The mother frequently found herself in the position of withholding from her husband information about Tal's misdeeds, explaining that her husband was accustomed to beating Tal for disobedience." Tal's father was "of course" sympathetic to Tal's problems, but, according to the mother, he would stand for "no nonsense" and certainly would beat Tal if Tal disobeyed his mother. With therapy, the father became "less punitive."

+ punitive
 yelling*

Complementing the father's role of beating Tal, the mother was in the habit of disciplining him by yelling and scolding. Tal was *so* negative she *had* to "yell at him a lot."

Behavioral Symptoms correlated with
adult punitive and excretory contacts with children

+ enuresis*

1. On occasion, Tal wet his bed.

+ excretory
 symptoms*

2. Tal went wild whenever he heard any reference to excrement even when he himself brought up the subject. No sooner had he mentioned the word "caca" during his therapy than he would become hyperactive, break loose and try to knock over the office furniture. To counteract these symptomatic reactions, Tal's therapist instituted a form of "desensitization therapy" during which Tal would talk about some aspect of excrement in his life while his therapist would quiet him, help him talk over his worries and offer him gentle controls. Eventually, Tal could talk of his enemas and of his "doing diarrhea all over the bathroom" and gradually he became able to refer to excremental words without his going

"berserk." Finally, he began even to be able to laugh at such thoughts.

+ compulsions*

In line with these concerns, Tal demonstrated a compulsion to *smell* different objects in the room, particularly crayons. At the same time he began to speak of a nurse in the hospital who had pushed "caca" in a child's face and how kids in the hospital ate excrement.[3] Tal also spoke of flatus. He questioned repetitively "what caused it" and confided how he would pass flatus at camp

+ excretory symptoms*

when "the boys" dared him to do so. Tal eventually was able to confide how he and his sister would play "doctor and nurse" when his sister would poke a stick into his rear end. As Tal talked over such concerns about excrement, he made references to a "clicking"[4] noise he would experience in his ears. He also re-

+ obsessions*

called how, at times, he couldn't stop thinking about sinking into mud. Once Tal acted out his preoccupation with mud by tricking girls to run after him in a muddy field with the hope that a girl would fall and become covered with mud.

+ hurt

3. Tal was expert in provoking his parents and his peers to hit him. Likewise, his parents were concerned at the time of his referral that Tal was constantly starting fights with a neighbor boy and then not defending himself. During his therapy hours, Tal re-enacted his habit of trying to induce others to "go after him." For example, he put chalk all over the blackboard and then tried to blow the chalk dust throughout the room and into his therapist's face. Expecting to be attacked, he tried throwing paper clips at his therapist until finally the therapist had to hold Tal's hands (see note 2). At other times, he would "accidentally" try to break a toy to see what would happen. In this con-

+ killing*

nection, Tal dreamed that he was "a monster who was wanting to *kill* people."

+ non-organic illness*
+ pains and aches*

4. Tal suffered from headaches and stomachaches severe enough to require a medical workup. The doctor's report indicated that there was "nothing organically wrong" and that the headaches were caused by "tension."

+ death*

Tal also was worried about *death*. For example, he did not want to *learn* the days or the months of the year because thinking of time made him think he was going to *die*.[5]

+ negative emotion

5. Even though Tal was a smiling, outgoing boy, his emotional negativism was his most outstanding trait. A typical therapeutic hour might begin positively, e.g., with Tal reaching out to invite his therapist to his home. However, soon he would start a series of complaints as he would go on to say, "the toys look stupid . . . it's a waste of time coming here. . . . I'd rather be with my father on the truck. . . . I don't like the smell of the clay. . . . There are no good toys around. . . . Dr. Z. is stupid, he needs a brain doctor. . . . I won't tell you my secret because you're not my friend." Likewise, when his therapist gave Tal a present which Tal had specifically requested, Tal at first was very pleased but as the hour progressed, he began criticizing it and finally decided he didn't want it.[6]

Later, when Tal's feelings toward his therapist became overtly positive, he turned his deluge of negative feelings upon himself. He was convinced he was "no good"; he was "just dirt"; he "couldn't do things."

+ negative
behavior

6. Tal's doing the opposite from what was requested of him, his opposition to authority, was one of his mother's chief concerns at the time of his referral. To quote the mother's complaints: "Tal has absolutely no respect for authority. . . . Tal does absolutely nothing that he is asked to do." Adding to his negative

+ lying*

symptoms, Tal began to lie to his parents in order to avoid being blamed.

+ learning*
(level 3)

With a background of such negativism and fears of learning about numbers and death, Tal developed a massive learning problem. At the age of ten, he was still doing only first grade work so that his perplexed parents were about to send him to a school for the retarded.

Sources of Stimulation:
children's tactile and visual erogenous contacts with the adult body

+ adult nudity

1. Tal would see his father's penis when he and the father were together in the bathroom or on camping trips.

+ adult genital
erotic*

2. Tal and his father were still wrestling together in their pajamas when Tal was already thirteen years old. The father would often hold him down in bed at such times of body contact.[7]

Behavioral Symptoms correlated with
children's tactile and visual erogenous contacts with the adult body

+ separation
hysterics*

1. Tal displayed school-phobic symptoms with stomachaches during his first year at school. As soon as he was allowed to stay home his stomachaches disappeared.

+ / − obsessive
fears*

2. Only after his third year of therapy did Tal finally speak of his obsessive fears about death and about sinking into mud.

+ irrational
tempers*

3. One of the mother's chief complaints regarding Tal's behavior at the time of his referral was his frequent bursts of temper both at home and in school.

+ sexual
problems*

4. Tal's sister, it will be recalled, would poke a stick into Tal's rectum during their childhood doctor-and-nurse games. Then for a period, when Tal was thirteen, he became involved with manipulating his sister's genitalia. With the help of therapy, this behavior was able to be controlled.

+ biting/cutting*

5. Tal expressed the angry thought that he would like to cut off a "certain big penis."

+ eyes*

6. Of all Tal's learning problems those involving *reading* were the most incapacitating .

+ fire*

7. At an early age, Tal was found lighting matches under a neighbor's

wooden patio. Tal's mother reiterated that this behavior never again occurred once she saw to it that Tal was severely spanked for his misdeeds.

NOTES

1 On numerous occasions, Tal's material referred to *ice* and *cold*, a theme suggestive of early deprivation. Tal, for example, drew a picture looking very much like a breast; he called it an "igloo" while noting it had a "deep-freeze" inside.

2 Tal acted out this scene during one therapy hour when he kept throwing paper clips at his therapist who finally tried gently to hold his hand in order to limit his attack. The moment Tal was "held down" he went wild, acting as he had during his enemas and during his traumatic operation, i.e., he broke loose kicking and spitting.

3 It was likely that Tal was referring to his own experiences and his own charged-up primitive thoughts and reactions pertaining to excrement being put into his mouth. See synopsis of Margaret Gerard's case of Mary, case 90.

4 Also, see case 13 of Joel with respect to a concurrent history of anal sexual play and symptoms involving a "clicking" noise in the head.

5 Compare with synopsis 98 of Editha Sterba's "Deli" regarding the coexistence of children's preoccupations with death and a history of frequent enemas.

6 See cases 17, 43, 92 and 93 of Ned, Kevin, William and Rosenblatt's Harold, which also illustrate the coexistence of (a) children's anal physical activities and (b) the children's tendencies to "socially smear," i.e., to devalue and find fault.

7 Such experiences of Tal's being "pinned down" must have reactivated feelings of panic Tal had experienced when he was tied down for his *tonsillectomy* as well as his emotional memories of having been held down for *enemas*.

Talbot
89

Stimulation-Symptom-and-Dream-Profile

	+ Separation Phobias
	Night Terrors, Twilight States
Sleep in Bed with Adult	+ Irrational Fears: Other
	+ Irrational Tempers
+ Adult Genital Erotic	+ Sexual Symptoms
	+ Biting/Cutting, etc.
View Adult Coitus	+ Eyes
	+ Fire

}   *content of dreams and symptoms*

	+ Learning Problems (levels 2 or 3, etc.)
+ Punitive Yelling	+ Lying and Delinquency
	Reversal of Affect
+ Beatings	+ Closing Down Upon, Kill
	Falling

}   *content of dreams and symptoms*

	+ Excretory Symptoms and Dreams
	Anal Masturbation
Preoccupation with Child's BM	+ Enuresis
	+ Illness, etc.
+ Anal Contacts	+ Pain
	+ Death
	+ Compulsions

}   *content of dreams and symptoms*

Case 90: Synopsis of Margaret Gerard's "Mary"

Mary, age four, I.Q. 117, was referred for psychoanalysis because of two main difficulties. (a) For the past year, she had repeatedly displayed a "sniffing" *tic* consisting of nose-wrinkling with a rapid inspiration that was followed immediately by a noisy expiration; (b) Mary was troubled by "tenacious constipation with moments of voluntary holding back of her feces" (*Psychoanalytic Study of the Child*, Vol. II, 1948, p. 150).

Sources of Stimulation:
children's tactile and visual erogenous contacts with the adult body

−/+ sleeping in bed with adults* (only sometimes)

1. Mary would sometimes awake crying at night and would then be taken into bed with her mother. Her mother felt this was the only way Mary could be induced to "relax" (p. 151).

Behavioral Symptoms correlated with
children's tactile and visual erogenous contacts with the adult body

+ separation phobia*

1. Fearing separation, Mary would not allow her mother to leave the house without her (p. 151).

+ nightmares

2. Mary suffered from nightmares which sent her to her mother's bed. The nightmares developed during her third to fourth year (p. 151, 152).

+ irrational tempers*

3. Mary's temper tantrums were rigidly punished by her mother (p. 151).

Sources of Stimulation:
adult punitive and excretory contacts with children

1-2. Punishment, in relation to defecation, occurred repeatedly during Mary's four-year history:

+ punitive bowel training

(a) Mary's bowel-training was begun as early as her fifth month of life. By the age of one year, she had been rigidly trained even for night-wetting (p. 152).

(b) Shortly after her little sister was born, Mary at the age of two and a half began to wet and soil herself for which she was punished by her nurse as well as by her mother (p. 151).

+ anal stimulation*

(c) The mother was meticulous in maintaining a routine for Mary's toilet functions. Therefore when Mary, at the age of three, became emotionally upset and constipated for six or seven days, the mother proceeded to give her an enema (p. 152).

(d) Mary's father was so punitive each time Mary soiled that Mary became fearful in his presence and gradually withdrew contact from him (p. 151).

(e) The mother was even more punitive toward Mary's soiling: for example, one day when Mary was three, the mother went to awaken her from her nap, only to find her smearing feces all over her face. Deeply shocked, the mother + beatings* slapped her and scrubbed her face so forcibly that Mary spluttered and gasped (p. 151).[1]

Behavioral Symptoms correlated with
adult punitive and excretory contacts with children

1. One of Mary's presenting symptoms was her tenacious and often voluntarily induced constipation: To maintain her constipation, Mary would "squat on the floor with her knees drawn up, her arms tightly circling her bent legs and + excretory would hold herself rigid. . . . Then she would suddenly relax and continue her symptoms* interrupted activity. . . . During the constipation period, she would never defecate in the toilet although she was placed there at least twice a day, but after the feces began to appear she would finally have a large hard stool in her panties" (p. 150).

As noted, Mary, at the age of three, smeared feces all over her face (p. 151). Then the mother pushed the same feces over the face as she roughly scrubbed it clean (p. 151). The feces smeared near or in the nose thus provided + tic a likely origin for Mary's sniffing tic which appeared the next day for the first time. The following year the tic became worse whenever Mary was anxious (p. 152).

2. Mary's voluntary constipation reflected not only a disturbance pertaining + negative to excrement but also negative withholding and restriction. Excessive restriction behavior soon began to invade Mary's capacity for learning, i.e., she now began to be + learning troubled by a hesitancy in learning new motor skills such as tricycle-riding, (level 1) climbing and similar activities (p. 151).

+ hurting 3. Mary became destructive during her temper tantrums (p. 151). She also liked to be mean to her sister. When Mary and her little sister were left alone together, Mary would make the sister cry (p. 152).

NOTES

1 Note the relation of (a) the *spluttering* and *gasping* as the mother forcibly scrubbed Mary's face covered with feces, and (b) the *inspiratory-expiratory* content of Mary's tic which made its first appearance the following day.

Gerard's "Mary"
90

Stimulation-Symptom-and-Dream-Profile

	+ Separation Phobias	
	Night Terrors, Twilight States	
Sleep in Bed with Adult	Irrational Fears: Other	
	+ Irrational Tempers	
Adult Genital Erotic	Sexual Symptoms	
	Biting/Cutting, etc.	} *content of*
View Adult Coitus	Eyes	} *dreams and*
	Fire	} *symptoms*

	Learning Problems (levels 2 or 3, etc.)	
Punitive Yelling	Lying and Delinquency	
	Reversal of Affect	
+ Beatings	Closing Down Upon, Kill	} *content of dreams and*
	Falling	} *symptoms*

	+ Excretory Symptoms and Dreams	
	Anal Masturbation	
Preoccupation with Child's BM	Enuresis	
	Illness, etc.	
+ Anal Contacts	Pain	} *content of dreams and*
	Death	} *symptoms*
	Compulsions	

Case 91: Synopsis of Harold Kolansky's "Ann"

Ann, at the age of three years, was brought to Dr. Kolansky for intensive psychoanalytic treatment. Among her presenting symptoms were stammering and a tic-like compulsion to slap herself while stamping her foot (*Psychoanalytic Study of the Child*, Vol. XV, 1960, p. 262).

The following timetable of significant events taking place in Ann's early life may shed some light upon the onset of her "neurosis":

Ann's Age	Events
27 months:	mother delivers twins; Ann receives *intensive bowel-training* from her grandmother
29 months:	*stammering* and *tic* begins
30 months:	father stops letting Ann see his penis
31 months:	one of the baby twins dies of pneumonia
36 months:	father stops allowing Ann to sleep in bed with him
37 months (approx.):	therapy begins

Sources of Stimulation:
adult punitive and excretory contacts with children

+ early deprivation and suffering

1. Ann was born with a defect of her left foot which from her second to her sixth month of life required a splint, day and night. During this period she displayed "questionable seizures" for which she was placed on an anti-convulsant drug until she was eleven months old (p. 266).[1]

Ann was breast-fed until the age of three and a half months when she became increasingly cranky as the result of a deficiency in the supply of her mother's milk. Until she mastered self-feeding at the age of ten months, she took very little food. To complicate matters, at eight months Ann was refusing

Gerard's "Mary"
90

Stimulation-Symptom-and-Dream-Profile

	+ Separation Phobias
	Night Terrors, Twilight States
Sleep in Bed with Adult	Irrational Fears: Other
	+ Irrational Tempers
Adult Genital Erotic	Sexual Symptoms
	Biting/Cutting, etc.
View Adult Coitus	Eyes
	Fire

Biting/Cutting, etc. ⎫ *content of*
Eyes   ⎬ *dreams and*
Fire   ⎭ *symptoms*

	Learning Problems (levels 2 or 3, etc.)
Punitive Yelling	Lying and Delinquency
	Reversal of Affect
+ Beatings	Closing Down Upon, Kill
	Falling

Closing Down Upon, Kill ⎫ *content of*
                        ⎬ *dreams and*
Falling   ⎭ *symptoms*

	+ Excretory Symptoms and Dreams
	Anal Masturbation
Preoccupation with Child's BM	Enuresis
	Illness, etc.
+ Anal Contacts	Pain
	Death
	Compulsions

Illness, etc. ⎫ *content of*
Pain   ⎬ *dreams and*
Death   ⎭ *symptoms*
Compulsions

Case 91: Synopsis of Harold Kolansky's "Ann"

Ann, at the age of three years, was brought to Dr. Kolansky for intensive psychoanalytic treatment. Among her presenting symptoms were stammering and a tic-like compulsion to slap herself while stamping her foot (*Psychoanalytic Study of the Child*, Vol. XV, 1960, p. 262).

The following timetable of significant events taking place in Ann's early life may shed some light upon the onset of her "neurosis":

Ann's Age	Events
27 months:	mother delivers twins; Ann receives *intensive bowel-training* from her grandmother
29 months:	*stammering* and *tic* begins
30 months:	father stops letting Ann see his penis
31 months:	one of the baby twins dies of pneumonia
36 months:	father stops allowing Ann to sleep in bed with him
37 months (approx.):	therapy begins

Sources of Stimulation:
adult punitive and excretory contacts with children

+ early deprivation and suffering

1. Ann was born with a defect of her left foot which from her second to her sixth month of life required a splint, day and night. During this period she displayed "questionable seizures" for which she was placed on an anti-convulsant drug until she was eleven months old (p. 266).[1]

Ann was breast-fed until the age of three and a half months when she became increasingly cranky as the result of a deficiency in the supply of her mother's milk. Until she mastered self-feeding at the age of ten months, she took very little food. To complicate matters, at eight months Ann was refusing to sleep at night (p. 266).

+ punitive
yelling*

2. Prior to therapy, the mother would hit and yell at Ann in order to discipline her (p. 268, 270). Once, in Dr. Kolansky's and Ann's presence, the mother was able to admit how wrong she had been to yell at Ann. On another occasion, the mother apologized for yelling and hitting Ann after Ann had thrown a cup of milk at a little boy (p. 264, 270). The mother pleaded: " 'You know I made a terrible mistake getting so angry and spanking you. It will never happen again' " (p . 270).

+ adult
defecation

Ann was permitted to see her parents urinate and defecate at the toilet until she was two and a half years old (p. 266).

+ punitive bowel
training

3. "When Ann was twenty-seven months old her mother went to the hospital in the middle of the night" to deliver twins. The next morning, Ann woke to find her mother absent and was told by the grandmother that the mother had "gone shopping." *It was during this period that Ann's grandmother worked intensely upon Ann to force bowel-training* (p. 263).

Behavioral Symptoms correlated with
adult punitive and excretory contacts with children

+ excretory
symptoms*

+ compulsions*

1. Ann was disturbed by any tactile or visual contacts suggestive of excrement. "Stickiness of her hands . . . became quite intolerable. In fact any dirtiness and the mixing of one food with another became equally unbearable. She could not eat vegetables nor foods of dark colors.[2] She became disgusted at the sight of raw eggs" (p. 262). In the same vein, Ann displayed a hand-washing compulsion when she was offered wet sand to play with. Gradually, with encouragement from her therapist, she became less upset by such fecal-like contacts (p. 270).

+ stammer

+ tic

2. At twenty-nine months of age Ann woke up one morning and greeted her parents "with a deeply troubled facial expression as she said 'D-d-d--daddy, M-m-m--mommy. I can't talk!' " From that point on she stammered almost continuously (p. 262). This restriction and partial *withholding* of speech was paralleled by a tic-like compulsion to slap her thigh and to stamp her foot (p. 262), behavior which later was found to be a restricted expression of a massive urge to hit and kick (p. 274).

+ negative
behavior

+ learning
(level 1)

A state of withdrawal accompanied Ann's disturbed speech and tic. Dr. Kolansky noted how Ann who had been an "intellectually and physically precocious little girl changed from an occasionally cranky child into a withdrawn . . . child who began to stay in her pajamas most of the day." Her interests narrowed. Her activities were restricted to watching television, taking repetitive naps or standing in a corner, thumb in mouth (p. 262, 263).

+ pain* (sting)

3. Ann experienced a nightmare about bees and suffered from a constant phobia of bees stinging her (p. 265, 274).[3]

+ death*

Ann disclosed to Dr. Kolansky her feeling that she had been *responsible* for the death of her sister (p. 276-77) even though this concern was not rational.

+ preoccupation with illness*

Reflecting a morbid preoccupation with death, Ann was upset by an advertisement showing a man suffering from *sinusitis*. Ann was convinced the man was *dead*. The deep black indentations beneath the man's eyes, "the holes," Ann said "made him dead" (p. 278-79).

Sources of Stimulation:
children's tactile and visual erogenous contacts with the adult body

+ / − sleeping in bed with adults*

1. Ann liked sleeping with her father, a practice which the father found expedient to stop when she was three years old (p. 267).

+ adult nudity
− / + adult genital erotic*
(− / + view adult coitus*)

2. "The parents were unconcerned about leaving their bedroom and bathroom door open" until Ann was two and a half years old, at which time she began repeating the word "penis" all day long. "After that, the father no longer permitted her to see his penis" (p. 266).

Behavioral Symptoms correlated with
children's tactile and visual erogenous contacts with the adult body

+ separation phobias*

1. Prior to therapy "the child was terrified to leave the house" (p. 265).

+ / − irrational tempers*

2. Ann displayed only an "occasional" fit of temper such as when she threw a cup of milk at a little boy (p. 262-63), or hit, bit and scratched her baby sister and mother (p. 265). Dr. Kolansky, however, concluded that for the most part Ann "did not express anger directly" (p. 263).

+ irrational fears*

3. Ann suffered from an insect phobia, a prominent symptom which was accompanied by a fear of Zorro (p. 265) who "looked like a flying 'bug' " (p. 277). "The child constantly called attention to specks or cracks in the ceiling." The specks and cracks she thought were insects (bees, lightning bugs or flies).[4] "When she saw an insect, she would freeze in terror with arms crossed in front of her and would scream, 'Mommy come quick' " (p. 265). Ann also was troubled by a phobia of being bitten by animals (p. 266, 271).

+ twilight states*

Ann's fearfulness sometimes became even more severe at night. On the evening following dental repair of a cavity, she had trouble sleeping and complained, "I seen faces. . . . I'm afraid" (p. 280).

+ biting/cutting*

4. Ann's phobia of being bitten by animals (p. 266, 271) was matched by the numerous phantasies she expressed about the dangers of being bitten. For example, during therapy: "She picked up a toy crocodile, and reassuringly said to herself: 'He is just a baby; he doesn't have *big teeth to bite*' " (p. 268). Similarly, when Ann and her mother were cutting paper animals out of a book, "the child asked with anxiety: 'Are you going to cut their legs, ears, or tail off?' " (p. 280).

These concerns about teeth and biting were paralleled by Ann's habit of *actively biting* others. Even at the age of three, she bit her baby sister and mother (p. 265), and attempted to bite her therapist (p. 278).

+ sexual
symptoms*

Ann did show a remnant of her earlier anxieties in the form of frequent masturbation which appeared after her therapy was terminated (p. 281).

Fortunately, the sources for pathological stimulation in Ann's home were brought under control: (a) The parents now closed their bedroom door (to ensure sexual privacy); (b) The father stopped sleeping with Ann and stopped appearing in her presence with his penis exposed; (c) The mother ceased hitting and yelling as a means of giving Ann controls. She no longer punished Ann for soiling. Furthermore, Ann was given an opportunity in therapy to talk over her upset problems derived from her past history of ill-advised stimulation. With these therapeutic measures, Ann became essentially free of her presenting symptoms (p. 281).

NOTES

[1] Thereafter there occurred no further signs of seizures.

[2] See case synopsis 1 of Freud's "Little Hans."

[3] Compare with cases 77 and 100 of Kurt Junior and Ronny regarding the relation of *bee* phobias, soiling and anal stimulation.

[4] Excretory connotations, see Table of Definitions in Appendix 2.

Kolansky's "Ann"
91

Stimulation-Symptom-and-Dream-Profile

	+ Separation Phobias	
	+ Night Terrors, Twilight States	
+ Sleep in Bed with Adult	+ Irrational Fears: Other	
	+ Irrational Tempers	
Adult Genital Erotic	+ Sexual Symptoms	
	+ Biting/Cutting, etc.	} *content of*
View Adult Coitus	Eyes	*dreams and*
	Fire	*symptoms*

	Learning Problems (levels 2 or 3, etc.)	
+ Punitive Yelling	Lying and Delinquency	
	Reversal of Affect	
Beatings	Closing Down Upon, Kill	} *content of* *dreams and*
	Falling	*symptoms*

	+ Excretory Symptoms and Dreams	
	Anal Masturbation	
Preoccupation with Child's BM	Enuresis	
	+ Illness, etc.	} *content of*
Anal Contacts	+ Pain	*dreams and*
	+ Death	*symptoms*
	+ Compulsions	

Case 92: William

At the age of ten, Willie started therapy following his parents' recent divorce. The mother thought therapy would be helpful because Willie now needed a good "father figure." Additionally, she was a "bit concerned" that Willie was acting too immaturely for his age and, despite his superior intelligence, was achieving only fair grades in school.

Sources of Stimulation:
children's tactile and visual erogenous contacts with the adult body

1. At the age of ten, Willie still liked to put his head on his mother's lap and to let her fondle his hair.

+ adult nudity

2. Willie and his father would share showers until Willie was nine, a year prior to the onset of therapy. Willie also would accompany his father to the "club" locker room where he would see many big "hairy" men nude. Willie expressed concern about "grey specks" he had seen on his father's penis and on some of the men's bodies.

+ / − adult genital
erotic*

3. The father was known to put his hands into his pants' pockets and rub his penis compulsively even in the presence of his children. On one occasion, Willie recalled seeing his father come out nude from his adolescent sister's room at night.[1]

Behavioral Symptoms correlated with
children's tactile and visual erogenous contacts with the adult body

+ separation
phobia*

1. When he was ten years old, Willie would become upset when his mother would have to leave him alone in the house.

Willie also did not like leaving home for school. He did not like getting on buses and wanted his mother to drive him to the school.

+ irrational fears*
(phobias)

2. Willie was beset by an array of fears. He was afraid of fire and used this as an excuse for begging his mother not to leave him alone at home. Willie also demonstrated fears of people behind him, fears of the dark and of being killed in the dark. He reasoned, "Maybe a guy with a knife will pop out of my sister's room[2] and get me in the back." He was petrified of the blades of the big ventilating fan in the attic; he was phobic about birds, frightened that they would peck his head.

391

+ twilight state*

When Willie was two years old he experienced a frightening hallucination. He recalled "seeing" a plane flying around his bedroom in the dark. The plane reminded him of his father's "electric batteries, lighter, and big yellow wheel."

+ sexual
symptoms*

3. Willie was compelled to masturbate. He would pick at a "grey spot" on his penis until it bled.

+ biting/cutting*

4. As noted, Willie suffered from fears that birds would *peck* him on the head and fears that the big fan in the attic also could *cut* him with its giant rotating blades.

+ fire*

Willie was especially phobic of fire. When he saw smoke from the incinerator he thought the house was about to burn. He was scared to light a match since he was sure the flame would shoot up and burn his hand.

Sources of Stimulation:
adult punitive and excretory contacts with children

+ anal
stimulation*

1. Willie suffered from an *anal fissure* which caused him to pick compulsively at his anus. Additionally, his mother "occasionally" inserted suppositories into his rectum to help him with his stomach upsets.

+ observations of
adults
defecating
+ punitive
yelling*

Willie still remained in the bathroom while his father urinated and defecated.

2. The parents fought throughout their marriage. Bickering often took place at the dinner table and sometimes would culminate in the father grabbing his plate and leaving the room in a rage.

Behavioral Symptoms correlated with
adult punitive and excretory contacts with children

+ excretory
symptoms*

+ excretory
dreams*

1. Willie displayed what might be referred to as "bi-fecal" vision. Wherever he looked and whatever he heard, he sooner or later thought of excrement. He thought the grey specks he saw on his father's penis looked just like excrement. He reported a dream about *gas* and then associated to information about his dog passing gas. "It really smelled." He added that he himself also passed gas and said "my farts are deadly." He figured fat people must have a belly full of gas. Then he dwelt upon an event during which his principal passed gas at school in front of his mother. This reminded him of a boy at camp whom they called "Little Brown Farthood" and who liked to let out gas. It also reminded him of a big fat counselor at camp, who, according to Willie, "has the biggest poop in the whole world." On another occasion, Willie reported how he took a trip to a foreign country where he found the latrine urinals loaded with feces. . . . Finally, he spoke of a fake piece of "doody" which he thought of putting into his mouth in front of his mother. "Boy!" he figured, "Would she have a fit!"

At the age of two and a half when Willie "saw" planes flying around his room in the dark, he remembered suddenly becoming frightened, whereupon he let out a "big doody." Since that time, Willie stated, he had soiled himself "about once a year." He recalled defecating on the rug as an older child. Once, at camp, he recalled the "doody" coming down his legs[3] while he was talking with a group of the children.

(+ anal masturbation*) But Willie's anal and fecal symptomatology was most directly expressed by his compulsive anal masturbation. Unfortunately, the anal masturbatory contacts served as a source for pleasurable erogenous stimulation reinforcing the maintenance and repetition of the associated behavior.

+ negative emotion 2. Willie expressed a continuum of negative feelings and complaints about the world. The following quotations offer a sample of Willie's thoughts extracted from his weekly interviews: ". . . I *hate* the social studies teacher. . . . I *hate* my teacher. She's *stupid*. She's mean when she should not be. If I have my hand up she tells me to put it down. She expects me to do so much, four hard pages. . . . I *hate* my sister. . . . I get *bored* at home. . . . The principal is *not nice*. He farted. He's a stinker. . . . My counselor at camp, he has *no* humor. . . . He's *not nice*. He does *not* treat you like anything. There are moles in the river at camp. They are *ugly* things. . . . My dentist is *no good*, he doesn't have a sense of humor. . . . The Japs or the Germans and the colored people, they're dirty. . . . Hitler was full of *hate*. . . . If there is somebody I don't like, I want to be their friend but I *can't*. Then I'm not nice to them. . . . The hockey kids *hate* me.[4]

+ learning* (referral problem) 3. Willie's hate for his teachers and his negative reactions account for his inadequate performance in school. The emotional origin of his learning problem was substantiated by noticeable improvement of his grades after only a year's therapy.

+ kill* 4. Willie was beset with a fear (already mentioned) that a man would come out of his sister's room in the dark and would *kill* him by putting a knife in his back. He also had the feeling that the "doody" wart on his penis would cause his *death* unless he picked it off. He continued to pick at the area even after his physician cauterized the wart off for him.

+ death*
+ compulsions*

NOTES

1 Information from Willie's sister indicated that the father had secretly tried to seduce her.

2 Note the equivalence of this fear and Willie's memory of seeing his father come out of his sister's room at night in the nude.

3 Note the equivalence of this fecal memory and that of Kevin, case 43.

4 Compare with almost identical statements of Kevin, case 43, and of Rosenblatt's "Harold," case synopsis 93.

Willie
92

Stimulation-Symptom-and-Dream-Profile

	+ Separation Phobias	
	+ Night Terrors, Twilight States	
Sleep in Bed with Adult	+ Irrational Fears: Other	
	Irrational Tempers	
+ Adult Genital Erotic	+ Sexual Symptoms	
	+ Biting/Cutting, etc.	*content of*
View Adult Coitus	Eyes	*dreams and*
	+ Fire	*symptoms*
	+ Learning Problems (levels 2 or 3, etc.)	
+ Punitive Yelling	Lying and Delinquency	
	Reversal of Affect	
Beatings	+ Closing Down Upon, Kill	*content of dreams and*
	Falling	*symptoms*
	+ Excretory Symptoms and Dreams	
	+ Anal Masturbation	
Preoccupation with Child's BM	Enuresis	
	Illness, etc.	*content of*
+ Anal Contacts	Pain	*dreams and*
	+ Death	*symptoms*
	+ Compulsions	

Case 93: Synopsis of Bernard Rosenblatt's "Harold"

"Harold was a small, pale, thin boy with a very worried look." Although he was almost fourteen years old at the time of his referral for psychoanalysis, he looked eleven (*Psychoanalytic Study of the Child*, Vol. XVIII, 1963, p. 566). Despite an I.Q. of 142, he was barely able to pass in school. Among Harold's other presenting symptoms were "fears that his mother would *die* and bad dreams in which his mother was *run down* by a car" (p. 562). Most disturbing, however, was Harold's symptom of poking his finger into his rectum in order to dig out his feces. This behavior was accompanied by great concern that "the feces would not come out" (p. 562).

Sources of Stimulation:
adult punitive and excretory contacts with children

+ early
deprivation

1. Harold's troubles began at the age of three weeks when he was beset with persistent vomiting and "looked dreadful." When he was approximately three months old, a diagnosis of pyloric stenosis[1] was finally offered. Until he was six months old, Harold was given atropine with each feeding in order to relax the muscular spasm. Although the vomiting thereupon ceased, Harold became constantly drowsy from his medication and he did not gain weight. Not until another doctor took him off the atropine and changed him to a normal diet was his weight finally corrected when he was a year old (p. 565).

Unfortunately, the mother became so preoccupied with Harold's visceral functions that she *continued* to treat him as a helpless, passive, sick baby. She ended up taking over his ego not only by being over-preoccupied with any signs of illness Harold would display (p. 574) but also by interfering with his sublimated activities, e.g., by insisting upon arranging his stamps in his stamp album for him (p. 587).

+ adult
preoccupation
with child's
BM*
+ anal
stimulation*

2. For fourteen years, Harold's mother was preoccupied with his bowel movements.[2] Regularly, she inspected his bowel movements and frequently discussed them.[2] Additionally, from infancy onwards and until therapy was instituted, Harold was subjected to frequent enemas administered to him by his mother.[2]

Contributing to this picture of fecal preoccupation, Harold's adolescent brother left his enormous bowel movements in the toilet for Harold to see (p. 571).

− / + punitive
yelling*

3. Harold was exposed to hearing his father and older brother argue explosively with one another (p. 577).

Behavioral Symptoms correlated with
adult punitive and excretory contacts with children

+ excretory
symptoms*

+ anal
masturbation*

1. A primary source for referral, Harold spent almost an hour on the toilet each morning and evening, while he compulsively poked his finger into his rectum in order to remove feces (p. 562). Harold very much wanted treatment because of his anal symptoms which he called "his trouble" (p. 563-64). In public, he was afraid that he would not be able to control a compulsion to scream out loud about his excretory problems (p. 568).

+ obsessions and
compulsions*

Additionally, "Harold was preoccupied with cleanliness in lavatories for a long time. The school lavatories were usually too dirty to meet his exacting standards." Likewise, he obsessively worried about the cleanliness of toilets at hotel resorts. Upon arriving at a hotel room, Harold's first task would be to inspect toilets (p. 563).

+ negative
emotion

2. Harold intensely *disliked* his math teacher. He phantasized that the teacher was anti-semitic or had a *prejudice* against boys (p. 576). Harold *hated* biology and complained bitterly about the "*stinks*" of chemistry (p. 576). He complained that he *disliked* French because the word endings changed irregularly (p. 594-95). Despite his excellence in French when he was much younger, he now managed to do extremely poorly in the subject (p. 594-95). In general, Harold felt it would be inappropriate for him to do well in his exams for it would make his brother look "*stupid*" and it would make the brother into a "*nothing*" (p. 578).

+ negative
behavior

+ learning
(level 1)

3. Harold's dislike for his math teacher was coupled with his doing his math exercises in an *opposite* way than his teacher recommended. Then, he would make simple arithmetic mistakes and be marked wrong for them (p. 576).

In still other ways Harold's negativism contributed to the establishment of a learning problem. He *turned away from his homework* which he found intolerable because of feelings that home and school should have "*nothing*"[3] to do with one another (p. 576).

+ pain*

+ preoccupation
with illness*

4. Harold hypochondriacally reinforced his mother's preoccupations with his body temperature, his aches, and pains (p. 567-68). He feared a sudden attack of appendicitis and was concerned that "something was growing in there" (p. 568).[4] Similarly, he was afraid that his bowels had "lost their strength" (p. 569).

+ killing*
(suicide)

+ falling*

Suicidal thoughts supplemented Harold's hypochondriacal preoccupations with his innards. Harold feared that he would commit suicide by throwing himself off a train (p. 577). He feared that "he would *fall out* of the train on his trips to and from school" (p. 563). He also feared that he would suffer a *heart*

+ preoccupation with illness*
+ death*
+ closing down upon destructively* (crush)
+ falling*

attack from too much masturbation (p. 585).

Harold's preoccupation with death extended to obsessive thoughts of his mother dying. He suffered bad dreams in which *"his mother was run over by a car"* (p. 562) and he struggled with thoughts that his father might *die* of a heart attack if he were shocked with Harold's good marks. He pictured his father standing on the deck of a boat and suddenly *falling* overboard into the water (p. 579).

+ freezing of emotion

Harold's emotional involvement with death extended to "a recurrent feeling that others were somewhat lifeless or unreal" (p. 570).

Sources of Stimulation:
children's tactile and visual erogenous contacts with the adult body

+ adult nudity

1. It was the custom for the father and Harold's eighteen-year-old brother to go about the house naked with their big genitals exposed. They also were accustomed to bathing and shaving with Harold present; they never closed the bathroom door except to keep out the cold (p. 588). In addition, Harold shared a bedroom with his adolescent brother (until, with the help of analysis, Harold finally moved into a room of his own) (p. 585).

Furthermore, the mother had the right to enter the bathroom at any time[5] (p. 588), e.g., when it was being used by fourteen-year-old Harold or his eighteen-year-old brother.

− / + adult genital erotic* (? seduction)

The mother encouraged Harold to be a woman to the extent that she gave him a sanitary napkin to put in his pants during an aeroplane trip in case Harold might soil himself (p. 593).

Behavioral Symptoms correlated with
children's tactile and visual erogenous contacts with the adult body

+ irrational fears*

1. Harold's fears were multifold. He feared his bowels would lose their strength (p. 569); "he feared he might lose control and shout out" about his anal poking during school assemblies (p. 568); he feared "his mother would die" (p. 562); he feared he would jump out of a train and commit suicide (p. 563, 577); he feared putting his head under the water (p. 595).

+ biting/cutting*

2. Harold stayed away from biology because of his concerns about *"cutting things up"* (p. 576).

+ sexual symptoms*

3. Harold became attracted to viewing "adult" sexual movies. During this period he *masturbated while watching* wrestlers on television (p. 581). At school, he wrestled with the boys to the point of rubbing penises with them through their trousers. One of his friends called him a sex maniac because he did not stop the activity as soon as the friend wanted (p. 593). Harold feared his genitals had been damaged by this mutual masturbation (p. 581).

4. Harold suffered specifically from "a severe reading inhibition, an inhibition which was all the more incongruous because of his excellent vocabulary and his precise use of language for expressive purposes" (p. 585). Of significance, he dreamt of a "peculiar disease of the *eyes.*"6(p. 590).

NOTES

1 *Pyloric Stenosis:* The pyloric muscle is situated at the junction of the stomach and the upper intestine. Spasm of the pyloric muscle results in a stenosis, a narrowing, of this exit from the stomach. Such a spasm, therefore, results in overfilling of the stomach with food to the point of subsequent vomiting.

2 Personal communication from Dr. Rosenblatt.

3 The likelihood that Harold's learning problem was neither constitutional nor organic is attested to by his great progress during his psychoanalysis. Eventually, in a physics exam, he earned the highest score in his class (p. 596).

4 Compare with case 79 of Murray.

5 Compare with case 94 of Louis.

6 The dream in full had to do with "a girl with spots; she had a peculiar *disease* of the *eyes.*" Compare Harold's dream with that of Freud's "Rat Man" (synopsis 87) who dreamed of patches of *dung over the eyes.* The dreams occurred in the minds of these patients who had been exposed to both fecal *and* erotic voyeuristic stimulation.

Rosenblatt's "Harold"
93

Stimulation-Symptom-and-Dream-Profile

	Separation Phobias	
	Night Terrors, Twilight States	
Sleep in Bed with Adult	+ Irrational Fears: Other	
	Irrational Tempers	
Adult Genital Erotic	+ Sexual Symptoms	
	+ Biting/Cutting, etc.	} *content of*
View Adult Coitus	+ Eyes	} *dreams and*
	Fire	} *symptoms*

	Learning Problems (levels 2 or 3, etc.)	
Punitive Yelling	Lying and Delinquency	
	Reversal of Affect	
Beatings	+ Closing Down Upon, Kill	} *content of* } *dreams and*
	+ Falling	} *symptoms*

	+ Excretory Symptoms and Dreams	
	+ Anal Masturbation	
+ Preoccupation with Child's BM	Enuresis	
	+ Illness, etc.	} *content of*
+ Anal Contacts	+ Pain	} *dreams and*
	+ Death	} *symptoms*
	+ Compulsions	

Case 94: Louis

Mrs. M requested psychiatric help for her fifteen-year-old son, Louis. She was concerned that Louis was teased by other children, provoked fights with them and talked back to his teachers.

Louis's mother, who as a child had been exposed to a history of punishment overstimulation, as an adult discharged her negative feelings of hate upon Louis's father by endless fault-finding.[1] She did her best to make the males in the family helpless. Whereas she rendered the father helpless by devaluation, she rendered Louis helpless by infantilization.[1]

The intake worker wrote: "I spent most of the time listening to the mother berate the father in front of me. The mother would say to the father 'The whole trouble is that you don't like the children and don't give them any attention.' The father then would smile and agree 'Yes, that's right. I'm not a good father, and not a very likeable guy.' The mother then went on to blame everyone: her mother, her husband, the teacher, the school, the principal, and the other school children. She said that she had been ill and all this made her feel worse. . . . She concluded that she and Louis's father never did get along that well and she knew there never would be a change."

At the same time, the mother treated Louis as though he were a baby. Throughout his childhood she continued to be preoccupied with his visceral functions. She kept Louis "on the bottle" until he was five years old. For the first seven years of his life, Louis was subjected to his mother's administration of enemas and suppositories, and even when Louis was fifteen years old, he was permitted to defecate and urinate in front of her while they shared the facilities of the bathroom.

Sources of Stimulation:
adult punitive and excretory contacts with children

+ early
deprivation

1. Louis's mother complained that she had lost forty pounds during the first two years of Louis's infancy and that caring for him led to the "general deterioration of her condition." It, therefore, was not surprising that Louis was ill during his infancy: by the time he was seven months old, Louis had been ill with whooping cough and pneumonia.[2] For three or four months, Louis suffered high temperatures. During this time his food intake was limited and he

was regularly subjected to needle injections of antibiotics. The mother meanwhile received very little support from Louis's father who was told by a psychiatrist that he was unable to give to his son "because" of the lack of understanding he had received from his own parents.

+ anal
penetration*

2. To make matters worse, Louis was born with a "small rectum." Difficulties in moving his bowels resulted in rupture of his rectum. At the age of three months, Louis required surgery for the rectal hernia. Following the operation, the doctor told the mother to insert her finger into Louis's rectum each day in order to dilate the orifice. The physician gave the mother detailed instructions: first, she was to use her small finger for the procedure, then gradually change from the small finger to larger fingers until she was able to insert her thumb. The mother described with pride her ability to do this for her child. She was delighted that she had succeeded in stretching the rectal orifice at least "one inch."[3] Following this achievement, enemas and suppositories had to be administered to Louis about once a week until he was four years old. This routine was resumed for another two years when, at the age of five, Louis became ill with the "Asian Flu." The administration of enemas was upsetting for Louis and he recalled with displeasure how his mother would "sneak up" with an enema bottle and push it into his back.

+ punitive
yelling*

3. Louis's mother admitted that she was very upset by the presence of her ailing elderly mother in her home. She wanted to explode at her mother but instead found herself exploding at her husband and Louis.

(wrestling with
adults)

4. Louis wrestled "a great deal" with his older adolescent brother.

Behavioral Symptoms correlated with
adult punitive and excretory contacts with children

+ negative
behavior

1. At home, Louis and his mother continually argued and disagreed. From kindergarten on, Louis was considered a nonconformist by his teachers and even though he achieved an I.Q. score of *135* on the Bellevue Wechsler Intelligence Test, his work and effort in class were described as "only mediocre." He was admitted to a high school for advanced students but was required to leave after doing relatively poor work there. Follow-up contacts after Louis's diagnostic revealed that he also was admitted to a college of high standing, but after a year was expelled for poor grades.

+ learning*
(level 2)

+ negative
emotion

2. The father described Louis as having a constant *chip on his shoulder.* Louis himself admitted to being "arrogant" even though he felt he really was not sure of himself. He confided: "I have a big mouth and I open it at the wrong time to the wrong people." In school, Louis kept finding fault with his teachers. He advised the principal, for example, to fire a certain teacher because the teacher seemed "unfair."[4]

+ hurt

3. Louis managed to get himself *beaten* up in school too often. A paranoid-like tendency to set others against him was also reflected in his very first memory

involving an event which took place when he was six or seven years old: in the memory, Louis was being thrown into a swamp[5] by the kids.

+ pains* (aches)
+ non-organic
  illness*

4. At the age of fifteen, Louis suffered from *stomachaches* due to his habit of overeating. Louis's mother remarked "this is what happens when you eat like a pig" and complained that Louis still was eating all evening long from the time the family finished dinner until it was time to go to bed.

+ excretory
  symptoms*

When he was away at camp for a month, Louis suffered from continual "dysentery."

Sources of Stimulation:
children's tactile and visual erogenous contacts with the adult body

− / + sleeping in
bed with adults*
− / + adult genital
erotic*

1. Louis stated that *"occasionally"* he would get into bed with his mother.

2. As noted, Louis at the age of fifteen still exposed his penis as he would urinate in front of his mother.

Behavioral Symptoms correlated with
children's tactile and visual erogenous contacts with the adult body

+ temper
  tantrums*

1. The parents stated that Louis was nervous, fidgeted and occasionally exploded with *"temper tantrums."*

+ biting/cutting*

2. Louis recalled a repetitive dream he experienced when he was young. In the dream, there was a man who turned into a *wolf* with sharp teeth: a were-wolf.

NOTES

[1] See also case 44 of Leon.

[2] See Spitz with respect to the predisposition to physical illness among infants subjected to early deprivation. *(Psychoanalytic Study of the Child,* Vols. I, II, VI)

[3] During this same period the mother underwent surgery for a rectal condition. When she was questioned about it, she vaguely referred to a troublesome rectal fissure.

[4] Again compare with case 44 of Leon.

[5] Recall this is the time Louis was still subjected to his mother's enemas. *"The swamp"* brings to mind Louis's *watery bowel movements* after his repeated enemas.

Louis
94

Stimulation-Symptom-and-Dream-Profile

	Separation Phobias	
	Night Terrors, Twilight States	
Sleep in Bed with Adult	Irrational Fears: Other	
	+ Irrational Tempers	
Adult Genital Erotic	Sexual Symptoms	
	+ Biting/Cutting, etc.	} *content of*
View Adult Coitus	Eyes	} *dreams and*
	Fire	} *symptoms*

	+ Learning Problems (levels 2 or 3, etc.)	
+ Punitive Yelling	Lying and Delinquency	
	Reversal of Affect	
Beatings	Closing Down Upon, Kill	} *content of* *dreams and*
	Falling	} *symptoms*

	+ Excretory Symptoms and Dreams	
	Anal Masturbation	
Preoccupation with Child's BM	Enuresis	
	+ Illness, etc.	} *content of*
+ Anal Contacts	+ Pain	} *dreams and*
	Death	} *symptoms*
	Compulsions	

Case 95: Synopsis of Otto Fenichel's "Patient"

Otto Fenichel summarizes the case of "P,"[1] "a married man, forty years old, who in spite of his neurosis was successful in his professional life and was the father of several children." P "loved his wife deeply and was very considerate and affectionate to her, but sexual intercourse with her left him unsatisfied. He could obtain gratification only in onanism; this he practiced with the accompaniment of either transvestite phantasies or more often actual transvestite behavior" during which he dressed himself in his wife's clothes." He suffered also from obsessional, hypochondriacal and paranoid symptoms (*The Psychology of Transvestism in the Collected Papers of Otto Fenichel*, Vol. I, 1930, p. 171).

The patient's "mother died early and his father soon married again. His father was a man of petty, fault-finding . . . character, while the stepmother was domineering, quarrelsome, and very strict with the children" (p. 171).

Sources of Stimulation:
adult punitive and excretory contacts with children

+ anal
stimulation*

    1. As a little boy, P suffered from a *prolapse of the rectum which "required" his mother's pressing back his rectum with her finger*. P recalled the tremendously pleasurable feelings he experienced during these contacts (p. 172). Adding to anal stimulation during his childhood, P was infected with *pinworms* causing itching of the anal orifice (p. 172). He also received *enemas* from his stepmother (p. 176).

Behavioral Symptoms correlated with
adult punitive and excretory contacts with children

+ excretory
symptoms*

+ falling*

    1. As a child, P *dreaded flushing the toilet* which he believed might wash away a finger or his whole body along with his excrement (p. 174). At the same time, P dreaded that his prolapsed rectum might *fall* into the lavatory pan after his mother pressed back his rectum (p. 175).

+ closing down
upon
destructively*

+ excretory
dream content*
(back)

    In his adult life, P continued to be deeply preoccupied with his back. In this connection, he dreamt " 'my wife had a disease of the lungs. A stout woman stabbed her in the *back* from *behind*. Thereupon I found myself in a theatre with the upper part of my body naked' " (p. 176). This dream differed little from P's memories of childhood when he experienced conscious wishes to "thrust something into father's 'behind' " (p. 177).

404

2. Whereas P dreamed that his wife had a disease of the lungs (p. 176), it

+ preoccupation
with illness*

is not surprising that he suffered from a dread of infection (p. 177). During a prolonged period of hypochondria, P also suffered an intense dread of *death* (p. 175). Of note, whenever P, as a little boy, thought of his stepmother "tending to" his father's *excretory functions*, P experienced conscious wishes that his

+ death*

father would *die* (p. 176).[2]

+ compulsions*

3. During his childhood, P *compulsively* had to *count his toes* and clutch his *penis* (p. 175). This compulsive behavior appears to have been connected with his panic that *one of his fingers* might have been carried down the bathtub drain (p. 173-74).

Sources of Stimulation:
children's tactile and visual erogenous contacts with the adult body

− / + sleeping in
bed with adults*
(how often?)

1. P experienced feelings of excitation when as a child he would lie in bed with his father (p. 177).

+ adult nudity

2. P recalled seeing his stepmother's genitalia (p. 173).

+ adult genital
erotic*
(adolescent
sister)

3. As a latency age child, P participated in the masturbatory activities of his adolescent sister (p. 172). He experienced dreams of the "primal scene" (though it is not exactly clear whether P actually saw his parents copulating) (p. 175).

Behavioral Symptoms correlated with
children's tactile and visual erogenous contacts with the adult body

1. As a child P dreaded having his long hair *cut*. He treasured the locks

+ biting/cutting*

once they were cut off (p. 175).

+ sexual
symptoms*

2. During his childhood play with his sister, he and the sister would change clothes with one another. This behavior had begun early when P's sister at the age of seven had decided to dress him up as a living doll (p. 172). These activities which ultimately involved mutual masturbation and sensations resembling orgasm continued until P's sister was thirteen. After this time the sister was less and less willing to practice these sexual games (p. 172). Once the games with the sister finally stopped P began secretly to put on the sister's clothes (p.172-73). When he was seventeen, dressing up in women's clothes became associated with (solitary) masturbation. It was at this time that P's perversion became confirmed (p. 173). As an adult, P's dreams continued to reflect the past childhood contacts between his sister and himself. Thus he would dream of "embracing a little boy, and saying to him, 'my little brother' " (p. 176).[3] Furthermore, as an adult, P found sexual satisfaction only from transvestite masturbation (p. 171).

+ irrational fears*

3. As mentioned, P was phobic of his *fingers* going down the bath water drain. Some of his other phobias — phobias which have been referred to as

being associated with his rectal prolapse — involved the flushing toilet, lung disease, poison and death (p. 173-74, 175, 176, 177).

NOTES

[1] P stands for "patient" since Fenichel offers no name.

[2] See synopsis of Editha Sterba's "Deli," case 98.

[3] In the dream, P apparently was doing to himself what his sister once had done to him (see also case 26 of Randy).

Fenichel's "P"
95

Stimulation-Symptom-and-Dream-Profile

	Separation Phobias	
	Night Terrors, Twilight States	
Sleep in Bed with Adult	+ Irrational Fears: Other	
	Irrational Tempers	
+ Adult Genital Erotic	+ Sexual Symptoms	
	+ Biting/Cutting, etc.	} *content of*
View Adult Coitus	Eyes	} *dreams and*
	Fire	} *symptoms*
	Learning Problems (levels 2 or 3, etc.)	
Punitive Yelling	Lying and Delinquency	
	Reversal of Affect	
Beatings	+ Closing Down Upon, Kill	} *content of* / *dreams and*
	+ Falling	} *symptoms*
	+ Excretory Symptoms and Dreams	
	Anal Masturbation	
Preoccupation with Child's BM	Enuresis	
	+ Illness, etc.	} *content of*
+ Anal Contacts	Pain	} *dreams and*
	+ Death	} *symptoms*
	+ Compulsions	

Case 96: Synopsis of Marjorie Sprince's "Debby"

Despite an I.Q. of 156, twelve-year-old Debby was barely able to function. At the time of her referral for psychoanalysis, Debby was suffering from a *"school phobia"* which had become full-blown a year after she started grammar school. A year prior to her referral, she also developed *night panics,* fears of sickness and an inability to go out without her parents (*Psychoanalytic Study of the Child*, Vol. XVII, 1962, p. 420).

The mother still bathed and dressed Debby and supervised her bowel movements (p. 420).

Simultaneous analysis of Debby's mother by Kata Levy revealed that the mother was reacting to Debby as she had to her own mother and sister: Debby's mother "spent much of her childhood nursing a sick mother and sister" (p. 422), "against whom she had harbored unconscious death wishes" (p. 426). In turn, she eventually *overindulged* and *infantilized* Debby.

Sources of Stimulation:
adult punitive and excretory contacts with children

+ adult preoccupation with child's BM*

+ anal stimulation*

1. Because the mother believed that a daily bowel movement was absolutely essential, she instituted measures for Debby's bowel-training immediately after birth (p. 423-24) and administered daily *oral purgatives* until the family doctor intervened when Debby was three months old. *Examinations of bowel products,* however, continued for the next *twelve years,* as did the mother's custom of regulating Debby's bowel movements by the frequent administration of *rectal suppositories* (p. 424). The mother would employ the services of the father, e.g., to hold Debby down while she inserted the rectal suppositories (p. 427). "Debby described how she sat on a pot for hours at a time waiting for purgatives or the suppositories to work . . . while mother, in a neighboring kitchen, awaited a knock on the wall to summon her to examine the product." Even when Debby was thirteen years old the mother continued to wipe Debby at the toilet during periods of illness. In Debby's words, " 'When I'm ill, mother is wonderful; she will sit up all night and wipe my bottom for me' " (p. 425).

+ adult defecation

In return, Debby's *mother would sit on the toilet and defecate in Debby's presence.* This "need to share the toilet with Debby" became evident when it was discovered that the mother was unable to lock the bathroom door while she was on the toilet (p. 429).

One particular event stood out in Debby's mind. At the age of six, after a

+ anal
stimulation*

bout of constipation, Debby was taken to a *hospital for unmarried mothers* (where an aunt happened to be a matron) and was given an enema by a strange nurse. With horror, Debby remembered this incident during which she completely lost control of her bowels (p. 424). In the home, Debby was subjected to enemas in addition to the routine suppositories and purgatives (p. 434).

+ early
"punishment"

2. When the doctor gave two-year-old Debby a "shot," the needle broke off in her arm. Abortive attempts to remove the needle were carried out without Debby receiving any anaesthetic (p. 424).

Behavioral Symptoms correlated with
adult punitive and excretory contacts with children

+ negative
behavior

+ learning
(level 1)

1. Debby's negativism involved her withholdingness in relation to time arrangements. "Time arrangements were never suitable and never kept; punctuality or regularity meant 'giving in' "; i.e., for Debby, punctuality meant being positive rather than negative and therefore was not tolerated (p. 426). In spite of Debby's I.Q. of 156, her headmistress considered her to be a dull, unsatisfactory student. "When treatment started her school life had come to a standstill" (p. 420).

Unfortunately, Debby's negativism interfered with her ability to use insights in therapy (p. 419). All means available to her (intellectual arguments, rationalization and aggressive attacks) were used negatively to oppose facing reality situations (p. 425).

+ negative
emotion

2. With extreme demandingness, Debby relentlessly *blamed* her desperate parents (p. 420).

+ reversal of
affect*

+ delusions

Her devaluing emotions were also directed toward her own self in alternation with inappropriate bursts of affect reversal. Marjorie Sprince noted: "Debby's feelings of inadequacy were so gross that she could only compensate by the use of reversal and withdrawal into fantasy" (p. 430). She would imagine herself to be of royal blood and would then walk through the streets nodding regally to passers-by. She also developed a method of becoming "famous" for bad characteristics while insisting that "it is better to be top of the bottom than never to be top at all" (p. 430).

+ preoccupation
with illness*

+ obsessions and
compulsions*

3. Debby's hypochondriacal preoccupation with sickness and her fears about sickness served as a nucleus for much of her disturbed behavior: her fears of *sickness* precipitated her night panics and her inability to go outside without her parents (p. 420). "Also fear of *sickness* necessitated special meals at special times" (p. 420). "Magical actions and formulas had to be repeated to ward off sickness . . . and she would spend hours at night making noises. . . ." Her obsessions and rituals demanded "her mother's constant participation" (p. 420).

Adding to the complexity of Debby's hypochondriasis were her attacks of *migraine*. Angry and jealous when others were sick, Debby became "more ill

+ pain*

than the sick person, from whom she invariably managed to wrest all attention. Even Debby's migraines could be more severe than her mother's" (p. 426).

+ death*

Debby's fears also dwelt upon ghosts (shadows of the *dead*). She needed to have the door open, the light on and the radio playing all night to ward off her dread of the ghosts (p. 431).

+ closing down upon destructively* (strangle)

Apropos of these morbid symptoms, Debby was preoccupied with phantasies of being *strangled* and of strangling (p. 435). She also phantasized herself being *locked up in a cupboard* and tortured by someone "sticking witch's thistles up her vagina" (p. 431).

+ excretory symptoms*

4. In reality, Debby joined a group of girls who would poke pencils into her rectum and would allow Debby to poke pencils into theirs (p. 431).

Sources of Stimulation:
children's tactile and visual erogenous contacts with the adult body

+ sleeping in bed with adults*

1. Night panics drove Debby to her mother's bed. Displacing her father, Debby would fall asleep snuggled close to her mother's body (p. 420).

+ adult genital erotic*

The mother frequently chided Debby for masturbating while the two were in bed together (p. 431). Despite such chiding, mutual masturbation was the outcome of "this close and satisfactory body-bound relationship between mother and child" (p. 430).

Even when Debby reached the *age of nineteen* with plans to be married, she succumbed on three occasions to outbursts of night terrors necessitating a *return to her mother's bed*. On one of these occasions, Debby slept nightly in bed with the mother for an entire week (p. 444).

+ adult nudity

+ adult genital erotic*

2-3. Debby was *seduced by her paternal uncle when she was five years old*. The adult uncle and Debby had gotten into the grandmother's double bed together, whereupon the uncle invited Debby "to suck" and to "manipulate" his penis. The activity was interrupted by Debby's grandmother's voice. Debby promised the uncle not to tell anyone of their activities (p. 432).

Behavioral Symptoms correlated with
children's tactile and visual erogenous contacts with the adult body

+ separation phobia*

1. At the age of twelve, Debby was faced with a long-term, full-blown school phobia and was unable to go outside without her parents (p. 420).

+ night terrors*

2. On several occasions during her childhood, Debby awoke at night terrified by phobic dream-like hallucinations of "broken bits of worms"[1] in her bed. At such times, she could be calmed by no one (p. 431).

+ irrational fears*

Debby also suffered from phobias of sickness (p. 420) and of ghosts (p. 431).

+ irrational
tempers*

3. Debby's temper outbursts made "her family life intolerable and her social life impossible" (p. 420). Neither parent could help Debby control her fury (p. 434).

4. Debby's sexual activities included episodes of her poking pencils into girls' vaginas and rectums and submitting to their poking pencils into her. She

+ sexual
symptoms*

also developed sexual activities with her dog and used his penis to masturbate as though it were her own (p. 431). In line with such homosexually oriented behavior, Debby would borrow and wear boys' clothes (p. 429).

At the age of thirteen, Debby was able to say " 'my trouble is that I love girls not boys' " (p. 433). Her homosexual preoccupations made working with women teachers impossible. When, for example, her school phobia made home teaching advisable, Debby became terrified by the possible effects of her own overt seductiveness with her women tutors (p. 433). She became more and more aware that her homosexual feelings interfered with her normal activities, schooling and friendships (p. 439). Beset by such concerns, Debby "had to chase boys in an attempt to prove that she was not homosexual" (p. 440).

Addendum

Debby's homosexuality may be understood to reflect her sharing a bed with her mother; her masturbation during the bed-sharing; the mother's rituals of inserting suppositories and enemas into Debby's rectum; the mother's involvement with bathing Debby and wiping Debby at the toilet. Furthermore, the uncle's seduction of Debby when she was five years old must have contributed to her fears of men so as to discourage a satisfactory heterosexual adjustment.

NOTES

1 The "broken bits of worms" must have closely resembled bits of excrement with which Debby was so overinvolved (p. 431).

Sprince's "Debby"
96

Stimulation-Symptom-and-Dream-Profile

	+ Separation Phobias	
	+ Night Terrors, Twilight States	
+ Sleep in Bed with Adult	+ Irrational Fears: Other	
	+ Irrational Tempers	
+ Adult Genital Erotic	+ Sexual Symptoms	
	Biting/Cutting, etc.	} *content of*
View Adult Coitus	Eyes	*dreams and*
	Fire	*symptoms*
	Learning Problems (levels 2 or 3, etc.)	
Punitive Yelling	Lying and Delinquency	
	+ Reversal of Affect	
Beatings	+ Closing Down Upon, Kill	} *content of*
	Falling	*dreams and symptoms*
	+ Excretory Symptoms and Dreams	
	Anal Masturbation	
+ Preoccupation with Child's BM	Enuresis	
	+ Illness, etc.	} *content of*
+ Anal Contacts	+ Pain	*dreams and*
	+ Death	*symptoms*
	+ Compulsions	

Case 97: Martin

At the age of six, Martin came to the clinic for his first diagnostic evaluation. At that time his intake summary read: "Martin is an adopted youngster. He has been showing symptoms of intense masturbation and pulling out tufts of his hair. He has shifted from a passive youngster to having violent temper tantrums. He is doing very poorly in school and is very clinging with his mother."

By the time of Martin's evaluation, his parents had been divorced for several years. His mother had demanded the divorce because of the father's sadistic treatment. In particular, she refused to submit to his sadistic demands during sexual intercourse. Following the divorce, Martin's father set up an apartment with a mistress. Martin would visit them weekly.

Sources of Stimulation:
children's tactile and visual erogenous contacts with the adult body

+ sleeping in bed with adult*

1. Martin at the age of six *regularly slept with his mother throughout each night* because, to quote his mother, "some of the older boys frightened him with threats of the boogie man." The mother also explained that she was compelled to take Martin into her bed because his room was so cold in the winter. Following her first interview at the clinic, however, the mother did initiate steps to limit the bed-sharing.

+ adult nudity

+ adult genital erotic*

2. Martin would see his mother as well as his father and the father's mistress without clothes. When Martin was little he and his father would urinate together into the toilet. The father and Martin would also bathe together. During his second diagnostic hour Martin went on to explain: "Remember when we talked about the pee pee in front and the bum in the rear, well I've seen some one put his *peepee* into a behind." He went on to say how he had done this with a little girl and how his father had tried to do it to him in the bathtub. Martin said he tried to put his hand over his rear to keep his father from poking him there.

(+ view adult coitus*)

Martin also reported to his mother how he had seen his father and the father's girl friend in bed together where they were doing "funny things."

Behavioral Symptoms correlated with
children's tactile and visual erogenous contacts with the adult body

+ separation phobia*

1. The mother was concerned because Martin would be very upset when she attempted to leave the house. If she went out to a meeting once or twice a

412

week for an hour in the evening he would become "hysterical." It is understandable, therefore, that Martin was frightened at school. Often he would leave class in the middle of the morning in order to run home.

2. Martin suffered from nightmares and fears of the "boogie man" which drove him to his mother's bed at night. The nightmares were so intense that Martin would wake up screaming.

+ night terrors*

+ eyes*

3. Martin presented a reading problem for many years. He didn't learn to read until he was in the fifth grade when finally his mother successfully prevailed upon the school to offer him remedial instruction.

+ temper
 tantrums*

4. A presenting symptom, as already noted, was the eruption of violent temper tantrums in this otherwise passive, compliant child.

+ sexual
 symptoms*

5. "Intense and compulsive masturbation" accompanied by hair-pulling and thumb-sucking[1] constituted another presenting symptom. Martin's continual masturbation resulted in his penis becoming very "sore."

Sources of Stimulation:
adult punitive and excretory contacts with children

− / + beatings*

1. Martin was spanked by his father to the extent that he phantasized it was because of these spankings that his mother asked for a divorce. Martin's maternal aunt would also severely punish him for his compulsive masturbation.

+ yelling* and
 violence

2. Martin was exposed to his parents' loud and violent fights during which his father would "beat up" his mother.

+ observances of
 adult defecating

+ anal
 stimulation*

3. The mother and father "taught" Martin how to defecate by giving him personal demonstrations on the toilet. In addition, it will be recalled, Martin's father attempted to place his penis to Martin's anus.

Behavioral Symptoms correlated with
adult punitive and excretory contacts with children

+ enuresis*

1. At the age of six, Martin was still wetting his bed.

+ negative
 behavior

2. In general, however, Martin's problems centered upon his negativism. First, Martin's negativism expressed itself in the form of his opposing directions in school. When he was asked during his diagnostic interview what he thought his "problem" was, Martin explained very seriously "when the teacher tells me to use the red crayon I use the green one; when she tells me to use the blue crayon I use the yellow one; BUT, when she tells me to use the brown crayon I use the brown."[2]

+ learning
 problem*
 (level 2)

With such negativism it is not surprising that Martin often refused to do his homework, could not seem to understand or follow directions and eventually developed a serious learning problem which required him to repeat second grade. Although he tried hard to be a good little boy and never was much of a behavior problem in school, he still performed unsuccessfully academically.

3. Unfortunately, against the clinic's advice Martin never was given an opportunity to receive therapeutic help for his problems. He was not seen again at the clinic until nine years later when he returned for a second diagnostic evaluation. By that time, Martin's negative reactions to authority figures had become + delinquency*   expressed by delinquent behavior. At the age of fifteen, Martin was picked up by the police for shoplifting.

4. Martin demonstrated no symptoms in relation to hurting himself or others. However, when he allowed himself to express some phantasies during his − / + kill*   first diagnostic meetings, he referred to killing and death. For example, just before telling of his baths with his father and his father's genital contacts with his anus, Martin told the story of a cow who went into the water and got killed.

NOTES

[1] It is likely that what Martin could not discharge upon his father's penis and pubic hair during close bodily contact in the bathtub, he completed upon his own body and hair: sexual forepleasure looking-grasping-mouthing syndrome was completed by his alternately masturbating, pushing his thumb into his mouth and grasping at the hair on his head (also see Buxbaum, *Psychoanalytic Study of the Child*, Vol. XV, 1960, p. 247, 253).

[2] Note the only *positive* response appears in relation to the color brown, the color of feces.

Martin
97

Stimulation-Symptom-and-Dream-Profile

	+ Separation Phobias	
	+ Night Terrors, Twilight States	
+ Sleep in Bed with Adult	Irrational Fears: Other	
	+ Irrational Tempers	
+ Adult Genital Erotic	+ Sexual Symptoms	
	Biting/Cutting, etc.	} *content of*
+ View Adult Coitus	+ Eyes	} *dreams and*
	Fire	} *symptoms*

	+ Learning Problems (levels 2 or 3, etc.)	
+ Punitive Yelling	+ Lying and Delinquency	
	Reversal of Affect	
Beatings	Closing Down Upon, Kill	} *content of*
	Falling	} *dreams and*
		} *symptoms*

	Excretory Symptoms and Dreams	
	Anal Masturbation	
Preoccupation with Child's BM	+ Enuresis	
	Illness, etc.	} *content of*
+ Anal Contacts	Pain	} *dreams and*
	Death	} *symptoms*
	Compulsions	

Case 98: Synopsis of Editha Sterba's "Deli"

Deli was seven and a half years old when she was brought to Editha Sterba in Vienna for psychiatric consultation (*Psychoanalytic Quarterly,* 1935, p. 137). This little girl, of average intelligence, had been suffering from a fear of dogs, a fear so intense "that she hardly dared leave the house and . . . refused to go to school." Even when Deli saw a dog at a distance she cried and screamed while she convulsively clutched her mother (p. 138).

Sources of Stimulation:
adult punitive and excretory contact with children

+ anal
stimulation*

1. Over a period of six weeks prior to the onset of her fears, Deli had been subjected to daily enemas. The enemas had been administered as part of treatment for a "severe digestive disturbance." The enemas were particularly disturbing because, at times, "Deli had not been able to retain their content for a sufficient length of time and was afraid of soiling her bed" (p. 138).

Of note, Deli had already been bowel-trained by the age of one (p. 138).

Behavioral Symptoms correlated with
adult punitive and excretory contacts with children

+ excretory
symptoms*

1. As she played a "tube game" during her therapy hours, Deli demonstrated an intense preoccupation with anal poking. The game consisted of her pushing a fountain pen filler over and over again into a doll's anal region. At the same time, she breathed heavily in evident sexual excitement (p. 141-42). Eventually Deli gained enough courage to say: " 'Why do I always have to think about the tube game . . . we shall have to find out why.' " Yet, when asked about a time that Deli must have *really* played the game, Deli "flew into a rage and demanded, 'How did you know about that?' " Finally, she was able to confide that she had tried to poke her finger and a tube into her sister's rectum but had been prevented from doing so when the sister cried and brought the mother to the scene (p. 146-47, 150).

+ anal
masturbation*

Deli also confided how she would poke her finger into her own rectum. She explained that a long time ago when she was little she often stuck her hands into her behind and shoved her fingers up and down. First, she would do this with her right hand and then with her left. When the mother wanted to know why Deli groaned at such times Deli "whispered it to her," whereupon the mother threatened that Deli would be put out of the house if she continued doing such

416

things (p. 151).

2. During her "tube game" Deli would reason that she would not have to be afraid of dogs anymore: for she could keep pushing the tube into the dog's behind until the dog died (p. 142). Soon, however, Deli became afraid not only of dogs but also of death (p. 145).

Deli's concerns about death must have been aggravated when her mother found her attempting to put an enema tube into her sister's rectum: at that time the horrified mother warned Deli, " 'You could injure your sister so severely with the tube that she might even die' " (p. 147). Deli also recalled her mother once sighing, " 'You'll be the death of me yet!' " Since that time, Deli could not get the tube game or dying out of her head. " 'I keep having to think about *dying* and the cemetery,' " she explained. When a school mate had scarlet fever, Deli became afraid she would catch the disease which she thought would be fatal. Not only was Deli afraid that *she herself would die* but that also her *teacher* as well as her *mother would die* (p. 145, 146). She "no sooner had admitted this anxiety than she began to weep bitterly . . . clasped her hands and beside herself with fear cried out . . . 'But please *Dr. Sterba* you won't *die* will you?' "

3. Deli's schoolwork was very poor. She failed one year and was required to repeat the grade, whereupon she did even *worse* than in the preceding year. Whereas arithmetic initially had not been a special problem, she now displayed a *total inability* to handle this subject (p. 143-44). Deli explained that anything to do with numbers now directed her thoughts to the number of months and years left before her teacher would *die* (p. 146).[1]

4. In Deli's phantasy games, children were beaten, *enchained* and *burned*. Deli also thought of binding her mother with "100,000 yards of cord" prior to burning her (p. 149). Deli displayed no *symptoms* or *dreams* pertaining to these concerns. However she did report a dream involving "falling," i.e., a dream of being thrown out of the window (p. 152).

Sources of Stimulation:
children's tactile and visual erogenous contacts with the adult body

1. When on one occasion Deli awoke screaming from dreams, her mother tried to quiet the child by resting with her in bed (p. 152). It is implied that Deli stayed in the mother's bed until she fell asleep.

2. Deli may have watched through the bars of her crib as her parents copulated (p. 152).

Behavioral Symptoms correlated with
children's tactile and visual erogenous contacts with the adult body

1. Deli was three and a half when her father scolded her for letting a dog playfully take her hand in its mouth (p. 139). Thereupon she developed a fear

+ irrational fear* of dogs which, however, remained insignificant until a few months prior to her referral for therapy (p. 138). Then she became so possessed by her fear that she trembled and became breathless after having been outside in the streets.[2] Visiting "the park was intolerable to her . . . and while her sister played with other children, Deli sat stiffly beside her mother on a bench . . . and whenever a dog appeared she began to scream with such anguish that everyone came running to the spot" (p. 138-39).

+ biting/cutting* 2. Deli was convinced that she would be bitten. "She . . . blurted out . . . 'The dog could peck me . . . he could stick his snout in and *bite* something off' " (p. 140). She also reported a *wolf* dream: " 'A wolf was in the room, then a big white man came and seized hold of me and wanted to throw me out the window' " (p. 152).

+ separation phobia* 3. Deli's fear of dogs led to school-phobic reactions and a tendency for Deli to remain excessively close to her mother. Like "Little Hans," she hardly dared leave the house. Upon being compelled to attend school she would become so paralyzed with fear that only with the utmost difficulty would she be able to gain some composure in the classroom (p. 139).

+ night terrors* 4. Deli on one occasion awoke screaming with such fear that her mother had to take her into bed to quiet her (p. 152).

+ sexual symptoms* 5. The mother was provoked by Deli's masturbating and sternly prohibited this activity when Deli was three years old (p. 154).[3]

NOTES

[1] See case 89 of Tal who was exposed to enemas and who also would not learn "numbers" because he was afraid to know at what age he would die.

[2] See Anny Katan's case 24 of Margaret.

[3] Once again, it is likely that parents copulated in front of a child and then felt entitled to scold the child for the activated masturbatory behavior. Likewise, the mother could stimulate Deli's rectum with daily enemas, yet could not understand Deli's anal masturbation.

Sterba's "Deli"
98

Stimulation-Symptom-and-Dream-Profile

	+ Separation Phobias	
	+ Night Terrors, Twilight States	
Sleep in Bed with Adult	+ Irrational Fears: Other	
	Irrational Tempers	
Adult Genital Erotic	+ Sexual Symptoms	
	+ Biting/Cutting, etc.	} *content of*
View Adult Coitus	Eyes	} *dreams and*
	Fire	) *symptoms*

	+ Learning Problems (levels 2 or 3, etc.)	
Punitive Yelling	Lying and Delinquency	
	Reversal of Affect	
Beatings	Closing Down Upon, Kill	} *content of* *dreams and*
	+ Falling	) *symptoms*

	+ Excretory Symptoms and Dreams	
	+ Anal Masturbation	
Preoccupation with Child's BM	Enuresis	
	+ Illness, etc.	} *content of*
+ Anal Contacts	Pain	} *dreams and*
	+ Death	) *symptoms*
	+ Compulsions	

Case 99: Philip

Five-year-old Philip, with an I.Q. of 104, was "impossible" at school where he consistently bit children, defecated in the classroom and urinated onto the classroom fire extinguisher. His mother had taken him to an inpatient diagnostic center, where, after a ten-day workup, it was decided he was a hapless psychotic who should be permanently hospitalized. Fortunately, his mother was infuriated by this decision, brought her son back home and then sought further diagnostic advice.

Sources of Stimulation:
children's tactile and visual erogenous contacts with the adult body

+ sleeping in bed with adult*

1. Prior to therapy, Philip often slept in bed with his mother, especially when his mother's boy friend, his new "father," was not around. The mother sometimes enjoyed close contact with Philip when they *snuggled together* in bed. On one occasion, she elaborated how at such times her body seemed to be becoming "bigger and bigger."

+ adult nudity

2. Philip would regularly see his "parents" without clothes when they were undressing and bathing.

(+ view adult coitus*)

3. Two years prior to therapy, when he had been sleeping in his mother's room, Philip witnessed his mother and her boy friend copulating.

However, over an extended period of time, Philip was exposed to sexual stimulation of far more serious proportions. The mother had brought Philip daily to a woman baby-sitter whose husband, Cecil, was a pedophile. Cecil exploited little Philip regularly from the time Philip was four until he was seven years old. Cecil would kiss Philip on the lips, and in front of Philip he would defecate on the bathroom floor or urinate into the bathtub. Following these exhibitionistic procedures, Cecil would practice anal intercourse upon Philip.

+ adult genital erotic*

Philip was also exposed to viewing this man practicing sexual intercourse with his own little daughter.[1]

Philip did not tell his mother about these activities. However, he did complain to her about his "sore bum." In response to this, his mother took him to a pediatrician who suggested that Philip had been sexually abused. The mother was indignantly enraged at this diagnosis and left the doctor in a huff, convinced that he was "a queer." However, when Philip's therapist informed her, at the beginning of therapy, that these activities were still going on, the mother

420

fell to her knees upon the floor and burst out sobbing.

For a year the mother superbly cooperated in therapy. Contacts with Cecil were immediately terminated, while the mother took special steps not to expose Philip to her nudity or that of her husband-to-be. Bed sharing and kissing were stopped. Interestingly enough, Philip's most severe symptoms cleared dramatically over the year's period. In school his behavior improved to the extent that Philip returned home with reports of A in learning and B in conduct. The mother was so impressed with Philip's progress she began proselytizing among her friends and acquaintances so as to help them not expose their children to excessive erotic stimulation.

Behavioral Symptoms correlated with
children's tactile and visual erogenous contacts with the adult body

+ temper
tantrums*

1. Prior to therapy, Philip would behave "like an angel," compliant and helpful when alone with his mother or other adults. However, as soon as he did not receive individual attention or when other children were around, he "changed radically." He would hit, spit, throw garbage all over the hall, kick the teacher, break windows, etc.

+ sexual
symptoms*

2. Part of Philip's disturbed behavior in school at the time of his referral was his penile exhibitionism: he urinated in the classroom closet, onto the fire extinguisher and into a wall socket so as to short the electrical system. Then, during the first year of therapy such sexualized behavior gradually disappeared. As long as Philip was able to verbally unload in therapy his sexual feelings and his sexual memories of Cecil's perverted behavior, Philip's sexual acting out remained at a minimum. At worst, he became involved with kissing another little boy friend.

However, Philip's surge of health turned out to be too much for his mother to tolerate. Having been a sexually abused child herself who during adolescence would often sleep in a church to avoid her uncle's sadomasochistic advances, she apparently experienced as an adult a need to have her childhood problems repeated. Perhaps it was for this reason that the mother suddenly demanded that Philip never speak again in therapy about the homosexual assaults to which he had been subjected. Likewise, she ordered that he stop the Mellaril medication which had been prescribed for his excitable disturbed behavior, this despite the dramatic progress he had demonstrated during his first year of therapy. The mother's excuse for her decision was based upon her conclusion that Philip had "outgrown" his problems and did not need the kind of therapy which reminded him of his past.

Unfortunately, Philip obeyed his mother's bidding. No longer would he talk in therapy about his sexual memories and wishes stimulated by Cecil's activities. What he could not talk about he began once again to act out. In school, he was found exposing himself in the "basement" where he hung around the urinals. In class, too, his disturbed behavior reappeared. Soon he was found urinating on the floor and leaving his feces under his chair — (all behavior, it will be recalled, quite similar to that of Cecil's exhibitionistic activities). At home, Philip simulated intercourse as he masturbated endlessly into a hole he had made into the mattress of his bed.

+ biting/cutting/
 stomach*

3. A presenting problem which had originally led to his being branded "incurably psychotic" was Philip's referral obsession with biting children's faces. These reactions of biting and devouring reappeared in his dreams. Philip reported the following dreams: "I was riding in a boat and a shark, he kissed me . . . there was a fish that said *'eat me, eat me'* "; and, "A scary monster, he went and killed me; so I was still alive in his *stomach*."

+ eyes*

4. With full force, Philip hurled his ball-point pen directly at his therapist's *eye*, in his words, "by accident." Even Philip looked frightened as the blood trickled down his therapist's face. The point of the pen had penetrated and became lodged in the flesh just below the therapist's right eye.[2]

This focus upon the eye also appeared within Philip's "make-believe" dreams: "We were riding along one day and there was a circle for traffic and we crashed and tipped over. My mother was killed and I went *blind*." "Once upon a time I had a beast. There was one thing about him, he didn't act right. He didn't see where he was going. He must have been *blind*. So I sent him to a doctor."

+ / − fire*

5. Philip was preoccupied with the classroom *fire* extinguisher. Urinating upon it constituted one of his bizarre presenting problems.

Sources of Stimulation:
adult punitive and excretory contacts with children

+ early
 deprivation

1. When Philip was an infant, his mother claimed that she did not have the time to pick him up. She, therefore, would prop his bottle for feeding. Furthermore, because she "needed money" she left him at night with a neighbor who was "irresponsible and frightened of kids." She felt this "was o.k. because Philip slept through the night."

+ anal
 stimulation*

2. Philip's three years of submission to *sodomy* involved not only tactile and visual contact with a sexually activated male body, but also intense anal stimulation accompanying rectal penetration. Philip also was exposed to seeing his seducer defecate upon the bathroom floor.

+ beatings*

3. Approximately twice a week, the mother's boy friend would take down Philip's pants and strap him with a belt. These punishments would frequently be incurred by Philip's saying "swears."

In turn, the mother was known for her explosive tempers during which she

+ punitive
  yelling*

would lose control of herself while yelling at Philip. She admitted that she "hollered at" Philip and beat him to no avail. She had tried every kind of punishment without success.

Behavioral Symptoms correlated with
adult punitive and excretory contacts with children

+ excretory
  symptoms*
(+ anal
  masturbation*)

1. Philip compulsively poked his finger into his rectum (repeating the erogenous feelings he experienced during anal intercourse) and smeared feces on his bathroom walls.[3]

+ negative
  behavior

2. When Philip was first asked during his diagnostic interview what he thought were his problems and worries he answered "I always *forget* what desk to sit in." Wherever he went, this problem of doing the "wrong" thing, the "opposite" of what he should do, continued to provoke others. Both at school and at day camp he opposed rules and authority to the point that his teachers and counselors were exasperated. Philip's "forgetting" very conveniently helped him in concealing his misdeeds. During therapy, Philip justified his withholding as he related a make-believe poem: "I am the King of Silence. Who will be my prince? Silence is my prince."

+ lying*

In addition to his withholding any reference to his misdeeds, Philip found no difficulty in reversing the truth in order to avoid punishment. Thus, despite complaints from his home and school with reference to his foul tongue, Philip claimed he *never* swore and that he was "shocked" to hear that boys would ever want to say a "naughty thing."

+ delinquency*

+ closing down
  upon
  destructively*
  (strangle)

+ pain*

3. At the time of his referral, Philip was hitting children in school, kicking the teacher and breaking the classroom windows. In his neighborhood, Philip was reported to have stabbed another child and was observed chasing a very tiny kitten with a large stick. He also was discovered *choking* an older child. At camp, he pretended to be kind to a blind[4] child while inducing the child to approach a hole and trip. At home, his mother discovered nails he had placed upright in her bedroom carpet. Apparently, he had hoped his parents would puncture their bare feet on the nails.

+ falling*

+ excretory
  dream content*
+ killing*
+ falling*
+ death*
+ killing*

Philip's *dreams* reflected similar themes pertaining to hurt, falling and death: "Elizabeth *fell* in the turpentine. She jumped in it and it was all *gas*. She drowned in the gas"; and a dream: "The monster went to *kill* me. . . . I fell asleep. I *fell* out of bed. I was trapped by the monster and they almost got me *dead*." . . . "A car crashed into us and we tipped over and my mother was *killed*."

+ reversal of
  affect*

4. Reversal of emotion appeared in several forms. Even though Philip essentially was a helpless little boy overwhelmed by excessive sexual and punishment stimulation, he took the stance of "Superman." Hour after hour he drew pictures of Superman (and with the S on his jersey reversed). Similarly, Philip

tried to give the appearance of the "nicest" "golden boy" one might ever want to meet, at which times he reversed his display of his ever-present hate. Philip revealed a realization of his reversal of emotion as he told the following story about "prettiness" covering up evil: "There was once a duck, the ugliest duck I ever saw. When he grew up he looked *pretty*. When he was old he still looked *pretty*. But when he died he looked *pretty* still. One thing though, he was supposed to go to heaven, but instead he went to hell."

NOTES

[1] Eventually, Cecil was sought by the police in connection with complaints of his pedophile activities.

[2] See case 100 of Ronny regarding a similar episode during which Ronny poked a prickly stick into a girl friend's eye.

[3] This behavior responded to therapeutic efforts to help Philip substitute a form of behavior which was not harmful and provocative: each week his therapist gave Philip a can of foam shaving cream with the suggestion that he could poke in the shaving cream and smear it on the bathroom tiles the same way he had smeared the feces.

Philip was helped to understand how the sexual activities with Cecil had been very exciting and, therefore, it was not his fault that he had come to find intense pleasure from anal poking. On the other hand, it was explained to him how he could get over many of his worries and problems if he could find a way to control his anal masturbation.

[4] Notice once again the appearance of a symptom pertaining to the *eye* (see above).

Philip
99

Stimulation-Symptom-and-Dream-Profile

	Separation Phobias
	Night Terrors, Twilight States
+ Sleep in Bed with Adult	Irrational Fears: Other
	+ Irrational Tempers
+ Adult Genital Erotic	+ Sexual Symptoms
	+ Biting/Cutting, etc.
+ View Adult Coitus	+ Eyes
	+ Fire

} *content of dreams and symptoms*

	Learning Problems (levels 2 or 3, etc.)
+ Punitive Yelling	+ Lying and Delinquency
	+ Reversal of Affect
+ Beatings	+ Closing Down Upon, Kill
	+ Falling

} *content of dreams and symptoms*

	+ Excretory Symptoms and Dreams
	+ Anal Masturbation
Preoccupation with Child's BM	Enuresis
	Illness, etc.
+ Anal Contacts	+ Pain
	+ Death
	Compulsions

} *content of dreams and symptoms*

Case 100: Ronny

Ronny, an eleven-year-old boy from a prominent professional family, displayed "perfect" manners during his first diagnostic hour. He gave the impression of a well-contained, sensitive and kindly boy. His family had requested therapy for Ronny's debilitating learning problem. Despite his average score (I.Q. 91) on the Bellevue Wechsler intelligence test, Ronny, at the age of eleven, was doing no better than first and second grade work and did not even know the months of the year.

Ronny was in treatment for four years. During this period his learning problem was resolved to the extent that at the age of fifteen he was doing seventh and eighth grade work.

Sources of Stimulation:
children's tactile and visual erogenous contacts with the adult body

1. At the age of eleven, Ronny still lay next to his mother on the bed to watch TV and during the following year continued to rest on the bed with her.

+ sleeping in bed with adults*

When he was about seven years old, Ronny would visit his grandmother on weekends and would sleep very close to her throughout the night. One of Ronny's adolescent brothers offered him additional frequent close physical contact in the form of tickling bouts while wrestling with Ronny.

+ adult nudity

2. During latency, Ronny shared a bedroom with his two brothers who were more than ten years older. They would walk around the room in the nude while they would tell Ronny "not to look."

The father would be seen walking around the house in just his undershorts, with his penis showing through. Ronny was particularly struck by his father's hairy buttocks when the father would appear nude on the toilet or in the bathtub.

During a weekend visit to his grandmother's, Ronny, at the age of seven, viewed his grandmother unclothed when he shared her bed. At that time, Ronny saw his grandmother urinate into a bedpan and was very much aware of her pubic hair.

A final example of Ronny's exposure to adult exhibitionism was his mother's habit of regularly leaving her girdle, slips, bra, nylon stockings and panties "stained with little lumps" to hang in Ronny's bathroom. Once Ronny opened

426

Philip
99

Stimulation-Symptom-and-Dream-Profile

	Separation Phobias
	Night Terrors, Twilight States
+ Sleep in Bed with Adult	Irrational Fears: Other
	+ Irrational Tempers
+ Adult Genital Erotic	+ Sexual Symptoms
	+ Biting/Cutting, etc.
+ View Adult Coitus	+ Eyes
	+ Fire

⎫ *content of*
⎬ *dreams and*
⎭ *symptoms*

	Learning Problems (levels 2 or 3, etc.)
+ Punitive Yelling	+ Lying and Delinquency
	+ Reversal of Affect
+ Beatings	+ Closing Down Upon, Kill
	+ Falling

⎫ *content of*
⎬ *dreams and*
⎭ *symptoms*

	+ Excretory Symptoms and Dreams
	+ Anal Masturbation
Preoccupation with Child's BM	Enuresis
	Illness, etc.
+ Anal Contacts	+ Pain
	+ Death
	Compulsions

⎫ *content of*
⎬ *dreams and*
⎭ *symptoms*

Case 100: Ronny

Ronny, an eleven-year-old boy from a prominent professional family, displayed "perfect" manners during his first diagnostic hour. He gave the impression of a well-contained, sensitive and kindly boy. His family had requested therapy for Ronny's debilitating learning problem. Despite his average score (I.Q. 91) on the Bellevue Wechsler intelligence test, Ronny, at the age of eleven, was doing no better than first and second grade work and did not even know the months of the year.

Ronny was in treatment for four years. During this period his learning problem was resolved to the extent that at the age of fifteen he was doing seventh and eighth grade work.

Sources of Stimulation:
children's tactile and visual erogenous contacts with the adult body

1. At the age of eleven, Ronny still lay next to his mother on the bed to watch TV and during the following year continued to rest on the bed with her.

+ sleeping in bed with adults*

When he was about seven years old, Ronny would visit his grandmother on weekends and would sleep very close to her throughout the night. One of Ronny's adolescent brothers offered him additional frequent close physical contact in the form of tickling bouts while wrestling with Ronny.

+ adult nudity

2. During latency, Ronny shared a bedroom with his two brothers who were more than ten years older. They would walk around the room in the nude while they would tell Ronny "not to look."

The father would be seen walking around the house in just his undershorts, with his penis showing through. Ronny was particularly struck by his father's hairy buttocks when the father would appear nude on the toilet or in the bathtub.

During a weekend visit to his grandmother's, Ronny, at the age of seven, viewed his grandmother unclothed when he shared her bed. At that time, Ronny saw his grandmother urinate into a bedpan and was very much aware of her pubic hair.

A final example of Ronny's exposure to adult exhibitionism was his mother's habit of regularly leaving her girdle, slips, bra, nylon stockings and panties "stained with little lumps" to hang in Ronny's bathroom. Once Ronny opened

426

the laundry hamper and found his mother's used bloody menstrual pad.

+ adult genital erotic*

3. During the period when he was sleeping weekends in bed with his grandmother and seeing her urinate, and when he was sharing a bedroom with his uninhibited adolescent brothers, Ronny allowed himself to be sexually seduced by an adolescent boy, Frank. Frank had persuaded Ronny to go with him into his cellar by promising Ronny a "big aeroplane" and a "big sword," then locked the cellar door and subjected Ronny to both oral and anal intercourse. These activities were repeated on "seventeen" different occasions. Ronny was extremely disturbed by his behavior but could not control himself from participating.

Behavioral Symptoms correlated with
children's tactile and visual erogenous contacts with the adult body

+ separation phobia*

1. When Ronny, age thirteen, was induced to leave his mother and home to go to camp, the tears poured down both his and his mother's cheeks. At camp his sobbing remained uncontrollable.

+ irrational fears*

2. Ronny was preoccupied with fears about hurt and dying. Although his ninety-three-year-old grandmother never liked him, Ronny was beside himself with fears of her dying. He bemoaned his grandmother's prospects of being buried in her grave and then begged "please don't talk about death, I can't stand it." Ronny also was afraid that he himself was going to die.

+ hallucinatory twilight state*

Ronny's fears were often accompanied by frightening eidetic imagery at night time when he was trying to go to sleep. He would see "colors" every night: "purples, reds, squares," and even when he was living in the residential center far away from his father, Ronny would keep hearing his father's punitive voice echoing in his ears.

+ sexual symptoms*

3. Ronny was obsessed with thoughts about his sexual encounters with Frank occurring "seventeen times." Ronny confessed that Frank had inserted his penis into his mouth and into his rectum to the point of Frank's orgasm and emission.

(+ hypochondria*)

Even though Ronny was seven when these activities had occurred, at the age of thirteen he still could not rid himself of the recurring images associated with his memories of these activities. He wept as he told his therapist how every day he thought of the teenager's penis in his mouth and "the fluid going down his throat." Then on the anniversary of the summer day that Ronny first submitted to Frank's advances, Ronny claimed that he could still, seven years later, taste "the stuff" in his mouth. He felt that some "yellow stuff" in his mouth had just come out "after all these years."

+ biting/cutting* (throat, teeth)

4. In one of Ronny's dreams, "two buffaloes *ate him up*"; in another, his "grandmother had a thing in her *throat*."

Ronny also struggled with fears that he would *cut* someone with the big knife in the kitchen . . . "it looked so big like a penis."

(+hypo-
   chondria*)

Furthermore, in answer to a diagnostic inquiry as to what Ronny felt were his "problems," he answered, "I have trouble with my *teeth*; they hurt when I eat things that are too cold or hot." Along with these concerns, Ronny presented auxiliary phantasies pertaining to teeth and cutting. He spent his second therapy hour talking about sharks' teeth. At another time, he drew two whales who bit another whale. Still later, he spoke of his grandmother's false teeth and in phantasy wondered if they could be used to bite a penis off. In relation to this preoccupation, he asked for a pair of false teeth for Christmas!

+eyes*

5. Shortly after his sexual episodes with the teenager had begun, i.e., during the period when he was exposed to viewing the teenager's penis, Ronny almost "blinded" a girl by "accidentally" poking a prickly stick into her eye.[1] She was taken to the hospital. Although the eye was bleeding badly, fortunately she was not blinded. While reporting this experience, Ronny complained that his own eye was sore even though physical findings were negative.

+fire*

6. Ronny's key drawing of a dream which helped him confess his sexual activities with the teenager focused upon fire. The drawing purportedly dealt with a hose watering the ground where some seeds had been planted. The hand is shown holding brown earth. The fire on the scene could not be explained. This picture actually turned out to portray a yellow colored penis squirting near a brown hole, the anus, while the hand was touching brown feces. The picture portrayed quite accurately what did happen to Ronny during his submission to the teenager's advances.

Sources of Stimulation:
adult punitive and excretory contacts with children

+early
   deprivation (of
   need
   fulfillment)

1. Ronny was placed in leg braces for his first two years of life in order to correct a "hip socket" defect which caused his feet to turn outwards. The resulting restriction and deprivation of pleasurable movement was accompanied by a retardation in Ronny's development. His mother became concerned that he "never seemed to want to master things too quickly."

+beatings*

2. The father would take "mental fits" of exploding and beating Ronny when Ronny did not behave. Ronny recalled that one time his father, "like a wild man," threw a barrel at him. It was the sudden unexpected, inappropriate character of the father's beatings which made them so dreadful. Ronny also recalled coming home from school one day and playfully giving his father a "Heil Hitler" salute. White with rage the father responded by forcibly striking Ronny in the face. On another occasion Ronny spilled some of the father's champagne on a rug during one of his parents' parties. In front of the guests the father responded with kindly understanding while assuring Ronny that he needn't feel badly or worry. Later that night, however, the father came into

Ronny's bedroom and beat him with a belt to teach him a lesson. On still another occasion, the father punished Ronny by lifting him up from the floor and shaking him by the neck.

+ punitive
yelling*

3. The father also punished Ronny by sharply yelling at him. One time the father threw his newspapers all over the living room and then ordered Ronny to pick them up. When Ronny refused to do this, the father screamed at him while the mother in turn screamed at the father for losing his temper. Ronny claimed that the battles between his mother and father were frequent. The yelling was so intense that Ronny complained the words would "blast" into his head where they would echo, over and over again.

+ adult
defecation

4. Ronny would find his parents' excrement in the unflushed toilet. Also, as already noted, he found his mother's used menstrual pad in the bathroom hamper.

+ anal
stimulation*

However, the principal source for anal-excremental stimulation occurred in relation to the teenager's completing sodomy upon Ronny. Thereafter, Ronny's anal stimulation continued in the form of bouts of anal masturbation which served to repeat some of the erotic reactions associated with his original sexual experience.

Behavioral Symptoms correlated with
adult punitive and excretory contacts with children

+ excretory
symptoms*

1. Ronny often was preoccupied with feces and the rectum: at the age of three he ate the "white colored doo-doo" he made in his pajamas. He first thought it would be good and "ate a lot of it and then threw up." Ronny later hated thoughts of "doody" taste in his mouth. He also put in his mouth his mother's used menstrual pad which he found in a hamper.

(+ anal
masturbation*)

Ronny would poke his finger into his rectum while he was in the shower to reactivate the exciting feelings which took place when Frank enacted anal intercourse upon him. This highly sexualized masturbation only gradually came under Ronny's control. The sensation of Frank's penis in his rectum was perpetuated in another way: Ronny would hold in his feces sometimes as long as four weeks with the result that a great deal of pressure would develop within his rectum. When he finally would have a bowel movement the stools were so large they would plug up the toilet. These activities paralleled his earlier experiences with Frank: after Frank had used him for anal intercourse, Ronny had held in his feces for four weeks, then experienced a frightening expulsion of excrement with blood splattering all over. Ronny thought he was dying but did not dare tell his parents for fear that they would truly kill him.[2]

+ negative
behavior

2. Ronny's behavior during therapy reflected his behavior in the outside world. Despite the large amount of material he eventually was able to bring to therapy, there also would occur long periods of withholding and restriction.

Despite his positive feelings towards his therapist, Ronny frequently would complain that he didn't want to come for his therapy hour. In his residential school Ronny displayed the same problem. "I don't want to do anything" he would say as he sat in front of the TV alone. He resisted participation in sports, group activities, games or intellectual pastimes.

+ learning*
(level 3)

Such restriction and negative passive withdrawal provided a basis for Ronny's presenting problems, his severe learning difficulties. At the age of thirteen he was performing four to five years behind his age level in school. His capacity to learn became manifest only after four years of therapy and an additional two years of education at a special school.

+ reversal of
affect*

3. Ronny's prolonged bouts of silliness too often were suggestive of "hebephrenic" behavior. Ronny would make use of his silliness to drive people "crazy." With manic laughter he would bump into children and counselors in the hall. Later he would upset his parents by acting like a "dunce" with his tongue sticking out or his hands wiggling next to his ears.

Eventually, Ronny was able to confide that every time he thought of the teenager's penis in his rear he would break out laughing and acting silly.

Ronny's hostile, negative silliness contributed to his setting it up for other children to dislike him: one of his presenting complaints was that "no one likes me."

+ death*

Ronny was obsessed with concerns about death and dying, hurting and killing.

The following list of his dreams reflects Ronny's preoccupation with disaster closing in upon him and with hitting, hurting, killing and death.

+ killing*

(a) "the monster started to come out and he was *killing* the people in the garbage trucks."

+ death*

(b) "about Floppy the hamster, at the end he died; someone was throwing Floppy around *dead*."

+ closing down
upon
destructively*

(c) "Steve was at my house and at night he *pushed me against* the wall." (Ronny's first association was how "we went to this place for ice cream; there was this *grave* yard across the way; we went to this *grave* stone.")

(d) "I was in a *prison* [closed in], they made me stay there."

+ kill*

(e) "Someone was going to *kill* me."

+ closing down
upon
destructively*
(crush)

(f) "all these guys came running down; they saw this old car; they got in it and started to go real fast; they *ran over* my cat and my dog, my mother, my father, my sister, my brother. . . . "

(g) "People were *hitting* someone; they were *beating* people up."

(h) "I got this thing for Christmas and some people *wrecked* it."

+ pain* (sting)
+ falling*

When he was thirteen, Ronny tried to justify his reluctance to leave his mother to go to camp. He claimed he might be killed there: "I might get run over by a big red truck or I might be killed by a bee[3] sting. . . . I might get hurt when they make you *go up high cliffs*; they're so dangerous."

+ death*

In particular, Ronny began to worry that his grandmother was dying and panicked when he thought that she would be enclosed within a grave. Ronny confided that when he had been sleeping with his grandmother and had seen her pubic hair during the same year he acted out with the adolescent boy, he had wished that she were dead. Later he feared that his wish might come true and that also he might himself die. On one occasion Ronny wept as he phoned his

+ closing down upon destructively*

therapist about his fears that he was going to die from *choking*. He also displayed his fears in his classroom where he kept talking with his teacher and the children about death.[4]

NOTES

1 Note the equivalence of the penis → eye contact (visual) and the stick → eye contact (visual and tactile).

2 Ronny's severe pathology might suggest the presence of some irreversible constitutionally determined homosexual disturbance. Contraindicating such a diagnosis, Ronny responded well to therapy. Not only did he make satisfactory advances in learning but he became socially oriented and was last reported to be enjoying the company of a steady girl friend.

3 See case 77 of Kurt Junior who also masturbated anally and was preoccupied with bee stings.

4 Ronny, Deli (case 98) and Tal (case 89), children who were exposed to sodomy or to frequent enemas, all were afraid to deal with numbers or to know the months of the year: they did not want to think of "time" leading to "death."

Ronny
100

Stimulation-Symptom-and-Dream-Profile

	+ Separation Phobias
	+ Night Terrors, Twilight States
+ Sleep in Bed with Adult	+ Irrational Fears: Other
	Irrational Tempers
+ Adult Genital Erotic	+ Sexual Symptoms
	+ Biting/Cutting, etc.
View Adult Coitus	+ Eyes
	+ Fire

+ Sleep in Bed with Adult

+ Adult Genital Erotic

   View Adult Coitus

+ Separation Phobias
+ Night Terrors, Twilight States
+ Irrational Fears: Other
   Irrational Tempers
+ Sexual Symptoms
+ Biting/Cutting, etc.   ⎫ *content of*
+ Eyes   ⎬ *dreams and*
+ Fire   ⎭ *symptoms*

+ Punitive Yelling

+ Beatings

+ Learning Problems (levels 2 or 3, etc.)
   Lying and Delinquency
+ Reversal of Affect
+ Closing Down Upon, Kill ⎫ *content of*
   ⎬ *dreams and*
+ Falling   ⎭ *symptoms*

   Preoccupation with Child's BM

+ Anal Contacts

+ Excretory Symptoms and Dreams
+ Anal Masturbation
   Enuresis
+ Illness, etc.   ⎫ *content of*
+ Pain   ⎬ *dreams and*
+ Death   ⎭ *symptoms*
   Compulsions

Appendix 1

NUMERICAL CASE INDICES
OF CLINICAL FINDINGS

APPENDIX 1 — TABLE 1

THE RELATION OF CHILDREN SHARING BEDS WITH ADULTS
and
CHILDREN'S SEPARATION PHOBIAS

Distribution of the 100 cases
Cases are designated by their case numbers

	+ Separation Phobias	− Separation Phobias
+ Bed	*19 cases* 2, 3, 4, 5, 7, 8, 21, 22, 25, 26, 44, 48, 66, 70, 76, 91, 96, 97, 100	*16 cases* 11, 16, 23, 30, 31, 35, 46, 51, 52, 58, 67, 71, 80, 81, 82, 99
− Bed	*19 cases* 1, 6, 9, 12, 14, 17, 18, 28, 29, 40, 41, 53, 68, 69, 88, 89, 90, 92, 98	*46 cases* 10, 13, 15, 19, 20, 24, 27, 32, 33, 34, 36, 37, 38, 39, 42, 43, 45, 47, 49, 50, 54, 55, 56, 57, 59, 60, 61, 62, 63, 64, 65, 72, 73, 74, 75, 77, 78, 79, 83, 84, 85, 86, 87, 93, 94, 95

APPENDIX 1 — TABLE 2

THE RELATION OF CHILDREN SHARING BEDS WITH ADULTS
and
CHILDREN'S NIGHT TERRORS/TWILIGHT STATES

Distribution of the 100 cases
Cases are designated by their case numbers

	+ Night Terrors/Twilight States	− Night Terrors/Twilight States
+ Bed	*19 cases* 2, 7, 16, 21, 22, 23, 25, 26, 30, 31, 46, 66, 70, 76, 81, 91, 96, 97, 100	*16 cases* 3, 4, 5, 8, 11, 35, 44, 48, 51, 52, 58, 67, 71, 80, 82, 99
− Bed	*18 cases* 9, 19, 20, 24, 27, 28, 29, 42, 54, 57, 63, 69, 75, 77, 84, 85, 92, 98	*47 cases* 1, 6, 10, 12, 13, 14, 15, 17, 18, 32, 33, 34, 36, 37, 38, 39, 40, 41, 43, 45, 47, 49, 50, 53, 55, 56, 59, 60, 61, 62, 64, 65, 68, 72, 73, 74, 78, 79, 83, 86, 87, 88, 89, 90, 93, 94, 95

THE RELATION OF ADULT GENITAL EROTIC CONTACTS WITH
CHILDREN
and
CHILDREN'S SEXUAL ACTIVITIES

Distribution of the 100 cases
Cases are designated by their case numbers

	+ Sexual Activities	– Sexual Activities
+ Adult Genital Erotic	*56 cases* 9, 10, 11, 14, 15, 17, 18, 19, 20, 21, 22, 23, 24, 25, 26, 27, 28, 29, 30, 31, 36, 37, 54, 57, 58, 61, 64, 65, 67, 68, 69, 70, 71, 72, 73, 74, 75, 76, 77, 78, 79, 80, 81, 83, 84, 85, 86, 87, 88, 89, 92, 95, 96, 97, 99, 100	*5 cases* 45, 47, 63, 66, 82
– Adult Genital Erotic	*18 cases* 1, 4, 5, 6, 7, 13, 16, 33, 39, 43, 44, 46, 53, 55, 56, 91, 93, 98	*21 cases* 2, 3, 8, 12, 32, 34, 35, 38, 40, 41, 42, 48, 49, 50, 51, 52, 59, 60, 62, 90, 94

THE RELATION OF CHILDREN VIEWING ADULT COITUS
and
CHILDREN'S SEXUAL ACTIVITIES

Distribution of the 100 cases
Cases are designated by their case numbers

	+ Sexual Activities	– Sexual Activities
+ View Coitus	*28 cases* 19, 21, 22, 23, 24, 25, 26, 27, 30, 31, 57, 58, 65, 68, 69, 70, 71, 72, 73, 75, 76, 77, 78, 79, 84, 85, 97, 99	*1 case* 66
– View Coitus	*46 cases* 1, 4, 5, 6, 7, 9, 10, 11, 13, 14, 15, 16, 17, 18, 20, 28, 29, 33, 36, 37, 39, 43, 44, 46, 53, 54, 55, 56, 61, 64, 67, 74, 80, 81, 83, 86, 87, 88, 89, 91, 92, 93, 95, 96, 98, 100	*25 cases* 2, 3, 8, 12, 32, 34, 35, 38, 40, 41, 42, 45, 47, 48, 49, 50, 51, 52, 59, 60, 62, 63, 82, 90, 94

APPENDIX 1 — TABLE 4

THE RELATION OF ADULT GENITAL EROTIC CONTACTS WITH CHILDREN
and
CHILDREN'S ANAL MASTURBATION

Distribution of the 100 cases
Cases are designated by their case numbers

	+ Anal Masturbation	− Anal Masturbation
+ Adult Genital Erotic	*16 cases* 10, 30, 37, 58, 64, 67, 69, 70, 73, 75, 76, 77, 88, 92, 99, 100	*45 cases* 9, 11, 14, 15, 17, 18, 19, 20, 21, 22, 23, 24, 25, 26, 27, 28, 29, 31, 36, 45, 47, 54, 57, 61, 63, 65, 66, 68, 71, 72, 74, 78, 79, 80, 81, 82, 83, 84, 85, 86, 87, 89, 95, 96, 97
− Adult Genital Erotic	*3 cases* 13, 93, 98	*36 cases* 1, 2, 3, 4, 5, 6, 7, 8, 12, 16, 32, 33, 34, 35, 38, 39, 40, 41, 42, 43, 44, 46, 48, 49, 50, 51, 52, 53, 55, 56, 59, 60, 62, 90, 91, 94

APPENDIX 1 — TABLE 5A

THE RELATION OF ADULT GENITAL EROTIC CONTACTS WITH CHILDREN
and
CHILDREN'S NIGHT TERRORS/TWILIGHT STATES

Distribution of the 100 cases
Cases are designated by their case numbers

	+ Night Terrors/Twilight States	− Night Terrors/Twilight States
+ Adult Genital Erotic	*30 cases* 9, 19, 20, 21, 22, 23, 24, 25, 26, 27, 28, 29, 30, 31, 54, 57, 63, 66, 69, 70, 75, 76, 77, 81, 84, 85, 92, 96, 97, 100	*31 cases* 10, 11, 14, 15, 17, 18, 36, 37, 45, 47, 58, 61, 64, 65, 67, 68, 71, 72, 73, 74, 78, 79, 80, 82, 83, 86, 87, 88, 89, 95, 99
− Adult Genital Erotic	*7 cases* 2, 7, 16, 42, 46, 91, 98	*32 cases* 1, 3, 4, 5, 6, 8, 12, 13, 32, 33, 34, 35, 38, 39, 40, 41, 43, 44, 48, 49, 50, 51, 52, 53, 55, 56, 59, 60, 62, 90, 93, 94

APPENDIX 1 — TABLE 5B

THE RELATION OF CHILDREN VIEWING ADULT COITUS
and
CHILDREN'S NIGHT TERRORS/TWILIGHT STATES

Distribution of the 100 cases
Cases are designated by their case numbers

	+ Night Terrors/Twilight States	− Night Terrors/Twilight States
+ View Coitus	*20 cases* 19, 21, 22, 23, 24, 25, 26, 27, 30, 31, 57, 66, 69, 70, 75, 76, 77, 84, 85, 97	*9 cases* 58, 65, 68, 71, 72, 73, 78, 79, 99
− View Coitus	*17 cases* 2, 7, 9, 16, 20, 28, 29, 42, 46, 54, 63, 81, 91, 92, 96, 98, 100	*54 cases* 1, 3, 4, 5, 6, 8, 10, 11, 12, 13, 14, 15, 17, 18, 32, 33, 34, 35, 36, 37, 38, 39, 40, 41, 43, 44, 45, 47, 48, 49, 50, 51, 52, 53, 55, 56, 59, 60, 61, 62, 64, 67, 74, 80, 82, 83, 86, 87, 88, 89, 90, 93, 94, 95

THE RELATION OF ADULT GENITAL EROTIC CONTACTS WITH CHILDREN
and
CHILDREN'S EYE SYMPTOMS AND DREAM CONTENTS

Distribution of the 100 cases
Cases are designated by their case numbers

	+ Eyes	− Eyes
+ Adult Genital Erotic	*44 cases* 9, 10, 14, 15, 17, 18, 19, 20, 22, 23, 25, 27, 28, 30, 36, 37, 47, 54, 58, 64, 65, 66, 68, 69, 70, 71, 72, 73, 74, 75, 76, 77, 78, 81, 83, 84, 85, 86, 87, 88, 89, 97, 99, 100	*17 cases* 11, 21, 24, 26, 29, 31, 45, 57, 61, 63, 67, 79, 80, 82, 92, 95, 96
− Adult Genital Erotic	*13 cases* 1, 7, 13, 16, 33, 34, 35, 40, 42, 52, 53, 56, 93	*26 cases* 2, 3, 4, 5, 6, 8, 12, 32, 38, 39, 41, 43, 44, 46, 48, 49, 50, 51, 55, 59, 60, 62, 90, 91, 94, 98

THE RELATION OF CHILDREN VIEWING ADULT COITUS
and
CHILDREN'S EYE SYMPTOMS AND DREAM CONTENTS

Distribution of the 100 cases
Cases are designated by their case numbers

	+ Eyes	− Eyes
+ View Coitus	*23 cases* 19, 22, 23, 25, 27, 30, 58, 65, 66, 68, 69, 70, 71, 72, 73, 75, 76, 77, 78, 84, 85, 97, 99	*6 cases* 21, 24, 26, 31, 57, 79
− View Coitus	*34 cases* 1, 7, 9, 10, 13, 14, 15, 16, 17, 18, 20, 28, 33, 34, 35, 36, 37, 40, 42, 47, 52, 53, 54, 56, 64, 74, 81, 83, 86, 87, 88, 89, 93, 100	*37 cases* 2, 3, 4, 5, 6, 8, 11, 12, 29, 32, 38, 39, 41, 43, 44, 45, 46, 48, 49, 50, 51, 55, 59, 60, 61, 62, 63, 67, 80, 82, 90, 91, 92, 94, 95, 96, 98

THE RELATION OF ADULT GENITAL EROTIC CONTACTS
WITH CHILDREN
and
CHILDREN'S SYMPTOMS AND DREAM CONTENTS
PERTAINING TO BITING AND CUTTING

Distribution of the 100 cases
Cases are designated by their case numbers

	+ Biting/Cutting	− Biting/Cutting
+ Adult Genital Erotic	*48 cases* 9, 10, 11, 14, 15, 17, 18, 19, 20, 21, 22, 23, 25, 26, 27, 28, 29, 30, 31, 36, 37, 45, 66, 67, 69, 70, 71, 72, 73, 75, 76, 77, 78, 79, 80, 81, 82, 83, 84, 85, 86, 87, 88, 89, 92, 95, 99, 100	*13 cases* 24, 47, 54, 57, 58, 61, 63, 64, 65, 68, 74, 96, 97
− Adult Genital Erotic	*20 cases* 1, 2, 3, 5, 6, 7, 8, 12, 13, 34, 38, 48, 50, 51, 55, 60, 91, 93, 94, 98	*19 cases* 4, 16, 32, 33, 35, 39, 40, 41, 42, 43, 44, 46, 49, 52, 53, 56, 59, 62, 90

THE RELATION OF ADULT GENITAL EROTIC CONTACTS WITH
CHILDREN
and
CHILDREN'S SYMPTOMS AND DREAM CONTENTS PERTAINING TO FIRE

Distribution of the 100 cases
Cases are designated by their case numbers

	+ Fire	− Fire
+ Adult Genital Erotic	*25 cases* 14, 15, 19, 25, 27, 29, 30, 45, 61, 65, 66, 67, 72, 73, 74, 79, 80, 81, 82, 83, 85, 89, 92, 99, 100	*36 cases* 9, 10, 11, 17, 18, 20, 21, 22, 23, 24, 26, 28, 31, 36, 37, 47, 54, 57, 58, 63, 64, 68, 69, 70, 71, 75, 76, 77, 78, 84, 86, 87, 88, 95, 96, 97
− Adult Genital Erotic	*5 cases* 43, 44, 48, 52, 62	*34 cases* 1, 2, 3, 4, 5, 6, 7, 8, 12, 13, 16, 32, 33, 34, 35, 38, 39, 40, 41, 42, 46, 49, 50, 51, 53, 55, 56, 59, 60, 90, 91, 93, 94, 98

APPENDIX 1 — TABLE 9

THE RELATION OF CHILDREN VIEWING ADULT COITUS
and
CHILDREN'S ENURESIS

Distribution of the 100 cases
Cases are designated by their case numbers

	+ Enuresis	− Enuresis
+ View Coitus	*13 cases* 22, 23, 25, 27, 30, 31, 70, 72, 73, 76, 78, 79, 97	*16 cases* 19, 21, 24, 26, 57, 58, 65, 66, 68, 69, 71, 75, 77, 84, 85, 99
− View Coitus	*15 cases* 6, 8, 15, 17, 34, 36, 41, 53, 55, 56, 60, 67, 74, 88, 89	*56 cases* 1, 2, 3, 4, 5, 7, 9, 10, 11, 12, 13, 14, 16, 18, 20, 28, 29, 32, 33, 35, 37, 38, 39, 40, 42, 43, 44, 45, 46, 47, 48, 49, 50, 51, 52, 54, 59, 61, 62, 63, 64, 80, 81, 82, 83, 86, 87, 90, 91, 92, 93, 94, 95, 96, 98, 100

APPENDIX 1 — TABLE 10

THE RELATION OF ADULT GENITAL EROTIC CONTACTS WITH CHILDREN
and
CHILDREN'S SYMPTOMS AND DREAM CONTENTS PERTAINING TO
KILLING/CLOSING DOWN DESTRUCTIVELY

Distribution of the 100 cases
Cases are designated by their case numbers

	+ Kill & Close Down Upon	− Kill & Close Down Upon
+ Adult Genital Erotic	*51 cases* 10, 14, 15, 17, 18, 19, 20, 21, 26, 27, 28, 29, 30, 31, 36, 37, 45, 47, 54, 57, 58, 61, 63, 64, 65, 66, 67, 68, 69, 71, 72, 73, 74, 75, 76, 77, 78, 79, 81, 82, 83, 85, 86, 87, 88, 89, 92, 95, 96, 99, 100	*10 cases* 9, 11, 22, 23, 24, 25, 70, 80, 84, 97
− Adult Genital Erotic	*20 cases* 2, 34, 38, 39, 42, 43, 44, 46, 48, 49, 50, 51, 52, 53, 55, 56, 59, 60, 62, 93	*19 cases* 1, 3, 4, 5, 6, 7, 8, 12, 13, 16, 32, 33, 35, 40, 41, 90, 91, 94, 98

APPENDIX 1 — TABLE 11

THE RELATION OF BEATINGS
and
CHILDREN'S SYMPTOMS AND DREAM CONTENTS PERTAINING TO
KILLING/CLOSING DOWN DESTRUCTIVELY

Distribution of the 100 cases
Cases are designated by their case numbers

	+ Kill & Close Down Upon	− Kill & Close Down Upon
+ Beat	*55 cases* 14, 17, 19, 21, 30, 34, 36, 37, 38, 39, 42, 43, 44, 45, 46, 47, 48, 49, 50, 51, 52, 53, 54, 55, 56, 57, 59, 60, 61, 62, 63, 64, 65, 66, 67, 68, 69, 71, 72, 73, 74, 75, 76, 77, 78, 79, 81, 82, 83, 85, 86, 87, 89, 99, 100	*11 cases* 5, 11, 13, 32, 33, 35, 40, 41, 70, 80, 90
− Beat	*16 cases* 2, 10, 15, 18, 20, 26, 27, 28, 29, 31, 58, 88, 92, 93, 95, 96	*18 cases* 1, 3, 4, 6, 7, 8, 9, 12, 16, 22, 23, 24, 25, 84, 91, 94, 97, 98

APPENDIX 1 — TABLE 12

THE RELATION OF BEATINGS
and
CHILDREN'S LEARNING PROBLEMS

Distribution of the 100 cases
Cases are designated by their case numbers

	+ Learning Problems	− Learning Problems
	39 cases	*27 cases*
+ Beat	13, 17, 19, 30, 32, 33, 34, 35, 36, 37, 38, 40, 41, 42, 43, 44, 45, 47, 50, 51, 52, 53, 54, 56, 59, 61, 62, 63, 65, 66, 69, 74, 78, 81, 82, 86, 87, 89, 100	5, 11, 14, 21, 39, 46, 48, 49, 55, 57, 60, 64, 67, 68, 70, 71, 72, 73, 75, 76, 77, 79, 80, 83, 85, 90, 99
	11 cases	*23 cases*
− Beat	7, 15, 16, 18, 20, 22, 27, 92, 94, 97, 98	1, 2, 3, 4, 6, 8, 9, 10, 12, 23, 24, 25, 26, 28, 29, 31, 58, 84, 88, 91, 93, 95, 96

APPENDIX 1 — TABLE 13

THE RELATION OF PUNITIVE YELLING
and
CHILDREN'S LEARNING PROBLEMS

Distribution of the 100 cases
Cases are designated by their case numbers

	+ Learning Problems	− Learning Problems
	39 cases	*28 cases*
+ Yell	7, 13, 16, 18, 19, 20, 22, 27, 30, 33, 34, 36, 37, 40, 41, 42, 43, 44, 47, 51, 52, 53, 54, 56, 59, 61, 63, 65, 66, 69, 74, 78, 81, 86, 89, 92, 94, 97, 100	4, 5, 6, 8, 9, 10, 11, 12, 14, 21, 25, 26, 39, 46, 48, 49, 55, 58, 60, 71, 72, 75, 76, 77, 79, 80, 91, 99
	11 cases	*22 cases*
− Yell	15, 17, 32, 35, 38, 45, 50, 62, 82, 87, 98	1, 2, 3, 23, 24, 28, 29, 31, 57, 64, 67, 68, 70, 73, 83, 84, 85, 88, 90, 93, 95, 96

APPENDIX 1 — TABLE 14

THE RELATION OF BEATINGS
and
CHILDREN'S DELINQUENCY SYMPTOMS

Distribution of the 100 cases
Cases are designated by their case numbers

	+ Delinquency or Lying	− Delinquency or Lying
+ Beat	*32 cases* 5, 19, 35, 36, 37, 38, 40, 43, 44, 47, 48, 49, 50, 51, 52, 53, 54, 57, 61, 63, 66, 68, 69, 73, 74, 78, 79, 82, 83, 86, 89, 99	*34 cases* 11, 13, 14, 17, 21, 30, 32, 33, 34, 39, 41, 42, 45, 46, 55, 56, 59, 60, 62, 64, 65, 67, 70, 71, 72, 75, 76, 77, 80, 81, 85, 87, 90, 100
− Beat	*4 cases* 15, 20, 25, 97	*30 cases* 1, 2, 3, 4, 6, 7, 8, 9, 10, 12, 16, 18, 22, 23, 24, 26, 27, 28, 29, 31, 58, 84, 88, 91, 92, 93, 94, 95, 96, 98

APPENDIX 1 — TABLE 15

THE RELATION OF BEATINGS
and
CHILDREN'S SYMPTOMS AND DREAM CONTENTS PERTAINING TO FALLING

Distribution of the 100 cases
Cases are designated by their case numbers

	+ Fall	− Fall
+ Beat	*41 cases* 11, 13, 14, 21, 32, 33, 34, 41, 43, 46, 47, 48, 50, 51, 52, 53, 54, 59, 60, 61, 62, 63, 64, 65, 66, 67, 69, 70, 72, 73, 74, 75, 77, 78, 80, 81, 82, 85, 87, 99, 100	*25 cases* 5, 17, 19, 30, 35, 36, 37, 38, 39, 40, 42, 44, 45, 49, 55, 56, 57, 68, 71, 76, 79, 83, 86, 89, 90
− Beat	*11 cases* 1, 2, 10, 12, 24, 25, 26, 84, 93, 95, 98	*23 cases* 3, 4, 6, 7, 8, 9, 15, 16, 18, 20, 22, 23, 27, 28, 29, 31, 58, 88, 91, 92, 94, 96, 97

APPENDIX 1 — TABLE 16

THE RELATION OF BEATINGS
and
CHILDREN'S SYMPTOMS AND DREAM CONTENTS PERTAINING TO FIRE

Distribution of the 100 cases
Cases are designated by their case numbers

	+ Fire	− Fire
+ Beat	*25 cases* 14, 19, 30, 43, 44, 45, 48, 52, 61, 62, 65, 66, 67, 72, 73, 74, 79, 80, 81, 82, 83, 85, 89, 99, 100	*41 cases* 5, 11, 13, 17, 21, 32, 33, 34, 35, 36, 37, 38, 39, 40, 41, 42, 46, 47, 49, 50, 51, 53, 54, 55, 56, 57, 59, 60, 63, 64, 68, 69, 70, 71, 75, 76, 77, 78, 86, 87, 90
− Beat	*5 cases* 15, 25, 27, 29, 92	*29 cases* 1, 2, 3, 4, 6, 7, 8, 9, 10, 12, 16, 18, 20, 22, 23, 24, 26, 28, 31, 58, 84, 88, 91, 93, 94, 95, 96, 97, 98

TABLE 17 *omitted*

APPENDIX 1 — TABLE 18

THE RELATION OF BEATINGS
and
CHILDREN'S REVERSAL OF AFFECT

Distribution of the 100 cases
Cases are designated by their case numbers

	+ Reversal of Affect	− Reversal of Affect
+ Beat	*35 cases* 11, 17, 30, 33, 34, 37, 38, 48, 49, 50, 51, 52, 53, 55, 56, 60, 64, 65, 66, 67, 68, 71, 72, 73, 74, 75, 77, 80, 81, 82, 85, 86, 87, 99, 100	*31 cases* 5, 13, 14, 19, 21, 32, 35, 36, 39, 40, 41, 42, 43, 44, 45, 46, 47, 54, 57, 59, 61, 62, 63, 69, 70, 76, 78, 79, 83, 89, 90
− Beat	*8 cases* 9, 15, 16, 22, 25, 28, 88, 96	*26 cases* 1, 2, 3, 4, 6, 7, 8, 10, 12, 18, 20, 23, 24, 26, 27, 29, 31, 58, 84, 91, 92, 93, 94, 95, 97, 98

APPENDIX 1 — TABLE 19

THE RELATION OF ANAL STIMULATION
and
CHILDREN'S EXCRETORY SYMPTOMS AND DREAM CONTENTS

Distribution of the 100 cases
Cases are designated by their case numbers

	+ Excretory Symptoms	− Excretory Symptoms
+ Anal Stimulation	*24 cases* 1, 5, 8, 19, 23, 29, 34, 40, 44, 55, 62, 77, 87, 88, 89, 90, 92, 93, 94, 95, 96, 98, 99, 100	*5 cases* 3, 20, 46, 85, 97
− Anal Stimulation	*37 cases* 2, 10, 12, 13, 14, 17, 22, 27, 30, 32, 36, 37, 42, 43, 48, 53, 56, 57, 58, 61, 64, 65, 67, 69, 70, 71, 72, 73, 74, 75, 76, 78, 79, 81, 82, 84, 91	*34 cases* 4, 6, 7, 9, 11, 15, 16, 18, 21, 24, 25, 26, 28, 31, 33, 35, 38, 39, 41, 45, 47, 49, 50, 51, 52, 54, 59, 60, 63, 66, 68, 80, 83, 86

APPENDIX 1 — TABLE 20

THE RELATION OF ANAL STIMULATION
and
CHILDREN'S OBSESSIVE-COMPULSIVE SYMPTOMS

Distribution of the 100 cases
Cases are designated by their case numbers

	+ Obsessional Symptoms	− Obsessional Symptoms
+ Anal Stimulation	*11 cases* 1, 19, 23, 87, 88, 89, 92, 93, 95, 96, 98	*18 cases* 3, 5, 8, 20, 29, 34, 40, 44, 46, 55, 62, 77, 85, 90, 94, 97, 99, 100
− Anal Stimulation	*9 cases* 13, 35, 37, 57, 60, 64, 68, 84, 91	*62 cases* 2, 4, 6, 7, 9, 10, 11, 12, 14, 15, 16, 17, 18, 21, 22, 24, 25, 26, 27, 28, 30, 31, 32, 33, 36, 38, 39, 41, 42, 43, 45, 47, 48, 49, 50, 51, 52, 53, 54, 56, 58, 59, 61, 63, 65, 66, 67, 69, 70, 71, 72, 73, 74, 75, 76, 78, 79, 80, 81, 82, 83, 86

APPENDIX 1 — TABLE 21

THE RELATION OF ANAL STIMULATION
and
CHILDREN'S PREOCCUPATION WITH PAIN

Distribution of the 100 cases
Cases are designated by their case numbers

	+ Preoccupation with Pain	− Preoccupation with Pain
+ Anal Stimulation	*17 cases* 3, 8, 19, 23, 34, 40, 44, 62, 77, 87, 88, 89, 93, 94, 96, 99, 100	*12 cases* 1, 5, 20, 29, 46, 55, 85, 90, 92, 95, 97, 98
− Anal Stimulation	*20 cases* 2, 7, 9, 10, 12, 13, 14, 15, 21, 25, 26, 37, 43, 48, 52, 57, 66, 75, 82, 91	*51 cases* 4, 6, 11, 16, 17, 18, 22, 24, 27, 28, 30, 31, 32, 33, 35, 36, 38, 39, 41, 42, 45, 47, 49, 50, 51, 53, 54, 56, 58, 59, 60, 61, 63, 64, 65, 67, 68, 69, 70, 71, 72, 73, 74, 76, 78, 79, 80, 81, 83, 84, 86

APPENDIX 1 — TABLE 22

THE RELATION OF ANAL STIMULATION
and
CHILDREN'S IRRATIONAL FEARS

Distribution of the 100 cases
Cases are designated by their case numbers

	+ Fears	− Fears
+ Anal Stimulation	*21 cases* 1, 5, 19, 20, 23, 29, 34, 44, 46, 62, 77, 85, 87, 88, 89, 92, 93, 95, 96, 98, 100	*8 cases* 3, 8, 40, 55, 90, 94, 97, 99
− Anal Stimulation	*33 cases* 6, 11, 14, 15, 16, 17, 18, 21, 22, 24, 26, 30, 33, 39, 45, 53, 56, 57, 58, 59, 64, 65, 68, 69, 71, 73, 75, 78, 79, 80, 84, 86, 91	*38 cases* 2, 4, 7, 9, 10, 12, 13, 25, 27, 28, 31, 32, 35, 36, 37, 38, 41, 42, 43, 47, 48, 49, 50, 51, 52, 54, 60, 61, 63, 66, 67, 70, 72, 74, 76, 81, 82, 83

Appendix 2

TABLE OF DEFINITIONS

EROGENOUS and/or PUNITIVE STIMULATION	DEFINITIONS
Erogenous or Erotic Contacts ("erotic" = "erogenous" with sexual emphasis)	
Bed sharing	child rests in bed with adult
*Bed sharing / Sleeping in Bed with Adults	*child shares bed with adult for the purpose of inducing the child's sleep (at least once weekly)
	*child sleeps in bed with adult (at least once weekly)
Adult Genital Erogenous Contacts (visual and/or tactile)	child observes adults dressing and undressing
	child observes male adult urinating
	child shares shower with adult (under one spray)
	child shares bath with adult
*Adult Genital Erotic Contacts (visual and/or tactile)	*child wrestles or is very physical with adult, in bed
	*child shares bed with nude adult
	*child shares bed with adults who are preparing for or performing sexual intercourse
	*child shares bed with adult who is masturbating
	*child contacts nude adult's genitalia in a shower or a bath
	*child observes adult penis during partial or complete erection
	*child observes adults copulating or masturbating

	*child observes adult's genitalia, breasts or buttocks during overt invitation for sexual play *child exposed to sexual contacts of adult fondling the child's genitalia or other erogenous zones *child exposed to direct sexual contacts of the genitalia of a parent or other adult *pre-adolescent child observes adult hard-core pornography
*Observations of Adults Copulating (to be investigated separately *and* as a sub-category of Adult Genital Erotic Contacts)	*children viewing exposed adults copulating *children viewing an exposed adult masturbating *children viewing hardcore pornographic depictions of such activities

Excretory Contacts

Fecal Sources of Stimulation	child observes an adult on the toilet in the process of defecating
*Fecal Sources of Stimulation (non-punitive)	*child aged five or older still wiped by adult *adult preoccupied with child's bowel movements
*Anal Sources of Stimulation	*child subjected to enemas or suppositories on repeated occasions *child observes an adult administering enemas *child has suffered from anal rashes, anal fistulas or pinworms of the anal orifice *child's anus or rectum contacted manually by an adult on repeated occasions *child's anus or rectum contacted by adult's or adolescent's genitalia

*Asterisks Indicate Statistical Investigation

APPENDIX 2 (*continued*)

SOURCES OF STIMULATION

EROGENOUS and/or PUNITIVE STIMULATION	DEFINITIONS
Punitive Contacts	
Extremes of Parental Negativism	extreme opposition to child's requests and needs negative, overcontrolling-interference with child's activities and acceptable goals
Early deprivation of empathic care and comforting; early exposure to parental punitive behavior including parental negativism (during infant's first year of life)	extreme opposition to infant's "requests" and neglect of the infant's needs overt rejection (e.g., not wanted, infant moved from family to family, not picked up) parental frozen affect during child's infancy, deficiency of parental empathy parental dislike for or unhappiness with the infant punitive interactions of parent and infant
Punitive Yelling	adults occasionally screaming to correct and punish child child occasionally hearing parents screaming at one another
*Punitive Yelling	*adults at least several times a week screaming to correct or punish child *child at least several times a week hearing parents screaming at one another
Hitting	occasional hitting with hand (one or two slaps) without loss of control and without violence; no marks, temporary or permanent
*Beatings and Beltings	*corporal punishment involving a strap, belt or utensil *prolonged or unquestionably violent hitting; kicking *parent hitting out of control *extremely painful punishments (e.g. involving tearing skin, sticking skin with pins; burns, blows which leave an imprint temporarily or permanently)

452

SYMPTOMS

SYMPTOM FORMATION	DEFINITIONS
*Separation Hysterics	*noisy, fearful and/or agitated display of emotions appearing in relation to separation, including school phobia
*"Irrational" Fears, Phobias, etc.	*affective or obsessive display of irrational concerns (other than separation hysterics, nightmares, night terrors or twilight states): *daytime phobias and obsessive fears *nighttime fears
Nightmares	nightmares
*Night Terrors and/or Other Hysterical Twilight States	*night terrors *sleep walking *fugues and hysterical twilight states *hysterical conversion symptoms *phobic hallucinations in transition from sleeping to waking *phobic hallucinations during periods of waking
*"Irrational" Temper Hysterics and Anger	*noisy tempers: agitated, angry screaming, thrashing or disorganized non-directed hitting or kicking (contrasts with "closing down upon" destructively)
*Sexual Activities	*compulsive masturbation *driven sexual activities, homosexual or heterosexual *anti-social sexual activities *sexual activities with animals *sexual fetishism

*Asterisks Indicate Statistical Investigation

453

APPENDIX 2 (*continued*)

SYMPTOMS

SYMPTOM FORMATION	DEFINITIONS
	*teenage sexual promiscuity *child's incestuous activities with siblings who are children *child's incestuous activities with a sexually mature partner *inhibited or absent sexual life during adulthood: impotence or frigidity
*Anal Masturbation (investigated both separately and as subcategories of sexual behavior and excretory activity)	*poking finger into anus or rectum *poking objects into rectum *wiping anus excessively
*"Biting" Symptoms, Dreams and Related Activities (does not include psycho-motor symptoms associated with infancy, e.g., thumb sucking, nail biting, anorexia and obesity)	symptoms or dreams involving: *biting *teeth *animals known for their sharp teeth and for biting and snapping (wolves, dogs, lions, tigers, birds with big beaks; sharks, alligators, crabs, lobsters, spiders) *cutting, chopping *cutting instruments (axes, knives, scissors used to cut rather than to impale) *effects of cutting (cuts, tears, sharp glass) *bodily processes associated with biting: swallowing, sensations in the throat or stomach *dreams of mouths and eating
*"Eye" Symptoms, Dreams and Related Activities	symptoms emphasizing "the eye": *psychogenic disturbances of the eyes including blurring, tics, difficulty in seeing; psychogenic blindness *psychogenic reading problems *child poking self or others in the eye, e.g., with sticks, pencils, arrows *dreams and symptoms involving the words "see," "look at," "staring" *dreams and concerns involving things stared at (TV, movies, stages, theatrical performances, etc.) *dreams and concerns involving light beams (lights, bulbs, rays of light, rays of sun, electrical flashes, X-rays)

*"Fire" Symptoms, Dreams and Related Activities

symptoms or dreams involving:
*fires
*firemen, firehoses, fire stations, fire extinguishers, fire alarms
*burns from fire; matches, fiery substances such as burning lava

Negative Behavior

child in general does opposite of what is requested (in numerous circumstances):

does not do when asked to do
does do when asked not to do
reverses order of performance (organic causes ruled out)

Learning Problems
(involving passive or active negativism)

learning problems level 1: (for child with potential I.Q. of 90 or above)
marks going down and the child is not performing up to his or her capabilities but child is able to be promoted on basis of satisfactory grades, no referral problem

*Learning Problems

*learning problems level 2: (for child with potential I.Q. 90 or above) the child has been left back once for learning difficulties and/or I.Q. has fallen 10 points or more

*learning problems level 3: (for child with potential I.Q. 90 or above) the child has been left back several times or more, or is performing significantly below his or her age group

*learning problems a referral complaint: (levels 1, 2, or 3); learning problems of children age five or less will not be evaluated statistically unless the learning problem has been presented as a "referral complaint"

*Asterisks Indicate Statistical Investigation

455

APPENDIX 2 (*continued*)

SYMPTOMS

SYMPTOM FORMATION	DEFINITIONS
*Delinquency and/or Lying (negative to social authority)	*socially harmful behavior on repeated occasions, breaking laws and/or frequent lying
Negative Affect	repetitive or irrational expressions of dislike, hate and fault finding
Freezing of Affect	inhibited empathy marked denial, e.g., accompanying reaction formations
*Freezing of Affect	*reduction of emotional hysterics (see section 17 of this chapter)
*Reversal of Affect	*laughter during punishment, pain, duress or disaster *pleasure when others are being hurt or unhappy *inappropriate clowning, silliness or nonsense talk, dreams of clowns
Hurting	symptoms and dreams pertaining to: hitting objects or people including the self breaking (biting and cutting are included under a separate heading)
*Closing Down Upon Destructively	symptoms and dreams pertaining to unrelenting "closing down upon": *being held down, cornered, hemmed in; clamped down, tied down; impaled *crushed, strangled, squeezed, choked, suffocated *objects associated with the above activities: chains, ropes, caskets; enclosures, cages and elevators which restrict and trap; crowds closing in, claustrophobia (does not include running away) *animate creatures or inanimate objects being run down by moving vehicles *solid objects thrown directly and destructively at another individual
*Killing as Content of Dreams and Symptoms	symptoms and dreams pertaining to: *killing, murder, suicide ("kill" focuses upon an attack vs "dying" and "death" which focus upon a passive state) *burns from acid, alkali or fire *violent explosions, earthquakes, tornados, hurricanes, volcanoes, crashes

456

*Falling

symptoms and dreams involving falling
*threatening heights and ledges, roof tops, from which a fall can easily take place
*objects falling or rolling downhill

*Excretory/Excremental Symptoms and Dreams

involvement with feces:
*soiling
*playing with feces
*eating feces
dreams or irrational symptoms involving:
*brown, black, dirty, smelly substances; itching
*the words "behind," "back," "end," "gas"; animals and insects which are dirty-looking or smell: bugs, vermin, lice, flies, dirty worms, rats and mice; conditions associated with dirt: dirty spots, pimples, boils, abscesses; garbage, refuse; enclosures which are "junky," e.g., a broken-down rusty car, an old dilapidated shoe, basement of a house
involvement with the anus and rectum:
*anal itching
*anal poking
*anal sexual play
*psychogenic fecal withholding
*psychogenic diarrhea

*Asterisks Indicate Statistical Investigation

SYMPTOM FORMATION	DEFINITIONS
*Illness (non-organic, etc.)	*illness which does not conform with organic patterns *illness which appears without evidence of organic pathology *self-induced illness *irrational preoccupation with organic illness or injury *preoccupation with innards, guts, poison likely to induce illness *hypochondriasis (does not include psychogenic organic diseases associated with early depriva- tion, especially respiratory and feeding difficulties associated with infantile failure to thrive, "hospitalism" and "marasmus")
*Death and Dying	symptoms and dreams pertaining to: *dying (focuses upon the passive state of dying vs "kill" which focuses upon active attack) *objects and situations closely associated with death: funerals, cemeteries, caskets, skeletons, bodies being buried, ghosts, poison likely to induce death
*Preoccupation with Pain	dreams and symptoms pertaining to psychogenic pains and aches: *headaches *stomachaches *backaches *oversensitivity to pains *interest in others suffering pain symptom and dream content involving: *instruments of pain, e.g., needles, nails, insects which sting (wasps, hornets, bees, etc.); does not include emotional insensitivity to pain: see freezing of affect and reversal of affect, sections 17 and 18 of chapter 2 of Vol. 1
Tics	tics
Stuttering	stuttering

| *Obsessive-Compulsive Neurosis | *obsessive-compulsive activities and thoughts which the subject consciously does not wish to occur; does not include addictions, e.g., involving drinking, eating or masturbation
*rituals |
| *Enuresis | *bed wetting after the age of three
*day wetting after the age of three |

*Asterisks Indicate Statistical Investigation